TALKS
TO
TEACHERS

TALKS TO TEACHERS

A FESTSCHRIFT FOR N. L. GAGE

EDITED BY

DAVID C.
BERLINER

BARAK V.
ROSENSHINE

RANDOM HOUSE   NEW YORK

This book was developed for Random House by Lane Akers Incorporated

First Edition
9876543
Copyright © 1987 by Random House, Inc.
All rights reserved under International and Pan-American Copyright Conventions. No part of this book may be reproduced in any form or by any means, electronic or mechanical, including photocopying, without permission in writing from the publisher. All inquiries should be addressed to Random House, Inc., 201 East 50th Street, New York, N.Y. 10022. Published in the United States by Random House, Inc., and simultaneously in Canada by Random House of Canada Limited, Toronto.

Library of Congress Cataloging-in-Publication Data

Talks to teachers.

  Bibliography: p.
  1. Teaching.   2. Teacher-student relationships—
United States.   3. Gage, N. L. (Nathaniel Lees),
1917–   . I. Gage, N. L. (Nathaniel Lees),
1917–   . II. Berliner, David C.   III. Rosenshine, Barak.
LB1025.2.T35   1987   371.1'02   86-29701
ISBN 0–394–35644–6

Cover design: Susan Phillips

Manufactured in the United States of America

FOREWORD

A FESTSCHRIFT FOR N. L. GAGE

A Festschrift (a collection of essays by the students and colleagues of a noted scholar) is a fine old European academic tradition. We are using it as intended, to honor the official retirement from academe of an emminent scholar and to commemorate his seventieth birthday, on August 1, 1987. We will not go on at great length about the many achievements of Nathaniel Lees Gage (although we could, and he would be both embarrassed and delighted if we did!). Instead, we will comment briefly about a few noteworthy characteristics that led his students and colleagues to honor him in this way.

Influence. An up-to-date listing of the published works of N. L. Gage can be found in the section of this book entitled About N. L. Gage. Through those works, as well as through presentations at professional meetings, consultation, direction of dissertations, teaching, conversing over wine, and in dozens of other ways, Gage has influenced both psychology and education. His early work was in educational and psychological measurement and in social psychology. But his attention was constantly drawn to issues in education. The study of teaching, ultimately, became the focus of his interests. In 1963 his scholarship resulted in the publication of a carefully conceptualized and exquisitely edited *Handbook of Research on Teaching*, a volume marking the beginning of the "modern era" of systematic, thoughtful, and careful scientific research on teaching. That volume, conceived by Gage and others, included a chapter by Donald Medley and Harold Mitzel that reviewed issues and methods of classroom observation. That chapter led to the improvement of virtually all subsequent research in the field and fostered a substantial increase in the number of studies that related teaching and classroom processes to student achievement. The research methods chapter in that volume, by Donald Campbell and Julian Stanley, became one of the most cited pieces in all of the social sciences. Additional chapters on teaching methods, teacher personality, social interaction in the classroom, and teaching in the content areas influenced researchers for at least the decade following this publication. This *Handbook*, which the field often refers to as "the Gage *Handbook*," was of singular importance in its influence on our field.

A second opportunity for Gage to greatly influence the field of research on teaching occurred in 1974 when he organized and chaired the National Institute of Education Conference on future directions for research on teaching. The reports of the conference, edited by Gage, all had influence on the ensuing research in the field, but two, in particular, stand out. One report led directly to the creation of the Institute for Research on Teaching at Michigan State University and the systematic study of teacher planning and thought processes. Another of the reports led directly to the funding of a program for research on language processes in the classroom. The liveliness of research now found in both fields has its roots, in part, in the conference and reports for which N. L. Gage was responsible.

Scholarship. Even the briefest examination of the list of Gage's published works (pages 390–398) makes clear the quantity and breadth of his writings. What is not so obvious is the exceptional scholarship shown in those written works. We think immediately of his early work on balance theory and the ratings of teachers; his methodological work on person perception and meta-analysis; his Teachers College lectures, published as *The Scientific Basis of the Art of Teaching;* his Phi Delta Kappa presentation published as *Hard Gains in the Soft Sciences;* and his review of open education. These, and many other works, display levels of scholarship that his colleagues admire and toward which his students aspire.

Commitment to improvement. A distinguishing feature of Gage's work has been his commitment to the improvement of teaching. He has had only passing interest in scholarship that describes educational phenomena. His praise is saved for those whose research can improve education. While favoring "improvers" over "describers," he only welcomes the small set of improvers whose ideas about practice are rooted in scientific investigations of teaching and learning. Society, says Gage, demands evidence of the effectiveness of teaching practices. Providing society with that evidence has been a consistent theme during Gage's career. His most recent scholarship is in that vein. He has recently finished a comprehensive review of experiments in classroom teaching that have been found to improve student achievement. He argues convincingly about the validity and usefulness of a great deal of the research on effective teaching completed in the last decade.

Wit, charm, and style. Virtually all of Gage's colleagues and students are aware of his view of heaven, "where everyone has had three martinis and smoking is good for you." His rhetorical style in written and oral presentations is also well known. When conceptual issues are argued, Gage often starts out his presentation slowly, clarifying an issue, then citing the opposition's argument. Soon he brings in some data and relevant quotes, accumulating evidence, bit by bit, that suddenly and clearly takes apart a contrary view, leaving his own ("obviously correct") position intact. A scientist who can articulately defend his position plays an important and delightful role in a field of study. Such a person helps you clarify issues in ways that enable you to take a position on matters where controversy exists. Gage does this extremely well and with great style. We all profit from his forthrightness. As for charm, can anyone with a wife like Maggie (Margaret Burrows Gage), four affectionate children, and the respect of his colleagues and students be without it? With wit, charm, and style, as well as aggressively high standards of scholarship, Gage has modeled for his students and colleagues the highest order of personal and academic behavior.

Editing. We would be remiss if we did not mention an aspect of Gage's scholarship and personality that all his students and colleagues remark about—his prodigious talent as an editor. No one who has submitted work to him for review has been spared his editorial talent. What was thought to be final copy has frequently become draft copy following a Gage review.

Gage is pleased to tell people that he is the founder of the Barak Rosenshine award for creative spelling, to honor one whose gift it is to invariably choose the wrong spelling whenever a choice could be made. Strangely, the annual winner of that award is David Berliner, whose gift it is not only to choose the wrong spelling whenever a choice can be made but to see choices where no one else discerns them!

We note for the record that Berliner and Rosenshine, with the help of professional copy editors, went over every chapter in this volume until every line was perfect. But then, since Nate cannot read without editing, we went back and put in a few errors, so Nate would thoroughly enjoy reading this book.

Students. Of all the accomplishments of an academic, perhaps the most important and enduring may be the number of highly productive, highly visible students he or she produces. Professor Gage's progeny (and now his grand-progeny) in the field of research on teaching are numerous and very active. Almost all who have studied with Professor Gage have come away enriched and committed to disciplined inquiry in some aspect of educational research.

Once at a meeting of researchers who study teaching, Nate was making a point. He started out, but with some hesitancy, declaring that "Someone has said . . . let's see . . . maybe it was a student of mine who said . . . I think it was a student of mine who said. . . ." At which point someone in the audience interrupted and said, "We're all your students, Nate." That sums it up nicely. For those who have been fortunate to work directly with him and for those who only know him through his record of scholarship, we state again: We are all your students, Nate.

We will end this foreword now. On behalf of all who have written here, and the much larger community of scholars who would have been pleased to join us if space had permitted, we thank you, Nate. We wish you a happy birthday and a most happy and productive retirement.

DAVID C. BERLINER   BARAK V. ROSENSHINE
TUCSON, ARIZ.   URBANA, ILL.

PREFACE

The title of this volume, *Talks to Teachers*, is the same one chosen by the great psychologist William James, who in the 1890s published the set of lectures he had been giving to teachers around the country. We approach the centenary of his lectures and their publication at about the same time that we honor N. L. Gage, who, like James, saw with clarity the relevance of psychology to education. We mean to honor James by remembering his prescience. We also mean to contrast this volume with his. His was a volume of erudite speculation that focused on learning. This is a volume primarily of research-based speculation that focuses on classroom teaching or issues related to teaching. The vast increase of research concerned with schooling, classrooms, and teaching, rather than just student learning, has provided teachers with more information worth considering seriously than ever could have been anticipated in James's day. This change is due, at least in part, to N. L. Gage.

1. Introduction. This volume begins with a talk to teachers about the contemporary research enterprise. David C. Berliner compares research on teaching to research in other fields, such as physics and medicine. Educational research comes away from that comparison looking extremely good. Some achievements of research on teaching are described, and a way for teachers and administrators to think about applying research findings is noted. Berliner asserts that a scientific base for the art of teaching has actually been achieved.

2. Classroom interaction. The next five chapters present the findings of classroom research. In the first of these, Greta Morine-Dershimer discusses the language of classrooms. Her research provides descriptions of the subtleties of and the problems that occur within classroom verbal discourse. Knowing how classrooms socially construct language systems that benefit some students but are detrimental for others should be a part of every teacher's knowledge about teaching in America's heterogeneous schools.

The management of classrooms is discussed next, in a chapter by Carolyn Evertson. She provides teachers with practical management guidelines about readying the classroom, determining class room rules and procedures, teaching rules and procedures, teaching student accountability, and developing a set of consequences for inappropriate student behavior. Evertson also discusses the implementation and maintenance of management systems.

In Barak Rosenshine's essay on classroom teaching, he begins by distinguishing two types of teaching: explicit, where all the steps can be specified, as in mathematics computation; and implicit, where steps cannot be specified, as in writing a term paper. Rosenshine summarizes the research on explicit teaching by organizing the findings within six sequential teaching functions: review, presentation of new material, guided practice, feedback and corrections, independent practice, and weekly and monthly reviews. He believes that student achievement in explicit areas of instruction can improve if the procedures he describes are used.

The next chapter, by David C. Berliner, also deals with teaching effectiveness. Berliner believes effective teachers simply deliver a curriculum matched to outcomes that are valued. His chapter elaborates on what it means to deliver a curriculum and why the match between curriculum and outcome is so important.

The final chapter in this set about effective classroom teaching is provided by Elizabeth Fennema and Penelope Peterson. They focus on the differences shown by teachers in classroom behavior toward boys and girls. Their findings suggest an explanation of why boys often score higher on mathematics tests than girls. Fennema and Peterson also describe the kinds of classroom environments in which the mathematics achievement of girls is high. Ways to achieve more equitable classrooms are suggested.

3. Observation, expectation, and motivation. The next three chapters are concerned with issues that are slightly removed from inter-action in the classroom. The first of these deals with observation in classrooms in order to improve instruction. Jane Stallings, Georgea Sparks, and Margaret Needels discuss observation instruments that can be used to provide specific information about details of classroom instruction. One instrument to record time off-task can inform teachers of the number of children who are off-task during each sweep of the classroom, the number of observations in each different kind of off-task category (such as *chatting, waiting, disruptive*), and the number of off-task events in different kinds of intended teaching activities, such as oral reading or seatwork. Another instrument enables one to record teacher behaviors (such as *asks a question, corrects a response*) and the students to whom they are directed. These instruments can be modified for different activities and to suit different subjects and grades.

In another chapter, on teacher expectancy, Thomas Good reviews how teachers behave differently toward high-achieving and low-achieving students in a classroom and how they react to high and low reading groups. Our insight into the power of expectancy is instantaneous when Good reports teachers saying, "I'll be over to help you slow ones in a minute," or "Hurry up, Robyn, even you can get this right." The chapter concludes with practical suggestions for working with low-achieving students.

The next chapter, by Jere Brophy, is both comprehensive and practical. He discusses a theory of motivation and ways of developing in students the expectancy that they can achieve. He discusses, as well, the concepts of extrinsic and intrinsic motivation and makes suggestions about capitalizing on both. In the final section of the chapter, on stimulating the students' own motivation to learn, he provides suggestions and classroom examples for inducing and teaching student motivation.

4. Student cognitions. Lynn Corno provides another chapter on motivation, from a different perspective. With her chapter we step aside from studies of interaction in the classroom and direct our attention to thinking about student cognition. Corno describes what it means to be a self-regulated learner. How students learn the strategies to process information intended for them to learn has implications for a wide range of educational issues. Ultimately, Corno reminds us, it is the students' responsibility to learn and to use appropriate cognitive strategies to ensure their own school success. Teachers can help students acquire and develop motivational and cognitive strategies for learning, but in the end it is the student's own volition with which we must be concerned.

Students' thoughts and motives also concern Philip Winne and Ronald Marks. In their chapter on student thinking they speculate on how a cognitive psychological view of the learner in the classroom can lead to recommendations about teachers' behavior that affect academic achievement and motivation to learn.

5. Instructional goals, testing, and planning. The next three chapters in this volume take another small step away from the classroom, and also back from the student. In the essay by Philip Jackson the goals of two types of teaching are discussed. The first is the teaching of explicit skills, knowledge, concepts, and (in particular) the narratives, which are basic to being an educated person in our culture. Jackson asks if one can really belong to a common culture without knowing the tales about Daniel Boone, Adam and Eve, Washington at Valley Forge, or the Gold Rush. The second, transformational teaching, refers to using education to transform our lives, to cause us to reconsider previous positions, to show students an aspect of themselves that they would not know about without benefit of a particular educational experience. Jackson argues that teachers do, and must always be able to, undertake activities "in the vague hope that something good—something transformative—may come of them."

The next chapter in this set, by Robert Glaser, deals with the integration of instruction and testing. Glaser points out that advances in the study of human cognition hold great promise for the fields of assessment. As notions of intelligence and competency are understood better, testing instruments are also being changed to reflect the new and more sophisticated meanings of these terms. Glaser concludes by predicting that we may soon have tests that lead teachers to decisions about how competence can be increased.

This section concludes with a discussion by Christopher Clark and Robert Yinger of the ways teachers plan. With knowledge about classroom instruction, ideas about the ways in which learners think and are motivated, and concepts about explicit and transformational instruction in mind, a teacher prepares plans of instruction. This area of research is a subset of the larger area of research on teacher thinking. Clark and Yinger review what we know about teacher thinking in planning and also during interactive teaching.

6. Conclusion. The final talk to teachers is by Lee Shulman, who discusses the wisdom of practice. Shulman talks about managing complexity in the fields of medicine and teaching. He reaches the conclusion any fair-minded observer of classrooms must reach—teaching is a far more complex activity than is the practice of medicine. With the melding of the research on teaching and the wisdom of practice, Shulman sees the possibility of positive educational change.

Scholars from humanistic and social science disciplines who write about teaching today have a greater knowledge base to draw on and a clearer focus about the critical issues in education than they did in William James's time. Our talks to teachers, while surely short of the erudition of James, reflect much of our learning about teaching. We have profited greatly in the 100 years since James first attempted to communicate the implications of psychology to education. The steady growth of disciplined inquiry, leading to ever sharper criticism of those inquiries, makes the study of teaching an exciting field today. All of us who work in this field thank James, Gage, and other scholars for teaching us. Now, if some of what we write here teaches others, their goals and our goals will have been met well.

CONTENTS

xiii

PART I

INTRODUCTION

CHAPTER 1

DAVID C. BERLINER

KNOWLEDGE IS POWER

A Talk to Teachers About a Revolution in the Teaching Profession

It is almost 100 years since the philosopher, psychologist, and consultant to educators William James talked to teachers about "psychology and the teaching art" (1983). Beginning in 1891, he regularly delivered memorable lectures to the teachers in the Boston area. In a moment of great insight he uttered words that stood unchallenged for most of these past 100 years:

> You make a great, a very great mistake, if you think that psychology, being the science of mind's laws, is something from which you can deduce definite programmes and schemes and methods of instruction for immediate schoolroom use. Psychology is a science, and teaching is an art: and sciences never generate arts directly out of themselves. An intermediary inventive mind must make the application, by using its originality. (p. 15)

I think that in the last few years we have come closer than ever before to providing direct scientific underpinnings for the art of teaching. In some cases, the need for highly inventive, creative minds has been lessened, as research provides ideas and technology that are *almost* directly applicable to classroom life.

A hybrid form of research has developed that relies on more than just laboratory findings from psychological science. This new research is broad in scope, using concepts and methodologies from all the humanities, as well as from all the social and behavioral sciences. The focus of these diverse approaches is teaching and learning as they occur in schools and classrooms. This relatively new research has provided findings, concepts, and technology undreamed of by William James. I believe James would now look a little more kindly on the relationship between

3

art and science and would see what we see—a genuine transformation in the profession of teaching as a scientific basis is developed for the art of teaching. No one I know denies the artistic component to teaching. I now think, however, that such artistry should be research based. I view medicine as an art, but I recognize that without its close ties to science it would be without success, status, or power in our society. Teaching, like medicine, is an art that also can be greatly enhanced by developing a close relationship to science. Let us explore these ideas about research and teaching by examining the knowledge base created in the past few years. I will start by examining one source of professional status in our society—professional knowledge.

KNOWLEDGE AND THE STATUS OF PROFESSIONS

Late in the last century, only a little over 100 years ago, there were three equally disreputable professions: medicine, law, and education. Doctors and hospitals, everyone thought, were the people and the places associated with pain and death. Only a few returned from medical treatment healthy, happy, and convinced that the medical professional was actually distinguishable from the local blacksmith or the visiting healer and snake-oil salesman. The true state of medical ignorance at that time has been well documented in a recent book entitled *Learning to Heal* (Ludmerer, 1985). For example, among Union troops during the Civil War, penetrating chest wounds incurred a 62 percent mortality rate, and abdominal wounds carried an 87 percent death rate. In contrast, during World War II, only about 3 percent of injured American soldiers failed to survive. The doctors of the Civil War period—120 years ago—believed that pus was part of the natural healing process, and thus infected wounds were rampant. Physicians themselves propagated much of the infection by probing wounds with fingers wiped on pus-stained aprons and towels. The importance of clean hands and sterilized equipment was simply not understood. Maggots were the most effective infection fighters of the war; they infested the wounds of the injured soldiers and ate only diseased tissue, leaving behind the healthy part of the wound. Although well known and often used in Europe, thermometers, stethoscopes, ophthalmoscopes, hypodermic syringes, and other simple instruments were rarely employed by American medical practitioners. The military physicians continued to give their patients dangerous doses of potent laxatives and emetics long after such substances had been proved absolutely ineffective or harmful. When a brave Union surgeon general, Dr. William Hammond, banned the use of two toxic drugs because he noticed they had severe side effects such as profuse salivation and development of putrid gangrene of the gums, mouth, and face, he was not only court-martialed by the military but condemned by the American Medical Association. The

Union Army had developed a medical exam to weed out the most incompetent doctors. The exam, however, only served to reveal that "the typical physician expressed vague and confused ideas in barbarous English that was at defiance with all rules of grammar."

The standard course of instruction at the nation's medical schools when William James was founding experimental psychology in America consisted of two four-month terms of lectures during the winter season, with the second term usually identical to the first. So ignorant of contemporary developments in medical science in 1871 was one of James's colleagues, a Harvard professor of pathology and anatomy, that he confessed his inability to use the microscope. At no school was there any gradation of studies or sequencing of subjects. There was simply no logical order. Instruction was didactic. Rote learning was emphasized. Students endured between six and eight hours of lectures daily, supplemented by textbook readings. There were few if any written examinations. To receive a medical degree, students merely needed to pass a brief set of casual, perfunctory oral questions. The age of 21 tended to be an official requirement for graduation, but not too much attention was actually paid to this regulation. State licensing did not exist. A graduate with a degree from any kind of institution could practice anywhere in the country. The ability to pay the fee was the single entrance requirement for many medical schools. Literacy was definitely not needed. Indeed, when Charles Eliot, the eminent president of Harvard (1869–1909), proposed written examinations for graduation from the university's medical school, he was vigorously opposed by the professor of surgery, who argued that more than half of Harvard's medical students could barely write. In fact, medical schools were so disreputable and the profession was so bad that the best students chose careers in law, the clergy, or *teaching!*

Eliot pointed out that "an American physician or surgeon may be and often is a coarse and uncultivated person devoid of intellectual interest outside of his calling and quite unable to either speak or write his mother tongue with accuracy." Harvard's medical school was described at the end of the last century as a "money making institution, not much better than a diploma mill." Eliot wrote, "The ignorance and general incompetency of the average graduate of American medical schools, at the time when he receives the degree which turns him loose upon the community, is something horrible to contemplate." Eliot tried to put into effect a scientific M.D. degree, but he was voted down by his faculty. After all, the faculty argued, medicine was an art, not a science. The scientific approach was a fad, simply glorifying the European practice and showing disdain for the clinical wisdom of America's physicians. Experimental research was roundly scorned. Some of the most eminent medical professors of the time stated that they did not accept the germ theory of disease and were opposed to animal vivisection. The handful of people doing research in the field either had to be independently wealthy or had to steal equipment for their laboratories.

Lawyers in those days, everyone also seemed to think, were despicable. The profession appeared to be run by the greedy and the conservative, though the lawyer often came from a "better class" of people than did the medical practitioner. Legal education was really no more rigorous than medical education. It did not take much in the way of apprenticeship, and one had only to read a few law books in order to be able to practice law.

It was also true in our recent past that everyone seemed to think that teachers were simply persons who were unfit for the rigors for farm, factory, or commercial life. What was clear was that to the vast majority of the American people there were three equally disreputable professions—medicine, law, and education—and this was only a mere 100 or so years ago.

It is interesting to reflect on why two of these three disreputable professions gained stature over the past 100 or so years. Doctors have become wealthy and respected, assuming the qualities of a priesthood (and at times of a deity) because they have acquired knowledge, skills, concepts, and technology in the form of pharmaceuticals that have allowed them to treat and cure illnesses. Lawyers, although some retain a rather unsavory image, have managed to climb the occupational hierarchy in terms of finance and prestige. In our modern society they possess the knowledge and skill to respond to the ever more complex legal issues in the areas of commerce, finance, taxes, and social behavior.

Now let us look at the third profession—education. I firmly believe that now it is our turn. We now have something that an ordinary person does not have—a knowledge base consisting of facts, concepts, and technology that can transform our profession as well. Although this is a time of intense criticism of education, it is also a time that gives us the greatest chance to reformulate our profession. The transformation we envision will put us on a scientific and technological track that will command the public's faith in and admiration of our competence. I believe we will get their full support when they believe that our services cannot be performed by ordinary, untrained, inexperienced members of society.

We in education are haunted by the public's erroneous belief that someone can walk in off the street and deliver a curriculum to 30 or so children. Raising any number of children and having gone to school for a number of years does not make an expert teacher. I believe we are on the threshold of creating a scientific basis for the art of teaching that will be acceptable to the general public as *truly specialized knowledge*. As the art of medicine has been enriched by a scientific underpinning, so is the art of teaching about to be enriched. I propose to subject my beliefs to a few direct questions about the issue:

1. How good is contemporary research in education in comparison to research in other fields?
2. What function does research in education serve with regard to the field of education?
3. Is any of the research that has been done of genuine practical value?
4. How should we interpret the findings of educational research?
5. How should we transmit the findings of educational research to teachers?

I will try to answer these questions in turn.

HOW GOOD IS RESEARCH IN EDUCATION IN COMPARISON TO RESEARCH IN OTHER FIELDS?

Educational research has suffered from criticism. Within and without the profession we hear people saying how awful it is and how much more insignificant it seems than in the hard sciences. Educational research suffers because education is not only a social science but an applied social science, meaning to some that the research work must necessarily be even "sloppier" than that conducted in the "purer" social sciences and certainly of less trustworthiness than that in the hard sciences.

A report by Larry Hedges (in press) of the University of Chicago debunks this myth. I would like to describe some of his data. It's very important that we put a quick end to this nonsense about the wonders of research in physics and chemistry and the abysmal state of research in the social sciences.

One source for examining the quality of data in the hard sciences is in the reviews of research that are done to see if the data collected are consistent over time, scientists, locales, and so on. A group of particle physicists at the University of California at Berkeley has been collecting experimental results on the properties of elementary particles for years. Their reviews are analyzed quantitatively as well as qualitatively. The field of particle physics engages some of the best physicists in the world. There is much current interest in this field, and literally billions of dollars are spent on the overall research enterprise. Millions of dollars may be spent on a single experiment. What I am going to show you next is the consistency of results for reviews of data of the so-called stable particles—that is, those particles that are judged stable against strong decay. This class of particles includes the familiar proton, neutron, and electron. The data presented are on the mass and lifetime of these stable particles. It is a well-understood research area. Let us now examine Table 1.

The 13 particles described in Table 1 include the muon, charged pion, lambda, omega, and so on. The property studied is either the lifetime or the mass of these particles. The number of studies included

Table 1. Summary of Homogeneity Statistics from 13 Particle Data Group Reviews.

Particle	Property	ALL STUDIES				STUDIES IN PDG REVIEW			
		Number of Studies	χ^2	p	R	Number of Studies	χ^2	p	R
Muon	Lifetime	10	29.496	0.000	3.28	9	11.602	0.170	1.45
Charged pion	Mass	10	20.034	0.018	2.23	7	2.046	0.915	0.34
Charged pion	Lifetime	11	34.139	0.000	3.41	10	14.280	0.113	1.59
Neutral pion	Lifetime	11	37.897	0.000	3.41	10	14.280	0.113	1.59
Charged kappa	Lifetime	13	17.633	0.127	1.47	7	14.937	0.021	2.49
Short-lived neutral kappa	Lifetime	13	18.524	0.101	1.54	10	11.415	0.248	1.27
Lambda	Mass	10	39.037	0.000	4.34	5	4.791	0.309	1.20
Lambda	Lifetime	27	70.676	0.000	2.72	3	4.929	0.085	2.46
Sigma +	Lifetime	21	9.834	0.971	0.49	19	8.101	0.977	0.45
Sigma −	Lifetime	16	24.252	0.061	1.62	14	16.808	0.208	1.29
Xi −	Mass	11	9.802	0.458	0.98	9	2.707	0.951	0.34
Xi −	Lifetime	17	11.058	0.806	0.69	11	7.724	0.656	0.77
Omega −	Mass	11	8.611	0.569	0.86	10	8.591	0.476	0.95
Mean		13.9		0.239	2.11	9.2		0.395	1.43
S.D.		5.1		0.343	1.28	4.1		0.363	1.05

NOTE: χ^2 is the chi-square statistic and R is Birge's ratio.

SOURCE: From Hedges (in press).

in a particular review is then given; for example, there were ten separate research studies of the lifetime of the muon. The next column presents a chi-square analysis of the results of these data. Chi-square is a statistic that can be used to see if data from different studies are homogeneous or heterogeneous. Chi-square gets very large when big differences occur among a set of findings and is very small when few differences occur among the findings. The probability of a chi-square can be estimated, and the next column in Table 1 gives that probability. We find that 6 of the 13 reviews showed statistically significant disagreement among the studies. That is, the findings of different studies were discrepant. The column R presents a statistic called the Birge ratio. That ratio is 1.00 when a set of studies yields consistent results. It departs from 1.00 as the studies get more divergent. The average Birge ratio across these 13 reviews, covering nearly 200 different studies, is 2.00, which is 100 percent larger than would be expected if the studies yielded consistent results. On the right of Table 1 are studies that the particle data group used for its special, most rigorous reviews. Thirty-four percent of the studies that were available were deleted because the particle data group decided they did not find the data trustworthy. What is noteworthy is that even with this more restricted set of studies, the Birge ratio is still nearly 1.5 and 2 of the 13 reviews showed, through chi-square analysis, that there were statistically significant disagreements among the studies. We are not knowledgeable physicists, and we can only admire what modern physics has accomplished. But it looks like it has accomplished its achievements with data sets that are not at all in agreement. Now we must ask how these data stack up against social science data. Let's turn to Table 2 and look at 13 reviews of social science data that Hedges has assembled. The data in reviews published in refereed journals tell us whether the data in some area are consistent or inconsistent across a series of replicated studies.

Five of these reviews come from the so-called hard areas of psychology—studies of sex differences and cognitive abilities, for example. Six of the reviews were selected from what are "soft" areas of educational psychology—studies of the effectiveness of open education. And two of the reviews examine the validity of student ratings of instruction and the effect of teacher expectancies on student IQ, which might be considered some middle ground between the hard and soft areas of educational research. What do we find in using the same statistics, either chi-square or the Birge ratio? For the social science reviews in the area of education and educational psychology, similar results were found as in the study of the physical science data sets. The chi-square analysis reveals that 6 of the 13 reviews showed statistically significant disagreement among the studies. In addition, the Birge ratio is more than 2.0. If some of the outliers in these studies making up these reviews are thrown out, as the particle data group did with its untrustworthy data, we find that none of the 13 reviews shows a significant chi-square. That is, the

Table 2. Summary of Homogeneity Statistics from 13 Social Science Reviews.

Review		ALL STUDIES				REVIEWS DELETING SOME STUDIES			
		Number of Studies	H	p	R	Number of Studies	H	p	R
Linn & Peterson	Spatial perception[a]	62	99.88	0.001	1.64	56	43.24	0.828	0.82
	Spatial visualization[a]	81	98.81	0.056	1.27	81	98.81	0.056	1.27
	Mental rotation[b]	29	43.34	0.024	1.61	29	43.34	0.024	1.61
Becker & Hedges	Verbal ability[a]	11	32.69	0.000	4.09	9	11.36	0.078	1.89
	Field articulation[a]	14	19.29	0.056	1.75	11	19.29	0.056	1.75
Hedges, Giaconia, & Gage	Reading achievement	19	105.60	0.000	5.87	16	25.68	0.054	1.65
	Math achievement	17	43.65	0.000	2.73	14	17.40	0.182	1.34
	Attitude to school	11	21.62	0.017	2.16	9	9.00	0.342	1.13
	Self-concept	18	23.66	0.129	1.39	18	23.66	0.129	1.39
Crain & Menard	Randomized	13	12.22	0.428	1.02	13	12.22	0.428	1.02
	Longitudinal	57	56.15	0.469	1.00	57	56.15	0.469	1.00
Cohen	Validity of student rating	67	104.62	0.002	1.59	65	79.48	0.092	1.24
Raudenbush	Teacher expectancy[b]	19	17.61	0.414	1.04	19	17.61	0.414	1.04
Mean		32.1		0.123	2.09	30.8		0.243	1.32
S.D.		25.0		0.183	1.42	24.8		0.239	0.33

NOTE: H is the chi-square statistic and R is Birge's ratio or a generalized Birge's ratio.
[a] A three-parameter fit is used.
[b] A two-parameter fit is used.

SOURCE: From Hedges (in press).

findings tend to agree among themselves, and the average Birge ratio is 1.3. As Hedges (in press) says:

> The data reported in Tables 1 and 2 are strikingly similar. When all studies actually conducted are included, reviews in both the physical science and social science domains suggest statistical inconsistency among research results. . . . When studies with [questionable characteristics] are deleted, research results in both domains are much more consistent.
>
> What is surprising is that the research results in the physical sciences are not markedly more consistent than those in the social sciences. The notion that experiments in physics produce strikingly consistent (empirically cumulative) results is simply not supported by these data. Similarly the notion that experiments in the social sciences produce relatively inconsistent (empirically noncumulative) results is not supported by these data either.

It is clear from these findings that research in the hard sciences is no better or no worse than in the soft sciences, if the criterion is consistency of results when studying the same area. That is, replication in the hard sciences is no easier to achieve than it is in the soft sciences.

Hedges goes on to point out that the social sciences also have a bad reputation because their measurement systems are so inaccurate—at least as compared to, say, physics or chemistry. The social sciences rarely have ratio scales to work with, while the physical sciences often do. But it looks like measurement problems plague the hard sciences, too. Table 3 shows some thermal conductivities of chemical elements and presents the values given in the *Metals Handbook* of 1961 and those given in the 1970 review of metals by the Thermochemical Properties Research Center. In a single decade, between 1960 and 1970, we find differences in measurement of carbon ranging as high as 8,000 percent, of indium ranging to 242 percent, of iridium to 151 percent, and so on. Once again, we see that the problems of the social sciences are the problems of other sciences as well.

My goal in presenting these data is not to pick at thermochemistry or physics. Surely the achievements of the physical sciences are well known and respected. But the fact of the matter is that social science data do not seem to be any poorer than those in the hard sciences and, furthermore, our measurement problems are no different than those in the physical sciences. We have unique problems in social science research and particularly in educational research, but the inherent quality of our studies and our measurement systems should no longer automatically be taken to be inferior to those in the physical sciences.

A second point that I must make about educational research data is that these data have the potential for being as compelling as research data in other fields. I would like to discuss this issue by using an argument made by the man we honor in this volume, our colleague N. L. Gage (1985). In 1982 Gage noted that the results of a large-scale experiment with a drug called propranolol were released to the public.

Table 3. Thermal Conductivities of Chemical Elements for Which There Are Relatively Large Differences Between the Data in the 1961 *Metals Handbook* and the 1970 Compilation by the Thermochemical Properties Research Center.

Element	TPRC (cut-off date December 1970)	Metals Handbook (1961)	Difference (%)
Antimony	0.247	0.19	30
Beryllium	2.04	1.46	40
Calcium	2.02[a]	1.26	60
Carbon (graphite)	0.057–19.6	0.24	−76–8000
Chlorine (gas)	0.000086	0.000072	19
Chromium	0.944	0.67	41
Cobalt	1.01	0.69	46
Erbium	0.143	0.096	49
Gadolinium	0.105	0.088	19
Indium	0.821	0.24	242
Iridium	1.48	0.59	151
Lithium	0.850	0.71	20
Neodymium	0.165[a]	0.130	27
Plutonium	0.067	0.084	−20
Rhenium	0.481	0.71	−32
Rhodium	1.50	0.88	70
Silicon	1.52	0.84	82
Tellurium	0.0343[b] 0.0199[c]	0.059	−58
Thallium	0.463	0.39	19
Thorium	0.543	0.377(373.2 K)	44
Titanium	0.220	0.167	32
Yttrium	0.172	0.146	18

[a] = Estimated value.
[b] = Parallel to c axis.
[c] = Perpendicular to c axis.
SOURCE: This table was adapted from Touloukian (1975) by Hedges (in press).

Propranolol is one of the family of so-called beta-blockers, a family of drugs intended to increase the rate of survival of people who have had at least one heart attack. Random assignment of about 3,800 people to either the drug or a placebo treatment took place. The investigators were quite thorough; they used double-blind procedures and spent about $20 million on this study. The results of this experiment are shown in Table 4.

After 30 months, 9.5 percent of the men who had received the placebo had died, while only 7 percent of those who had received the beta-blocker had died. The drug reduced the percentage of fatalities by only 2.5 percent. Such a result would certainly be regarded as trivial in research on teaching. If 2.5 percent more children score above grade

Table 4. Beta-Blocker Study.

After 30 Months	Received Propranolol (N = 1,900)	Received Placebo (N = 1,900)
Percentage dead	7.0	9.5
Percentage alive	93.0	90.5
	100.0	100.0

Correlation obtained from these data = .045.
Percentage of variance explained = .2.

level or remain in regular classrooms due to an educational program, we do not run out and shout with glee. But in the medical arena, the results of the propranolol study were regarded as so important that the experiment was discontinued on ethical grounds; the researchers felt that their data were so strong that it was unethical to continue denying treatment to the control group. Their results led to the recommendation that propranolol be used, with a potential saving of about 21,000 lives per year in the United States alone.

In 1984 news of a similar experiment was released. This seven- to ten-year-long experiment cost $150 million and dealt with the lowering of cholesterol levels through diet and the use of a drug. These results are shown in Table 5.

Of the men who received the placebo, 9.8 percent had a definite fatal or nonfatal heart attack. Of the men who received the experimental treatment, only 8.1 percent had a definite heart attack. The result was front-page news in the *New York Times* and the *Boston Globe* and led to a cover story in *Time* and an article in *Science*, which held that the results would "affect profoundly the practice of medicine in this country." But the treatment produced only a 1.7 percent difference.

Now, let us ask the questions that are most often asked in educational research. That is, what is the correlation? and how much variance is

Table 5. Effects of Cholesterol Lowering.

Results After 9 Years	Experimental (N = 1,906)	Placebo (N = 1,900)
Percentage definite fatal or full heart attack	8.1	9.8
Percentage no fatal or definite heart attack	91.9	90.2
	100.0	100.0

Correlation obtained from these data = .03.
Percentage of variance explained = .1.

accounted for by the treatment effects? If we go back to the study of the miracle drug propranolol we find out that the correlation between longevity and treatment is .045. The percentage of variance explained is .2. If we look at the effects of lowering cholesterol levels, we find that the correlation is a minuscule .03 between heart-attack rate and the type of treatment received. The percentage of variance explained is a trivial .1. These data lead to statements about medical miracles, but data of greater magnitude in the field of education are often simply disregarded. As Gage pointed out, correlations or differences do not need to be large in order to be significant. In education we may not be influencing life or death, but we are influencing dropout rate, literacy, placement in special classes, love of learning, self-esteem, and the ability to integrate many facts and concepts in complex ways. The implications of research for practice depend *not* on the size of the effects but on whether we see any benefits, whether change in practice results in a change we value. When we deal with the many millions of students in our classrooms, even small differences result in significant amounts of overall change in the lives and productivity of our students.

With this as background for the interpretation of the research literature, what have we discovered over the last dozen or so years? Let us take a look at the second question.

WHAT FUNCTION DOES RESEARCH IN EDUCATION SERVE?

I believe that five characteristics are indicative of a productive scientific community. First of all, a productive scientific community should verify ideas and practices believed to be effective by most people. Second, a productive scientific community should discover new ideas and practices. Third, there should be an expression of ideas that actually complicate everyone's lives. This is because I believe a scientific community should not flinch from ideas that make our tasks more complicated than we would like. Fourth, there ought to be an elucidation of ideas that simplify everyone's lives. And finally, there ought to be the discovery of ideas and practices that are counterintuitive. It seems to me that if these characteristics exist in educational research, we can talk of a very productive scientific community. Let me try to give you some examples under each of these headings.

Verifying Existing Ideas

First of all, our research community has verified ideas and practices known to be effective by most people. The president and the Department of Education recently released a report called *What Works*, a description of 41 research-based findings about how to help students and schools achieve better (U.S. Department of Education, 1986). In this little book are a number of ideas that verify things many people already know. For example, the report states that well-designed homework assignments that relate directly to classwork extend student learning beyond the classroom. It goes on to say that homework is most useful when teachers carefully prepare the assignment, thoroughly explain it, and give prompt comments and criticisms when the work is completed. Although the report does not tell us how teachers are supposed to fit time for the correction and feedback into an already busy day, the findings are quite clear: homework of this type improves achievement. Another verification of ideas known to be effective is the research in the last decade or two on how time spent on a task is a strong predictor of classroom achievement. I was responsible for some of that research, and I well remember people asking us why we would study the obvious. Everyone knows that time is related to learning, we were told. What we found, of course, was that time was not spent equally in classrooms. That is, there was incredible variation across classrooms in the way time spent on a task occurred, and it was this incredible variation that was the predictor of achievement. Still another recent finding that verifies something we all know is that new learning is best remembered when it is related to old learning. This goes back at least as far as the Greek philosophers and became a "modern" theory during Herbart's time in the mid-nineteenth century. New research on "schema theory" and learning verifies the ideas and practices that educators have held for years. Research will, I am sure, continue to provide scientific underpinnings to ideas that are now called "common sense." That is good. Common practices need such justifications, and we have learned, time and time again, that common sense is not always common practice.

Finding Out New Things

Is our scientific community coming up with any new ideas and practices? I think the answer here is yes. For example, Annmarie Palincsar and Ann Brown (1984) have recently written about reciprocal teaching, a new method of teaching whereby students who have deficits in comprehension skills are taught ways to ask questions of text so that their comprehension improves. With the teacher and other students, they take turns creating different kinds of questions until they have developed metacognitive skills—that is, the habit of reflecting upon what they are reading. Reciprocal teaching works. It holds much promise for helping students who are able to decode but have trouble comprehending reading.

Another new idea brought forth by Walter Doyle (1983) deals with the negotiation of low-risk tasks in classrooms. While many teachers are criticized for keeping the intellectual level low, Doyle finds that the blame for this can often be found in students' demands for low-risk, highly convergent work that allows them to achieve well. Doyle describes classrooms as places where students perform in order to earn grades. A class, therefore, can be viewed as an economic system. In such a setting, when the teacher tries to raise the level of discussion, then the students lose some certainty about the way to achieve their grades in the system. Students then begin engaging in acts that bring the task down to a low level, providing them with the security they want. They ask questions like, "How long an assignment should this be?" "Do you want our names in the upper right-hand corner?" "Do you want a library reference?" "Can we work on it together?" and so on. While the critics of education talk about how classrooms are not creative, Doyle has pointed out that, if in fact this is true, the fault lies at least as much with our students and the systems of schooling we have as with the teachers. These fresh ideas change the way we look at classroom interaction.

Findings That Complicate Things

I also said a productive scientific community would expound ideas that would complicate everyone's lives. Two such research findings come quickly to mind. One of them has to do with the fact that truly bilingual children have a cognitive advantage over monolingual children. We keep trying in this country to make bilingual education a program that changes a foreign speaker into an English speaker as quickly as possible. We keep forgetting that bilingual means "speaking two languages." We do nothing to preserve the native languages of the children who come to the United States speaking another tongue. We engage in such peculiar activities as squelching foreign-language speakers in elementary school in order to teach foreign languages in high schools. The findings that are emerging, however, are that truly bilingual children have cognitive advantages and gain economic advantages over monolinguals. Now we have to find a way to accommodate those findings in a system that is not designed to preserve a foreign speaker's native tongue. I am not sure anyone is using this research to guide policy on this matter.

A second example of findings that complicate life is that for low-income children, parent-involvement programs seem to work well. Asking middle-class teachers to deal with lower-class parents, who might also be racially or ethnically different from the teachers, makes for difficulty. Nevertheless, an emerging body of literature shows that when schools and teachers work with parents on educational programs for children, those children seem to achieve much better. These findings complicate things because our teachers and schools are not particularly geared to work closely with parents. Schools have been isolated islands in communities and may now need to redefine themselves, particularly in neighborhoods serving lower-class students.

Findings That Simplify Things

I also said that a productive scientific community should elucidate ideas that simplify everyone's life. This occurs when we find that one of the variables that schools can control is opportunity to learn. Researchers have found that opportunity to learn, or content covered, is one of the best predictors of student achievement. (For reviews, see Rosenshine & Berliner, 1978; Rosenshine, 1979.) This is a simple idea that can guide practice. Another bit of research that seems to call for simplification is the recent work describing the "shopping mall high school (Powell & Farrar, 1985), or, as someone else characterized it, the "cafeteria approach" to high-school education. Research is emerging that questions the proliferation of dozens of elective courses in high schools. Such courses may not have helped American education but harmed it. We probably need students to learn more about particular subjects rather than have them spread their knowledge thin across all sorts of subjects. In the reorganizations and reforms in education that are going on at the present time, we can expect that this research will help simplify course offerings in our public schools.

Counterintuitive Findings

Finally, I said that a productive scientific community should yield ideas and findings that are counterintuitive. One of these findings, which flies in the face of much current thinking, has to do with promoting students who have not passed the work of their present year in school. Schools are under great fire for what is called "social promotion." In this country, therefore, there is a wave of leaving back students who have not completed their year's work. The research, however, goes directly against this trend. The preponderance of research indicates that if there are two children who have not passed an elementary grade and you choose to hold one back and promote the other one, at the end of the next year the one who was promoted will probably be achieving about 15 percentile points above the one who was left back (Holmes & Mathews, 1984). Furthermore, the one who was left back has a lower self-concept and lower overall attitude toward school; he or she generally shows poorer personal adjustment as well. It is estimated that 1 million children will be left back this year because of the belief that children should not be passed if they have not completed their studies. The logic sounds fine, but the research does not support it.

Another example of counterintuitive findings is that young children apparently need very high rates of success in order to learn academic subject matter (Berliner, 1985). A good many people seem to have felt that children learn when they are "stretched," that some intermediate level of difficulty is needed. Perhaps this is because adults seem to learn as often from their errors as from their successes. But the research seems reasonably clear that such is not the case for young children. In approximately the first through fifth grades, a number of researchers are estimating that children's homework assignments and workbook assignments ought to yield a success rate of 90 percent or better and that the questions asked in classroom discourse and recitation should probably yield 80 percent or more successful responses.

One of the oldest examples of counterintuitive ideas in the research literature has to do with the status of "eggheads." Common folklore says that the brightest students are somehow "nerdy" in their appearance and in their social relationships, that they have maladjustments through life, and so on. There is a continuing pervasive belief that the most brilliant children are the least well adjusted. The evidence against this was produced by Terman in his monumental longitudinal study of the gifted that began in the 1920s (Terman, 1925). These children of genius were, in general, more physically attractive than the general population and in better health than the general population. They needed glasses less often, engaged in sports more often, had better social relationships, and were class stars more often and class isolates less often.

It is my belief that research in education has already passed the test of being a productive endeavor. It verifies ideas and practices known to many, it provides new ideas and practices, it promotes ideas that complicate life, it promotes ideas that simplify life, and it provides research that is counterintuitive. Let us move on, then, to the third question.

IS ANY OF THIS EDUCATIONAL RESEARCH OF PRACTICAL VALUE?

I would like to discuss the practical value of educational research by citing findings, concepts, and technology that educational researchers have developed in the last few years. A brief but representative set of findings that show the very practical nature of contemporary educational research includes studies on success rate, structuring, academic feedback, monitoring, motivating, expectancy, and wait-time.

Success Rate

I have already discussed the high success rate that young children need and how the research findings in this area have been counterintuitive. I might also add that the data supporting the value of a high success rate for young children seem to be more impressive with lower-class children, and the data also appear to be more impressive when the nature of the curriculum is hierarchical. That is, unless a child has been successful in learning addition, he or she will have trouble in learning multiplication, and unless the child has been successful at subtraction, he or she will have difficulty in learning long division. Moreover, the necessity for high success rates for young students, where curriculum has been carefully matched to the student so that the student can succeed at it, seems to be the precursor for the development of a positive academic self-concept (Shavelson & Bolus, 1982). The evidence from educational research appears to be quite clear: positive self-concept as a learner *follows* successful experiences as a learner.

How do effective teachers obtain these high success rates? This topic is discussed in Chapter 4. Some of the answers that have been learned from studying effective teachers include: presenting new material in small steps followed by student practice; directing initial student practice through problems and questions; continuing practice until students are confident; and providing for additional, spaced practice to the point where student responses are automatic.

Structuring

Another important research finding is that structuring behavior (providing clear directions, objectives, reviews, and advance organizers for material to be presented) improves classroom achievement. Research shows this to be true. When the distinguished psychologist Jerome Bruner looked at American schools after having spent about a decade in England (Bruner, 1981), he thought that one of the key factors for improving education in America would be to tell children what is expected of them. He saw many children unable to figure out what to do at what time, or where to be, or whom to study with. My own experience of reading protocols of lessons led me to the same conclusion. I spent a good deal of time reading transcripts or protocols of the lessons of teachers who had been classified as either highly effective or less effective. While reading the transcripts, I tried to put myself into the mind of a second- or a fifth-grader. I asked myself whether I could simply understand from the record of classroom instruction what was going on. If the answer was yes, I had almost always identified an effective teacher. If the answer was no—because there were too many interruptions, or the lesson was disjointed, or I could not see where the lesson structure was—the teacher almost always turned out to be less effective. Thus I learned about the practical importance of structuring.

Academic Feedback

We have also learned that effective teachers provide academic feedback. It can be positive or negative feedback, as long as it is academic in its focus. Negative feedback sometimes gets confused with criticism, and criticism *is* harmful to students. Academic feedback that is negative and task-oriented, however, is a positive predictor of achievement. There is a big difference between saying to a child "You write badly" and "The essay you wrote is not good, for the following reasons." Teachers who give a higher rate of academic feedback produce higher levels of achievement than their colleagues who give a lower rate of academic feedback (Fisher, Berliner, Filby, Marliave, Cahen, & Dishaw, 1980). In order to provide such feedback at high rates, there is a need for creative time management by teachers. But creative interpretations of the research are not as necessary as William James had thought. Some of these findings are much less in need of translation to practice than were the findings James had to offer the teachers in his day.

Monitoring

Effective teachers also engage in monitoring during seatwork. An effective teacher does not sit in a corner working with one student in a tutorial. An effective teacher does not grade papers or perform other relevant or irrelevant activities while seatwork is occurring. Effective teachers walk the classroom answering questions privately, working with students privately, and maintaining attention. Effective teachers also provide contingent reinforcement. They do not say "Good" to everything. They do not give out gold stars easily. They make sure behavior and reinforcement are related.

Motivating Students

Effective teachers introduce people to tasks in ways that are positively motivating (see Chapter 9). However, Brophy, Rohrkemper, Rashid, and Goldberger (1983) observed six intermediate grade classrooms 8 to 15 times during reading and mathematics instruction and found that not one teacher ever mentioned that students might derive any personal satisfaction from a learning task. Only a third of the introductory statements included comments likely to have positive effects on student motivation, and most of these were brief general predictions that the students would enjoy the task or would do well on it. One hundred hours of classroom observation yielded only nine task introductions that included substantive information about motivation. None of these went into enough detail to be very meaningful or memorable for most students.

Expectancy

Another set of findings from research on teaching suggests that expectations for performance do actually affect performance. In comparison to students for whom teachers hold high performance expectations, the students perceived to be low performers are more often seated farther away from the teacher, are treated as a group rather than as individuals, are smiled at less, are engaged in eye contact less, are called on less to answer questions, are given less time to answer those questions, have their answers followed up less frequently, are praised more often for marginal and inadequate answers, are praised less frequently for successful public responses, are interrupted in their work more often, and so forth. This kind of differential treatment between students for whom teachers hold high and low expectations appears common enough to worry about and is discussed at length in Chapter 8.

Wait-Time

This finding is particularly interesting. Wait-time is usually defined as the amount of time a teacher waits between asking a good, meaty, higher-order question and calling on students. Researchers have completed at least 16 studies on the topic of wait-time (Tobin, in press). The results clearly indicate that when teachers learn to wait 3 seconds before calling on a student, instead of their customary 0.8 second, some wondrous things happen. The following seven events have been found to be connected with increased wait-time when a good, strong, higher-order question is asked:

1. The length of student response increases.
2. The number of unsolicited but appropriate responses increases.
3. The failures to respond decrease.
4. The complexity and cognitive level of student responses increase.
5. The number of alternative explanations increases.
6. The incidence of child-to-child interactions increases.
7. Student achievement in science and mathematics increases.

No negative side effects are known. The positive effects seem to be many. Yet the behavior is not in the repertoire of most teachers.

It is important to remember that the findings of these 16 studies have the power of the medical research we discussed earlier. The causal connections with achievement are persuasive. The amounts of variance accounted for are persuasive. In medicine, such findings would make their way into accepted practice in just a few years. But in education we do not implement our findings. This does not mean to say that every time a teacher asks a question he or she should wait. What I do mean is that teachers ought to have this behavior in their repertoire, and know how to justify the use and nonuse of wait-time as they work through their lessons. Thoughtful application of our findings in educational research is what is needed, not blanket, unthinking application.

Now let us look at another kind of useful information derived from research. These are the concepts that help us organize our world better—

by helping us to name things, by giving us a technical vocabulary that we can then use with colleagues as we describe classroom phenomena. Concepts need to be easily accessed by teachers if they are to help teachers organize the myriad phenomena present in classrooms. A representative set of practical concepts is discussed, and these include a number of time concepts, which are discussed further in Chapter 5.

Allocated Time

The first of these concepts is a simple one—allocated time. It turns out that allocated time is a positive predictor of achievement because there is enormous variation in the amount of time allocated for instruction in each classroom. We have studied classrooms in which allocated time ranges from 16 to 50 minutes a day in mathematics instruction and from about 45 to 137 minutes a day in reading instruction. These are variations of 2:1 and 3:1 in the amount of time allocated for instruction. This is the kind of concept we must have easy access to in our minds when we think about instruction. When the public criticizes us—when they say children do not know how to write, or they do not comprehend well, or they are not getting enough science—the public is asking whether we as educators have allocated enough time for writing, comprehension, and science activities. Whenever we hear someone criticize the schools in this way, we should ask ourselves whether we are allocating sufficient time. If we are not allocating sufficient time, then students do not have the opportunity to learn the skills the public is asking for. This is a very useful concept for thinking about what instruction is actually offered to students.

Engaged Time

A second time concept that contributes to our technical vocabulary is engaged time. Engaged time, or time-on-task, or attending time, is also a positive predictor of achievement, again because enormous variation has occurred. We find 40–50 percent time-on-task in one classroom, while next door, perhaps with children of the same socioeconomic group, we may see 90 percent time-on-task. These are enormous differences in the amount of curriculum the children are exposed to. We have learned by organizing our observations around these kinds of time concepts that some elementary classrooms cannot even deliver 100 hours of time-on-task over the course of the school year in reading and mathematics combined! This happens, for example, because the school year is not really a year but is in fact nine months. The nine months are not a full nine months; they are really 180 days of instruction. However, the 180 days of instruction must be reduced by the number of days on which there are plays, field trips, strikes, bus breakdowns, snow days that are not made up, mental-health days for teachers and students, and genuine illness of teachers and students. We might end up, if we are lucky, with 140 *real* days of instruction. If mathematics is taught 30 minutes a day—which is very common in, let us say, second grade— we end up with a total allocated time for mathematics of 70 hours for the year. With a low engaged time rate, say 50 percent, the curriculum delivered is 35 hours. All the mathematics for the year is 35 hours! Reading may be double that, about 70 hours, and the whole year may total about 100 hours of engaged time. It should be obvious, therefore, that engaged time is an important concept for thinking about instructional activities in the classroom.

I think that time is the single most important resource over which schools have control. Time concepts, therefore, are important concepts for thinking about curriculum and instruction. They are the yardstick by which we can measure and judge if we are doing what we are trying to do as educators. Research informs us that these concepts are of major importance. Thus they need to be learned well by teachers. I would argue that teachers need to have easy access to these concepts when thinking about their instructional activities.

Curriculum Alignment

Another concept of great utility is variously called curriculum alignment, or overlap, or congruence. This is a very powerful concept in a test-oriented (perhaps test-crazy) society such as ours. The concept refers to the alignment between what is taught and what is tested. Schools, we think, are vastly underestimating their students' performance by using tests mismatched to the curriculum (Freeman et al., 1980). Research informs us, for example, that if a school district is unfortunate enough to have chosen the Stanford Achievement Test as a criterion and uses the Addison-Wesley fourth-grade Mathematics Curriculum Series, there will be an estimated 47 percent overlap. That is, items on the test will have been found to correspond to items in the text about 47 percent of the time. That means, of course, that 53 percent of the items on that test will have been unfamiliar to the students unless the teachers have taken extraordinary action. Even in the best case, with the Scott-Foresman series and the Metropolitan Achievement Tests, the overlap is only about 70 percent. If you ever want to underestimate what your students learn, simply teach one thing and test another! This concept holds for classes as well as districts. If you ever want to get students angry, teach A, test B. In college we get rebellions; in public schools you get anger, hostility, and high dropout rates. This is a very important concept. It helps remind teachers each day that what they do in class should match the outcome measures they use or, *more important*, that the outcome measures they use should match what they do in class.

Concepts to Guide Small-Group Work

Some concepts serve primarily descriptive purposes. They mostly help us organize our world better by rendering that world more comprehensible. Conductance and resistance in electricity; social class in sociology; ego, id, and superego in psychology; and homeostasis in biology are concepts of this kind. These kinds of concepts enrich our lives by helping us describe phenomena. In pedagogy we are also developing a wonderfully descriptive conceptual language from our research endeavors. For example, let us consider the teacher who might choose to work in small groups on a lesson in, say, social studies. He or she may have to use many different techniques simultaneously in order to have successful instruction. The techniques of modern cognitive science have been used to explore teachers' decision making during such interactive group work (Marland, 1977). It was found that teachers who engage in small-group instruction seem to be simultaneously attending to five principles of teaching:

1. *Compensation*, or favoring the shy, the quiet, the dull, or the culturally different.
2. *Strategic leniency*, or ignoring some of the inappropriate behavior of special children.
3. *Power sharing*, whereby the teacher selectively reinforces certain students in order to enlist their aid in sharing responsibility.
4. *Progressive checking*, in which the teacher makes a special effort to check the problems and progress of low-ability students.
5. *Suppressing emotions*, which many teachers feel is appropriate during certain kinds of teaching. Their reasoning is that showing emotion could lead to higher levels of emotionality among the students, which creates management problems in some of the curriculum areas.

Thus the apparently simple task of running a small group, when examined from a cognitive science perspective, requires complex decision making about the application of many principles, and this kind of decision making makes considerable cognitive demands of a teacher. Many rich concepts are used to perform the task.

We have only recently been able to describe exactly how complex the job of teaching really is: researchers have found that teachers make about 30 nontrivial decisions per hour. They are decisions about whether Johnny should stop fractions and go on to decimals, or whether Jane should be moved into the fast mathematics group. These complex, professional, nontrivial decisions take place in environments where teachers can have 1,500 distinct interactions per day with different children on different issues, in different classes where aggregates of students need to be supervised all the time. We are just beginning to uncover the concepts that help us to describe how experienced teachers make decisions in the face of this kind of enormous complexity. We are expanding our practical knowledge base very rapidly.

To conclude these comments on practical concepts, let me remind you that these concepts are the names of things, and that by naming and defining things we thereby organize our world and render it more manageable. When we have a precise concept like "allocated time," or descriptive concepts like "gifted" or "learning-disabled," or even that wonderful concept given to us by Jacob Kounin (1970) and called "withitness," we are developing our technical vocabulary and our language to communicate with each other. The development of a technical language goes hand in glove with the development of our science and the ability to earn more respect from the general public. We in teaching need our unique pedagogical concepts to develop our technical language.

Now let us discuss briefly the new technology we have developed that was totally unforeseen by William James in the 1890s.

Cooperative Learning

In the last decade we have created the technology for producing cooperative behavior among students and between the students and teachers (see Slavin, 1983). These techniques have also given rise to higher self-esteem for the learners, as well as higher rates of proacademic behavior and, even more astounding, higher academic achievement. These recent experiments in cooperative learning environments have involved thousands of students in thousands of classrooms. In the process we have learned how certain teaching techniques can help to integrate handicapped children into the mainstream of the classroom, help to integrate minority students into the majority culture, and help to produce more nearly equal performance of students of different social classes. Such technology has been developed and field-tested only in the last ten years. This is the kind of technology to be taught to preservice and practicing teachers throughout the country. It should influence teacher behavior directly.

Classroom Management

In classroom management, we also have new technology. This is the area that the press and the public love to criticize teachers about, and it is the area that teachers themselves are most afraid of when they begin to teach. We have made unbelievable strides in the last decade. We have identified many of the teacher behaviors that lead to smooth-running, on-task, cheerful classrooms. The original research was first reported only in 1970. Others verified the findings through the 1970s and transformed them into teacher-training materials during the early 1980s (see Chapter 3). These materials, based on empirical research, have been field-tested recently by the American Federation of Teachers. In New York and elsewhere, the results have been amazing. Teachers who had failed to meet the criteria of good management were in complete control of their classes for the first time in their professional lives. One twenty-year veteran of the New York City schools said that the training produced nothing short of a miracle.

Outcome-Based Learning

Let us look at one last example of recently created technology. This technology has to do with outcome-based or mastery strategies (Spady, 1984). We think first of the California Achievement Test data in reading for Johnson City, New York, a small blue-collar community, that has used Bloom's mastery concepts for a number of years. The data we have seen are for 1978, 1979, and 1980. Over time the students do better and better in relation to grade-level norms. By the time students finished eighth grade in 1980, they were two and half years above grade level. On the California Achievement Test in mathematics, Johnson City students gained greater amounts relative to national averages the longer they stayed in the system. In fact, in 1979 and in 1980 students finished about three years above grade level. Similar data are available from another town.

In Red Bank, New Jersey, in 1978, the average eighth grader scored 1.5 years below grade level in reading on the Metropolitan Achievement Tests. In 1983, the eighth graders were 1.5 years above grade level. In mathematics, from 1978 to 1983, the eighth-grade class went from a mean of 1.5 years below grade level to a mean of almost 2.5 years above grade level. In five years of a special program in Red Bank, the mean achievement level in mathematics went up four years on the Metropolitan Achievement Tests. A similar program was found in an elementary school in New Canaan, Connecticut. The overall results showed that about 15 percent of the graduating sixth graders in that school finished half of Algebra 1. About 60 percent of the sixth graders scored at the 99th percentile on the mathematics section of the Metropolitan tests. About 30 percent of the fifth graders scored at the 99th percentile. In the entire school in the last seven years, only about two students per year scored under grade level on this standardized achievement test. The programs in use in these very different schools are outcome-based mastery-type programs. This technology must be understood in order to decide whether to use it or to reject it. Since there are impressive data to support its utility, we all should take this kind of technology very seriously.

In summarizing this discussion of the usefulness of research for practitioners, we can conclude that we have a strong research tradition and a strong research base with which to build bridges to practice. Our scientific base grows richer every month. Our findings, our concepts, and our technology are becoming more advanced every year. Our research is every bit as good as, or better than, that in the medical profession. Our kind of research, however, is much tougher to do. Our colleague N. L. Gage was dining not long ago with a Nobel laureate in biology. The Nobel laureate was very interested in the kind of research that we do in education. Gage asked him, "Why don't you join us? Why don't you become an educational researcher? We need your talent!" The Nobel laureate looked Gage in the eye and said, "God, what an awful thought! That kind of research is much too difficult to do!" This brings us to the fourth question that needs to be asked about research in education.

HOW SHOULD WE INTERPRET EDUCATIONAL RESEARCH FINDINGS?

We have a number of problems in interpreting educational research. These problems limit the generalizability of our findings in a way that does not occur in other professions. Classrooms are complex, dynamic environments. They are kept together by a delicate balance of forces. Sometimes these forces favor us; sometimes they conspire to do us in. Our classrooms are constantly changing: the time of year, current events, special needs of our students—these and other factors sometimes all plot to throw up barriers to implementing educational research in ways that will prove its usefulness. We also have the problem of new brooms in education. That is, we are subject to fads, new curricula, new textbooks, new demands for accountability, new state tests, new superintendents, principals, or curriculum consultants. Findings that have held up in one place, therefore, may not always hold in another place when new events absolutely must be dealt with.

It is also true that we have size problems in education. Technology that might work in tutorial sessions or in small groups of 8 students may not work in a class of 27. Concepts that are useful to describe a group of 8 students may be useless to describe a heterogeneous class of 28. As William James noted only too wisely, educational research needs to be implemented by a thoughtful, reflective practitioner. Our practitioners are very human, and this means that a teacher's personal relationships and personal status sometimes get in the way of implementing programs of research. For example, to implement the mastery program requires hours and hours of preparation time. A teacher who is also a single parent may not be able to spare that time. Teachers who do other kinds of work in the evenings or on weekends may simply not be able to provide the feedback necessary to allow homework assignments to improve achievement in the ways that research says it might. My point is that because of problems such as the delicate balance of classrooms, the way new brooms sweep, the size of the enterprise, and the personal status and relationships of the people involved, the generalizability of educational research is problematical. I believe that in physics and chemistry the relationship of the investigator to what is being studied affects the findings only slightly. In medicine we find more problems when we discover how individual differences affect the course of treatment. We learn, for example, that penicillin works, but not for everybody. In educational research, we are at the other end of the continuum. We work in settings where the investigator, the subjects, and the context all interact in confusing ways. In comparison to some other fields, educational research is much more fragile.

But note: fragility does not imply uselessness. In our culture, fragility means that something should be handled with care. And that is the point. Educational research needs to be taken seriously but handled with care. I am not sure whether educational research will generalize as well as physical and biological findings often seem to. Nevertheless, when we find some conditions under which these findings hold, we are obligated as professionals to take them very seriously. The job of teachers, as William James noted, is to use their minds creatively to apply those findings.

Now, if we are to take the body of findings, concepts, and technology seriously, how should we think about communicating that body of knowledge to practitioners? This brings us to the final question.

HOW SHOULD WE COMMUNICATE RESEARCH KNOWLEDGE TO PRACTITIONERS?

The educational philosopher Gary Fenstermacher (1980) has talked about two ways to put research findings, concepts, and technology into practice: through rules and through discussion of evidence. One of these ways enhances the lives of teachers and one does not.

Communicating Research by Rules

Rules may serve as the means for bridging educational research and practice. This happens when the results of research are converted to imperatives for teachers to follow. For example, from the findings of one study, we learned that "more substantive interaction between the student and an instructor is associated with higher percentages of student engagement." A person engaged in bridging research and practice could use this finding as a rule to govern teacher practice. A principal I know, for example, having read this study, asked his staff to devote not less than half the time available in a given instruction period to teacher-led small-group instruction. In taking this action, the principal bridged research and practice by converting a finding to a rule and requesting compliance with that rule. The principal's school board thought well of him. Nevertheless, a request by someone in authority is often viewed as a command by those who have less authority. That is, there is always a veiled suggestion that doing X will be a factor in a person's evaluation; thus the request to do X can turn into a most demanding requirement. In every case, there is an expectation that one will modify one's behavior according to some other person's interpretation of the research finding. When using rules to communicate, the recipient of the command is not asked to consider the research finding itself but rather is asked to behave in ways suggested by the finding. Communicating research findings by means of rules brings little, if any, advantage to practitioners and makes most researchers angry. It takes research findings out of context, and it also ignores the limits to generalization that concern researchers deeply. Perhaps the most debilitating aspect of communication by rules is its effect on a practitioner's perception of his or her stature and competence. Persons expected to change their behavior on the basis of rules imposed by others are denied a portion of their freedom to think and act independently. If practitioners are ever to have the opportunity to grow as professionals, other means of communicating research to practitioners may be far more productive. Dewey (1929) recognized the temptation to communicate by rules and cautioned that "no conclusion of scientific research can be converted into an immediate rule of educational art." He was, and is, right. William James, as I noted earlier, said that teachers would make a great mistake if they thought that psychological science would provide them with prescriptions for how to act in classrooms. Developing rules is not a style of communicating knowledge that we can approve.

Communicating Research Through Discussion of Evidence

There is another way to communicate knowledge, however, and that is through serious discussion of evidence. A good use of evidence occurs when the results of research are used to test the beliefs that teachers hold about their work. For example, a teacher might argue that it is perfectly acceptable for students to make mistakes. "After all, how can you learn if you don't make mistakes?" A teacher who believes this may be quite casual about preparing classroom or homework assignments for students, thinking that they can always ask questions if they are confused or that their confusion will make them think harder. Findings from one of the studies discussed earlier stated that "tasks which produce low error rate result in higher achievement as measured by standardized tests." This finding casts doubt on the adequacy of our hypothetical teacher's belief about the acceptability of errors. It may not always be possible, or always advisable, to provide error-free tasks, but the findings suggest that the teachers should be more careful in developing and assigning learning tasks, homework, and seatwork to young children. What the research findings do is call into question the reasonableness of the practitioner's beliefs. This is good. This is how we grow. The point made by Fenstermacher, with which I agree, is that a confrontation with evidence (such as having teachers thoughtfully discuss the meaning of findings, concepts, and technologies that researchers have generated) does not require a teacher to modify his or her beliefs automatically every time research findings are presented. It requires only that the teacher weigh the results of the research seriously. To insist on more would be to place greater confidence in educational research than it legitimately commands. In this respect, William James was right. The translation of research findings into practice will always take a creative and inventive mind. For example, consider again the finding that "tasks which produce low error rate result in higher achievement." Now suppose the teacher is teaching long division (or fractions, or the skill of identifying the topic sentence in a paragraph). Simply stating this finding, or even giving two examples, does not tell the teacher how to present the lessons in long division. Even though the research of today is closer to the world of practice, we are still faced with the fact that research rarely can be applied automatically and directly to solve classroom problems.

Our research findings may often conflict with the beliefs held by teachers—beliefs that are supported on the basis of other reasonable grounds. Thus we are well aware that a teacher may at any time be quite justified in choosing to modify or ignore certain findings. They are required, however, as professionals, to reject or adapt research findings thoughtfully. This is what we hope new professionals in teaching will be able to do. They should have a great deal of knowledge about our findings and our concepts. They should have had practice in using our technology. And they should also know when not to use such findings, when such concepts are inadequate, and when such technology is inappropriate.

Given this discussion, we can compare and contrast the two forms of communicating research: rules versus serious discussion. Rules are imposed with the expectation of obedience, while discussion of findings, concepts, and technologies derived from research leads to serious consideration. Rules are imprecise representations of research findings because their construction requires the rule maker to interpret the findings; discussion conveys to the practitioner precisely what has been learned from research studies and lets *them* interpret the data. To adapt or ignore a rule is frequently regarded as an act of subversion, whereas evidence may be freely and openly accepted, rejected, or modified. The imposition of rules can leave a teacher's beliefs, whether sound or unsound, unaffected, while a consideration of evidence encourages the clarification and assessment of one's prior beliefs. Discussing evidence accords the practitioner the status of a thinking, reasoning person; communicating rules treats the practitioner as if he or she were little more than an automaton. The remainder of this book discusses research findings by people who are engaged in the process of creating knowledge. They are talking directly to practitioners. They also hope that the arguments they make will be checked by practitioners who will seek out and read the original research. Through analysis of the original research and discussion of the conclusions of that research, teachers will confront evidence that may or may not support their beliefs about teaching. The result of that confrontation is bound to be good. If teachers do not weigh the evidence brought forth by this research and critically analyze it, someone else is likely to take the findings, concepts, and technologies reported on in this volume and develop rules for teachers to follow. No one engaged in research wants that to happen.

SUMMARY

I have talked about three professions—medicine, law, and education—that were equally disreputable 100 or so years ago. In my analysis, knowledge and skill are what gave the first two the high level of status they now hold. Knowledge is clearly power, a kind of social power. It commands respect and confers status in our technologically oriented society.

Educational research is fully prepared to bring that kind of power to the teaching profession. I hope I have made clear how our research has power, like medical research, if we simply choose to treat it seriously. I hope I have communicated that we have a productive scientific community that provides practical findings for teachers to think about. I hope I have convinced you that despite our problems with generalizability, the educational research produced thus far has to be taken very seriously. And finally, I hope I have convinced you that the communication of research findings to practitioners has to be done in a way that benefits and strengthens the practitioners.

The research reported in this volume is only a part of the broader research that is being developed to transform the teaching profession as it prepares for the twenty-first century. William James would not have recognized the current productivity and creativity in educational research. He probably would still be considered right when he commented that no research findings will tell a teacher what to do with Johnny on Monday morning. But at the same time, he could also be considered to be out of date. The educational research community is providing practitioners with more and more findings, concepts, and technologies that are closely related to their performance as teachers in the classroom. I believe that it no longer requires a great leap of faith to do what James said was impossible—"to deduce definite programmes and schemes and methods of instruction for immediate schoolroom use." The research community of today, so heavily influenced by N. L. Gage, is working with creative teachers everywhere to transform the teaching profession into one in which artists interpret science in ways that allow rapid and successful implementation of research into the schoolroom.

REFERENCES

Berliner, D. C. (1985). Effective classroom teaching: The necessary but not sufficient condition for developing exemplary schools. In G. R. Austin & H.
Garber (Eds.), *Research on exemplary schools.* Orlando, FL: Academic.

Brophy, J. Rohrkemper, M., Rashid, H. & Goldberger, M. (1983). Relationships
between teachers' presentations of classroom tasks and student engagement
in those tasks. *Journal of Educational Psychology, 74,* 544–552.

Bruner, J. (1981, August). *On instructability.* Paper presented at the annual
meeting of the American Psychological Association, Los Angeles.

Dewey, J. (1929). *The sources of a science of education.* New York: Liveright.

Doyle, W. J. (1983). Academic work. *Review of Educational Research, 53,* 159–
199.

Fenstermacher, G. D. (1980). On learning to teach effectively from research
on teacher effectiveness. In C. Denham & A. Lieberman (Eds.), *Time to learn.*
Washington, DC: National Institute of Education, U.S. Department of Education.

Fisher, C. W., Berliner, D. C., Filby, N. N., Marliave, R., Cahen, L. A., & Dishaw,
M. (1980). Teaching behaviors, academic learning time, and student achievement: An overview. In C. Denham & A. Lieberman (Eds.), *Time to learn.*
Washington, DC: National Institute of Education, U.S. Department of Education.

Freeman, D., Kuhs, T., Porter, A., Knappen, L., Floden, R., Schmidt, W., &
Schwille, J. (1980). *The fourth-grade mathematics curriculum as inferred from
textbooks and tests.* IRT Report No. 82. East Lansing, MI: Michigan State
University, Institute for Research on Teaching.

Gage, N. L. (1985). *Hard gains in the soft sciences: The case of pedagogy.* Bloomington, IN: Phi Delta Kappan.

Hedges, L. V. (in press). How hard is hard science, how soft is soft science:
The empirical cumulativity of research. *American Psychologist.*

Holmes, C. T., & Mathews, K. M. (1984). The effects of non promotion on elementary and junior high school pupils: A meta-analysis. *Review of Educational
Research, 54,* 225–237.

James, W. (1983). *Talks to teachers on psychology and to students on some of
life's ideals.* Cambridge, MA: Harvard University Press.

Kounin, J. (1970). *Discipline and group management in classrooms.* New York:
Holt, Rinehart & Winston.

Ludmerer, K. M. (1985). *Learning to heal.* New York: Basic Books.

Marland, P. W. (1977). *A study of teachers' interactive thoughts.* Doctoral dissertation, University of Alberta, Alberta, Canada.

Palincsar, A. M., & Brown, A. L. (1984). Reciprocal teaching of comprehension-
fostering and comprehension-monitoring activities. *Cognition and Instruction, 1,* 117–175.

Powell, A. G., & Farrar, E. (1985). *The shopping mall high school.* Boston: Houghton Mifflin.

Rosenshine, B. (1979). Content, time, and direct instruction. In P. L. Peterson & H. J. Walberg (Eds.), *Research on teaching.* Berkeley, CA: McCutchan.

Rosenshine, B., & Berliner, D. C. (1978). Academic engaged time. *British Journal of Education, 4,* 3–16.

Shavelson, R. J., & Bolus, R. (1982). Self concept: The interplay of theory and methods. *Journal of Educational Psychology, 74,* 3–17.

Slavin, R. (1983). *Cooperative learning.* New York: Longman.

Spady, W. G. (1984). Organizing and delivering curriculum for maximum input. In *Proceedings of three state conferences: Making our schools more effective.* San Francisco, CA: Far West Laboratory for Educational Research and Development.

Terman, L. M. (1925). Mental and physical traits of a thousand gifted children. In L. M. Terman et al., *Genetic studies of genius,* Vol. 1. Stanford, CA: Stanford University Press.

Tobin, K. (in press). The role of wait time in higher cognitive level learning. *Review of Educational Research.*

Touloukian, Y. S. (1975). Reference data on thermodynamics. In H. A. Skinner (Ed.), *International review of science, physical chemistry: Vol. 10, Thermochemistry and thermodynamics.* London: Butterworth.

U.S. Department of Education. (1986). *What works.* Washington, DC.

PART II

CLASSROOM
INTERACTION

CHAPTER 2

GRETA MORINE-DERSHIMER

CAN WE TALK?

When the comedienne Joan Rivers asks, "Can we talk?" audiences enthusiastically answer in the affirmative. They understand her to mean, "Can I be frank, share a little gossip, express my feelings, reveal some personal information?" They encourage her because they expect to be entertained by her comments.

When students in our schools ask, "Can we talk?" however, teachers frequently answer in the negative. A variety of meanings can be attached to the question as asked by students, and teachers discourage student talk for a variety of reasons. But the primary reason is that neither students nor teachers are in school to be entertained.

Teachers have known for years that unbridled pupil talk is damaging to classroom learning. Loose lips not only sink ships (as we were taught in World War II), they also torpedo lessons. However, a classroom in which pupils never talked would be a dull place indeed. Between these two extremes there are many intermediate points, as revealed by recent research. These are classrooms where pupil talk is an important contributing factor in the learning process. Teachers in these classrooms have developed useful rules for determining when to say yes and when to say no when students ask, "Can we talk?" Research has also revealed some interesting characteristics of classrooms that lie nearer to the two extremes. These are classrooms where the rules that permit and prohibit pupil talk may be detrimental to student learning.

This "talk to teachers" about classroom talk examines the different meanings pupils may attach to the question "Can we talk?"; discusses the decisions teachers have made in responding to this perpetual pupil question; and considers the consequences of those decisions.

TALK AS CONVERSATION

Audiences are entertained (and sometimes shocked) by Joan Rivers because she says publicly what most of us reserve for private conversation. For her, to talk means to share personal information. Joan Rivers is not alone in assigning such a special meaning to the term *talk*. Elementary-school pupils who regularly participate in class discussions solemnly report that they do not *talk* during lessons. In one California study of six classrooms, pupils completed a series of sentences, reporting their perceptions of rules for talking in their classrooms. Almost unanimously, they stated that "during a lesson, I talk to . . . nobody" (Morine-Dershimer, Galluzzo, & Fagal, 1980). These pupils were quite clear in their belief that answering questions and talking were two entirely different activities.

Actually, in Joan Rivers's sense, the pupils were fairly accurate in their belief. Out of more than 1,000 responses that students gave to teacher questions, in 36 lessons videotaped in these 6 classrooms, fewer than 300 involved any expression of feelings or "personal" information (that is, information about their personal experiences or opinions). Instead, pupil comments typically contributed academic information (Morine-Dershimer, Ramirez, Shuy, & Galluzzo, 1980).

This is hardly to be wondered at, since lessons are designed to convey academic information. But it illustrates one way in which teachers commonly say no to the frequently unspoken question "Can we talk?" Teacher questions typically invite students to display knowledge of facts and only occasionally encourage them to share personal experiences or opinions.

A number of studies indicate that this type of questioning strategy is quite effective in promoting academic achievement. Teachers who ask many factual questions at a level of difficulty that ensures a high accuracy rate (that is, questions students can answer correctly 85–90 percent of the time) register greater student gains on standardized tests of achievement in reading and mathematics. This is particularly true of teachers who work with pupils who are in the primary grades, or are low achievers, or come from minority or poor families (Brophy & Evertson, 1976; Stallings & Kaskowitz, 1974). Teachers who have been trained to use this "direct instruction" approach have been able to improve the achievement gains of their pupils (Anderson, Evertson, & Brophy, 1979; Stallings, Needels, & Stayrook, 1979). Thus teacher questions that focus on factual academic information clearly contribute to pupil learning.

Some teachers and administrators have interpreted this research to mean that teachers should concentrate almost exclusively on factual talk in lessons. But this is not necessarily the case. Research also provides us with examples of the effectiveness of teachers who encourage conversation.

In the California study noted above, one teacher was particularly effective in integrating a conversational style with a direct instruction approach (Morine-Dershimer & Tenenberg, 1981; Morine-Dershimer, 1985). Mrs. Flood taught a fourth-grade class in a school that served mainly lower-achieving, lower-socioeconomic-status, multiethnic pupils. Her language arts lessons always focused on academic content, but she typically included opportunities for pupils to talk about their own experiences and to relate these to the topic under discussion. For example, a lesson on changing statements to commands was introduced by having students make statements about what they did when they got up in the morning ("I brush my teeth"; "I eat my breakfast"; "I get dressed"). Similar statements were transformed into commands ("Brush your teeth"; "Eat your breakfast"; "Get dressed"), and then students practiced changing textbook statements into commands. In another lesson Mrs. Flood helped students interpret a textbook poem about an embarrassing incident by asking them to recount some of their own embarrassing experiences.

Mrs. Flood's students viewed classroom talk as conversational. They reported that Mrs. Flood, like their parents and their friends, asked questions because she wanted to know something. Students in other classrooms reported that their teachers asked questions because they wanted to teach or tell them something; thus they saw classroom talk as instructional rather than conversational. The interesting thing about these classroom differences was that Mrs. Flood was more effective in promoting pupil achievement gains than most other teachers in this study. Her technique of asking some questions that encouraged expression of personal feelings, experiences, and opinions *related to the subject matter* of the lesson was a useful method for integrating conversational talk into direct instruction. This enabled her to say yes regularly to the question "Can we talk?"

TALK AS TURN-TAKING

Another important meaning of the question "Can we talk?" refers to getting a turn in class discussions. Much of the early research on classroom talk focused on the degree to which teacher talk dominated lessons. Flanders (1970) coined the "two-thirds rule," which summarized the findings that, in a typical lesson, two-thirds of the time someone was talking, two-thirds of the time that someone was the teacher, and two-thirds of that teacher talk was "direct" (i.e., giving directions, presenting information, and asking factual questions as opposed to encouraging students to come up with ideas). More recent research has investigated the opportunities that students have to participate in lessons and the "rules" that teachers follow in distributing these turns to talk (Green, 1983).

One important finding of this research is that turns to talk are not distributed equally. In the classroom, as in the world at large, more privilege accrues to those who are already advantaged. Boys get more opportunities to talk than girls, and higher achievers get more opportunities than lower achievers (Brophy & Evertson, 1976; Morine-Dershimer, 1985). This tendency to favor certain pupils appears to stem from teachers' principles of instructional management (Morine-Dershimer, 1983). Every experienced teacher is guided by principles of the "if-then" type. Thus a teacher may believe *"If* I call on them *then* my less attentive students may stay alert."* In fact, many teachers report that they use turn-taking to keep students alert and on task during a discussion, and in these instances they usually need to call on boys more than girls. Teachers also report that they work to maintain the pace of a lesson, therefore want to ensure a high proportion of correct answers, and so may call on higher achievers more often than lower achievers. It is interesting to note, however, that many teachers will wait longer for higher achievers to respond to a question (Brophy & Good, 1969). This is apparently related to teacher expectations that higher achievers will be able to get the right answer if given time to think, but it is another way in which teachers may favor more advantaged students. Still other teachers report calling only on pupils who volunteer, because they do not want to embarrass pupils who may not know the right answer. In lessons featuring factual questions with one right answer, higher-achieving pupils are apt to volunteer more frequently than lower achievers. This is in line with pupil beliefs that you should raise your hand only if you know the right answer (Morine-Dershimer, 1985). Thus teachers who are trying to apply research on direct instruction may use several procedures that lead them to distribute turns to talk unequally.

This unequal distribution of opportunity may be detrimental to the very students who most need to learn. There are indications that participation in class discussions is an important contributor to pupil achievement. In the California study mentioned earlier, pupils who participated frequently scored significantly higher in reading achievement at the end of the school year than those who participated infrequently, even after controlling statistically for entering achievement (Morine-Dershimer, 1985).

This does not mean that strictly equal distribution of turns to talk is necessarily a good rule to follow. One of the teachers in the California study followed this rule with adverse results (Morine-Dershimer, 1983). Mrs. Estes called on pupils in a fairly random fashion, so that turns were distributed fairly equally across achievement levels. She encouraged all pupils to contribute their ideas in a discussion. However, her lessons were not sharply focused on academic content. She seemed to encourage talk for its own sake, rarely denoting answers that were correct or that contributed well to development of the lesson topic.

Students in this classroom had equal opportunity to express their ideas, but the ideas were not clearly related to subject matter content and discussions did not operate to explicate or reinforce important concepts.

Mrs. Estes's students scored significantly lower than Mrs. Flood's students in achievement gains. In Mrs. Flood's class, higher-achieving students had more turns to talk, but lower-achieving students had many opportunities as well. Two features of talk in Mrs. Flood's classroom were associated with student achievement gains. First, class discussions were focused on academic content, and student ideas that contributed to development of that content were clearly denoted by teacher praise. Second, while higher-achieving pupils talked more frequently, lower-achieving pupils had opportunities to participate. Giving students turns to talk is an important way for teachers to say yes to the question "Can we talk?" But the talk must relate to academic content.

TALK AS A COMMUNICATION TASK

Another sense in which students may raise the question "Can we talk?" is revealed by the research on the types of communication tasks that confront students in classrooms. Not only do these tasks vary widely from lesson to lesson, but they may also vary within a single lesson and from one ability group to another (Cazden, 1985). Green (1983) notes that teacher expectations about what type of talk is appropriate in a given lesson are often expressed implicitly, so that students must infer the exact nature of the communication task at the same time that they are attempting to learn the academic content embedded in the task. Given this complexity, some students may be confused about how and when they are permitted or obligated to talk. This is important because communicative behavior that does not accord with teacher expectations may result in negative judgments about pupil ability. Several studies illustrate problems associated with differences in teacher and pupil expectations related to communication tasks.

In a pioneering study, Susan Philips (1983) examined classrooms in a Native American community. Teachers were concerned about students' seeming inability to respond to questions. Philips noted that patterns of interaction in the community were quite different from those in the classroom. In the community, questions did not carry an obligation of immediate response but might be answered several minutes later. Since a comment was not necessarily topically related to the preceding comment, speakers had more control over when they spoke and what they said, and their turns to talk were not controlled by others in the discussion group. The patterns of communication that children had learned at home led to confusion about the communication task associated with answering teacher questions in the classroom. Teachers attributed student patterns of response (or nonresponse) to low ability or lack of comprehension.

Michaels (1981, 1983) studied "sharing time" in primary classrooms. She noted that black and white children used different narrative styles. White children were topic-centered (that is, their whole stories would relate to one topic or event), while black children did more topic associating (that is, their reports would move from topic to topic, rather than focus on a central theme). The white teachers judged the topic-associating style to be less appropriate and conveyed this by interrupting the black children's narratives to ask questions and make comments. In a later study, Michaels and Cazden (1986) conducted an experiment in which both styles were recorded on tape, masking the race and social-class origin of the narrators. White teachers considered stories presented in topic-associating style to be poorly formed and judged students using this style to be low achievers. Black teachers were more apt to judge both types of stories positively and to rate the narrators as capable. These studies show that teacher and pupil differences in interpretation of a communication task can lead to negative teacher judgments of pupil ability.

Au (1980) showed that a teacher could redesign the classroom communication task to conform more closely to the expectations of Hawaiian children, which were based on communication patterns they had learned at home. In this study, the teacher encouraged a cooperative response mode where several children answered in unison, rather than singling out one pupil at a time to talk. This mode was a familiar interaction style for pupils, and pupil achievement improved with its use. Thus, as teacher and pupil expectations about the communication task became more similar, pupil achievement increased.

In another interesting study (Carrasco, Vera, & Cazden, 1981), a teacher judged a Mexican-American girl to be of low ability, based on her behavior in class and on the fact that she was repeating first grade. Researchers videotaped an episode in which the girl was helping a Mexican-American boy to practice spelling. Unobserved by the teacher, the girl performed this communication task very competently, keeping the boy on task and helping him to correct his errors. The videotape showed that the girl had greater cognitive and intellectual competence than the teacher realized. In this case, when the communication task was varied, so that the student took on a new role and greater responsibility, pupil performance and teacher evaluation both improved.

Tenenberg (1987) provides information on what may be a more common source of pupil confusion about the communication task. He examined teacher questions, focusing particularly on instances in which the same question was asked of several pupils. This pattern of questioning could occur under at least three types of instances: (1) where the first response was wrong and the teacher wanted a correct response from another pupil; (2) where the first response was correct but incomplete, and the teacher wanted additional information from another pupil; and (3) where the question allowed for a number of different correct responses so that, while the first response was appropriate, the teacher wanted to get several additional responses from other pupils. In each of these three cases the communication task was different, yet teachers rarely provided cues to help pupils identify which of the three conditions pertained. Furthermore, Tenenberg noted, when teachers asked several students to state their opinions on a topic (the third condition described above), they frequently praised some contributions and merely accepted others. While the teacher question implied that all opinions were equally valid, the teacher reaction suggested that "some were more equal than others." Tenenberg saw this as a potential source of confusion for pupils about the real nature of the communication task.

In the California study discussed earlier, two teachers were particularly adept at defining the communication task clearly for pupils. Both these teachers had higher pupil-achievement gains than other teachers in the study (Morine-Dershimer, 1985). Mrs. Flood, as noted earlier, used a conversational style, so that the communication task was similar to patterns children had learned at home. In addition, after asking a question that invited a series of alternative appropriate responses, she tended to accept all responses as valid, rather than confusing pupils by selecting some for special praise. Finally, when she invited pupils to report on their experiences, Mrs. Flood frequently modeled an appropriate response by telling some story about her own experience, thus clarifying the communication task.

Mrs. Brown, another teacher in this study, used a variety of questioning strategies but carefully provided cues about each communication task. For example, the pupils' task in one lesson was to ask questions to solve a puzzle. As in the game Twenty Questions, all questions had to be phrased so the teacher could answer yes or no. In this situation, when the teacher answered no to a student question, the "no" conveyed useful information. It was not a negative evaluation of the pupil's idea, as it would be in a more typical classroom questioning sequence. The first several times that she responded no to a pupil question, Mrs. Brown immediately added, "but that's a good question." Thus she worked to clarify the new communication task for her pupils.

These studies show that teachers can improve pupil achievement and encourage pupil talk in lessons by defining the communication task clearly, by recognizing communication patterns that pupils have learned at home, and by designing classroom communication tasks that build on these patterns. Pupils can infer from these behaviors that teachers are responding with a resounding yes to the question "Can we talk?"

TALK AS EXERCISING COMMUNICATION SKILLS

One further meaning of the pupil question "Can we talk?" deserves exploration. Research shows that children bring certain important communication skills with them when they come to school, skills that can be useful in lessons (Green, 1983; Cazden, 1986). These skills are exhibited in peer-group interaction and are used to advantage by some pupils in instructional settings. Important communication skills involve both speaking and listening. Selective attention, attention getting, information giving, and information getting are skills that children use in play settings as well as in lessons. These skills have been associated with both social and academic success.

In the California study (Morine-Dershimer, 1985), children were observed in both lessons and play settings, and their attention to and interpretation of language was investigated. In both settings children exhibited selective attention. In play groups, they were particularly attentive to directive language ("Pour the sand in the cup"; "Now let's change places"), while they tended to ignore attention-getting language ("Watch me"; "Listen to me"). In lessons they were particularly attentive to pupil responses to questions, while they tended not to recall teacher questions and directions. In both settings, use of selective attention was related to success. Socially successful children (those high in status with peers, as measured by a sociometric test) paid more attention to directive language in play groups and in lessons than did less successful students. One characteristic of the high-peer-status student was his or her ability to lead or direct the play activities, and apparently being alert to the directive or controlling language of others was associated with this ability. Academically successful pupils (high in reading achievement) were more attentive during lessons to teacher questions and the responses of other academically strong pupils than were their less successful peers. These were the questions and responses that conveyed most of the academic content of the lesson, so skill in attending to them could well contribute to academic success.

Attention getting was another communication skill associated with success in both play groups and lessons. In play groups, bids for attention were verbal ("Lookit!" "Hey, you guys!"), and observers noted that children of low peer status, particularly low-status boys, were less adept at getting the attention of their playmates than children of high peer status. In lessons, bids for attention were nonverbal, as children raised (or waved) their hands to request a turn to talk. Children of low academic status were less apt to be called on, or recognized, by the teacher. Thus inability to gain the attention of others was associated with lack of success in both social and academic settings.

Information giving was also an important communication skill in both play groups and lessons. In play groups, children initiated informative comments, frequently reporting to others about the activities in which they were engaged, and these comments were attended to closely by the other participants. In lessons, children provided information in response to teacher questions, and this information was also carefully attended to by other children. In both settings, children had opportunities to learn from the information that their peers provided, and, in lessons, the information given by the more academically successful students was more apt to be heard by other children.

A fourth communication skill exhibited by children in both play groups and lessons was information getting. In the California study (Morine-Dershimer, 1985), the information traced was sociolinguistic in nature (who said what to whom). High-peer-status children gathered more sociolinguistic information in both play groups and lessons than did lower-peer-status children. Thus skill in tracking the social aspects of language was associated with social success.

A study by Wilkinson and Calculator (1982) focused on children's skill in getting academic information in peer-directed reading groups. Children in these groups read silently or aloud and completed worksheets or other tasks associated with the reading. They were permitted to ask each other for assistance. Higher-achieving students were more clear and explicit in requests for information and were more successful in obtaining compliance with their requests. Thus, skill in gathering academic information was associated with academic success.

These studies show that skill in communication is closely associated with social and academic success. Yet those children who are less adept at the essential communication skills of selective attention, attention getting, information giving, and information getting rarely receive instruction designed to improve these skills. Children who have learned important communication skills may take advantage of every opportunity to practice these skills in lessons. Children who have not yet developed these skills may need to hear teachers give a more explicit yes to the question "Can we talk?"

LOCATING THE REAL LIMITS ON TALK IN CLASSROOMS

Research on teaching demonstrates that classroom talk is highly patterned. In fact, it is so patterned that it was dubbed a "language game" by Arno Bellack and his colleagues (1966). The question-response-reaction cycle of classroom discussions or recitations is so pervasive that it has been found to be a stable characteristic of teaching for more than 50 years (Hoetker & Ahlbrandt, 1969) and in many different countries (Bellack, 1973).

When classroom talk fits the typical pattern, the teacher initiates interaction by asking a question. Teacher questions tend to be "convergent," aiming to elicit a single correct answer. They tend also to be "known-information" questions (Mehan, 1979), in that the teacher knows the answer before he or she asks the question. Student responses tend to be contributed by one person at a time. They generally provide nonpersonal information, and they frequently consist of single words or brief phrases rather than full sentences (Morine-Dershimer, 1985).

Each of these characteristics has important positive aspects. When teachers are the primary source of questions, they are in control of the flow of content. They can design lessons to present tasks that gradually increase in cognitive complexity, and they can ensure a pace that permits coverage of all essential content. When the questions are convergent and the correct answers are plainly marked by teacher acceptance or praise, students receive clear signals designating the information that is to be learned. When "known-information" questions predominate, teachers have clear guidelines to apply in judging which answers require corrective feedback and which students may be having difficulty mastering the material.

When one student at a time responds, teachers can identify individual students who have learned or failed to learn the concepts being discussed. When responses are focused on academic, rather than personal, information, more academic content can be covered. When responses are brief, the pace of the lesson is maintained and student interest is sustained. All of these factors can contribute to greater pupil achievement gains (Brophy & Good, 1986).

However, each of these characteristics of classroom talk also has certain negative aspects. When the teacher is the principal source of questions, students have few opportunities to develop their own skill in asking questions, and this is a critical skill for productive inquiry or successful problem solving. When teacher questions are chiefly convergent, students have few opportunities to develop skill in divergent or creative thinking, yet this is also an essential problem-solving skill. When "known-information" questions strongly predominate, classroom communication tasks are sharply differentiated from patterns of communication learned at home, and children who do not perform according to teacher expectations may be inaccurately judged as lacking in ability.

When student responses to teacher questions are restricted to one student at a time, the number of opportunities any one student has to participate is necessarily restricted as well, yet frequency of participation is associated with achievement gains. When student responses are limited to nonpersonal information, children may come to view academic discourse as distinct from and irrelevant to real-life experiences. When student responses consist primarily of one- or two-word utterances, the communicative competencies that children develop at home and at play are neither used nor expanded. In short, when severe limits are imposed on patterns of classroom talk, students have little opportunity to develop the complex thinking and communication skills needed for effective adult functioning.

But, contrary to some beliefs, teachers can reap the rewards of direct instruction techniques *without* imposing severe limits on classroom talk. Not all lessons need to be taught by direct instruction, and, even during direct instruction, teachers can vary communication patterns to some degree.

HOW TEACHERS SAY YES EFFECTIVELY

Studies of classroom talk have identified effective teachers who have developed procedures that enable them to say yes enthusiastically to the pupil question "Can we talk?" These procedures can be used in conjunction with direct instruction techniques and in some cases are closely associated with these techniques.

Clarifying the Communication Task

One set of procedures teachers have been observed to use involves clarification of the communication tasks in which children are engaged. These procedures are basic to direct instruction techniques and can be used effectively in other types of lessons as well.

Effective teachers regularly orient students to the procedures to be used and the content to be covered in a lesson. They introduce their lessons by briefly outlining or describing the activities to be pursued and the topic to be discussed. For example, in the California study (Morine-Dershimer, 1985), Miss DeLuca oriented students as follows:

> Here's what we're going to do. We're going to build mental pictures in our heads. . . . We're going to see mental pictures . . . to practice using our imagination . . . everybody's pictures will probably be different. You'll close your eyes to see it, to see the thing in your head. And then, when you're picturing in your mind, you can ask—what do you see? What do you feel? What do you hear? Tell us about what you saw at that moment. . . . Now, after I do about three with you, I'm going to let you be the teacher, and you're going to get to come up and ask the class to build a mental picture. . . . Okay? Let's try one.

Effective teachers frequently model the procedures they want students to follow. This is particularly important when a new communication task is being introduced. For example, in the California study, Mrs. Brown wanted students to compare two dissimilar objects, to develop skill in creative thinking. She modeled the process herself by comparing two similar things (two girls in the class), being careful to note several different ways in which they were similar (both girls, both wearing blue, both liking to jump rope, both sitting at the same table) in order to demonstrate that in this communication task, each question would have several right answers.

Effective teachers typically provide praise, corrective feedback, and probing questions that indicate what *kinds* of answers are appropriate, as well as which specific answers are correct. This is critical when new communication skills are being learned. For example, in Miss DeLuca's lesson on building mental pictures, she used praise and probing questions to denote that detailed, imaginative responses were appropriate, as well as stating specifically that a variety of answers would be correct.

MISS DELUCA: I can see something that is red and running. Do you see something that is red and running in your mind? Okay. Open up your eyes. Who would like to tell us about it? Ray?

RAY: A red fox running.

MISS DELUCA: A red fox running. Robert?

ROBERT: I saw red bricks, and when I moved my eyes, it made them move.

MISS DELUCA: Wow! Everyone will have different answers, won't they? Mark?

MARK: I saw a red roadrunner.

CHRIS: I seen a red rabbit.

MISS DELUCA: Chris saw a red rabbit. All of these are very good. Ysa?

YSA: A red clown.

MISS DELUCA: What was he doing? Was his face red too?

YSA: He had red all over him and red buttons, and he was juggling.

Mrs. Brown also used praise, corrective feedback, and probing questions well in a lesson where pupils were developing skill in asking good questions.

MRS. BROWN: I am thinking about a teacher at this school, and I want you to ask me some good questions that will help lead you to the answer. Now, don't just guess, don't just ask, "Is it Mrs. Hart?" I don't want that kind of question. Darren.

DARREN: Is it a third-grade teacher?

MRS. BROWN: Is it a third-grade teacher? No, it is not. Good question, though. Good question. Now you can eliminate third-grade teachers. All right. Madeline.

MADELINE: Is her hair blonde?

MRS. BROWN: No, her hair is not blonde. Good question. Arthur.

ARTHUR: Is she pretty?

MRS. BROWN: Yes. Melanie.

MELANIE: Is it Miss DeLuca?

MRS. BROWN: Do you have enough information to ask that question? What color is Miss DeLuca's hair?

AMANI: Blonde.

MRS. BROWN: And what did Madeline ask me before?

MADELINE: If her hair was blonde.

MRS. BROWN: And what did I say?

KEVIN: No.

MRS. BROWN: So you also have to be a very good listener in this game. A very good listener. Frank.

FRANK: Is her hair brown?

MRS. BROWN: Yes.

In these examples teachers are using techniques identified as effective in direct instruction lessons to clarify communication tasks that are new to pupils and that are not typical of tasks presented in direct instruction lessons. These procedures can be used to clarify both familiar and unfamiliar communication tasks. When teachers orient students to procedures and content to be dealt with in a lesson, when they model the procedures to be used, and when they provide praise, corrective feedback, and probing questions that delineate appropriate responses clearly, pupils are less apt to be confused about what is expected of them and are more apt to believe that they can participate, or talk, in lessons.

Varying the Communication Task

The above examples involve lessons in which the basic communication task was somewhat atypical (that is, not focused on convergent, "known-information" questions). Occasional use of such lessons provides variation that can be effective in developing communication skills and maintaining student interest and attention in lessons (Flanders, 1970; Morine-Dershimer, 1985). In addition, studies show that many teachers are skillful at varying the communication task within a single lesson (Green, 1983).

Effective teachers design lessons in which the questions asked and the communication tasks practiced become progressively more difficult. Each task builds on the preceding task in ways that maximize student success.

Effective teachers also demonstrate ability to ask questions that encourage students to share personal experiences and opinions without losing the content focus of the lesson. Their lessons have a conversational tone as well as a content orientation.

In the California study (Morine-Dershimer, 1985), Mrs. Flood taught a lesson that illustrates both techniques. The topic was how to change statements to commands. Selected segments demonstrate the sequence.

TASK	INTERACTION
Sharing personal information	MRS. FLOOD: In the morning when you get up, what are all the things that you do? What's one of the things that you do? Mike?
	MIKE: Eat breakfast.
	MRS. FLOOD: You eat breakfast. Kim.
	KIM: I make my bed.
	MRS. FLOOD: All right. Rachel.
	RACHEL: I put my clothes on my bunk bed, and I get dressed on my bunk.

Reading aloud from chalkboard	MRS. FLOOD: Now, I put a few sentences on the board this morning. Brandon, would you read the first one for us?
	BRANDON: You will brush your teeth.
	MRS. FLOOD: All right. The next one, Karen?
	KAREN: You will put on your clothes.
Comparing and contrasting sentences	MRS. FLOOD: Now I'd like you to look at those four sentences and see what you can see about them that's the same. Nina.
	NINA: "You will . . ."
	MRS. FLOOD: Okay. Kris, do you think you could come over and erase those two words she just mentioned? . . . Now, how are these sentences different from the four that were up there before?
	SHAWN: They're demands.
	MRS. FLOOD: They're demands. And we call them commands. They're demands that you do something.
Changing oral statements to commands	MRS. FLOOD: Do you see the difference between a statement and command? Let's see if you can change some for me. "You will go out to recess today if it doesn't rain." Can you make that a command? Nina.
	NINA: Go out to recess if it doesn't rain.
	MRS. FLOOD: Let's try another one.
Changing textbook statements to commands	MRS. FLOOD: Let's see if we can change a few in your textbook. The very first one on the top of the page says, "You will feed the rabbit a carrot." Kendra.
	KENDRA: Feed the rabbit a carrot.
	MRS. FLOOD: Good. The next one. Kim.
Generating commands appropriate for a familiar situation	MRS. FLOOD: Now, this is something you might actually see happening. Can you think of a command to fit this? A dog is running after a ball out in the street, and there's a car coming. What command might you say? Think about it for a minute. What could you say? John?
	JOHN: Get back here!
	MRS. FLOOD: Get back here. What were you thinking about, Don?
	DON: Get out of the street!
	MRS. FLOOD: Fine. Another command? Bob?

In this lesson the tasks that confronted students gradually increased in difficulty, and the teacher asked questions related to students' personal experience, as well as "known-information" questions. These techniques serve to vary the communication tasks that students practice within a given lesson and can also help to increase students' opportunities to participate.

Maximizing Opportunity to Participate

Research indicates that pupil opportunity to participate is related to achievement in two ways. Pupils who participate more in class discussions show greater gains in achievement than pupils who refrain from participating (Morine-Dershimer, 1985). Also, pupils who are lower achievers may be given fewer opportunities to participate (Brophy & Good, 1969). This can include being called on less frequently, being given less time to respond to a question when called on, and having partial answers accepted, rather than probed to elicit a full response. Teachers who work to maximize pupil opportunities to participate have been observed to use a variety of techniques.

Effective teachers make use of questions that invite a variety of appropriate responses, carefully signaling to students that more than one answer is expected (Tenenberg, 1987). This provides opportunities for several students to respond to the same question and may encourage more students to participate by relieving pressure to respond with the "right" answer.

Effective teachers also use a longer wait-time after asking a question, thereby providing students some time to think of an answer (Swift & Gooding, 1983; see also Chapter 1). This can lead to longer answers, more relevant responses, and more overall student talk. Not only are more students willing to volunteer to respond, but in responding with longer answers, they are using more complex communication skills. When a teacher asks a question and then pauses about three seconds before calling on a student, beneficial results usually occur.

Effective teachers vary the procedures they use for turn-taking and clearly indicate the participation rules to be followed in a given lesson (Cazden, 1985; Green, 1983). They may call on one volunteer at a time they may allocate turns in a "round robin" sequence, or they may invite choral responses. Whatever the procedure, they are alert to the importance of providing opportunities for lower-achieving students to contribute useful information to the lesson (Morine-Dershimer, 1985). In addition, they are aware of patterns of participation used at home by children of different cultural backgrounds (Au, 1980; Michaels, 1981; Philips, 1983), thus avoiding the trap of misjudging the intellectual ability of students who may misinterpret classroom communication patterns.

These fairly simple techniques enable teachers to increase pupil participation in classroom talk by maximizing the opportunities that various pupils have to participate. The procedures that serve to clarify the communication tasks and vary communication tasks within a lesson also increase the probability that pupils will understand how to contribute appropriately to class discussions. Thus they help to maximize opportunity to participate.

CONCLUSION

Research on classroom talk shows that pupils may attach a variety of meanings to the seemingly simple question "Can we talk?" Talking in classrooms may mean engaging in real conversations about personal experiences. It may mean getting a turn to respond to a teacher's question. It may mean exercising communication skills that children have developed at home and at play that are rarely practiced in lessons or accepted as appropriate behavior by teachers.

Research on effective teaching has demonstrated that direct instruction procedures can increase pupil achievement. The patterns of teacher questioning and pupil response that are typical of direct instruction need not limit teachers' ability to say yes to the question "Can we talk?" Effective teachers clarify the communication task for pupils, vary communication tasks between and within lessons, and maximize pupil opportunity to participate. These techniques enable students to engage in real conversations, get frequent turns to talk, and exercise a variety of communication skills. In sum, effective teachers can and do emulate the audiences of Joan Rivers, encouraging their students to ask, "Can we talk?" and answering enthusiastically in the affirmative.

REFERENCES

Anderson, L., Evertson, C., & Brophy, J. (1979). An experimental study of effective teaching in first-grade reading groups. *Elementary School Journal, 79*, 193–223.

Au, K. (1980). Participation structures in a reading lesson with Hawaiian children: Analysis of a culturally appropriate instructional event. *Anthropology and Education Quarterly, 11*, 91–115.

Bellack, A. (1973). *Studies in the classroom language.* New York: Teachers College Press.

Bellack, A., Hyman, R. T., Smith, F. L., & Kliebard, H. M. (1966). *The language of the classroom.* New York: Teachers College Press.

Brophy, J., & Evertson, C. (1976). *Learning from teaching: A developmental perspective.* Boston: Allyn & Bacon.

Brophy, J., & Good, T. (1969). *Teachers' communication of differential expectations for children's classroom performance: Some behavioral data* (Texas Research and Development Center for Teacher Education, Report No. 25). Austin: University of Texas.

———. (1986). Teacher behavior and student achievement. In M. C. Wittrock (Ed.) *Handbook of research on teaching,* 3rd ed. New York: Macmillan.

Carrasco, R., Vera, A., & Cazden, C. (1981). Aspects of bilingual students' communicative competence in the classroom: A case study. In R. Duran (Ed.), *Latino language and communicative behavior*. Discourse processes: Advances in research and theory, Vol. 4. Norwood, NJ: Ablex.

Cazden, C. (1986). Classroom discourse. In M. C. Wittrock (Ed.), *Handbook of research on teaching*. 3rd ed. New York: Macmillan.

Flanders, N. A. (1970). *Analyzing teaching behavior*. Reading, MA: Addison-Wesley.

Green, J. L. (1983). Research on teaching as a linguistic process: A state of the art. *Review of Research in Education, 10*, 151–252.

Hoetker, J., & Ahlbrandt, P. A. (1969). The persistence of recitation. *American Educational Research Journal, 6*, 2.

Mehan, H. (1979). "What time is it, Denise?": Asking known information questions in classroom discourse. *Theory into Practice, 18* (4), 285–294.

Michaels, S. (1981). "Sharing time": Children's narrative styles and differential access to literacy. *Language in Society, 10*, 423–442.

———. (1983). Influences on children's narratives. *Quarterly Newsletter of the Laboratory of Comparative Human Cognition, 5*, 30–34.

Michaels, S., & Cazden, C. (1986). Teacher/child collaboration as oral preparation for literacy. In B. B. Schieffelin (Ed.), *Acquisition of literacy: Ethnographic perspectives*. Norwood, NJ: Ablex.

Morine-Dershimer, G. (1983). Instructional strategy and the "creation" of classroom status. *American Educational Research Journal, 20*, 645–661.

———. (1985). *Talking, listening, and learning in elementary classrooms*. New York: Longman.

Morine-Dershimer, G., Galluzzo, G., & Fagal, F. (1980). *Rules of discourse, classroom status, pupil participation, and achievement in reading: A chaining of relationships*. Participant perspectives of classroom discourse, Final report, Part III. Syracuse, NY: Syracuse University Division for the Study of Teaching.

Morine-Dershimer, G., Ramirez, A., Shuy, R., & Galluzzo, G. (1980). *How do we know?* (Alternative descriptions of classroom discourse). Participant perspectives of classroom discourse, Final report, Part IV. Syracuse, NY: Syracuse University Division for the Study of Teaching.

Morine-Dershimer, G., & Tenenberg, M. (1981). *Participant perspectives of classroom discourse* (Final report NIE G–78–0161). Washington, DC: National Institute of Education.

Philips, S. U. (1983). *The invisible culture*. New York: Longman.

Stallings, J. A., & Kaskowitz, D. H. (1974). *Follow-through classroom observation evaluation, 1972–73*. Menlo Park, CA: Stanford Research Institute.

Stallings, J., Needels, M., & Stayrook, N. (1979). *How to change the process of teaching basic reading skills in secondary schools*. Menlo Park, CA: SRI International.

Swift, N., & Gooding, T. (1983). Interaction of wait time, feedback, and questioning instruction on middle school science teaching. *Journal of Research on Science Teaching, 20* (8), 721–730.

Tenenberg, M. (1987). Diagramming question cycle sequences. In J. L. Green & J. Harker (Eds.), *Multiple-perspective analyses of classroom discourse*. Norwood, NJ: Ablex.

Wilkinson, L. C., & Calculator, S. (1982). Requests and responses in peer-directed reading groups. *American Educational Research Journal, 19*, 107–120.

CHAPTER 3

CAROLYN M. EVERTSON

MANAGING CLASSROOMS
A Framework for Teachers

Sara Smith awakened early. It is the first day of school, and she has a dozen last-minute chores to do before she is ready to greet her new students. This will be her first year of teaching second grade. For the past several weeks she has been decorating the room, making lists, collecting materials, developing lesson plans, and trying to think of a good way to arrange her classroom. She hopes her students will like her, will enjoy school, and will want to work hard. She is not sure how well things will go. "I'll just have to do my best and wait and see," she says, keeping her fingers crossed.

Doug Jones will have five classes of high-school history this year. He has taught history before in another school. He enjoys his subject, and he wants his students to like it also. He makes a note to check on the textbooks for his classes and to find out where his class rosters are. He has collected some amusing posters to brighten up the bulletin boards. School begins in three days, and he is hoping the year will go well.

Most teachers have been in Sara Smith's or Doug Jones's shoes at some time, anticipating the opening of the school year and facing the task of finding workable ways to set up and organize their classrooms. Even the most accomplished and confident teachers have felt the anxiety of needing to begin "somewhere" to deal with the problem of order in their classrooms and to sort through the myriad of practical details required to conduct lessons. One of the enduring truths of schooling is that most teachers do get through that first day of school and the days that follow. Most will even look back when school comes to a close and speculate about what went well, what did not, and what they wish they had done differently, such as spending more time with Robert to help him overcome his fear of fractions, or working more with Melanie to help her work more independently, or requiring that all students turn in homework when it is due instead of giving extensions. Most of us who teach use this hindsight to give us renewed determination to get a better start when school opens again in the fall and to do some things differently the next time.

Classrooms are busy, crowded, and complex places. The demands placed on teachers and the environmental press for rapid decisions often leave little time to think before having to act. Philip Jackson's (1968) observation that teachers may engage in as many as 1,000 interactions in a single day will come as no surprise to most teachers.

For the most part, teachers have been left on their own to solve the problems inherent in teaching a large group, or several large groups, of students on a daily basis. Sara Smith and Doug Jones are caring teachers with good intentions. Until fairly recently, classroom research has offered little guidance, leaving teachers to fall back on the traditional practical wisdom: "You have to find whatever works for you," or "You really have to like kids," or "Clamp down at the beginning and lighten up later." We are not suggesting that this advice is not often correct. We are saying that it, by itself, does not provide a guiding framework with which to make decisions about the complex job of managing classrooms.

Finding ways of creating predictable, orderly classrooms, establishing rules, gaining student cooperation in tasks, and coping with the procedural demands of the classroom have largely been left to the inventiveness and good intentions of the classroom teacher. As Lortie (1975) describes the teacher's task:

> The teacher . . . is expected to elicit work from students. Students in all subjects and activities must engage in directed activities which are believed to produce learning. Their behavior, in short, should be purposeful, normatively controlled, and steady; concerns with discipline and control, in fact, largely revolve around the need to get work done by immature, changeful, and divergent persons who are confined in a small space. (p. 151)

The purpose of this chapter is to provide an overview and general framework for helping teachers to develop their own approaches to managing their classrooms. What we outline here should not be considered a complete guide to teaching; it should be seen as a starting point. The suggestions summarized here have also been presented in books written particularly for teachers (Emmer, Evertson, Sanford, Clements, & Worsham, 1984; Evertson, Emmer, Clements, Sanford, & Worsham, 1984).

RESEARCH ON CLASSROOM MANAGEMENT

Some of the first and most important research on the management of classroom groups was done by Jacob Kounin (1970). He started by studying how a teacher's handling of misbehavior influences other students who have witnessed it but were not themselves participants. Kounin called this the "ripple effect" and concluded that ways in which teachers handle misbehavior once it has occurred have little effect on student behavior. It is instead the means by which teachers prevent problems from occurring in the first place that differentiate effective from less effective group managers. Kounin described the more effective group managers as possessing, among other things, "withitness" (the ability to communicate an awareness of student behavior), "smoothness" (the ability to move in and out of activities smoothly), and "momentum" (the ability to sustain a good lesson pace avoiding sudden starts, stops, or digressions). Effective managers also used "group alerting" to keep their students attentive during lessons. Most often these techniques were designed to keep the rest of the group attentive while one student was reciting (for example, calling on listeners to comment on a response, selecting students randomly, looking around the group before choosing someone to recite). Effective group managers also used techniques for keeping students accountable for paying attention by having them show work, by circulating and checking performance, or by calling on individuals.

Findings from this and other work on effective teaching also supported the relationship between well-managed classrooms and student achievement (Good, 1979; Medley, 1977). In studies of effective teaching in second- and third-grade classrooms, Brophy and Evertson (1976) found that teachers whose students consistently gained in achievement organized classrooms that ran smoothly, with a minimum of disruption. Their results supported many of Kounin's earlier findings. Teachers in these classrooms also actively taught their students the procedural skills needed to participate in class lessons, such as how to complete assignments, obtain supplies, or get a turn at answering.

We became interested in how teachers who had well-run, stimulating, and task-oriented classrooms accomplished this from the first day of school. This interest led us and our colleagues to begin a series of research studies that addressed the following objectives:

1. To discover what principles of management, organization, and group processes were most important for beginning the year.
2. To determine if these principles were related to effective management throughout the year.
3. To collect a number of highly descriptive and rich examples that illustrated how effective managers implemented skills and techniques related to good management.

Findings of these studies are described briefly below.

Studies of Elementary-School Classrooms

Twenty-seven self-contained third-grade classrooms were observed extensively starting with the first day as well as the first weeks of school, then periodically for the remainder of the year (Emmer, Evertson & Anderson, 1980; Evertson & Anderson, 1979). Observers were trained to collect information using a variety of instruments that assessed student engagement, classified behavior, and captured a sequence of events in narrative form. These included establishing rules, routines, and expectations, strategies for gaining student cooperation in academic tasks and activities, and control of student behavior. From this information we could identify teachers who were especially effective at managing their classrooms and those who were less so. Several characteristics distinguished the better managers:

1. *Analyzing classroom tasks.* Better managers were able to analyze in precise detail the procedures and expectations required for students to be able to function well in the classroom.
2. *Teaching the going-to-school skills.* Better managers included instruction in rules and procedures as an important part of the curriculum in the first weeks of school and provided opportunities for practice and feedback.
3. *Seeing the classroom through students' eyes.* Better managers could analyze their students' needs for information about how to participate in class activities. This information was signaled in ways that were predictable and consistent.
4. *Monitoring student behavior.* Better managers kept their students in view and dealt with problems quickly.

Studies of Junior-High-School Classrooms

Because of departmentalization in most secondary schools, we believed that the organizational and managerial tasks facing secondary-school teachers were likely to be different from those confronting elementary-school teachers. Another exploratory study was conducted in junior-high-school classes (Evertson & Emmer, 1982; Sanford & Evertson, 1981). Fifty-one mathematics and English teachers were observed in two of their regularly scheduled classes. Collection of information in these classes was done in a similar way to that used in the elementary-school classes just mentioned. Observations began on the first day of school and continued extensively for the first three weeks, then less often for the rest of the year. Fourteen one-hour observations were made in each teacher's two classrooms. Classrooms were compared on a variety of measures, and differences between good and poor management could be detected. Better management could be distinguished in the following ways:

1. *Explaining rules and procedures.* Better managers had explicit rules, procedures, expectations, and rationales that were developed into a coherent system and communicated to students.
2. *Monitoring student behavior.* Better managers were more consistent in support of their management system. They were aware of and dealt with disruptive behavior and potential threats to their system.
3. *Developing student accountability for work.* Better managers developed a detailed system for keeping track of student academic work.
4. *Communicating information.* Effective managers could present information clearly, reduced complex tasks to their essential steps, and had a good understanding of student skill levels.
5. *Organizing instruction.* More effective managers preserved their instructional time and had more students engaged in academic work.

Training Teachers in Classroom Management

Additional studies were conducted to determine if the findings from the elementary- and secondary-school classrooms could be developed into training materials for teachers (Evertson, Emmer, Sanford & Clements, 1983; Emmer, Sanford, Clements, & Martin, 1983; Evertson, 1985). Results from these studies showed that not only could the findings be used for teacher in-service programs, but that teachers who used the management suggestions for planning and establishing rules, procedures, and routines were able to establish better student engagement in their classrooms, with less off-task behavior and less inappropriate and disruptive behavior.

Findings from these studies were used to develop in-service workshops for teachers. In one such program, adopted by the state of Arkansas (sponsored by the Arkansas Department of Education), 150 (45 percent) of the state's school districts have used a classroom-management model based on these findings to train teachers in their schools (Evertson & Smylie, 1986; Evertson, Weade, Green, & Crawford, 1985).

A FRAMEWORK FOR MANAGING CLASSROOMS

In the remainder of this chapter, we will describe several guidelines for developing an effective management system. These points are organized into the following major areas:

1. Planning before the year begins.
2. Getting started during the first few weeks (implementing the plan).
3. Maintaining the management system throughout the year.

It is important to note that although the use of this framework will help teachers to manage their classrooms more productively, they should be seen primarily as an enabling set of plans, strategies, and techniques that can set the stage for learning to occur. Each of these steps will be discussed briefly, along with key points to consider. Each section will conclude with a set of questions to guide thinking about your own system.

PLANNING BEFORE SCHOOL BEGINS

Use of Space (Readying the Classroom)

A natural place to start planning for the school year is with the arrangement of the classroom and its furnishings. As many teachers already know, there are few "ideal" classrooms with an abundance of space for students, work areas, and storage. For most teachers, the task of planning the physical arrangement of desks and furnishings in the space they are allotted is one of making trade-offs between what they would like to have and what they must work with. How the available physical space is used can have important implications for how students participate in class activities and how they may interact with the teacher and with each other.

Provisions for seating students, access to needed storage areas, and locations for posted assignments, equipment, and materials will convey to students how the room will be used and what the teacher's expectations are. Classrooms that function in support of instructional goals appear to have been arranged with the following considerations in mind:

1. *Visibility*. Students should be able to see the instructional displays. The teacher should have a clear view of instructional areas, students' work areas, and learning centers to facilitate monitoring of students.
2. *Accessibility*. High-traffic areas (areas for group work, pencil sharpener, door to the hall) should be kept clear and separated from each other.
3. *Distractibility*. Arrangements that can compete with the teacher for students' attention (seating students facing the windows to the playground, door to the hall, face to face with each other but away from the teacher) should be minimized.

Some teachers may not have an assigned classroom, but must conduct their lessons in shared space or in space ordinarily allocated for other purposes. While choices may be limited in a "borrowed" classroom, how the space is used and what materials are needed to teach are still of prime importance. Much of the teacher's plan will be concerned with compensating for the many routine things normally available in the permanent classroom. For example, assignments may have to be written on chart paper and brought to the class each time, along with materials and supplies. If the temporary space does not allow some students to be easily monitored, the teacher will have to allow for this and make certain to keep eye contact with students.

Questions to think about:

• What areas in the classroom are likely to cause congestion—pencil sharpener, teacher's desk, or a materials center?
• How can frequently used materials be stored for easy access?
• Will the teacher be able to see and to monitor students easily?
• Are high-traffic areas clear so students can reach the teacher for help and vice versa?
• Are display and instructional areas easily visible to all students?
• Are students who need special help seated so they can receive assistance easily? Are they seated away from distractions that could compete for their attention?

Determining Classroom Rules and Procedures

General Classroom Rules.   Rules are a fact of life. They govern our behavior in numerous ways. The requirements for living in a social world and working in group settings mean that some individual freedoms must necessarily be regulated to accomplish the goals of the group or society at large. Classrooms are no different from other social settings in this regard. Rules in classrooms may be explicitly stated by the teacher or may be negotiated with students. Nevertheless, well-managed classrooms do not operate without them.

Effective classroom managers in both elementary and secondary schools have well-developed classroom rules and procedures and spend much of the time at the beginning of the school year teaching these to their students, in much the same way they would teach an academic lesson. Classroom rules, particularly in the upper grades, can be written rules that are either posted, given to students to copy, or provided on ditto sheets for their notebooks. Rules differ from classroom procedures (discussed in the next section) in that they define general expectations or standards for behavior. For example, the general rule "Be in your seat and ready to work when the bell rings" defines a set of behaviors that should always be practiced. Classroom procedures, on the other hand, communicate expectations for behavior but are usually directed at accomplishing specific activities as opposed to defining general behavior or prohibiting some action.

Each teacher must decide just what rules are the most important and appropriate in his or her classroom. These decisions will depend on instructional goals, the developmental level of the students, and expectations and attitudes regarding appropriate behavior, among other things. Nevertheless, a few guidelines that can help in planning a reasonable set of classroom rules are listed below.

First, rules should be stated clearly so that students will know precisely what behavior is expected of them. For example, a rule such as "Be in the right place at the right time" is ambiguous. A likely consequence of this ambiguity is that much time can be devoted just to clarifying and interpreting what it means before students can comply. A better statement might be, "Be in your seat and ready to work when the bell rings."

Second, rules should be supported by rationales that are necessary and beneficial for a positive class climate. An overly arbitrary or negatively stated set of rules can convey negative expectations, discourage student responsibility, and lead to teacher-student conflicts that defeat the goals of a positive, productive class.

Third, keep the list of rules as short as possible. Usually four or five well-planned rules will cover most areas. Avoid long lists of "do's" and "don't's" that may challenge students to test the system in those areas that the list of rules does not specifically cover.

Fourth, classroom rules should be consistent with school rules and policies. Some behaviors that are expressly required, such as having hall passes for trips outside the classroom, or expressly forbidden, such as running in the halls, will need to be reinforced in each classroom.

Finally, many teachers prefer to involve students in rule setting. This strategy can promote student responsibility for good behavior and encourage ownership in helping the class function well. This strategy can be useful and can work in several ways. First, rationales for rules and their meanings can be the basis for class discussions. During discussions, students have an opportunity to check their understanding and to voice any concerns they may have. Second, students can be provided with choices within reasonable limits—such as free choice in seating, as long as the general rule of not disturbing others is followed. Finally, in some matters, students may actually be able to vote or to reach a consensus—for example, on where or when to take a field trip or to use particular materials.

Although it is important to keep the number of classroom rules short and manageable, the actual number of rules is not as critical as the development of these rules into a systematic set of expectations that is consistently reinforced and followed.

It is also important to plan time during the year to review the classroom rules. Students may need reminders, and some rules that are not consistently followed may have ceased to function and should be re-examined. By the same token, new classroom tasks and activities that have been implemented as the year progresses may need new rules.

Points to consider in developing rules:

- Are class rules consistent with school policy?
- Are they specific enough to be easily understood?
- Do they address all the major areas that need to be covered?
- Which rules can students have a part in developing?
- What positive examples can be used to illustrate the rules?

Procedures for Specific Activities.   Procedures, as we have said, communicate expectations for student behavior, but usually refer to accomplishing a specific activity, such as collecting assignments, moving to the reading group, obtaining a hall pass, or checking out of or returning books to the library.

We have already discussed planning the use of classroom space. However, the ways that the space will be used are equally important. The accommodation of 25–30 people in a confined space such as the typical classroom necessarily means planning for physical movement in and out of the room or in and out of small groups within the classroom. Specific routines promote smooth and quick transitions between activities and thus add to instructional time. Such routines also reduce disruption that can lead to behavior problems. They help maintain lesson flow, continuity, and student engagement in academic work. A carefully prepared list of classroom procedures can facilitate the establishment of these routines.

Table 1.   Checklist of Classroom Procedures.

Area	*Procedures or Expectations*
I. Room use	
A. Teacher's desk and storage areas	
B. Student desks and storage for belongings	
C. Storage for class materials used by all students	
D. Drinking fountains, sink, pencil sharpener, wastebasket	
E. Bathrooms	
F. Centers, stations, or equipment areas	
II. Transitions in and out of room	
A. Beginning the school day	
B. Leaving the room	
C. Returning to the room	
D. Ending the day	
III. Procedures during group work	
A. Getting class ready	
B. Student movement	
C. Expected behavior in group	
D. Expected behaviour out of group	

Table 1 (Continued)

Area	Procedures or Expectations

IV. General procedures
 	
  A. Distributing materials
  B. Behavior during interruptions
  C. Bathrooms
  D. Library, resource room, school office
  E. Cafeteria
  F. Playground or school grounds
  G. Fire and disaster drills
  H. Class helpers	

V. Other general procedures for secondary-school classrooms
  A. Beginning the period
    1. Attendance check
    2. Previously absent students
    3. Late students
    4. Expected student behavior
  B. Out-of-room policies
  C. Materials and equipment
    1. Pencil sharpener
    2. Other room equipment
    3. Student contact with teacher's desk, storage, other materials
  D. Movement of student desks
  E. Ending the period	

VI. Seatwork and teacher-led instruction
 	
  A. Student attention during presentations
  B. Talk among students
  C. Student participation
  D. Obtaining help
  E. Out-of-seat procedures
  F. Tasks after seatwork is completed	

SOURCE: Adapted from Emmer et al. (1984) and Evertson et al. (1984) with permission.

Even a cursory look at the many specific behaviors required of students in a typical elementary- or secondary-school classroom will reveal a wealth of specificity and detail that the teacher must address. Space does not permit an extensive discussion of the number and types of procedures that teachers can employ. Table 1 is a checklist that includes major areas that will need some type of procedure in most elementary and secondary classrooms.

For example, classroom procedures for room use in Table 1 include the teacher's desk, student desks, storage areas, and so on. Most teachers have specific requirements regarding whether or when students may have access to the teacher's desk. Students may be required to keep their desks neat and clean and to respect the privacy of other students' desks. If drinking fountains are in the hall rather than in each classroom, provisions for student drinks must be planned for.

In secondary-school classrooms, teachers may require that students leave desks in a specific arrangement and that they put away equipment or materials in preparation for the next class. If so, this requirement must be spelled out for students, and time must be allocated for them to do it.

At the beginning of each class period, most secondary-school teachers have administrative routines associated with keeping records for a large number of students. Expectations for what students are to be doing as the teacher completes these tasks should be made clear to them. "Warm-ups" or other short-term activities can keep students occupied during this time.

While many of the common procedures needed in most classrooms are included in the checklists, you may think of others. Take some time to go over these checklists carefully. As you think about these specific areas, it may also remind you of other classroom procedures that you may need.

Activities and questions to think about:

- Use the checklist in Table 1 and list as many specific procedures as possible for each of the main areas.
- What areas in the classroom will need special procedures?
- How will these procedures be taught to students?
- What school-wide procedures do students need to know about?
- What procedures will be needed later on in the year that should be planned for now?

Procedures for Managing Student Academic Work. One of the most persistent features of schooling is that much academic work that students do revolves around the completion of assignments. Sometimes assignments are to be finished in class, as in the case with seatwork, and sometimes at home. Sometimes assignments are seen by students as "for a grade" instead of "just for practice." The nature of these and other learning activities will differ by grade level or subject area; however, teachers must still consider carefully, specifically, and in advance just how they will handle student work, how they will check it, and what portion of students' grades will be based on tests, daily assignments, homework, or special projects.

Effective teachers in the classrooms we studied often provided initial "warm-up" activities at the beginning of the class period, as students were entering the room. In math classes, these might be one or two new problems; in English classes, they might be a scrambled sentence or new vocabulary words to define. Students worked on these, and they became part of the daily grade. "Warm-ups" accomplished several purposes. One was to establish a content focus; another was to use the first few minutes of the class period when the teacher was tending to administrative details; a third was reinforcement of skills and concepts and provision of practice. The fact that "warm-ups" were checked and counted as part of the total grade supported their being taken seriously by students.

Effective teachers also made sure that they checked student work regularly, provided feedback and correctives, and rechecked to make certain students were learning concepts correctly. They found ways to accomplish this close monitoring by having students check each other, by continually moving around the room during seatwork and looking over each student's work, or by having students check their own papers and then turn them in. Sometimes students placed their work in folders that were checked weekly; sometimes students routinely turned in daily work for informal checking. In secondary-school classrooms where teachers often had five separate classes to teach, it became doubly important to find efficient ways to check student progress.

Table 2 is a general checklist of procedures teachers should consider in deciding on good ways to monitor and evaluate student work. While these procedures are appropriate for most classrooms, additional ones will probably be required for special situations such as science labs, physical education classes, or art and music classes. Look over the areas on the list, and use them to guide thinking about what procedures are needed for your classes.

Activities and questions for managing students' academic work:

- Fill out the checklist in Table 2. Share your ideas with another teacher, and see if you can add more options to your list.
- How frequently should I check on student work?
- What kinds of feedback can I give students about their progress?
- How quickly should I provide feedback?
- How can I provide ways for students to check themselves?
- How shall I assess student effort as well as progress on assignments?
- What are the school's policies regarding the reporting of grades?

Identifying Consequences

It would be ideal if all that was needed to establish a smoothly running classroom was a good set of rules and procedures. Unfortunately, just because there are classroom rules and procedures to be followed, not all students will necessarily follow them just because they are asked

Table 2. Checklist of Accountability Procedures.

Area	Notes
I. Communicating assignments and work requirements	
A. Where and how will you post assignments?	

B. What will be your standards for form and neatness?
    —Pencil, color of pen
    —Type of paper
    —Erasures
    —Due dates
    —Headings
    —Incomplete work
    —Late work	

C. What are your procedures for make-up work?
    —Assignment list or folder
    —Time for completion
    —Where to turn in
    —Help for absentees	

D. What grading criteria or other requirements will be described?	
II. Monitoring progress and completion of assignments	
A. What procedures will you use to monitor work in progress?	
B. What checking procedures will you use?	
C. How will you determine whether students are completing assignments?	
D. What records will you keep of students' work?	
E. How will you collect completed assignments?	
F. What records of their work will students keep?	
G. When and how will you monitor projects or longer assignments?	

Table 2 (Continued)

Area	Notes
III. Feedback A. What are your school's grading policies and procedures? B. What kinds of feedback will you provide, and when? C. What will you do when a student stops doing assignments? D. What procedure will you follow to communicate with or send materials home to parents? E. Where might you display student work? F. What records, if any, of their own work will students keep?	
IV. Grading system A. What components will your grading system have? B. What will be the weight or percentage for each component? C. How will you organize your grade book? D. Will you allow extra credit assignments? If so, when? How much will they count?	

SOURCE: Adapted from Emmer et al. (1984) and Evertson et al. (1984) with permission.

to. Rules and norms for appropriate behavior have implicit consequences for compliance or noncompliance in order to function as rules. If teachers fail to make clear to students the consequences of their behavior, students will eventually try to determine these for themselves. Teachers recognize this as "testing the limits." One way to anticipate potential problems is to discuss with students rules and procedures, the rationales for these regulations, and the accompanying rewards and penalties, as we mentioned in the previous section on classroom rules. Another essential part of planning for the first weeks of school includes determining what the consequences will be for appropriate and inappropriate behavior.

For each of your general classroom rules and for each of the procedures shown in Table 1, decide what rewards and penalties are appropriate in your classroom. Types of rewards can vary from the concrete, such as symbols or tokens, to recognition. The rewards and penalties you consider will depend on the age of your students. For example, public praise may backfire in a secondary-school classroom, but can motivate younger children if used properly. You should also consider how rewards and penalties will function to promote the desired behavior and how much effort they will require to administer fairly. Some systems require a great deal of teacher time and effort for accurate recordkeeping, such as some types of token systems in which students earn points toward a larger reward. Others may require relatively little, such as smiles, symbols on papers, or private praise.

We will not attempt a complete discussion of rewards and penalties here; a great many writers have discussed the appropriate types of rewards and penalties, how frequent they should be, and how they function in helping or hindering students to learn self-control (see Chapter 9). The point for the teacher is that rules and procedures are more likely to be followed if students have a clear idea of the expected behaviors and the consequences for their cooperation or noncooperation. Ultimately, our goal for students is to help them develop self-control and to manage their own behavior. A clear understanding of the consequences of their behavior can be a step toward this end.

Points to consider in developing consequences:

- What district or school policies might affect my choice of rewards and penalties?
- Are my rewards and penalties suitable for the age level of my students? Are they of sufficient variety? Do they encourage the desired behavior?
- Can I be consistent in applying the rewards and penalties I have chosen, or will the system be difficult to administer?
- Have I encouraged positive ways for students to reinforce their own behavior?

Readying the classroom, determining general classroom rules and specific procedures, developing procedures for managing student work, and determining consequences for behavior are key areas for teacher planning prior to the first day of school. The next section offers some suggestions for implementing what you have planned and for beginning the school year.

IMPLEMENTING YOUR SYSTEM

Getting Started on the First Day of School

The first day of school has special significance for both teachers and students. It is at this time that rules, routines, and expectations are established. Students' first impressions about their classrooms, their teachers, and what standards are expected can have a lasting effect on their attitudes and on the ways they will engage in classroom tasks. Effective classroom managers appear to understand the importance of orienting students to the setting and consistently communicating these expectations. The teacher's task becomes one of gaining student cooperation in following the rules and procedures and in completing assignments.

Some beginning activities for elementary-school classrooms might include the following:

1. *Greeting students.* Teacher provides nametags, designated places to sit, a place for belongings.
2. *Introductions.* Teacher and students tell something about themselves.
3. *Describing the room and how to use it.* Teacher points out major areas of the room, their use, and any procedures associated with them.
4. *Get-acquainted activities.* Teacher provides ways for students and teacher to know each other better, uses sharing activities.
5. *Discussing rules, procedures, and consequences.* Teacher presents these and provides some opportunities for students to practice them. Actively teaching young children the rules and procedures is an important part of instruction during the first day and the first weeks. This includes describing and demonstrating the desired behavior, having students practice, and providing feedback about how well they did.
6. *Teaching a procedure.* Teacher begins to instruct students in one of the class procedures that they will need to know, such as heading papers or locating materials and replacing them. Keep in mind the following steps in teaching a procedure:
   a. *Describe and demonstrate the desired behavior.* Explain precisely what is acceptable and what is not; provide a model. Let students also demonstrate the procedure for the class.
   b. *Rehearse.* Let students practice the behavior or the correct method. If procedures are complex, break them down into their components and let students practice each part and then put them all together.
   c. *Provide feedback.* After students have had a chance to practice, let them know if they have done it properly. If improvement is needed, point that out, too, and give them a chance to try again.
7. *Content activities.* Teacher provides early content activities that students should be able to accomplish. Engaging students in these activities can supply important information about completion rates and skill levels.

In secondary-school classrooms, activities for the first day will differ in some ways. The teacher in junior high or high school will usually be confined to specific class periods and will teach several groups of students within each of those times. These students will probably not require as much instruction in rules and procedures as will elementary-school students, although they may require instruction in some of the procedures for doing assignments. Additionally, they can perform many administrative tasks such as filling out class cards. It is important to be visible, available, and in charge as soon as students enter class, even before the bell.

Activities for secondary-school classrooms could include:

1. *Introductions.*
2. *Administrative tasks* (completing course cards, taking attendance, checking rosters, school paperwork, learning correct pronunciation of names).
3. *Discussing course requirements.*
4. *Discussing classroom rules and procedures.*
5. *Content activity* (brief review and introduction of new course content).

It may not be possible to accomplish all of these tasks on the first day. If class periods are short or if there are interruptions, some of these activities can be handled on the second day of school and consistently followed up thereafter. Time invested in establishing a comprehensive system at the beginning will pay handsome dividends throughout the year.

MAINTAINING THE SYSTEM THROUGHOUT THE YEAR

Careful planning and care in instructing students about classroom rules, procedures, routines, and expectations are essential to a good start, as we have said. However, continued and consistent efforts toward maintaining your management system are just as crucial as the year progresses. There are a few things to remember about keeping things going; these are consistent monitoring, keeping students accountable for academic work, and dealing with inappropriate behavior.

Monitoring Student Work and Behavior

Monitoring requires that teachers regularly survey their class or group and watch for signs of student confusion. It also involves checking for understanding in other ways, such as having students demonstrate the steps, questioning them, or other means of detecting potential problems with academic material.

Teachers are unlikely to be able to deal with student inattention or stop misbehavior before it spreads if they do not see it in the first place. Likewise, teachers can appear inconsistent in reinforcing their classroom rules and procedures if they are not aware of infractions. If some students are consistently out of the teacher's line of sight, it may signal to these students that they are not as accountable for their work or behavior as others in the class. All of these things can lead to management problems that can become more severe as time goes on.

Still, the importance of monitoring does not lie only in the detection of potential behavioral problems. It also provides teachers with important information about student performance, the appropriateness of assignments (are they too easy? do students finish too quickly? are they too difficult, so that students cannot complete them?). Teachers who make a practice of routinely checking students and attending to nonverbal cues can often catch problems before they continue too long and before errors are practiced and reinforced.

Monitoring tips to consider:

- Make a practice of routinely scanning the room.
- Keep a whole-group focus, particularly when giving instructions meant for everyone.
- Avoid spending too much time with one student or a group of students such that you lose eye contact with the rest of the class.
- Keep alert for the early signs of avoidance of seatwork or student confusion about assignments.

Dealing with Inappropriate Behavior

Much student behavior can be dealt with by letting students know what is expected of them. In this chapter, we have stressed a preventive approach that includes careful preparation and development of routines, procedures, and expectations that are systematically taught and modeled for students. These steps will go a long way to ensure student cooperation and compliance. Threats to a good system can still develop, however, and teachers will have to intervene to stop inappropriate behavior.

Most inappropriate behavior should be handled promptly to avoid its continuing and spreading. Behaviors such as persistent inattention, avoidance of seatwork, and obvious violations of classroom rules and procedures need to be dealt with. Ways of doing this include redirecting the student's attention to tasks, making eye contact or moving nearer the student, reminding the student of the correct procedure, or directly asking the student to stop. It is important to maintain a calm, reasoned approach and to avoid overreacting. Some inappropriate behaviors are of short duration and not serious (for example, momentary whispering, brief visual wandering) and would be more disruptive to deal with than to call attention to.

More serious misbehaviors, such as rudeness or hostility toward the teacher, chronic avoidance of work, or fighting, will require both immediate and long-term strategies. Extensive reviews of the various disciplinary and intervention approaches that can be used are beyond the scope of this chapter. However, we can give some general guidelines. First, the teacher will need to consider both short- and long-term responses to the misbehavior. The first step in addressing the problem will be to remain calm and to avoid power struggles with students. Get help if needed. Over the long term, it may be necessary to find out what triggered the problem and to work with the student on an individual basis to help improvement. This also may mean enlisting the help of other school staff members, counselors, or special education resource teachers.

Points to consider:

- What positive techniques can I use to deal with difficult students?
- Am I being consistent in dealing with student behavior?
- Do I have a plan for handling problems when they occur?
- What is my long-range plan for dealing with persistent misbehavior?

ENDING THE SCHOOL YEAR

With much of our focus on getting off to a good start at the beginning of the school year, the end of the school year may seem to be the least of our concerns. But teachers in our studies have often mentioned that endings as well as beginnings have their special meanings. Students and classes that were at one time cooperative and productive sometimes became apathetic, lethargic, and uncooperative. Teachers mentioned difficulties with enthusiasm and increases in inappropriate behavior and disruptive behavior, even in classes that were formerly running smoothly and were task-oriented. Stanford (1977) points to the feelings of both students and teachers that can accompany the ending of the term or school year. In some cases, students may experience a sense of loss of both relationships they have developed and opportunities that have passed by; in other cases, they need to assign a value to their year-long efforts.

How these experiences and feelings are dealt with is of great importance in determining what aspects of the past experience can be retained and used in the future. Paradoxically, the more successful the teacher has been at promoting a cohesive and positive classroom climate, the more likely some of the anxieties of separation will occur.

Teachers need to be sensitive to things that can be done to modify these effects. Activities that highlight successful projects, special student shows or fairs where work is displayed, awards, parties, or other tangible proofs of accomplishment help to commemorate the significance of student efforts. These events can help to affirm to students and teachers the value of their mutual work and can provide positive experiences that can be reflected on at a later time. Many teachers intuitively plan these events as a fitting capstone to the year. Before the school year progresses too far, it will be useful to begin to plan suitable activities with which to conclude the year.

SUMMARY

Some first steps in developing a system for organizing and managing classrooms have been presented. The uniqueness of each classroom and the variety and complexity of tasks that teachers face make it impossible to prescribe specific techniques. The purpose of this chapter has been rather to provide a framework for thinking about these important areas.

The initiation of any activity or set of activities will necessarily involve some planning, implementing, and maintaining. Although our discussion has centered around the specific steps teachers can take to develop and install a management system, these steps should be viewed as interrelated, cyclical, and dynamic. For example, the introduction of a new unit of work may require that students participate in the classroom in different ways; changes in expectations for participation can mean changes in the classroom arrangement. This in turn could require different rules, procedures, and expectations for academic performance and may alter the ways students can demonstrate their knowledge. Each of these shifts in classroom tasks and activities can mean new cycles of planning, implementing, and maintaining. We have also suggested that concluding events play a part in this cycle.

The teacher's task remains one of orchestrating these events in ways that serve curriculum goals. Skill in managing classrooms doesn't just happen. It takes time, reflection, systematic analysis, and willingness to participate in personal inquiry to adapt good strategies. Effective use of these strategies can support teaching at its very best and enable the creation of the optimal conditions for student learning.

REFERENCES

Brophy, J., & Evertson, C. (1976). *Learning from teaching: A developmental perspective.* Boston: Allyn & Bacon.

Emmer, E., Evertson, C., & Anderson, L. (1980). Effective management at the beginning of the school year. *Elementary School Journal, 80,* 219–231.

Emmer, E., Evertson, C., Sanford, J., Clements, B., & Worsham, M. (1984). *Classroom management for secondary teachers.* Englewood Cliffs, NJ: Prentice-Hall.

Emmer, E., Sanford, J., Clements, B. & Martin, J. (1983). *Improving junior high classroom management.* Paper presented at the annual meeting of the American Educational Research Association, Montreal.

Evertson, C. (1985). Training teachers in classroom management: An experiment in elementary school classrooms. *Journal of Educational Research, 79* (1), 51–58.

Evertson, C., & Anderson, L. (1979). Beginning school. *Educational Horizons, 57,* 164–168.

Evertson, C., & Emmer, E. (1982). Effective management at the beginning of the school year in junior high classes. *Journal of Educational Psychology, 74,* 485–498.

Evertson, C., Emmer, E., Clements, B., Sanford, J., & Worsham, M. (1984). *Classroom management for elementary teachers.* Englewood Cliffs, NJ: Prentice-Hall.

Evertson, C., Emmer, E., Sanford, J., & Clements, B. (1983). Improving classroom management: An experiment in elementary school classrooms. *Elementary School Journal, 84,* 173–188.

Evertson, C., & Smylie, M. (1986). *Research, training, and practice: Outcomes and implications for staff development.* Paper presented at the annual meeting of the American Educational Research Association, San Francisco.

Evertson, C., Weade, R., Green, J., & Crawford, J. (1985). *Effective classroom management and instruction: An exploration of models.* Final report (NIE-G-83-0063), Washington, DC: National Institute of Education.

Good, T. (1979). Teacher effectiveness in the elementary school: What we know about it now. *Journal of Teacher Education, 30,* 52–64.

Jackson, P. (1968). *Life in classrooms.* New York: Holt, Rinehart & Winston.

Kounin, J. (1970). *Discipline and group management in classrooms.* New York: Holt, Rinehart & Winston.

Lortie, D. (1975). *Schoolteacher: A sociological study.* Chicago: University of Chicago Press.

Medley, D. (1977). *Teacher competence and teacher effectiveness: A review of process-product research.* Washington, DC: American Association of Colleges for Teacher Education.

Sanford, J., & Evertson, C. (1981). Classroom management in a low SES junior high: Three case studies. *Journal of Teacher Education, 32,* 34–38.

Stanford, G. (1977). *Developing effective classroom groups: A practical guide for teachers.* New York: Hart.

CHAPTER 4

BARAK V. ROSENSHINE

EXPLICIT TEACHING

The research on effective teaching conducted since 1974 has revealed a pattern that is particularly useful for teaching a body of content or explicit skills. This pattern is a systematic method of teaching that includes presenting material in small steps, pausing to check for student understanding, and requiring active and successful participation from all students.

Although this pattern came primarily from research in reading and mathematics instruction in elementary and junior high schools, the results are applicable to any explicit or "well-structured" (Simon, 1973) body of knowledge whose objective is to teach skilled performance or mastery of a body of knowledge. Specifically, these results are most relevant to areas such as teaching mathematical procedures and computations, reading decoding, explicit reading procedures (such as distinguishing fact from opinion), science facts and concepts, social studies facts and concepts, map skills, grammatical concepts and rules, and foreign language vocabulary and grammar.

These findings are less applicable for teaching in areas that are less well structured—that is, those in which skills do not follow explicit steps or where concepts are less identifiable and distinct (Spiro & Meyers, 1984). Thus the results of this research are less relevant for teaching composition, writing of term papers, reading comprehension, analysis of literature or historical trends, or discussion of social issues or concepts such as liberalism or modernity (Spiro & Meyers, 1984). (The research on explicit teaching also has some value for teaching these implicit skills, but that is a tale for another time.)

RESEARCH ON EXPLICIT TEACHING

In general, researchers have found that when effective teachers teach well-defined concepts and skills, they:

- Begin a lesson with a short statement of goals.
- Begin a lesson with a short review of previous, prerequisite learning.
- Present new material in small steps, with student practice after each step.
- Give clear and detailed instructions and explanations.
- Provide a high level of active practice for all students.
- Ask many questions, check for student understanding, and obtain responses from all students.
- Guide students during initial practice.
- Provide systematic feedback and corrections.
- Provide explicit instruction and practice for seatwork exercises and, when necessary, monitor students during seatwork.
- Continue practice until students are independent and confident.

The major components include teaching in small steps with student practice after each step, guiding students during initial practice, and providing all students with a high level of successful practice.

School-Based Origins

These results come from research in real classrooms with real students and represent the practices of the most successful teachers. This research was conducted in two steps. First, the investigators gave pretests and posttests—for example, in second-grade reading—to students in about 25 classrooms. Using these data, and making appropriate adjustments for the initial ability of the students, the investigators were able to identify those teachers whose classes made the highest achievement gain in reading and those teachers whose classes made the least gain. The investigators then studied the teaching behavior of the teachers in the two groups. For example, they counted the number of questions, types of questions, quality of student answers, amount of time spent in presenting new material, and amount of time spent in review. They used this information to identify the behaviors that the most successful teachers used more frequently than did their less successful colleagues. The distinguishing behaviors of the most successful teachers are discussed in this chapter.

Second, experimental studies were conducted. The investigators developed a manual for teaching based, in part, on the behaviors of the successful teachers. One group of teachers received the manual and was taught the behaviors, whereas the control teachers were asked to continue their regular teaching. These studies have shown that the teachers who received the manual performed many of the behaviors it mentioned. For example, they asked students more questions and spent more time presenting new material. The investigators also found that students of these teachers achieved higher than did students of teachers in the control group. Thus the experimental studies support the findings of the earlier correlational studies. The results of both sets of studies form the major part of this chapter.

Use and Limits

It would be a mistake to say that this systematic, small-step approach applies to all students or all situations. It is most important for young learners, slow learners, and all learners when the material is new, difficult, or hierarchical. In these cases, each presentation is relatively short and is followed by student practice. However, when teaching older, brighter students, or when teaching in the middle of a unit, then the steps are larger—that is, the presentations are longer, less time is spent in checking for understanding or in guided practice, and more of the independent practice can be done as homework because the students do not need as much help and supervision. But even in these situations, it is more efficient to return to small-step instruction when the material becomes difficult.

Information-Processing Research

One way to understand the need for systematic explicit teaching is to look at the recent research on human information processing. The results of these studies deal with three areas: the limits of our working memory, the importance of practice, and the importance of continuing practice until the students are fluent.

First, current information process theories suggest that we are "limited-capacity processors." That is, there are limits to the amount of information we can attend to and process effectively. We can only process a few pieces of information (about seven) in our working memory at one time. When we are presented with too much information at once, or when the processing demands on us are too great, our working memory becomes swamped, we become confused, and we omit or skim material and do not process it (Tobias, 1982). This is why, when teaching new or difficult material, a teacher should teach only a small amount and arrange for student practice after each part. In this way, the amount taught at any time is manageable for working memory. Further, a teacher can help students by reviewing relevant learning and by providing an outline so that students can focus on major points more readily.

Second, we have to process new material in order to transfer it from our working memory to our long-term memory. That is, we have to elaborate on, review, rehearse, or summarize the material. This suggests that a teacher should provide active practice for all students. Such practice is facilitated if the teacher guides processing by asking questions, requiring students to summarize main points, having students tutor each other, and supervising students as they practice new steps in a skill.

Finally, extensive practice and frequent review are needed after the material is first learned so that the material can be recalled effortlessly and automatically in the future. When prior learning is automatic, space is left free in our working memory to be used for application and higher-level thinking.

We might summarize these three points by saying that it is important for the teacher to provide "instructional support" when teaching students new material (see Tobias, 1982). Such support occurs when the teacher: (1) breaks material into small steps in order to reduce possible confusion; (2) structures the learning by giving an overview or behavioral objective; (3) gives the learner active practice in each step in order to move the new learning into long-term memory; and (4) provides for additional practice and overlearning so that the learners can use the new material or skills effortlessly.

SIX TEACHING FUNCTIONS

In summarizing the studies on explicit teaching, I have divided the results into six teaching functions: review, presentation of new material, guided practice, feedback and corrections, independent practice, and weekly and monthly reviews. Similar functions have also been developed by Good and Grouws (1979) and Russell and Hunter (1981). These results are summarized in Table 1.

These teaching functions represent what Gage (1978) calls "the scientific basis of the art of teaching." Even though these findings came from the study of actual classrooms, a great deal of deliberation is required in order to apply these findings to daily lessons. Before and during teaching, a teacher has to make decisions on the amount of material that will be presented at one time, the way in which it will be presented, how guided practice will be conducted, how specific errors made by specific students will be corrected, the pace and length of the lesson, and how he or she will work with different students. Thus a great deal of thought, creativity, and flexibility is needed to apply these results to specific instances of teaching lessons on long division, on the Constitution, on grammar, and on reading comprehension.

These six functions are not new. All teachers use some of these functions some of the time, but effective teachers apply the effective behaviors in these functions consistently and systematically, while the less effective teachers, indeed, use each function less effectively. The remainder of this chapter, then, will discuss more effective and less effective ways of implementing each of the six functions.

Table 1. Teaching Functions.

1. Review

   Review homework
   Review relevant previous learning
   Review prerequisite skills and knowledge for the lesson

2. Presentation

   State lesson goals and/or provide outline
   Teach in small steps
   Model procedures
   Provide concrete positive and negative examples
   Use clear language
   Check for student understanding
   Avoid digressions

3. Guided practice

   More time
   High frequency of questions or guided practice
   All students respond and receive feedback
   High success rate
   Continue practice until students are fluid

4. Corrections and feedback

   Give process feedback when answers are correct but hesitant
   Give sustaining feedback, clues, or reteaching when answers are incorrect
   Reteach when necessary

5. Independent practice

   Students receive help during initial steps, or overview
   Practice continues until students are automatic (where relevant)
   Teacher provides active supervision (where possible)
   Routines are used to give help to slower students

6. Weekly and monthly reviews

Daily Review

Effective teachers begin the lesson with a five- to eight-minute review of previously covered material, correction of homework, and review of prior knowledge that is relevant to the day's lesson. The goal is to ensure that the students have a firm grasp of the prerequisite skills for this lesson. The teachers' activities can include: reviewing the concepts and skills necessary to do the homework; having students correct each others' papers; asking about points at which the students had difficulty or made errors; and reviewing or providing additional practice on facts and skills that need overlearning. Daily review could also include a short test on items similar to the homework assignment.

Daily review is particularly important for teaching material that will be used in subsequent learning. Examples include reading sight words, grammar, math facts, math computation, math factoring, and chemical equations.

One example of effective daily review is in a successful reading program (Reid, 1978). In this program five minutes are spent in daily review of previously and soon-to-be-learned words from stories in the reader. The students go over the word lists, in unison, until they are fluent. Because the students are reading fluently, and easily, at the rate of about a word a second, it is possible to review 150 sight words in less than 4 minutes. Similar review procedures can be used in other reading programs or in other subject areas.

Daily review was also part of a successful experiment in elementary-school mathematics (Good & Grouws, 1979). In this study, the teachers who received training in daily review conducted review and checked homework 80 percent of the days they were observed, whereas teachers in the control group did so on only 50 percent of the days. Thus, although daily review is important, it is not as common a practice as we would have thought.

Presenting New Material

One difference between more and less effective teachers of mathematics is that effective teachers spend more time in presentation of new material and guided practice than do less effective teachers (Evertson et al., 1980; Good & Grouws, 1979). For example, Evertson et al. (1980) found that the most effective mathematics teachers spend about 23 minutes per day in lecture, demonstration, and discussion, in contrast to 11 minutes for the least effective teachers. The effective teachers use this extra time to provide additional explanations, give many examples, check for student understanding, and provide sufficient instruction so that the students can do the independent practice with minimal difficulty. In contrast, the less effective teachers give much shorter presentations and explanations and then ask the students to practice independently. Under these conditions, the students make too many errors and have to be retaught.

At the start of the presentation, effective teachers focus the students' attention on what they are to learn and do. They do this by providing the students with a short behavioral objective such as, "At the end of this lesson, you will be able to distinguish among metaphor, simile, and personification," or, "Today you will be able to do problems using two-digit multiplication." These objectives help to focus the students and reduce the complexity of what is being presented to them. In addition, such objectives help the teacher to stick to the subject matter and avoid confusing digressions.

Effective teachers then proceed by teaching one point at a time. They do this by giving a series of short presentations using many examples. The examples provide the concrete learning and elaboration that are useful for processing new material. As we noted above, presenting too much material at once may confuse students because their short-term memory will be unable to process it.

Researchers have also found that our processing is enhanced if points are made explicit. Such clarity helps to focus the learner and reduce the amount of ambiguous processing. It is also important for the teacher to avoid ambiguous phrases, such as "sort of" and "a few," or phrases that may easily be misinterpreted, such as "as you can see" and "it is obvious that." These phrases are vague and may confuse a student when learning new material (Smith & Land, 1981).

Effective teachers also stop to check for student understanding. They ask questions, ask students to summarize the presentation to that point or to repeat directions or procedures, or ask students whether they agree or disagree with other students' answers. This checking tells the teacher whether he or she needs to reteach the material. The wrong way to check for understanding is to ask, "Are there any questions?" and to assume that what is taught has been learned when no student asks anything. Another error is to ask a few questions, call on volunteers to hear their (usually correct) answers, and then assume that the class understands and has learned from the volunteers.

The following suggestions for effective presentation have emerged from the experimental and correlational classroom literature:

Organize material so that one point can be mastered before the next point needs to be introduced.

State lesson goals.

Give step-by-step directions.

Focus on one thought (point, direction) at a time, completing one point and checking for understanding before proceeding to the next.

Model behaviors by going through the directions.

Avoid digressions.

When presenting new material, the main point to remember is that students become confused when too much material is presented. Hence, it is better to proceed in small steps, pause to check for student understanding, and allow students to process the material. Digressions should be avoided, however interesting they may be, because they can frequently confuse the students by giving them too much to process. The main problems with unclear presentations appear to be giving directions too quickly, assuming everyone understands because there are no questions, and introducing more complex material before the students have mastered earlier material.

Conducting Guided Practice

After the presentation, or after short segments of the presentation, the teacher conducts guided practice. Major purposes of this activity are to supervise students' initial practice on a skill and to provide the active practice, enhancement, and elaboration that are necessary to move new learning from working memory into long-term memory.

The appropriate length of the segment prior to guided practice is open to debate and deliberation. Some people advocate that when teaching explicit concepts, such as metaphor and simile, or explicit skills, such as two-digit multiplication or determining least common multiples, the guided practice should begin after a short presentation and that this pattern of short presentation and guided practice continue throughout the presentation phase. Others advocate presentations of eight to ten minutes before beginning guided practice. Because little research focuses directly on this issue, a teacher might experiment with different lengths and learn which is most effective for his or her class. One might expect that with younger, slower students, or when the material is new and/or different, that shorter segments of presentation would be more effective.

During guided practice, students actively participate by working problems and/or answering teacher questions. A number of correlational studies have shown that teachers who are more effective in obtaining student achievement gain ask a large number of questions (Stallings & Kaskowitz, 1974; Stallings et al., 1977; 1979; Soar, 1973; Coker, Lorentz & Coker, 1980). During successful guided practice, two types of questions are usually asked: questions that call for specific answers and process questions, which call for an explanation of how an answer was found. In a correlational study of junior-high-school mathematics instruction (Evertson, Anderson, Anderson, & Brophy, 1980), the most effective teachers asked an average of 24 questions during the 50-minute period, whereas the least effective teachers asked only 8.6 questions. The most effective teachers asked 6 process questions (questions about how students do their tasks) per period, whereas the least effective teachers asked only 1.3. In two other experimental studies (Anderson et al., 1979; Good & Grouws, 1979), teachers were taught to follow the presentation of new material with guided practice, using a high frequency of questions. In both studies, the students of teachers in the experimental groups achieved higher than did students of teachers in the control groups.

Frequent Practice. In all of these studies, it is the frequency of practice that is perhaps most important. Students need a good deal of practice when learning new material, and effective teachers find ways to provide this practice. For example, when teaching concepts such as metaphor, simile, and personification or past, present, and future participles, the guided practice could consist of the teacher giving examples—say, "Is the statement 'My love is like a red, red rose' a metaphor, simile, or personification?"—and having the students respond and explain their answers; later, students could be asked to give their own examples. At each step, the guided practice continues until the students are fluent.

When teaching procedures such as two-digit multiplication, guided practice should consist of going over the skills in small steps with teacher supervision. Some students practice at the board, while others work at their seats. When the teacher feels they are ready, the students proceed to the next step. If they are not ready, then he or she gives additional practice. In this way, there is sufficient practice on one step before the students go to the next.

When teaching a more elaborate skill, such as dissecting a frog, using a computer package, or solving a geometry problem, students might first be asked to restate the steps that were taught. If the material is difficult, it might be best for the teacher to ask the students to state the steps one at a time, so that he or she can resolve any confusion. The steps might be repeated until all students are fluent. Then the teacher can supervise the students as they begin the actual practice, guiding them through each procedure until they can perform each step without errors.

It is inappropriate to spend only a short time in presentation or guided practice in the belief that "after I told it to them, they have learned it and are able to apply the skills." Research on information processing has revealed that, in order to learn new material, we have to spend a lot of time processing it—that is, rephrasing, rehearsing, and summarizing the new material so that we can readily retrieve it from our long-term memory when applying it to new situations.

Of course, all teachers spend time in guided practice. However, the most effective teachers spend more time in guided practice, more time asking questions, more time correcting errors, and more time having students work out problems with teacher guidance.

High Percentage of Correct Answers. Not only is the frequency of teacher questions important, but the percentage of correct student responses is also significant. Effective teachers also have a high success rate of student responses (Fisher et al., 1978; Anderson et al., 1979; Gerstein, Carnine, & Williams, 1981). For example, in a study of fourth-grade mathematics, Good and Grouws (1979) found that 82 percent of the answers were correct in the classrooms of the most successful teachers, whereas the least successful teachers had a success rate of 73 percent. The optimal success rate appears to be about 75–80 percent during guided practice, suggesting that the effective teachers combine both success and sufficient challenge. The most effective teachers obtained this success level by combining short presentations with supervised student practice, and by giving sufficient practice on each part before proceeding to the next step.

Active Participation. Students need to practice and process new learning actively. Teachers often lead this process by asking questions of individual students during presentation and guided practice. For instance, they may ask students to repeat directions, procedures, or main points, or they may ask many questions on facts and procedures. Instead of only calling on one student at a time, imaginative teachers increase the amount of active participation by involving *all* students in answering questions. Examples include having each student:

1. Tell the answer to a neighbor.
2. Summarize the main idea in one or two sentences, writing the summary on a piece of paper and sharing this with a neighbor, or repeat the procedures to a neighbor.
3. Write the answer on a slate that he or she then holds up.
4. Raise their hand if they know the answer (thereby allowing the teacher to check the entire class).
5. Raise their hand if they agree with an answer someone else gave.
6. Raise different colored cards when the answer is a, b, or c.

Active group participation is particularly useful when teaching students to identify parts of things, such as parts of a plant, book, or dictionary, or to discriminate among related concepts, such as metaphor, simile, and personification or adverbs and adjectives. In this type of practice all students can signal an answer, or one student can answer and the other students can then signal whether they agree or disagree.

The purpose of all these procedures (cards, raising hands, writing answers) is to provide active participation for the students and also to allow the teacher to check to see how many students are correct and confident. If you feel that these overt procedures are too childish, an alternative would be to have students write their answers and have them immediately grade each others' papers. This procedure should still allow for the necessary active practice and should still give the teacher feedback on whether additional instruction or practice is needed.

Other teachers use choral responses to provide sufficient practice when teaching new vocabulary or lists of items. This makes the practice seem more like a game. To be effective, however, all students need to start together, on a signal. When a group start is not used, then only a few students answer, and the others do not receive adequate practice.

Student participation, of course, should take place throughout the lesson and should also include responding to teacher checks for understanding, active work on the skills or concepts during guided practice, supervised independent seatwork where the students work alone but can receive help from the teacher or peers, and independent practice at home.

Provide Feedback and Correctives

During guided practice, during checking for understanding, or during any recitation or demonstration, how should a teacher respond to a student's answer?

Research has shown that if a student is correct and confident, then the teacher can simply ask another question, or give a short statement of praise (such as "Very good") while maintaining the momentum of the practice. However, if the student is correct but hesitant, then it is important to tell the student that the answer is correct. In such cases, it is also useful to give process feedback. *Process feedback*, a term developed by Good and Grouws (1979), refers to the teacher saying, "Yes, that's right, because . . . ," and then proceeding to re-explain the process one goes through to arrive at the correct answer. Process feedback gives the student the additional explanation he or she sometimes needs when correct but hesitant.

When a student has made an error, then it is appropriate to help him or her by simplifying the question, providing hints, or reteaching the material. Whether one uses hints or reteaching, the important point is that errors should not go uncorrected. When a student makes an error, it is inappropriate simply to give the correct answer and then move on.

In their review of effective college teaching, Kulik and Kulik (1979) found that instruction is more effective when (a) students receive immediate feedback on their examinations, and (b) students have to study further and take another test when their quiz scores do not reach a set criterion. Both points seem relevant to this discussion: students learn better with feedback—as immediately as possible; and errors should be corrected before they become habitual.

Conduct Independent Practice

Students may be expected to do the steps correctly but hesitantly at the end of guided practice. The next step, independent practice, provides the additional review that students need to become fluent in a skill and to work without the cues that were present during guided practice. This need for fluency and independence applies to many of the procedures that are taught in school: using a rule to measure widths, adding decimals, reading a map, conjugating a regular verb in a foreign language, proofreading copy for errors, writing major chords, completing and balancing a chemical equation, operating equipment, and applying safety procedures. This need for fluency also applies to facts, concepts, and discriminations that must be used in subsequent learning. After substantial practice, students reach a stage where they perform rapidly, successfully, and automatically and no longer have to think through each step (Anderson, 1983; Bloom, 1986). Students who reach this stage can devote their full attention to comprehension and application.

The independent practice should involve the same material as the guided practice. That is, if the guided practice dealt with identifying types of sentences, then the independent practice should deal with the same topic or, perhaps, with creating individual compound and complex sentences. It would be inappropriate to follow this example of guided practice with an independent practice assignment that asked students to "write a paragraph using two compound and two complex sentences," because the students have not been adequately prepared for such an activity.

Similarly, if one is teaching students how to add decimals through the thousandths place, then the guided practice *and* the independent practice should include this activity. In other words, students need guided practice in an activity before they are assigned independent practice. For example, it may be appropriate for a teacher to practice in class some of the homework problems (guided practice) before the students take the work home (independent practice). When the material to be learned is difficult, more time should be spent in supervised independent practice; when easier, more of the independent practice can be done as homework.

Managing Independent Practice.   Investigators have found that students are more engaged during seatwork when their teacher circulates around the room and monitors and supervises their work (Fisher et al., 1978). However, research suggests that these contacts should be relatively short, averaging 30 seconds or less.

Another finding has been that teachers who spend more time in guided practice have students who are more engaged during seatwork (Fisher et al., 1978). This suggests the importance of adequately preparing students *before* seatwork. In contrast, when teachers have to give a great deal of explanation *during* seatwork, then student error rates rise (Fisher et al., 1978). Having to provide abundant explanations during seatwork indicates that the initial explanation and guided practice were not sufficient. In summary, students are more engaged during independent practice when the teacher circulates and when there has been sufficient explanation in guided practice beforehand.

Students Helping Students.   Some investigators have developed procedures by which students help each other during seatwork (see Johnson & Johnson, 1975; Sharan, 1980; Slavin, 1980b). Research shows that all students tend to achieve more in these settings than do students in regular settings (Slavin, 1980b); a manual (Slavin, 1980a) explains how these procedures can be used in classrooms. Presumably, some of the advantage comes from having to explain the material to someone else and/or having someone else (other than the teacher) explain the material to the student (Webb, 1982). These cooperative/competitive settings are also valuable for helping slower students in a class by providing extra instruction for them during seatwork.

Weekly and Monthly Review

Some of the successful programs in elementary schools provide for frequent review. For example, Good and Grouws (1979) recommend that teachers review the previous week's work every Monday and the previous month's work every fourth Monday. These reviews and tests provide the additional practice that students need to become skilled, successful performers who can apply their knowledge and skills to new areas.

Kulik and Kulik (1979) found that, even at the college level, classes that had weekly quizzes scored better on final exams than did classes that had only one or two quizzes per term.

In sum, instruction in explicit, well-structured areas is a process in which the teacher initially takes full responsibility for performing a task, but gradually relinquishes responsibility to the students (Lohman, 1985; Pearson & Gallagher, 1983). This progression can be seen as a continuum that begins with full teacher control and in which the teacher diminishes control through the lesson so that at the end students are working independently. This progression moves from teacher modeling, through guided practice using prompts and cues, to independent and fluent performance by the students.

MODIFICATIONS TO SUIT DIFFERENT SITUATIONS

When the material is difficult and possibly confusing, or when it involves a complicated series of steps, then it is more effective to break the instruction into smaller steps and have a series of sequences of instruction, guided practice, and independent practice during a single period. Thus the teacher: (1) provides an explanation; (2) checks for understanding; (3) leads the students through guided practice; and (4) supervises independent practice for the first step and then repeats the procedure for each subsequent step. This procedure is particularly effective for difficult material and/or slower students. However, the optimal length for such a sequence is not known, and the teacher needs to attempt different lengths and reflect on the results he or she achieves.

For example, when teaching a lesson in computer programming, it may overtax the students' short-term memory to go through all the package-use steps at once. It may be more efficient to break the learning into a series of small segments consisting of the presentation of a first procedure—say, inputting the disc—guided practice on that step,

Table 2. Modifications to Suit Different Students.

SLOWER STUDENTS	FASTER STUDENTS
More review	Less review
Less presentation	More presentation
More guided practice	Less guided practice
More independent practice	Less independent practice

MODIFICATION FOR DIFFICULT MATERIAL

Presentation

Guided practice

Supervised independent practice

independent practice, and only then go on to the next segments, entering the program itself and outputting in the same manner.

Multiple steps could also be used when teaching percentages. Students would first be taught and receive practice in converting percentages into a decimal. Then they would receive instruction and practice in setting up the multiplication problem and in doing the multiplication. Finally, they would receive practice in putting the decimal in the right place. Before they did the final problems, the students would be asked to restate the steps. This procedure is not necessary for all material. Rather, it is an example of how to break down difficult material into small steps when necessary.

The time spent in these six functions should also be modified to suit different learners (see Table 2). When students are faster or older, or when the material is less difficult, then less time needs to be spent in review and more time can be spent on new material (although we often overestimate how much new material can be learned at a given time). Similarly, in such cases, there is less need for guided practice and less need for independent practice in class. More of the independent practice can be done as homework because the students do not need as much help and supervision.

On the other hand, when the learners are younger and slower, or when the material is difficult for all students, then more time ought to be spent in review, less time in presentation of new material, and more time in both guided and independent practice. During independent practice, there should be more supervision, and a greater emphasis on all students becoming quick and accurate. When material is particularly difficult, some teachers (Evertson, 1982) use a series of cycles of short presentation, guided practice, and independent practice.

Teaching in Implicit Areas

Although we know a good deal about teaching in explicit and well-structured areas, we know much less about instruction in areas that involve implicit skills—that is, skills that cannot be specified. Such areas include composition, writing term papers, analysis of literature, and interpreting social issues discussed in newspapers.

Need for Extensive Prior Knowledge. Some insight into how to help students acquire implicit procedures has come from studying the thought processes of experts in a field, people who have demonstrated an ability to solve problems in a specific domain. This research has shown that such people have well-organized background knowledge in their field and are fluent in the skills and procedures needed in their field (Glaser, 1984). Thus the development of a large body of content knowledge, with well-formed connections among the parts, is a necessary, but not sufficient, first step (Anderson, 1983). This content knowledge can be developed using the systematic procedures described above.

Explicit Teaching. Durkin (1978–1979; 1981) noted that neither teachers nor basal readers provide explicit instruction in comprehension skills. That is, they do not explain or teach a process that a student might use to answer questions about characterization, inference, or main ideas. Rather, the dominant activity consists of asking students questions without explaining a process they might use to answer.

Subsequent to these studies, a number of investigators have attempted to develop procedures that students might use to help them answer comprehension questions (Carnine, Kameenui, & Maggs, 1982; Carnine, Kameenui, & Woolfsen, 1982; Hansen, 1981; Hansen & Pearson, 1983; Paris, 1986). They have shown that such training can facilitate responses to comprehension questions. Although they have not been able to specify all the steps to follow when answering these questions, the investigators are virtually unanimous in concluding that teachers need to explicitly teach students what processes to use when answering comprehension-type questions.

Extensive and Varied Practice. In order to develop implicit skills, students also need extensive and varied practice in the given area. Thus, in addition to learning comprehension skills, students need to spend a large amount of time reading, reflecting on what they have read, and making connections among parts of the text. In addition to learning grammar and vocabulary, learners need to spend extensive time writing and revising (Graves, 1983). In math, learners need to spend extensive time solving problems in a variety of areas. Transfer of problem-solving skills to new areas is promoted when students practice in a variety of areas (Spiro & Meyers, 1984).

Metacognition. In one of the most exciting new fields, investigators are developing metacognitive procedures that students can use while they learn. For example, students are taught to ask themselves different types of questions as they read—questions about detail, main idea, prediction, and clarification (Palincsar, 1984). Or students are taught to specify what a question is asking—whether then to search the text or their mind for the answer (Raphael, 1980). Or students are taught the structure of expository text—whether it is problem and solution, compare and contrast, or rule and example (Cook & Meyer, 1983). In each case, below-average and average students who were taught metacognitive procedures gained more in reading achievement than did control students who were not so taught. However, above-average students did not improve compared to controls, probably because they already had these metacognitive skills.

SUMMARY

Current research on teaching in explicit, well-structured areas has shown that it is most effective to teach in a systematic manner, providing instructional support for the students at each stage of learning. The effective teacher begins with a review of prerequisite skills, relating the current material to past learning, and then teaches the new material in small steps. He or she uses short presentations and follows each presentation with questions. After the presentation, the teacher guides the students as they practice the new skill and continues this guidance until all students have been checked and received feedback. Guided practice is followed by independent practice, which is continued until students can perform the new skill independently and fluently.

What is new is that the above ideas now have a research base that draws on experimental studies conducted in ordinary classrooms with ordinary teachers teaching ordinary subject matter. The results have consistently shown that when teachers modify their instruction so that they do more systematic teaching, then student achievement improves. In addition, researchers frequently note gains in student attitudes toward school or self. Thus, these practices derived from research are recommended for your consideration.

ACKNOWLEDGMENT: My thanks to Nancy Thomas and Sheila Valencia.

REFERENCES

Anderson, L. M., Evertson, C. M., & Brophy, J. E. (1979). An experimental study of effective teaching in first-grade reading groups. *Elementary School Journal, 79*, 193–222.

Anderson, J. R. (1983). *The architecture of cognition.* Cambridge, MA: Harvard University Press.

Bloom, B. S. (1986, February). Automaticity. *Educational Leadership, 56*, 70–77.

Carnine, D., Kameenui, E. T., & Maggs, A. A. (1982). Components of analytic assistance. *Journal of Educational Research, 75,* 374–377.

Carnine, D., Kameenui, E. T., & Woolfsen, N. W. (1982). Training of textual dimensions related to text-based inferences. *Journal of Reading Behavior, 14,* 335–340.

Coker, H., Lorentz, C. W., & Coker, J. (1980). Teacher behavior and student outcomes in the Georgia study. Paper presented to the annual meeting of the American Educational Research Association, Boston, MA.

Cook, L. K., & Meyer, R. E. (1983). Reading strategies training for meaningful learning from prose. In M. Pressley & J. Levin (Eds.), *Cognitive strategies training and research.* New York: Springer-Verlag.

Durkin, D. (1978–1979). What classroom observation reveals about reading comprehension instruction. *Reading Research Quarterly, 14,* 481–533.

———. (1981). Reading comprehension instruction in five basal reading series. *Reading Research Quarterly, 16,* 515–544.

Evertson, C. E. (1982). Differences in instructional activities in higher- and lower-achieving junior high English and math classes. *Elementary School Journal, 4,* 329–350.

Evertson, C. E., Anderson, C., Anderson, L., & Brophy, J. (1980). Relationship between classroom behaviors and student outcomes in junior high mathematics and English classes. *American Educational Research Journal, 17,* 43–60.

Evertson, C. E., Emmer, E. T., & Brophy, J. E. (1980). Predictors of effective teaching in junior high mathematics classrooms. *Journal of Research in Mathematics Education, 11,* 167–178.

Fisher, C. W., Filby, N. M., Marliave, R., Cahen, L. S., Dishaw, M. M., Moore, J. E., & Berliner, D. C. (1978). *Teaching behaviors, academic learning time, and student achievement: Final report of Phase III-B, Beginning Teacher Evaluation Study.* San Francisco, CA: Far West Educational Laboratory for Educational Research and Development.

Gage, N. L. (1978). *The scientific basis of the art of teaching.* New York: Teachers College Press.

Gerstein, R. M., Carnine, D. W., & Williams, P. B. (1981). Measuring implementation of a structured educational model in an urban school district. *Educational Evaluation and Policy Analysis, 4,* 56–63.

Glaser, R. (1984). Education and thinking: The role of knowledge. *American Psychologist, 39,* 93–104.

Good, T. L., & Grouws, D. A. (1979). The Missouri mathematics effectiveness project. *Journal of Educational Psychology, 71,* 143–155.

Graves, D. H. (1983). *Writing: Teachers and children at work.* Exeter, NH: Heineman.

Hansen, J. (1981). The effects of inference training and practice on young children's comprehension. *Reading Research Quarterly, 16,* 391–417.

Hansen, J., & Pearson, P. D. (1983). Improving the inferential comprehension of fourth grade good and poor readers. *Journal of Educational Psychology, 75,* 821–829.

Johnson, D., & Johnson, R. (1975). *Learning together and alone.* Englewood Cliffs, NJ: Prentice-Hall.

Kulik, J. A., & Kulik, C. C. (1979). College teaching. In P. L. Peterson & H. J. Walberg (Eds.), *Research on teaching: Concepts, findings, and implications.* Berkeley, CA: McCutchan.

Lohman, D. F. (1985). *Teacher higher-order thinking skills.* Elmhurst, IL: North Central Laboratory for Educational Research and Development.

Palincsar, A. S. (1984). Reciprocal teaching. Paper presented at the annual meeting of the American Educational Research Association, New Orleans, LA.

Paris, S. (1986). Teaching children to guide their reading and learning. In T. E. Raphael (Ed.), *The context of literacy.* New York: Random House.

Pearson, D. P., & Gallagher, M. C. (1983). The instruction of reading comprehension. *Contemporary Educational Psychology, 8,* 317–344.

Raphael, T. E. (1980). The effects of metacognitive awareness training on students' question answering behavior. Doctoral dissertation, University of Illinois.

Reid, E. R. (1978–1982). *The Reader Newsletter.* Salt Lake City, UT: Exemplary Center for Reading Instruction.

Russell, D., & Hunter, M. (1981). Planning for effective instruction: Lesson design. In *Increasing your teaching effectiveness* (pp. 63–69). Palo Alto, CA: Learning Institute.

Sharan, S. A. (1980). Cooperative learning in small groups. *Review of Educational Research, 50,* 241–271.

Simon, H. A. (1973). The structure of ill-structured problems. *Artificial Intelligence, 4,* 181–201.

Slavin, R. E. (1980a). *Using student team learning,* rev. ed. Baltimore, MD: Center for Social Organization of Schools, Johns Hopkins University.

———. (1980b). Cooperative learning. *Review of Educational Research, 50,* 317–343.

Smith, L., & Land, M. (1981). Low-inference verbal behaviors related to teacher clarity. *Journal of Classroom Interaction, 17,* 37–42.

Soar, R. S. (1973). *Follow-through classroom process measurement and pupil growth (1970–71): Final report.* Gainesville, FL: College of Education, University of Florida.

Spiro, R. J., & Meyers, A. (1984). Individual differences and underlying cognitive processes. In P. D. Pearson, R. Barr, M. L. Kamil, & P. Mosenthal (Eds.), *Handbook of reading research* (pp. 471–505). New York: Longman.

Stallings, J. A., Gory, R., Fairweather, J., & Needels, M. (1977). *Early childhood education classroom evaluation.* Menlo Park, CA: SRI International.

Stallings, J. A., & Kaskowitz, D. (1974). *Follow-through classroom observation.* Menlo Park, CA: SRI International.

Tobias, S. (1982). When do instructional methods make a difference? *Educational Researcher, 11,* 4–10.

Webb, N. M. (1982). Student interaction and learning in small groups. *Review of Educational Research, 52,* 421–446.

CHAPTER 5

DAVID C. BERLINER

SIMPLE VIEWS OF EFFECTIVE TEACHING AND A SIMPLE THEORY OF CLASSROOM INSTRUCTION

In this chapter I will define what an effective teacher is and discuss the ways in which effective teachers run their classrooms. I will also describe academic learning time, a concept or variable that I believe has great heuristic value for helping to decide whether or not a teacher is likely to be effective. These ideas will be used to demonstrate that we can now predict who will be an effective teacher and who will not when achievement-test scores are used as the standard by which we judge effectiveness. We will also develop a simple theory of classroom instruction, a theory that increases our understanding of what teacher behaviors and classroom activities might contribute to teacher effectiveness.

A DEFINITION OF EFFECTIVENESS

Some scholars would call a teacher effective if the correlation between social class and achievement in his or her classroom was near zero. Such a definition, however, makes the judgment of effectiveness dependent on test performance that shows nearly equal levels of achievement for economically disadvantaged and economically privileged children in the same classroom. Since socioeconomic status is related to family values and behavior, and since such family values and behavior also relate to school achievement, it is not easy to eliminate the correlation between socioeconomic indicators and school achievement.

Another definition would designate as an effective teacher someone whose class is one standard deviation or more above the mean achievement level of similar classes. This definition equates effectiveness with a standard of classroom performance—the eighty-fifth percentile rank (or higher) on an achievement test. The cut-off point is, of course, an arbitrary one. And by setting the cut-off point relatively high, one ensures that only a small number of teachers (15 percent) will ever be considered effective in a single study or in a single year.

The definition of effectiveness that I propose to use is a much looser one. I define an effective teacher as one whose students end up possessing at least the knowledge and skills judged to be appropriate for that particular type of student (say, fourth graders, low-ability general mathematics students, or advanced placement biology students). In other words, effectiveness here means simply that teachers get most of their students to learn most of what they are supposed to learn.

The Difference Between Good Teaching and Effective Teaching

Note that this definition of effectiveness requires an understanding of what students are supposed to learn. That is, one must have clear ideas about the outcomes expected from a given instructional activity. The issue of outcomes is one of the oldest in education. Determining what knowledge is of most worth sparks continuous debate. Because of the complexity of this question and the difficulty of ever adequately resolving such a fundamentally philosophical matter, schools and teachers within the same district may not share the belief that particular outcomes are expected for students at a given grade level or in a particular course. When schools and teachers share no common beliefs about what constitutes a desired set of outcomes for particular grades or courses, the issue of effective schooling or effective teaching is irrelevant because the concept of effective teaching or schooling directly implies a set of criteria. But "good" teaching implies no such criteria. A teacher who starts a lecture on time, provides a review, gives an advance organizer, emphasizes important points, asks higher-order questions throughout, cracks a good joke, and the like, may be judged to be a "good" teacher, whether or not his or her students learn. Good (and poor) teaching and schooling are determined by values and by knowledge of the standards of good practice, independent of effectiveness. The concept of good teaching always requires an understanding of normative behavior, while the concept of effective teaching always requires an understanding of the expected outcomes of instruction. These concepts need not be mutually exclusive, but the distinctions between these two concepts are very important to maintain.

Cautions in Judging Teacher Effectiveness

Our purposefully loose definition of effectiveness—that most students learn most of what they are supposed to learn—is one that requires considerable reliance on human judgment, with all its frailty. Such judgments should take into account the kinds and numbers of students a teacher has worked with and the kinds and numbers of outcomes associated with instruction at a particular grade level or in a particular course. A knowledgeable judge evaluating teachers' effectiveness is expected to possess well-grounded beliefs about what might be reasonable levels of performance under the conditions that exist in a particular instructional setting. Our definition of effectiveness is not dependent on arbitrary cut-off points or statistical correlations between measures of achievement and of socioeconomic status; it should always be the result of a deliberative process by knowledgeable judges who use much more than test scores as indicators of student achievement. These judges must look beyond these scores because society asks teachers to do far more than have students achieve well. Students should learn to love learning, desire to go on and take more courses in science and mathematics, read on their own out of school, want to attend school regularly, giggle often, and so forth. These outcomes of instruction are hard to measure in any formal way. When making judgments about a teacher's effectiveness, then, it is best to look at the academic performance of his or her students as merely one of a great number of indicators.

In research we usually adopt a very narrow view of effectiveness, often confining ourselves to or overly depending on student performance on standardized achievement tests. The simple conception of effective teachers presented below is based on this kind of restricted view. Those who evaluate teacher effectiveness to determine teacher retention, promotion, merit, and so forth must keep the limitations inherent in this conception in mind. The researcher looks for neat, clean, simple definitions of effectiveness to reduce the complexity of the research task and to communicate clearly with his or her colleagues. The evaluators of classroom teachers—principals, curriculum coordinators, peers— should take the researchers' ideas about effectiveness seriously, but at the same time they *must* take a broader perspective about the nature of teacher effectiveness than we will discuss here.

THE CLASSROOMS OF EFFECTIVE TEACHERS

The simplest summary of how the classrooms of more effective teachers differ from those of less effective teachers is that the more effective teachers deliver a curriculum that matches agreed-on outcomes. In the classrooms of the less effective teachers, either the curriculum is not delivered in sufficient quantity, or the curriculum that is delivered is not well matched to the desired outcomes.

Clearly, we need to explore this assertion, which may sound too commonsensical, or too much of a truism to be useful, or too down to earth, or too vague. To such criticisms, I offer two replies. First, simple ideas may have considerable utility. Second, from extensive observation in classrooms, I have learned that commonsense knowledge does not always result in either common (that is, widespread) or sensible practices. Let us start to unravel these ideas about effective teachers by discussing, again, the outcomes of instruction.

Instructional Outcomes and Opportunity to Learn

Any discussion of effectiveness, as we noted above, requires an understanding of the outcomes of instruction. The effective teacher knows these outcomes and provides his or her students with the opportunity to learn the knowledge and skill that they are expected to acquire. The effective teacher ensures that the curriculum and the desired outcomes are aligned, that they are congruent. The effective teacher sees to it that students are provided with the opportunity to learn the things they are supposed to learn. That this "opportunity to learn" is a necessary condition for learning to occur is one of the most consistent findings and points of agreement in our field (Carroll, 1963; Cooley & Leinhardt, 1980). A teacher must seek from or plan with district administrators statements that reflect the goals and objectives of instruction at a particular grade level, for a particular course, in a particular community. In no way does this imply that teachers need 97 objectives for reading, 74 objectives for mathematics, and a few hundred others for science, prosocial behavior, and physical education. The behavioral objectives movement in education fostered an overly molecular and rational view of teaching, often trivializing teaching and learning. But one need not throw out the baby with the bath water. It appears that the development of 10–15 objectives for reading, another dozen or so for mathematics, and another dozen or so for the rest of the curriculum are reasonable aspirations. For a single course, as in junior or senior high school, a dozen or more objectives are all that is necessary to proceed with any kind of study or program to determine teacher effectiveness.

Naturally, if test instruments are used to assess instruction, they must also be matched to the goals and objectives of the school district. It is impossible for teachers to be found effective if they teach one thing but find themselves tested on another. It is unfortunate that school districts and teachers have, far too frequently, been foolish enough to be trapped in this kind of untenable position. Standardized achievement tests that are poorly matched to the curriculum are often unthinkingly accepted as indicators of the effectiveness of schools and teachers. Such tests, we should note, must necessarily vastly underestimate the effectiveness of instruction. (See the discussion of curriculum alignment in Chapter 1.) They underestimate because they provide no assessment of the many other things teachers may have taught.

Providing students with an opportunity to learn what is supposed to be learned is the key concern. If a test is used as an indicator of the things a student was supposed to learn, then the test must reflect the objectives of instruction in the same way that the curriculum must reflect the objectives of instruction. Teachers judged to be effective find ways to match the objectives, curriculum, and testing practices. Ineffective teachers do not. They do not offer their students the same opportunity to learn. This may sound simple, but it really is not. If it were simple to align the curriculum with the outcome measures, most of these teachers would gladly do so. For reasons we do not yet fully understand, some teachers do not perform this task well.

Delivering the Curriculum

Let us unravel our simple view of effective teachers further. We said the effective teacher delivers a curriculum that is matched to outcomes. I would consider a curriculum to be "delivered" when students have the opportunity to spend sufficient time engaged in and succeeding at tasks that are related to the desired outcomes. *Engagement* and *success* are the key concepts. They are discussed next, along with the concepts of *allocated time* and *academic learning time,* concepts that help clarify our discussion of the ways effective teachers run their classrooms.

The concept of *allocated time* was presented in Chapter 1. The salient fact uncovered in the research on how elementary teachers allocate time was that the variability across classes was enormous. One teacher would allocate 20 minutes a day to mathematics; another teacher would allocate 71 minutes. One teacher would allocate about three-quarters of an hour to reading and language arts each day; a second teacher would allocate about 2 hours. This range in allocated time in classrooms is consistently associated with variations in student achievement on tests. Thus allocated time must enter into our concern about teacher effectiveness.

Because teachers do not usually keep track of how they allocate classroom time, some teachers probably spend too little time per day on the subject matter they are committed to teaching. When teachers allocate too little time to a subject, the achievement scores of students will be low. The effective teacher, at a minimum, allocates sufficient time for learning a subject. The decision about how much time to allocate to a curriculum area is a decision about what opportunity to learn a student will have. Since opportunity to learn is a crucial variable in discussions of classroom teaching, time allocated to instruction takes on special significance.

Important decisions about how to allocate time must also be made by junior and senior high-school teachers. However, these decisions are concerned with content areas within a particular subject area. Both elementary- and secondary-school teachers must make choices about how much time to allocate to each content area of the curriculum they teach. For example, when teaching mathematics, how much time should be allocated to fractions? word problems? linear measurement? probability?

One study of teachers found unexpectedly large teacher differences in these more specific time-allocation decisions (Dishaw, 1977a, 1977b; Berliner, 1979). For example, one teacher spent ten times as much time on creative writing in a school year than another did. And one teacher spent no time teaching fractions, while another teacher in the same grade allotted nearly 7 hours to that topic.

The relationship between allocated time and effectiveness makes common sense and has been confirmed many times. When the data show that the teacher of one class allocates more than 50 hours to comprehension activities during reading and language arts periods, while another teacher allocates fewer than 6 hours to such activities, we can guess at the impact this might have on student achievement. When students from the two classes take a test that requires choosing the best title for a paragraph they have just read (a common way to measure comprehension), we can make a safe bet about which class will perform better. The class with the higher amounts of time allocated to reading comprehension will appear to have had a more effective teacher. As we have noted, effective teachers provide an opportunity to learn. Allocated time is one way to account for whether that opportunity was provided. In this way, time is used as a way to measure students' opportunity to learn.

In discussing the relationship between allocated time and perceived teacher effectiveness, we seem to be saying that more allocated time is better. If this rule is not adhered to blindly, it is, within limits, often true. Certainly we must remember that more is better only up to some point. Beyond that point, "more" is bound to be boring. Nevertheless, effective teachers seem to keep the fact clearly in mind that some curriculum areas will never be learned well if enough time is not allocated to them. For example, most of us could not translate .66667 into the fraction two-thirds (⅔) or into 67 percent if some teacher had not allocated enough time for us to learn these equivalencies in mathematics.

How much time should be allocated to each content area of the curriculum? Only a teacher can decide how to answer this question. That decision is made in cooperation with the school district personnel, with concern for the outcomes that a district values, and with intimate knowledge of the characteristics of the students in the class. Such decisions are very difficult to make, which is why every teacher is not an effective teacher. It is not always recognized that the decision about how much time to allocate to each curriculum area or instructional activity is also a way of checking to see whether a teacher is putting into effect his or her personal philosophy of education. A philosophy that values inquiry over rote learning in biology instruction, for example, should result in the kind of classroom where we observe more time being spent by students in inquiry activities rather than in, say, worksheet or other facts-and-figures activities. A belief in the usefulness of whole language approaches to reading ought, in some way, be made manifest in the classroom. Observations should reveal that less time was spent in activities that resemble decoding activities and that more time was devoted to silent reading of prose or other comprehension activities. Philosophy-as-espoused is mere talk. Philosophy-in-action results in an activity having some measurable duration. An educational philosophy is translated into action when it can be observed in classrooms and measured by allocated time. The effective teachers seem to find ways to have their beliefs become realities in their classrooms. The opportunities for learning in the classroom of an effective teacher are those that are compatible with that teacher's beliefs about instruction.

Engaged time was also discussed in Chapter 1 and identified as an important practical concept for thinking about instruction. Classrooms generally range along a continuum from about 50 percent to 90 percent time-on-task by students. Effective teachers are at the higher end of this range. Their students are on the tasks they are supposed to be on 75, 85, or 90 percent of the time. If engaged time with the curriculum is too short, students will not have the opportunity to learn what they are supposed to learn. When a teacher's management system or motivational system breaks down, time-on-task plummets, and little curriculum is actually delivered to the students. We have learned that when we find large differences among classes in engaged time with a curriculum, we also find substantial differences in achievement in that curriculum area.

Data collected by Rossmiller (1982) make this point quite clearly. They reveal that for low-ability children, the variance in reading and mathematics achievement accounted for by engaged-time variables can reach as high as 73 percent! Even for the highest-ability groups, the mean variance accounted for in reading and mathematics achievement was about 10 percent. (These data should be contrasted with the amount of variance accounted for in some medical research studies discussed in Chapter 1.) Thus engaged time also appears to be an important predictor of achievement.

A high rate of engagement is a characteristic of classrooms managed by effective teachers. It should also be noted, however, that the desired levels of engagement within a classroom are more easily attained in schools where the entire staff is concerned about this issue. It is easier to be an effective teacher if one is in an effective school—one that promotes safety, order, a businesslike atmosphere, high expectations for achievement, and rewards for such achievement.

Success rate was also discussed in Chapter 1 as a variable of some importance when thinking about schooling. Until recently, many educators had argued that teachers should work hard to develop a high self-concept for their students and that a student's achievement in academic areas would develop after his or her self-concept was positive and secure. The research now supports the opposite view. It is now thought likely that a high level of success in a learning environment causes students to develop an enhanced self-concept as a learner. Thus, to build a positive self-concept, a teacher needs to design environments and make assignments so that students can have experience at attaining high levels of success.

Besides building self-esteem, a higher-than-average success rate in instruction during the school year has been associated with higher achievement on test scores in the spring, better retention of learning over the summer, and more positive attitudes toward school (Fisher et al., 1978; 1980). It should be noted, however, that the positive effects of highly successful school experiences, where very low error rates occur, are probably confined to younger children and to lower-achieving children of all ages.

The importance of success rate in the learning process is more understandable if one thinks about the cyclical nature of learning. We may think of most learning in a classroom as a process of moving from not knowing something to knowing it. When new material is introduced, the student most likely will not understand it completely and will make some errors. Guided practice or explanations by an instructor help the student to understand. He or she comes to make fewer errors. Eventually, the student will perform correctly, although probably with some effort. Learning eventually becomes well established with practice or review. This stage of practice and review can be thought of as one in which learning is consolidated. At some later point, the student knows the material so well that further practice is of minimal value. At that time, the teacher would be wise to move on to something new. The results of a study by Fisher et al. (1978; 1980) suggest that for learning basic skills in the elementary grades, the stage of consolidation, characterized by successful practice, is particularly important to the thorough mastery of concepts and procedures. (See Chapter 4 for a further discussion of the importance of such activities.) Therefore, teachers need to give considerable thought to planning for a stage of consolidation in the learning process.

We have discussed the importance of a high-success rate in fostering achievement and seen how effective teaching requires attention to fostering success experiences, particularly in young students. But the research also shows an important effect associated with a low success rate. It is not surprising to find that, when students have had many low-success experiences, their achievement is lower. We define low success experiences as those in which a student makes errors more than 80 percent of the time. The student in such a situation is experiencing excessive failure. Most teachers are very sensitive to failure by students and take pains to avoid having a student spend too much time in such frustrating situations. Thus most teachers see to it that students spend only 0–3 percent of their time in such a stressful environment (Fisher et al., 1978). Yet the same study that found generally low amounts of time spent in failure experiences also found that students in some classes were observed being assigned to activities or materials that resulted in a low-success experience 10 percent or more of the time. It appears that some teachers are not monitoring the instructional situation carefully enough and are allowing students to spend relatively large amounts of the school day in what must be a very frustrating environment. Self-concept and achievement are bound to be lower when large amounts of time are spent in low-success activities.

It should not really be surprising that high and low success rates in the classroom predict higher and lower performance on achievement tests. If the curriculum and tests are matched to any degree at all (and they really should be matched quite well), then the knowledge and skills derived from the materials and activities a student works on in the class should be related to the knowledge and skills needed to answer the test items. If a student is successfully accomplishing workbook activities, answering worksheets correctly, and answering teacher questions correctly, then that student should also be able to answer correctly test items related to that material and to those classroom activities. Similarly, if the student is not answering teacher questions correctly, performing poorly on worksheets, and unable to follow instruction, then he or she is likely to answer similar items on tests incorrectly. When curriculum and tests are aligned, a student's classroom success rate predicts his or her test performance.

Now that we have discussed the outcomes of instruction, allocated time, engaged time, and success rate, we are ready to discuss the concept of *academic learning time (ALT)*. This concept has great heuristic value for thinking about classroom instruction and predicting who might be an effective teacher. We shall define ALT as *that part of allocated time in which students are engaged with materials or activities related to the outcome measures that are being used and in which students experience a high success rate.* ALT is, to me, one of the more useful concepts for judging whether student learning is taking place at a particular moment in some particular curriculum area. It is a variable we can observe and measure in the classroom, and it has known relations with student learning. Thus it is a sensible variable to use when trying to decide if a teacher is going to be effective or not.

All of the variables discussed so far as correlated with or causally related to measures of achievement are incorporated into this single variable. Allocated time, engaged time, success in class, and the relationship of classroom activities to outcomes are all incorporated in the definition of ALT. The utility of ALT is based on the concept's logical nature and the successful demonstration that achievement can be predicted with it. For example, in that part of the research by Fisher et al. (1978) concerned with second-grade achievement, 17 outcome measures were identified. These included decoding blends and long vowels, comprehension, addition and subtraction with regrouping, and linear measurement. The variables that make up ALT—allocated time, engaged time, and success rate in a given content area—were used to predict achievement in the 17 content areas. *Allocated time* was a positive predictor of achievement in the 17 different areas 14 times. *Engaged time* was a positive predictor of achievement 15 times. *High success rate* was a positive predictor of achievement in the 17 areas every time. *Low success rate* was a negative predictor of achievement 14 times. Many of these relationships were statistically significant. Furthermore, when we examined how much of the variance in these 17 different measures could be accounted for by the ALT variables taken as a set, we found further support for the idea that ALT is an important concept. After we statistically removed the effects of the students' entering ability, on a variety of measures we were able to account for between 1 percent and 22 percent of the variance in student achievement. On average, across all sorts of content areas and in different grades, ALT consistently accounted for about 10 percent of the variance in students' achievement. (This should be compared to the medical research reported in Chapter 1.) Thus ALT has proven to be a useful concept or variable for thinking about classroom instruction.

Effective teachers seem to keep ALT in mind as they instruct, though they rarely call it by this name and rarely make their cognitive processes conscious so deliberately. Effective teachers seem to know the outcome measures used for instruction, assign activities related to those outcome measures, see to it that enough time is allocated for students, find ways to keep students engaged, and ensure that the younger or lower-achieving students spend large percentages of time in high-success experiences. In short, the students of effective teachers accumulate a good deal of ALT. Empirically, students and classes that accumulate high levels of ALT are those that are likely to achieve more than students or classes that accumulate lower amounts of ALT.

Let us return now to our initial simple statement about what constitutes effective teaching. We stated that the effective teacher delivers a curriculum that is linked to certain outcomes. Delivery of the curriculum requires the teacher to find ways to ensure that allocated time and especially engaged time are sufficient for learning and that the materials and activities students are engaged in lead to high success. That is, an effective teacher controls ALT, providing students with the chance to learn what they are supposed to learn. Perhaps, at this abstract verbal level, the definition of an effective teacher is as simple as I have stated it—it is simply a person who delivers to students a curriculum related to valued outcomes.

CAN SIMPLE VIEWS OF EFFECTIVE TEACHING PREDICT EFFECTIVE TEACHERS?

A good test of whether or not one's views about some phenomenon are useful to a scientific community is to see if they can predict that phenomenon. Scientific theories are often validated in this way. For example, when Einstein predicted early in the twentieth century that light would bend, due to the gravitational pull of a heavenly body, his colleagues were dubious. At that time, no measurement system existed to test his theory. About 15 years later, however, his theory was verified, and his views about light and gravitational forces had to be taken much more seriously. Prediction is thus a way to validate a scientist's ideas. Successful prediction will *not* tell us if ideas or theories are "true." Someone who might predict the summer solstice very accurately might also believe that a sun god changes direction on that day. Thus accurate prediction and the "truth" of a theory are not the same thing. But an accurate prediction makes you want to take someone's ideas more seriously than if those ideas could not be used to predict the phenomenon on which they focused.

Two separate tests of how the ALT conception of the way effective teachers operate their classrooms were undertaken by students of mine, David Lynn and Michelle Ellis Schwabe. In both studies, observers were given minimum training in the use of observation instruments concerned with allocated time, engaged time, success, the teacher's classroom behavior, classroom climate, and so forth. In both studies, about 25 teachers of second through sixth grades were studied. Observations ranged from three to eight visits in each class. Reading and mathematics instruction were the focus of the observations. Performance on the California Achievement Test was the outcome measure used in both studies. Tables 1 and 2 present the results of these two small studies, which were instructive, though, in many ways, not well designed. They were our first attempts to see whether the variables we thought were related to teacher effectiveness could really be used to predict which teachers would be and which teachers would not be effective in producing gains on the standardized achievement tests used by these school districts. From the magnitude of the multiple correlations (the columns labeled multiple R), we see that the set of variables that we thought would predict performance on standardized tests actually did so. When we examine the total amount of variance accounted for (the columns labeled multiple R^2) we see that this set of predictors accounts for substantial amounts of the variation in the achievement scores of these students. When we go on to ask whether there is a unique contribution to the prediction of achievement that certain clusters of the variables make, we see that the time and success variables—that is, the ALT variables—often uniquely account for some of the variance in achievement. These data also inform us that the time and success variables

Table 1. Prediction of Test Performance by ALT Variables: Study 1.

Outcome Measure: California Achievement Test	OVERALL PREDICTION		VARIANCE ACCOUNTED FOR UNIQUELY		
	Multiple R	Multiple R²	Time and Success Variables	Teacher Behavior Variables	Classroom Climate Variables
Math applications	.79	.62	.32	.11	.20
Math computation	.64	.41	.32	.15	.16
Math concepts	.51	.26	.13	.13	.07
Word study skills	.37	.14	.09	.07	.05
Reading comprehension	.81	.65	.13	.52	.00
Vocabulary	.76	.58	.13	.30	.08
Total mathematics score	.38	.14	.11	.04	.08
Total reading score	.74	.19	.03	.13	.05

Number of elementary-school classrooms = 25.
Approximately 5 observations per classroom.
SOURCE: Unpublished study by David Lynn, 1980.

do not always predict achievement, and they sometimes predict achievement for some outcome measure but not for others. This means we should be cautious in how we interpret our findings. Nevertheless, these studies lead us to be optimistic overall.

We would argue that with a well-polished study, with carefully trained observers, and perhaps with as few as five or seven observations per classroom, we might be able to predict effective teachers quite well. If classroom observations could be made, say, between October and December in an academic year, and analyses of the data could be

Table 2. Prediction of Test Performance by ALT Variables: Study 2.

Outcome Measure: California Achievement Test	OVERALL PREDICTION		VARIANCE ACCOUNTED FOR UNIQUELY		
	Multiple R	Multiple R²	Time Variables	Teacher Variables	Classroom Process Variables
Mathematics: spring-spring gain in scale scores	.62	.38	.33	.06	.00
Mathematics: residualized scores	.51	.26	.12	.04	.03
Reading: spring-spring gain in scale scores	.78	.60	.04	.02	.21
Reading: residualized scores	.79	.62	.03	.02	.19

Number of elementary school classrooms = 18.
Approximately 5 observations per classroom.
SOURCE: Unpublished dissertation by Michelle Ellis-Schwabe, 1986.

made over the Christmas break, then the most and least effective teachers in the sample observed could be identified by the beginning of January. Identifying those teachers who are predicted to be ineffective—that is, identifying those teachers and classrooms that are somehow "at risk"— means that some forms of remediation might be tried throughout the spring to help those classrooms achieve better. It does not take a high multiple correlation in a prediction study to be useful in identifying the top and bottom 10–20 percent of the teachers in a particular sample. Multiple correlations as low as .30 would be more than enough to identify accurately the teachers who would be highly effective and highly ineffective.

From these two small and imperfect studies, which used the ALT concept and related variables as predictors, we see that the development of a system to identify the most and least effective teachers in a sample is quite feasible from a technical standpoint. It would be sensible and in the best interests of students to identify teachers who are at risk in a particular academic year and to target the school district's scarce in-service dollars to those teachers. Although they are predicted not to have their students score well on standardized achievement tests, such teachers might be helped throughout the second half of the academic year to solve the instructional or management problems that led to the prediction of ineffectiveness. But it is likely that social and political problems involved in implementing such a system may prevent its use. The labeling of teachers as "at risk" is likely to lead to all the problems that have been noticed when labels such as "slow," "learning disabled," or "culturally deprived" are applied to a child. Technically, though, by relying on ALT, such a predictive system now appears to be feasible. The ALT variables do forecast which teachers will and which teachers will not be effective, accounting for important amounts of the variance in students' achievement. Thus we have evidence that requires us to take the ALT concept seriously.

Academic Learning Time, Achievement, and Quality Instruction

It would be nice to find a school system that regularly studies classroom instruction to find ways to accurately identify teachers who might need extra help in a particular school year. But even without systematic use of the ALT concept as part of an ongoing assessment of classrooms, we may still find that concept useful as we view our own teaching or as we enter the classrooms of others. In fact, because ALT impels us to think about both allocated and engaged time, success rate, and the alignment of the curriculum with outcomes, it is the best variable we can use for thinking about actual student achievement.

We could choose, as we often did in the past, to rate a teacher's grooming when we visit a classroom, or we could rate the neatness of the bulletin board, or the care with which students handle equipment and supplies. But the relationship of those observable classroom variables to student achievement has never been very clear. On the other hand, the relationship to achievement of each of the variables subsumed by ALT is much clearer. Therefore, as a proxy or stand-in for the actual measured achievement of a class on standardized tests, ALT has much to recommend it. But, in addition, ALT may also be considered a way of thinking about that most elusive concept of "quality" instruction.

It has been easy for some critics to dismiss the notion of ALT as simple-minded. Some critics regard the empirical relationship of ALT to achievement as a mere technical or engineering fact unrelated to the real issues of schooling, which are those of quality (see Berliner & Fisher, 1985; Jackson, 1985; Phillips, 1985). But I would argue that the concept of ALT is intimately tied to the concept of quality. I look at it this way. If I enter a classroom and I see students who for the most part are engaged in activities or with materials that I judge to be related in some sensible way to outcomes that are valued, and that the students are for the most part succeeding at what they are doing, then what I am seeing is high-quality classroom instruction. If, in addition, the teacher allocates what appears to be sensible amounts of time to these endeavors, we would find high rates of ALT in the content areas being taught. I would argue that when high levels of ALT are found, as they would be in this case, we are simultaneously witnessing high-quality instruction. Judgments of quality and measures of ALT are intimately related. A measure of ALT can stand both as a proxy for achievement on standardized tests (because it accounts for considerable amounts of the variance in such tests), and it can also be an indicator of the quality of instruction that is taking place (because it conforms to our notions of what a quality instructional setting should be like). To me, ALT is an indicator of both the products of instruction and of the processes of instruction that we value in our society.

DEVELOPING A SIMPLE THEORY OF CLASSROOM INSTRUCTION

Dozens of findings have emerged from correlational and experimental studies of teacher effectiveness (see Wittrock, 1986). These predictors of effectiveness are sensible, for the most part. In looking them over, I thought I saw a way that a simple theory fit the existing data. I believe that the teaching variables associated with effectiveness probably affect student achievement by affecting one of the components of ALT—allocated time, engaged time, success, or the congruence of tasks with outcome measures. That is, one way we may understand the findings that keep emerging from studies of teacher effectiveness is to ask how these findings might be related to one of the known correlates of achievement. Stating this as a theory, I would simply hypothesize that effective teachers deliver a curriculum that is matched to outcomes. Effective teachers provide their students with better opportunities to learn what it is they are supposed to learn, and they do so by attending to time variables and success variables and by matching the curriculum and the outcome. Let us briefly test how this theory might be applied.

When we find out, for example, that *pacing* is a consistently positive predictor of achievement, and that effective teachers characteristically go through the curriculum at a faster pace than their less effective colleagues do, we can easily satisfy one goal of science, that of prediction. When we hypothesize that pacing is a consistent predictor of achievement because it results in preventing or allowing students the opportunity to learn the things that they are to be held responsible for learning, we are striving to attain another goal of science—namely, understanding. Prediction, we noted earlier, can occur without much understanding. But when you feel you understand why some instructional phenomenon occurs—when you "make sense" out of the myriad things that go on during instruction, when you order them or see how they fit together—then you are developing a theory of instruction (see Snow, 1973).

Structuring is another variable that has been found to be a predictor of teacher effectiveness. Teachers who share the goals of a lesson with students, who provide clear directions at the start of a lesson, who provide introductions, advance organizers, reviews, and summaries, and who, in general, *structure* the activity for students in an unambiguous way are usually more effective than teachers who do not engage in such activities. These findings provide us with data to predict effectiveness. To understand why structuring acts as it does is a bit harder. In line with our simple theory, however, we would hypothesize that structuring works because of a number of factors. When a teacher provides clear directions, a reduced error rate occurs because students are aware of what they are supposed to be doing. The teacher who often gives intelligible and short directions at the start of an activity is also ensuring higher engaged time. Since students know what they are to be doing, they cannot easily act befuddled or honestly remain unengaged. Summaries and reviews help keep error rates down by enabling students to check what they have done. The overviews, summaries, and reviews also expose students to key ideas and information, possibly increasing the congruence of the curriculum to the tests used to measure achievement in that subject area. Reminding students about the reason they are doing certain tasks decreases students' feelings that tasks are mindless, thus increasing their motivation to learn, resulting in higher rates of engaged time in class and possibly higher allocations of overall time if students choose to work on such tasks when they have uncommitted time. I think our theory helps us in understanding how this reliable predictor of achievement might work.

Monitoring is another variable found to correlate with achievement. In the United States, elementary-school students work independently, in workbooks and on worksheets, a good deal of the time. It is not unusual for independent seatwork activities to occupy 40–60 percent of the time that students work on academic curriculum in the elementary grades. While students are working independently at their desks, a teacher may or may not circulate and monitor the classroom. Those teachers that do such monitoring generally have classes that achieve higher. Monitoring probably correlates with achievement because it acts to keep error rate down and engagement rate up. A teacher who roams the classroom can catch students' mistakes before they are practiced too long and can also minimize off-task behavior simply by his or her presence. Thus monitoring is a predictor of achievement by affecting ALT variables and, therefore, the students' opportunity to learn.

This list could go on, but by now the outline of how we might come to understand (rather than predict) effective teaching practices should be clear. Teacher behaviors, classroom processes, and school-level variables that affect achievement probably do so by affecting ALT and therefore by influencing students' opportunity to learn. Thus not only can we predict teacher effectiveness, in my opinion, but we now also can *understand* how many of the findings related to effectiveness actually must be applied. The roots of our theory are in J. B. Carroll's (1963) model of school learning and the work of the Beginning Teacher Evaluation Study (see Fisher & Berliner, 1985). As simple as this theory may appear, we believe it to be a powerful one for understanding effective classroom teaching.

CONCLUSION

We have discussed how effective teachers earn their reputations. They find ways to deliver a curriculum to their students that matches the desired outcomes. They accomplish this task by managing academic learning time. The concept of academic learning time subsumes four other concepts or variables: allocated time, engaged time, success rate, and curriculum alignment. Each of these variables singly, or in combinations, has been a consistent correlate of achievement across many grade levels and curriculum areas. In two independent small-scale inquiries into whether ALT could be used to predict classroom gain on standardized tests, this concept was found to be useful. It appears that the most and least effective teachers in a sample can be reliably identified even before their classes are assessed. Moreover, we argued, ALT is tied to classroom processes that ordinarily are taken as indicators of instructional quality. Finally, we argued that the teaching variables or instructional activities that individuals identify as related to achievement are likely to be significant predictors of achievement because they affect ALT. Variables or programs of instruction that affect achievement will generally do so by affecting allocated time, engaged time, success rate, or the relationship between what is taught and what is tested. Teachers who control ALT, or the set of variables subsumed by that concept, are teachers whose students will achieve well, at least on our traditional measures of student achievement.

We have come a long way in our understanding of effective teachers since William James started advising teachers about how to think about their art. We have simple ideas of considerable utility with which to think about instruction. These ideas infuse the art of teaching with rich concepts so that classroom experiences can be ordered and discussed in meaningful ways and so that predictions can be made and verified. These ideas are beginning to provide a scientific underpinning to the complex and dynamic art of teaching.

REFERENCES

Berliner, D. C. (1979). Tempus educare. In P. L. Peterson & H. J. Walberg (Eds.), *Research on teaching*. Berkeley, CA: McCutchan.

Berliner, D. C., & Fisher, C. W. (1985). One more time. In C. W. Fisher & D. C. Berliner (Eds.), *Perspectives on instructional time*. New York: Longman.

Carroll, J. B. (1963). A model of school learning. *Teachers College Record, 64*, 723–733.

Cooley, W. W., & Leinhardt, G. (1980). The instructional dimensions study. *Educational Evaluation and Policy Analysis, 2* (1), 7–25.

Dishaw, M. M. (1977a). *Descriptions of allocated time to content areas for the A-B period*, Technical Note IV-11a, Beginning Teacher Evaluation Study. San Francisco, CA: Far West Laboratory for Educational Research and Development.

———. (1977b). *Descriptions of allocated time to content areas for the B-C period*, Technical Note IV-11b, Beginning Teacher Evaluation Study. San Francisco, CA: Far West Laboratory for Educational Research and Development.

Fisher, C. W., & Berliner, D. C. (1985). (Eds.). *Perspectives on instructional time*. New York: Longman.

Fisher, C. W., Berliner, D. C., Filby, N. N., Marliave, R. S., Cahen, L. S., & Dishaw, M. M. (1980). Teaching behaviors, academic learning time, and student achievement: An overview. In C. Denham & A. Lieberman (Eds.), *Time to learn*. Washington, DC: National Institute of Education.

Fisher, C. W., Filby, N. N., Marliave, R. S., Cahen, L. S., Dishaw, M. M., Moore, J. E., & Berliner, D. C. (1978). *Teaching behaviors, academic learning, and student achievement*. (Final Report of Phase III-B, Beginning Teacher Evaluation Study, Tech. Rep. V-1). San Francisco, CA: Far West Laboratory for Educational Research and Development.

Jackson, P. W. (1985). Time-off-task at a time-on-task conference. In C. W. Fisher & D. C. Berliner (Eds.), *Perspectives on instructional time*. New York: Longman.

Phillips, D. C. (1985). The uses and abuses of truisms. In C. W. Fisher & D. C. Berliner (Eds.), *Perspectives on instructional time*. New York: Longman.

Rossmiller, R. A. (1982, September). *Managing school resources to improve stu-*

dent achievement. Paper presented at the State Superintendent Conference for District Administrators, Madison, WI.

Snow, R. E. (1973). Theory construction for research on teaching. In R. W. Travers (Ed.), *Handbook of research on teaching*, 2nd ed. Chicago: Rand McNally.

Wittrock, M. C. (1986). (Ed.). *Handbook of research on teaching*, 3rd ed. New York: Macmillan.

CHAPTER 6

ELIZABETH FENNEMA

PENELOPE L. PETERSON

EFFECTIVE TEACHING FOR GIRLS AND BOYS
The Same or Different?

Several years ago, a first-grade teacher described to us a pageant that her class put on for parents every year. In this pageant, the children portrayed famous people whom they had studied during the school year. For each month of the year, a famous person who was born in that month would appear on the stage and recite his accomplishments. As the teacher described the scenario, she mentioned only famous men who were portrayed by boys in her class. We thus inquired naively, "What roles do the girls have in the class pageant?" The teacher replied, "Oh, the girls play the months. Each girl dresses up like the month of the year and comes on stage holding a sign with the name of the month. Then the boy portraying the famous man born in that month comes on stage and recites." As she talked, the teacher seemed blithely unaware of the message that she was communicating to girls and boys about what they might be when they grew up. Further, she was unaware of biographical information on famous women whom she might include in her class's study of famous persons. We quickly remedied this situation by providing her with some first-grade curriculum materials on famous women.

This teacher has since retired, and when we observe in classrooms these days, we seldom see such overt examples of sexism. However, inequities in educational outcomes still exist for girls and boys, particularly in the area of mathematics.

Girls continue to achieve at lower levels in mathematics than do boys. Male superiority in mathematics begins in the upper elementary-school years and increases throughout high school. The gap between sexes in mathematical achievement widens as the difficulty level of mathematics increases (Fennema, 1984). However, as early as 9 years

111

of age boys score higher than girls on mathematics achievement tests that require high-level thinking, such as application or interpretation of mathematical knowledge (Fennema & Carpenter, 1981). Further, even when they are equal in mathematical ability to boys, girls have less confidence in their mathematical competence. Girls develop more negative attitudes about themselves and about mathematics than do boys. (See Fennema, in press, for a complete review.) Because of these negative attitudes and lower achievement, girls often feel that any mathematics-related career is not an option for them. Consequently, girls select a mathematics-related career less frequently than do boys. Girls, more so than boys, do not achieve important goals that mathematics teachers set.

Why do these gender-related differences in mathematics continue to exist? They have been documented for at least a decade (see Fennema, 1984, for a decade's review). Some would argue that parents are at fault, or that society as a whole must assume responsibility. Others place the blame on genetic or biological factors. (See Bleier, 1984, for a complete review of the data about genetic/biological factors.) Yet none of these responses provides a mechanism whereby educators might address these inequities. However, if processes that occur in classrooms contribute to these gender-related differences in mathematics achievement and teachers had more knowledge about these classroom processes, then they could take the initiative to eliminate any inequities.

In this chapter we focus on behaviors of students and teachers within classrooms, and, in particular, we examine those behaviors that might explain gender-related differences in learning mathematics. We begin with an overview of findings from classroom research on teaching effectiveness. Then we discuss some findings from our own classroom research and the research of others that addresses gender-related differences in learning mathematics. We conclude with some guidelines for teachers.

FINDINGS FROM RESEARCH ON TEACHING

During the past decade, researchers have gained increased knowledge about what teachers and students do in classrooms. The purpose of their research has been to increase teacher effectiveness and has been called process-product research. In the first stage of process-product research, researchers observe and record overt behaviors of students and teachers during the school year. Second, they measure the amount of learning that has taken place during the school year by computing gains in student achievement on standardized tests from the beginning to the end of the year. Third, they examine the relationship between these achievement gains and the number of times a specific teacher or student behavior occurred in the classroom. Finally, they identify those behaviors that are most highly related to the achievement-gain scores and thus appear to be most important for increasing student learning. In a subsequent study, the researcher might provide a new group of teachers with information about the behaviors that were highly related to learning. The researcher would teach the teachers to implement the behaviors and would then observe the teachers and students to see if the behaviors were used and if learning was increased.

From process-product research, we have gained important new knowledge. One behavior found to be important is the amount of time students are engaged or not engaged in a mathematics activity during class. Not surprisingly, researchers have reported that classes in which students are engaged more in academic activities are also classes in which students learn more. The teaching behaviors that seem to be most important are "direct teaching" behaviors, in which the teacher takes an active role in telling students what they are to learn and how they are to do various academic activities, followed by close monitoring to ensure that students do the activities as directed. In summarizing process-product research, Brophy and Good (1986) concluded that "students learn more efficiently when their teachers first structure new information for them and help them relate it to what they already know, and then monitor their performance and provide corrective feedback during recitation, drill, practice, or application activities" (pp. 363–364; see also Chapter 4).

Good, Grouws, and Ebmeier (1983) conducted a process-product study of teaching, which has had the greatest impact on mathematics teaching. During the first year of this study, they identified a set of behaviors used by fourth-grade teachers whose children's scores on an academic achievement test had risen more than had those of other teachers' children. They then taught this set of behaviors, called "Active Teaching," to other teachers who used them during the second year of the study. Active Teaching included spending specified amounts of time on review and development of mathematical concepts and skills and on monitoring seatwork and homework closely. In other words, teachers clearly told children what to learn, related new learning to old learning, and actively monitored all practice. Good et al. observed the second-year teachers, measured the achievement scores of their children at the end of the year, and reported that children achieved more in the classrooms of the teachers who used Active Teaching.

Process-product researchers have taught us a lot. For example, they have provided strong evidence that what teachers and students do in the classroom is important. However, the research findings are limited in several ways (see Peterson, 1979a, 1979b). First, researchers have used narrow outcomes or product measures as criteria for effective teaching. Typically, they have used standardized tests, which tend to emphasize the measurement of students' low-level cognitive thinking, such as computational skills, and de-emphasize the measurement of students' high-level cognitive thinking. Researchers have not often attempted to differentiate achievement at various cognitive levels but have used the total score on a standardized achievement test as an indicator of learning. Thus we do not know whether behaviors that facilitate low-level cognitive learning are the same as those that facilitate high-level cognitive learning.

What are the important differences between high-level and low-level cognitive learning in mathematics? Low-level mathematics activities require the student to apply a routine procedure, such as addition or subtraction, to find an answer. Figure 1 presents some examples of low-level problems. For a low-level problem, teachers usually teach students a mechanistic way to arrive at a solution. While it is possible that the low-level problems in Figure 1 might require very young children to engage in high-level cognitive thinking to solve them, most children are able to solve these problems using a routine procedure by the time they reach fourth grade.

While low-level mathematical tasks require the student to recall a specific fact or to use a memorized algorithm, high-level cognitive tasks in mathematics require the student to understand, interpret, or apply mathematical knowledge. Thus the mental demands are greater for high-level mathematics problems than for low-level problems. To solve a high-level problem, the student must first figure out *how* to solve the problem; the student cannot use a prelearned procedure.

In addition to not differentiating high-level from low-level cognitive achievement in mathematics, researchers have not considered other important outcomes of education, such as students' motivation, confidence, and attitudes. Further, researchers have not investigated whether classroom behaviors that are effective for one group of students are equally effective for other groups of students.

The limitations of process-product research seem severe for educators who are concerned with gender-related differences in mathematics. To date, process-product researchers have ignored those student outcomes on which gender-related differences are most apparent: in students' high-level cognitive mathematics learning and in students' motivation and attitudes toward and confidence in learning mathematics. Indeed, one is left with several unanswered questions. Do gender-related differences exist because:

1. Girls are not engaged in mathematics as much as boys?
2. Girls engage in different activities than boys during mathematics classes?
3. Teachers use more effective teaching behaviors with boys than with girls?
4. Effective teaching behaviors for girls are different than effective teaching behaviors for boys, and teachers carry out instruction primarily for boys?

In the remainder of this chapter, we discuss findings from some new research that provide partial answers to these questions.

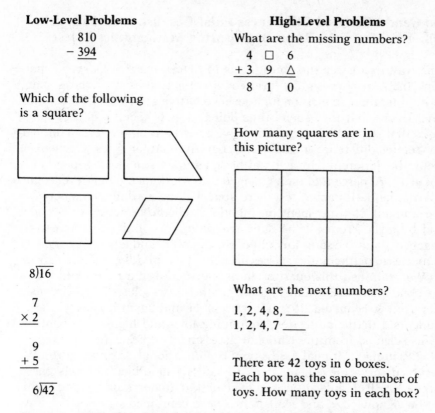

Low-Level Problems

$$810$$
$$-\;394$$

Which of the following is a square?

$$8)\overline{16}$$

$$7$$
$$\times\,2$$

$$9$$
$$+\,5$$

$$6)\overline{42}$$

High-Level Problems

What are the missing numbers?

$$4\quad \square\quad 6$$
$$+\,3\quad 9\quad \triangle$$
$$8\quad 1\quad 0$$

How many squares are in this picture?

What are the next numbers?

1, 2, 4, 8, ____
1, 2, 4, 7 ____

There are 42 toys in 6 boxes. Each box has the same number of toys. How many toys in each box?

Figure 1. Examples of low-level and high-level mathematics problems.

Do Gender-Related Differences Exist Because Girls Are Not Engaged in Mathematics as Much as Boys?

Several researchers have investigated this question (Reyes, 1981; Koehler, 1985; Peterson & Fennema, 1985). The answer is *no!* Both girls and boys spend about the same percentage of time in class actively working on mathematics. Reyes (1981) reported that fourth-grade boys and girls were thus engaged about 65 percent of the time. In a study of 36 fourth-grade mathematics classes, Peterson and Fennema (1985) found that both girls and boys were engaged about 75 percent of the time. Koehler (1985) reported that she observed no differences between boys and girls in academic engagement in beginning algebra classes.

These findings conflict with traditional beliefs. Many teachers believe that girls are more attentive in class than boys. However, at least as evidenced in their overt behavior, girls and boys appear to spend about the same percentage of time in class working on mathematics.

Do Gender-Related Differences Exist Because Girls Engage in Different Activities Than Boys During Mathematics Classes?

One way to answer this question is to determine if girls spend more time than do boys on low-level cognitive activities while boys spend more time than do girls on high-level cognitive activities. Because children learn what they spend time doing, if girls spend less time doing tasks that require high-level cognitive activity, then the reason for gender-related differences in high-level cognitive mathematics achievement would be apparent. However, although students in classes spend only about 15–20 percent of their engaged time working on high-level cognitive mathematics activities, there appear to be no differences between the amount of time spent on high-level cognitive activities by boys and by girls. From all the data available, boys and girls seem to be engaged about the same amount of time in high- and low-level cognitive activities in mathematics classes in elementary, middle, and high school.

We examined this question in greater detail in a recent study that we conducted in 36 fourth-grade mathematics classes in Wisconsin (Peterson & Fennema, 1985). In December and again in May, we gave students a mathematics test containing low- and high-level cognitive items selected from the National Assessment of Educational Progress (NAEP) items (National Assessment of Educational Progress, 1979). We designed the achievement items to assess four difficulty levels based on the NAEP classification: knowledge, skill, understanding, and application. Knowledge and skill items were combined to form the low-level items, and understanding and application items were combined to form the high-level items. Figure 1 shows examples of low-level and high-level problems. In general, the low-level problems required that a student recall a specific fact or be able to manipulate an algorithm but did not require that the student understand, interpret, or apply mathematical knowledge. During January through April, six randomly selected girls and six randomly selected boys were observed in each class. Using a 60-second time sampling procedure, the observers recorded the cognitive level of the mathematics activity—low-level or high-level—as defined above, and whether or not the students were engaged in mathematics activities.

Girls were observed to be engaged in mathematics about 77 percent of the time (15 percent high-level cognitive activities and 62 percent low-level activities). Boys were observed to be engaged in mathematics about 75 percent of the time (15 percent high-level, 60 percent low-level). Students were most typically engaged at a low cognitive level, using symbols (numerals and mathematical signs) rather than pictures or materials that represented mathematics (such as counters). While students were engaged in mathematics, there was little helping going on, and the mathematics activity was usually neither competitive nor cooperative. When students were not engaged in mathematics, they were most often engaged in either off-task behavior or in interim activities such as passing out papers, sharpening pencils, or waiting for the teacher to begin class. Off-task behavior included daydreaming, getting a drink of water, or social talking of which the teacher did not approve. Boys were observed to be engaged in off-task behavior slightly more often than were girls, although this difference was not statistically significant. Interim activities occupied about 9 percent of the time during mathematics class. Girls and boys did not differ in the percentage of time they were observed to be engaged in these activities.

In sum, girls and boys apparently spend their time in mathematics classes engaged in about the same things. Thus differential engagement in mathematics activities does not explain gender-related differences in mathematics.

Do Gender-Related Differences Exist Because Teachers Use More Effective Teaching Behaviors with Boys Than with Girls?

Differential treatment of girls and boys by teachers is well documented. Boys participate in more interactions with the teacher, receive more feedback, receive more help from the teacher, are scolded more and receive more praise, and have more informal contacts with the teacher (see, for example, Brophy, 1985). Because of the disproportionate amount of time that teachers spend with boys, many have assumed that this is a major reason for girls' underachievement in mathematics.

In our study, we also observed many facets of interactions between students and teachers, such as the cognitive level of the interaction, whether teacher or student initiated the interaction, and whether the interaction was private or public. When we examined the average frequency per day for boys and girls on the 26 major teacher-student interaction categories, we found consistent differences between boys and girls on 9 of them. Teachers initiated more public and private interactions with boys than with girls concerning classroom behavior. Similarly, teachers initiated more private procedural interactions with boys than with girls; procedural interactions involved classroom management, directions, and procedures. Also, teachers initiated more private and public social interactions with boys than with girls. Further, they received and accepted more "called out" answers to low-level mathematics questions from boys than from girls. These are all findings that have been reported previously by other researchers (see, for example, Brophy, 1985). Most important, teachers engaged in significantly more interactions dealing with mathematics with boys than with girls. Teachers initiated significantly more low-level and high-level interactions with boys than with girls. For example, when working on word problems, teachers more frequently called on boys than girls for both the answers and the explanations of how the answers were obtained. Further, our data showed that the differences in teacher-student mathematics interactions with girls and boys were due to gender-related differences in teacher initiations, not due to gender-related differences in student initiations. Girls and boys did not differ in the number of times that they initiated mathematics interactions with the teacher, such as asking the teacher a question on a mathematics word problem.

Does the higher frequency of interactions with teachers in these categories result in greater achievement for boys? To gain some information about this, we computed correlation coefficients between the various interaction categories and both high- and low-level cognitive achievement gains for boys and girls. For the purposes of our discussion, the important correlations were the positive correlations between teacher-initiated high-level mathematics interactions, total high-level mathematics interactions, and girls' mathematics achievement on high-level problems. The more that teachers asked high-level mathematics questions and interacted about mathematics at a high cognitive level with girls, the more girls learned about a higher cognitive level of mathematics. When we recall that teachers interacted more on high-level mathematics with boys, and when we consider the finding that high-level mathematics interactions are important for girls' learning of high-level cognitive mathematics, then we begin to hypothesize that a partial explanation of girls' lower mathematics achievement may be that girls are interacting less with teachers on the type of mathematics that leads to the ability to do high-level cognitive tasks in mathematics. Once again, let us point out that it is the teacher who is not initiating "why" and "how" questions with girls. We wonder whether, if teachers did ask girls more of these types of questions, their achievement would increase.

Another important question is "Why do teachers interact less with girls than with boys?" Our data do not address this question. Perhaps boys demand more attention, or perhaps teachers are afraid that if boys are not called on they will disrupt the class. Alternatively, girls may be demanding less attention because of lowered confidence in their ability to do mathematics. Maybe teachers believe that it is more important for boys than for girls to learn mathematics, and thus they call on boys more often to ensure that they learn.

If teachers make sure that they interact with girls on high-level mathematics, will girls learn more? Although we cannot answer these questions definitively from currently available research, we would conclude that increasing interactions with girls on high-level cognitive mathematics will do no harm and will likely improve girls' mathematics achievement.

Do Gender-Related Differences Exist Because Effective Teaching Behaviors for Girls Are Different Than Effective Teaching Behaviors for Boys? Do Teachers Carry Out Instruction Primarily for Boys?

If the answer to the first question is yes, then perhaps teachers should organize instruction in one way for girls and in another way for boys.

After all, educators have been concerned about making classrooms effective for individual students for a long time. If boys and girls learn differently, shouldn't teachers set up some situations in which girls learn best and other situations in which boys learn best? However, the question of different learning situations for different people is a troublesome one. Think of what happened as separate schools were developed for blacks and whites. Indeed, it is now illegal to develop separate schools for identifiable subgroups. Thus, if we as teachers systematically treat girls and boys differently, we may be in violation of some laws and contribute to inequitable educational outcomes. We will discuss some of our findings with respect to these issues.

Let us begin by looking in more detail at what boys and girls are actually doing in mathematics classes and how their classroom activities and interactions with the teacher are related to their learning. In our study, we found that, although there were few differences in the percentage of time that girls and boys were engaged in various activities, their participation in various activities and interactions with the teacher were differentially related to their mathematics achievement. Consistent gender-related differences appeared in five areas: (1) competitive mathematics activities; (2) cooperative mathematics activities; (3) helping by the teacher; (4) approved social interactions with peers; and (5) teacher praise and feedback. We turn now to a discussion of each of these areas. (For a complete presentation of results, see Peterson & Fennema, 1985; and Fennema & Peterson, 1986.)

Competitive Mathematics Activities. For girls, being engaged in a competitive mathematics activity was negatively related to learning of low-level cognitive mathematics activities. The more competitive the situation in mathematics class, the less girls learned. This finding was confirmed by another analysis. When we were analyzing our data, we noticed that some classrooms appeared to be favorable for girls' learning, some classrooms were favorable for boys' learning, while other classrooms seems to be equally favorable for boys' and girls' learning. Using some statistical procedures, we selected six classes where the mathematics achievement-gain scores were higher for girls than boys (girl-gain classes), six classes where the gain scores were higher for boys than girls (boy-gain classes), and six classes where there was little if any difference. We did this twice: first for high-level cognitive learning and then for low-level cognitive learning. Then we looked at the student engagement within these classrooms. Interestingly, classes that made high or low gains on high-level cognitive outcomes were usually not the same as those that made high or low gains on low-level cognitive outcomes.

Classes in which boys gained more on low-level mathematics measures than did girls spent significantly more time in competitive activities. We found 2½ times more competitive mathematics activity in the boy-gain classes than in the girl-gain classes. The more the girls were engaged in competitive mathematics activities, the less lower-level mathematics skills they learned. However, the more the boys were engaged in competitive mathematics activities, the more they learned these lower-level skills.

Why might competition cause negative gains for girls and positive gains for boys? Informal observations of the mathematics classrooms in our study help to explain these results. The teachers in the fourth-grade classes spent a significant amount of time each day during the school year working on getting students to master the multiplication tables. Learning the multiplication tables involves drill and practice, but this drill and practice may take several forms, including having students complete timed tests or play games. Typically, the mathematics games were either competitive or both competitive and cooperative.

One of the mathematics games that was often played to learn the multiplication tables was called Around the World. The teacher designated one student as "it." This student began the trip "around the world" by standing next to the desk of another student. The teacher then fired a multiplication question at the pair of students. The two students competed to be the first one to give the correct answer. The winner then proceeded "around the world" by standing beside the next student in the row for the next turn. The winner of the game was the student who successfully made it around the room by beating out each of the other students individually. It appeared that winning Around the World was often determined not only by the student's knowledge of the multiplication tables, but also by the student's verbal aggressiveness. In other words, whoever said the answer loudly and quickly won the right to move on.

Psychological research on competitiveness has been inconclusive with respect to sex differences, but when sex differences are found, research usually shows boys to be more competitive (Maccoby & Jacklin, 1974). Moreover, reviews of research have indicated that the greater aggressiveness of the male is one of the best-established and most pervasive of all psychological sex differences. Males are more aggressive than females both nonverbally and verbally. Thus males would tend to excel in situations that require greater verbal aggressiveness to achieve success.

Boys may have benefited from and enjoyed a highly competitive game like Around the World, and they may have learned the multiplication tables better due to playing the game. Indeed, our results suggest that boys' low-level mathematics achievement was enhanced by participation in competitive mathematics games that emphasized drill and practice of low-level skills. On the other hand, our results suggest that girls' low-level achievement may have been harmed by participation in competitive mathematics games.

Why do teachers use competition in classrooms? Many teachers say that they do so because the students enjoy activities that include competition. We wonder if this is so. Do girls enjoy competition? Our findings suggest that competition does not facilitate girls' learning. Perhaps it is the boys who enjoy competition, and teachers are making instructional decisions based on boys' preferences. Cooperative activities are often suggested as an alternative to competitive activities. Let us now turn to a discussion of cooperative mathematics activities.

Cooperative Mathematics Activities.   Being engaged in cooperative activities was negatively related to boys' high-level mathematics achievement. The more boys were in a cooperative situation in mathematics, the less they learned. For girls, the correlation was positive and differed significantly from the negative correlation found for boys.

We defined cooperative mathematics activities as those in which two or more students work together on a task to achieve the same goal. Such activities were negatively related to boys' high-level achievement. On the other hand, working in a small group of boys and girls was positively related to girls' high-level mathematics achievement gains. This type of activity occurred infrequently. Why didn't it occur more often if cooperative, small-group activity is so favorable for girls? Were teachers aware that such activities were not good for boys? Do teachers make decisions about structuring their classroom environments with only the boys in mind?

The idea that cooperation facilitates learning is not new. Many researchers have investigated cooperative learning situations and have found positive effects on student achievement (see Slavin, 1983, for a review). However, these researchers have not usually looked at either gender differences or at high- and low-level cognitive mathematics learning.

Our results suggest that, like the use of competitive mathematics activities, a teacher's decision to use cooperative mathematics activities may also have different effects on girls' and boys' learning of the subject. Although girls' mathematics achievement may be enhanced by participation in cooperative learning situations, boys' achievement may be impeded by participation in such situations. The boy who achieves well in high-level mathematics may do so because of his ability to think and work independently. Indeed, we have suggested elsewhere that independence is an important characteristic related to mathematics achievement on high-level problems (Fennema & Peterson, 1985). High-level cognitive problems, such as those shown in Figure 1, require complex thought before they can be solved. Each problem requires a unique solution. However, once a student figures out or is told how to do the problem, the problem no longer requires much thought. Thus we believe that the important part of finding the answer is figuring out how to do it, not actually arriving at the answer itself. For high-level learning to occur, this figuring needs to be done on an individual basis or independently, not cooperatively. What happens all too often in a cooperative group is that one student figures out how to do the problem, and then the other students use the procedure that the first student has figured out.

A boy who performs well on high-level mathematics problems may be one who is unlikely to seek out a cooperative learning situation. In other words, participation in a cooperative learning situation may be the result of a lack of independence and also may increase dependent behavior that could lead to less high-level thinking in girls. Other situations provided some support for the idea that independence may be an important consideration in explaining gender-related differences in mathematics, such as helping situations.

Helping Situations. Waiting for help was negatively related to girls' high-level achievement gains. Girls who spent more time waiting for help from the teacher may have been those who were dependent on someone else to help them to solve problems and to do other high-level cognitive tasks. Perhaps these girls had failed to develop the independence required to do well in such activities.

Do gender-related differences in mathematics arise partially because girls do not develop the independence that is required to perform well in high-level cognitive mathematics? We think so. Results from another category provide more support for our hypothesis. We coded when a student was being helped by the teacher, being helped by another student, or not being helped at all. Girls and boys were in a "no help" situation about the same percentage of the time overall (75 percent and 73 percent for girls and boys, respectively). The "no help" category was correlated to achievement gains about the same for boys and girls. However, when the boy-gain classes were compared with the girl-gain classes, we found that the sex that gained more was the one that was in a helping situation less often. In boy-gain classes, boys were being helped 19 percent of the time and girls 22 percent of the time. In the girl-gain classes, girls were being helped 25 percent of the time, compared to 29 percent for boys. In the boy-gain classes, boys and girls were working alone about 41 percent of the time. In girl-gain classes, girls and boys were working alone about 49 percent of the time. In other words, in classes where girls learned more than boys, they were working more independently. We now examine another category that may be related to girls' lack of independent learning behavior—social interactions with peers.

Approved Social Interactions with Peers. We coded "approved social interaction with peers" whenever a student was supposed to be working on mathematics but was actually chatting with a peer, with the teacher permitting the socializing to continue. We found that the more girls engaged in this type of social interaction with peers, the lower they achieved on high-level mathematics problems. Although teachers typically discourage socializing between students when they are supposed to be working, teachers may be more likely to accept socializing by girls than by boys. From personal experience and observation, we know that boys' social behavior often leads to disruption of the class because it is noisy and troublesome. Girls' social behavior may be quieter and less disruptive. However, the more girls participated in such behavior—quiet though it may have been—the less they learned.

In sum, this result suggests that the social-affective aspects of mathematics class may be significantly related to girls' learning. This conclusion is substantiated further by our findings for teacher praise and feedback.

Teacher Praise and Feedback.　In our observations of teacher-student interactions, we recorded the teacher's reaction following a student response to a mathematics question by the teacher. We found that teacher praise of a correct mathematics answer was particularly important for girls' mathematics achievement. Examples included the teacher saying "very good," "right," or "great" following a student's correct answer to a mathematics question. Perhaps girls more than boys are influenced by positive affective responses from the teacher because they are less confident than boys of their mathematics ability and need the teacher's affirmation of their ability when they do well. Alternatively, this finding again suggests the tendency for girls to be more dependent than boys in their classroom behavior.

Some additional findings about teacher feedback also seem to relate to girls' dependence/independence. We found a difference in what seemed to be the most effective teacher reaction following a student's correct response to a teacher's question on a low-level mathematics problem. For boys, correcting the answer was significantly positively related to mathematics achievement. For girls, the teacher's prompting the answer or strategy was significantly related to mathematics achievement. Prompting was coded whenever the teacher asked the student to continue or elaborate on his or her response and provided a clue or hint about what the answer should be or what strategy should be used to solve the problem.

We hypothesized that teacher feedback about the mathematics strategy would be particularly important and effective for high-level responses and for increasing high-level achievement. Our results supported our hypothesis. Focusing on the strategy rather than the answer was particularly important following a girl's high-level mathematics response and encouraged girls' high-level achievement. Focusing on the strategy may be effective because in most high-level mathematics responses, more than one right strategy can be used to obtain the answer. Thus the student needs to learn to focus on the strategy to solve the high-level problem. For girls, following an incorrect or a partly correct high-level response, prompting the strategy was important for high-level achievement. In contrast, for boys, correcting the answer was significantly related to high-level achievement. These results suggest the need for teachers to focus girls' attention on being more divergent and independent in their thinking by providing hints on the strategy that the girl might use to solve the problem, and then encouraging the girl to solve the problem on her own.

CONCLUSIONS

Is effective teaching the same for boys and girls? The answer is not a simple yes or no. We think that we have evidence to suggest that several dimensions of classroom instruction hold promise for decreasing gender-related differences in mathematics. Teachers might place more stress on cooperative mathematics activities and less stress on competitive mathematics activities when girls are instructed. Teachers should not tacitly accept socializing by girls during mathematics class. Teachers should ensure that girls attend to mathematics tasks fully as much as do boys. Teachers need to increase their interactions with girls on high-level cognitive mathematics activities, to expect girls to be able to figure out the mathematics answers, and then to praise them for doing so. Further, when girls respond incorrectly in mathematics class, the teacher needs to encourage their divergent and independent thinking by giving them hints on the strategy they might use to solve the problem, rather than telling them the answer or the strategy. Perhaps the most important thing that a teacher can do is to expect girls to work independently. Teachers should encourage girls to engage in independent learning behavior and praise them for participating in and performing well on high-level cognitive mathematics tasks. The learning of mathematics, particularly the skills required to perform high-level tasks, does not develop quickly. Rather, students develop these skills over many years by participating many times in the activities necessary for performing the high-level tasks. Indeed, a very circular path is required. One learns to do high-level tasks by choosing, persisting, and succeeding at high-level tasks.

If teachers take these guidelines to heart, then gender-related differences in mathematics achievement may diminish. Moreover, if the differences in mathematics achievement are reduced, girls' beliefs about themselves and mathematics will improve. Teachers are important agents of change, and they, more than anyone else, can help girls to achieve equity in mathematics.

ACKNOWLEDGMENTS: The research reported in this chapter was funded by a grant from the National Science Foundation (Grant No. SED 8109077). The opinions expressed in this chapter do not necessarily reflect the position, policy, or endorsement of the National Science Foundation.

We thank Deborah Harris, Peter Kloosterman, Mary Koehler, Margaret Meyer, and Lindsay Tartre, who assisted with data collection and analyses. The contributions of the authors of this article are equal.

REFERENCES

Bleier, R. (1984). *Science and gender.* New York: Pergamon Press.

Brophy, J. E. (1985). Interactions of male and female students with male and female teachers. In L. C. Wilkinson & C. B. Marrett (Eds.), *Gender influences in classroom interaction.* Orlando, FL: Academic.

Brophy, J. E., & Good, T. L. (1986). Teacher behavior and student achievement. In M. Wittrock (Ed.), *Handbook of research on teaching,* 3rd ed. (pp. 363–364). New York: Macmillan.

Fennema, E. (1974). Mathematics learning and the sexes: A review. *Journal for Research in Mathematics Education, 5* (3), 129–164.

———. (1984). Girls, women and mathematics. In E. Fennema & M. J. Ayer (Eds.), *Women and education.* Berkeley, CA: McCutchan.

———. (in press). Sex-related differences in education: Myths, realities and intervention. In V. Koehler (Ed.), *Education handbook: Research into practice.* New York: Longman.

Fennema, E., & Carpenter, J. (1981). The second national assessment and sex-related differences in mathematics. *Mathematics Teacher, 74* (7), 554–559.

Fennema, E., & Peterson, P. L. (1985). Autonomous learning behavior: A possible explanation of gender-related differences in mathematics. In L. C. Wilkinson & C. B. Marrett (Eds.), *Gender influences in classroom interaction* (pp. 17–35). Orlando, FL: Academic.

———. (1986). Teacher-student interactions and sex-related differences in mathematics. *Teaching and Teacher Education, 2* (1), 19–42.

Good, T. L., Grouws, D. A., & Ebmeier, H. (1983). *Active mathematics teaching.* New York: Longman.

Koehler, M. C. S. (1985). *Effective mathematics teaching and sex-related differences in algebra one classes.* Doctoral dissertation, University of Wisconsin–Madison.

Maccoby, E. E., & Jacklin, C. (1974). *The psychology of sex differences.* Stanford, CA: Stanford University Press.

National Assessment of Educational Progress (NAEP). (1979). *The second assessment of mathematics, 1977–1978: Released exercise set.* Denver, CO: NAEP.

Peterson, P. L. (1979a). Direct instruction: Effective for what and for whom? *Educational Leadership, 37* (1), 46–48.

———. (1979b). Direct instruction reconsidered. In P. L. Peterson & H. J. Walberg (Eds.), *Research on teaching: Concepts, findings, and implications* (pp. 57–69). Berkeley, CA: McCutchan.

Peterson, P., & Fennema, E. (1985). Effective teaching, student engagement in classroom activities, and sex-related differences in learning mathematics. *American Educational Research Journal, 22* (3), 309–335.

Reyes, L. H. (1981). *Classroom processes, sex of student and confidence in learning mathematics.* Doctoral dissertation, University of Wisconsin–Madison.

Slavin, R. E. (1983). *Cooperative learning.* New York: Longman.

PART III

OBSERVATION, EXPECTATION, AND MOTIVATION

CHAPTER 7

JANE A. STALLINGS

MARGARET NEEDELS

GEORGEA MOHLMAN SPARKS

OBSERVATION FOR THE IMPROVEMENT OF CLASSROOM LEARNING

"Bill, sit down and be quiet! You must finish those pages before the bell rings or no recess for you!" It is the last 10 minutes of a 60-minute reading lesson in Ms. Burns's third-grade classroom. Seven children in the highest reading group are seated around a table reviewing their work with Ms. Burns. The 18 students in low and average reading groups have been given silent reading or written assignments to be accomplished independently. The students' desks are arranged in rows, and Ms. Burns is seated so that she can see all of the classroom. She intermittently calls the names of Joe, Hazel, Sarah, and Bill, urging them to finish their work. A visual scan of the room indicates that eight other children are waiting with their hands up or are wandering around the room. Ms. Burns's last cajoling of Bill has left Ann in the middle of her turn to read aloud. Ann continues her reading, but the continuity is lost.

Ms. Burns has been teaching school for three years. During this time, she has learned to group children by levels of ability and to arrange the physical environment so that she can see most of the children most of the time. She does manage to call each group to the reading circle each day, and each group receives daily lessons and assignments according to the textbook chosen for their reading level.

What then is the problem? Clearly, some students in Ms. Burns's class are misusing the 60 minutes provided for reading every day. In fact, in a recent evaluation, Ms. Style, the school principal, who has been studying the time-on-task literature, strongly suggested that Ms. Burns develop strategies to keep more of her children involved in their work more of the time. Ms. Style gave Ms. Burns a timed observation record of which children were off-task during which activities and the nature of their off-task behavior. Ms. Burns was asked to study the report and to fill in a summary sheet. She was then to discuss the problems and possible solutions with Mr. Kesey, the other third-grade teacher. Mr. Kesey is in his ninth year of teaching, but this is his first year of teaching third grade. He has previously only taught sixth grade. He, too, has been recently observed by the principal. The two teachers were to develop a plan for increasing the amount of time students spend on meaningful reading activities. The evaluation and assignment with a peer were of great concern to Ms. Burns.

OBSERVING THE CLASSROOM: A CASE STUDY

From the off-task record that the principal made when she scanned the classroom every five minutes, Ms. Burns noticed that all of the children had been off-task during some part of the period (see Figure 1). She noticed that Joe, who was trying to be good due to the principal's presence, was still off-task 6 out of 12 times when the principal scanned the room. Appendix A describes how to use the off-task observation system.

Following the principal's directions, Ms. Burns completed the observation summary sheet (see Figure 2). This summary made clear that during the first 20 minutes, most of the children were doing what they were supposed to do. From then until the end of the period, the group became increasingly off-task. Most of the off-task behavior occurred during transitions or toward the end of the period, when the children were supposed to be reading silently or completing written assignments. Ms. Burns identified each child by reading group to see when each group was off-task most often. One surprising fact was that even the high achievers were waiting or uninvolved nearly 15 percent of the time, as were the average achievers. The low achievers were off-task 31 percent of the time (see Figure 2). A few children accounted for most of the chatting and the disruptive behavior. Moving their seats closer to Ms. Burns's desk would probably improve this situation. Children like Orin, Sarah, and Hazel, who were off-task but not bothering anyone, were greater mysteries. This very specific off-task observation gave Ms. Burns much to think about.

During a physical education period, Ms. Style arranged for the two third-grade teachers to meet and discuss their observation charts. She made it clear that their conversation was to be confidential. The purpose of the meeting was to improve student use of time. Each teacher was asked to answer the following questions:

What was the predominant off-task behavior?
    What might be the cause?
    How can this be corrected?
During which activity did most off-task behavior occur?
    What might be the cause?
    How can this be corrected?

During which sweeps were most students off-task?
> What might be the cause?
> How can this be corrected?
Which students were off-task most often?
> What are possible reasons?
> What are possible solutions?
What overall recommendations would you make?

At their first meeting, both teachers studied Ms. Burns's observation record and then Mr. Kesey's. They tried to think of a solution to the high rate of off-task behavior during the last part of the period (see Figure 2).

A glance at Ms. Burns's summary sheet revealed that, on the average, children spent 5 minutes getting organized, received 15 minutes of instruction, and were expected to be involved in independent written seatwork for 40 minutes. Mr. Kesey noticed that most of the children in Ms. Burns's low group were on-task during the first 15 minutes of their independent seatwork time. This did not surprise him. It was the time at the middle and end of the seatwork activity that was the problem. He remembered, however, a report by Stallings, Goodman, and Johnson (1986) indicating that working with the lowest achievers in the middle of the period helped them stay on-task for more of the period. The organization of successful groups in that study looked like this:

9:00	Explain assignments and expectations to all groups; help low group get started (have all assignments on chalkboard).
9:05	Instruct average group.
9:20	Assign seatwork to average group and answer individual student questions.
9:25	Instruct low group.
9:45	Assign seatwork to low group and answer individual student questions.
9:50	Instruct high group.

Stallings, Goodman, and Johnson found that third- and fourth-grade students on the average stayed on-task during seatwork from 15 to 20 minutes; then they wandered off-task. First-grade children stayed on task an average of 10–12 minutes. These findings suggest that students should have a number of well-structured, short, engaging activities in addition to a worksheet. These might include library reading, writing activities, and working in pairs on developing fluency in reading passages or sight words.

Mr. Kesey also mentioned a study by Stallings, Needels, and Stayrook (1979) that indicated students were most on-task and achieved more when class activities were varied, allowing children to use several different ways of working and answering questions; seatwork needed

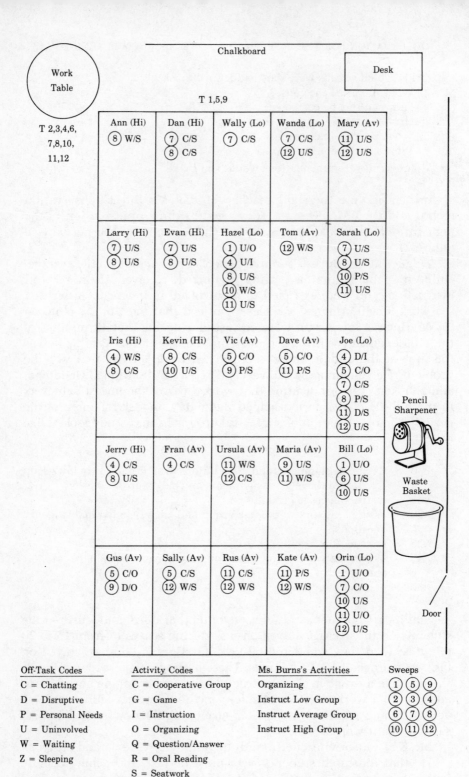

Figure 1. Off-task seating chart for Ms. Burns's students.

Figure 2. Ms. Burns's off-task seating chart summary sheet.

Sweeps	1	2	3	4	5	6	7	8	9	10	11	12	Total
Observation 1	3	0	0	5	5	1	8	10	3	5	10	9	59

Off-task behaviors	Chatting	Disruptive	Personal needs	Uninvolved	Waiting	Total
Observation 1	16	3	5	25	10	59

Students should be on task during these activities.

Activities	Organizing	Instruction	Question/Answer discussion	Oral reading	Seatwork	Games	Total
Observation 1	9	2	0	0	48	0	59

Off-task rates for achievement groups

High (Hi) $\dfrac{13 \text{ off-task}}{7 \text{ students} \times 12 \text{ opportunities} = 84} = 15\%$

Average (Av) $\dfrac{20 \text{ off-task}}{11 \text{ students} \times 12 \text{ opportunities} = 132} = 15\%$

Low (Lo) $\dfrac{26 \text{ off-task}}{7 \text{ students} \times 12 \text{ opportunities} = 84} = 31\%$

to be more than filling in blanks. For example, a mix of silent reading, a search for main ideas, and cooperative academic games, which allowed students to reinforce vocabulary, all seemed to help students stay on-task.

Based on her and Mr. Kesey's analysis of her observation record, Ms. Burns developed a plan that allowed her low achievers to do some vocabulary worksheets and flash cards first, receive instruction during the middle of the period, or do silent reading, and go to the listening center at the end of the period. Ms. Burns and Mr. Kesey shared ideas for diversifying the written seatwork activities and for making certain the work was appropriate—not too hard, not too easy, not too long.

While these new plans comforted Ms. Burns somewhat, she remained concerned about the amount of time the average and high achievers spent uninvolved or waiting. The principal had given her an article by Robert Slavin and his colleagues (Madden, Stevens, & Slavin, 1986) describing the effects of cooperative work groups. In this study, student reading groups were made up of high, middle, and low achievers (see Figure 3). The children were taught to help each other quickly, quietly, and efficiently. By changing the order of the reading groups and assigning seats according to these groups, all children would have someone to help them with an unknown word or unclear directions. More time-consuming, complex problems would be answered by the teacher during the question period between groups. To signal that help was needed and to reduce the time students spent waiting with their hands up, Ms. Burns planned to make "help flags" that students could place upright on their desks. Children would be instructed to continue with some part of their assignment until Ms. Burns was free to answer their questions. Thus the small group receiving reading instruction could expect to receive the teacher's full attention; the students at their seats knew how to receive help and when the teacher would be available.

Mr. Kesey noted from his observation record that many students were off-task during the oral period. Off-task activity occurred during the fourth, fifth, sixth, seventh, and eighth sweeps. He had six students reading a play aloud. The others were supposed to follow along, but many were uninvolved. His sixth-graders had enjoyed reading plays aloud, but these younger students did not stay with it. Mr. Kesey also found that his students were off-task during the organizing time at the third sweep. The principal had given him some materials by Emmer, Evertson, and Anderson (1980) that were supposed to help with procedures for getting a class started. He vowed to study these suggestions. Clearly, he needed some help with getting these third-graders organized and started in their lessons.

Overall, Ms. Burns and Mr. Kesey felt encouraged by their analysis of the observations and by the positive ideas that their discussion fostered. They both predicted that the plans they had developed would

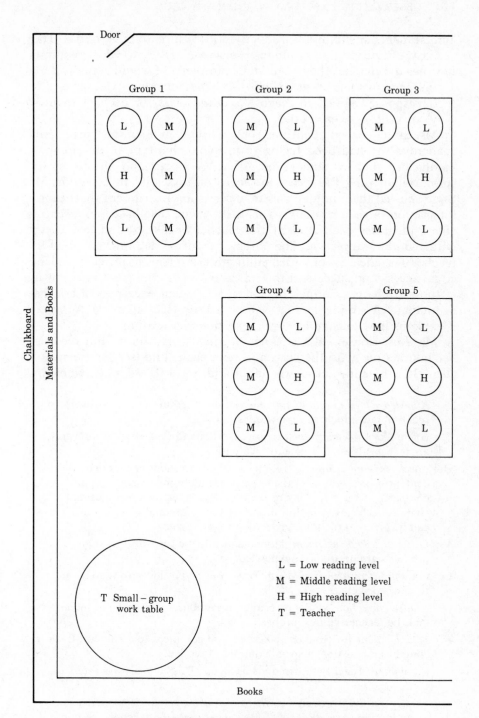

Figure 3. A plan for cooperative work groups.

help students spend more productive time on reading activities. They asked Ms. Style for permission to observe each other in order to examine whether the changes they would try to implement would actually make a difference in their students' on-task behavior. Ms. Style, pleased by their response, agreed to teach a reading class for each of them so they could observe each other.

Ms. Style learned about peer observations in a summer principals' academy. She had been trying to promote this type of development among her staff for some time. After Ms. Burns and Mr. Kesey felt comfortable using the forms to record off-task student behavior, Ms. Style showed them how to use an observation instrument that records interaction in the classroom. This instrument, also based on a seating chart, identifies each student the teacher speaks to and defines the nature of the interaction. The observer records each interaction of the teacher with the class or with an individual student. To provide students equal access and success in the classroom, it is important to be aware of those students who may be lost in the urgent eagerness of a few to participate. A simple coding system is used (see Figure 4). Appendix B explains how to conduct the interaction observation.

Mr. Kesey observed Ms. Burns during a math class and recorded her interactions with the class and with each child (see Figure 5). It is clear that the entire class was often addressed through questions and

? = *Knowledge-level questions* (*direct questions*): require a right answer, simple recall of facts; include review questions.

? = *Higher cognitive questions:* require students to think, apply, interpret, analyze, synthesize, create, or evaluate.

? = *Checks for understanding:* require students to show they understand the content or procedures of the lesson; call for summarizing, explaining, comparing. Students may respond orally, in writing, or by using hand signals, flash cards, or slates. Checks for understanding or comprehension can be given to the total group or to individuals.

+ = *Praise or acknowledgment:* students' academic responses, actions, or products are praised or acknowledged.

C = *Correction:* students' academic responses or products are wrong, and teacher corrects them.

G = *Guided correction:* students' academic responses are wrong or incomplete, and the teacher guides, probes, restates.

✓ = *Social comments:* teacher makes a social comment to a student. Even if stated as a question, a social comment is coded.

− = *Reprimand:* Teacher reprimands *behavior*. This code always refers to behavior.

* = *Student initiates:* students sometimes initiate remarks or questions to the teacher. These are all coded *. Be sure to code the teacher's response if there is one.

Figure 4.   Interaction codes.

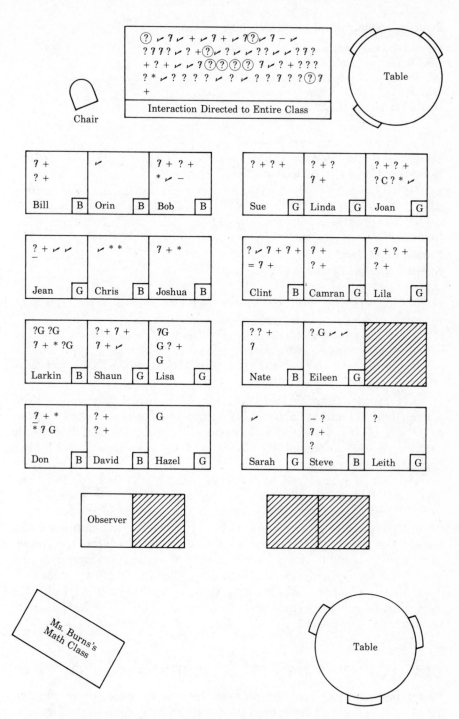

Figure 5. Interaction seating chart.

137

Figure 6. Summary of interaction observation.

How many students were in the class? __23__
How many students were spoken to? __23__
Where was the student most spoken to sitting? left-hand side of teacher, 2nd row
Where were the students not spoken to sitting? last row, mostly
Was there any pattern? __No__

	CLASS	INDIVIDUALS	TOTAL
Number of Direct Questions asked?	24	27	51
Number of Checks for Understanding asked?	11	17	28
Number of Open-Ended Questions asked?	8		8
Number of Guides?		9	9
Number of Corrections?		1	1
Number of Praises?	5	30	35
Number of Reprimands?	1	6	7

Recommendations for this teacher might include:

1. Moving the teacher up and down the rows periodically.
2. Using 3 x 5 cards with students' names and calling on students when their card turns up in the deck.
3. Keeping a tally sheet of each time Orin, Hazel, and Sarah are spoken to.

checks for understanding. However, Hazel, Sarah, and Orin were seldom spoken to individually. Each teacher completed a summary chart (Figure 6) for his or her own interaction-observation record. Ms. Burns, for example, asked a total of 51 knowledge-level questions and 8 higher cognitive questions.

Each teacher analyzed his or her own data to look for patterns. The level of questions addressed to high and low achievers was examined. Teachers are always surprised at the number of students who do not participate in lessons and how a few students dominate the lessons (Stallings, 1985). An interaction chart, such as the one shown in Figure 5, helps develop an awareness of interaction patterns and provides a focus for developing strategies that are likely to induce all students to participate. Research by Morine-Dershimer (1983) indicates that even low achievers can respond effectively to higher-order questions when given the opportunity.

DEVELOPMENT OF A PEER OBSERVATION SYSTEM

Peer observation of the type desired here is an effective method to develop awareness of classroom processes and to promote teacher self-development. Research by Mohlman (1982) indicates that teachers involved in an ongoing program of peer observation changed their behavior more in recommended ways than did a group of teachers who received coaching. Subsequent studies by Stallings (1985) also found that the attitudes of the teachers who took part in peer observation were consistently positive.

Teachers gave two primary reasons for liking peer observation. The first related to being observers, the second to being observed. As observers, teachers in Mohlman's (1982) study said: "I had a chance to see how someone else works"; "I saw how Mary's room arrangement works better than mine"; "It helped me to see how well Greg [a student] behaved in math—he doesn't pay attention in my English class"; "I liked the game John [the teacher] used at the end of math class. He kept everyone involved right up until the bell rang."

As observees, teachers said: "I stopped being afraid to be observed when I knew the records were confidential and were for my own use"; "I liked being able to raise questions about specific children's behavior based on the time-on-task record"; "I liked looking at the 'data' and raising my own questions rather than having someone else telling me what's right and wrong"; "The seating chart helped me see which students I spoke to and which ones I missed. It helped me plan so that all children have a chance to speak each day"; "I actually liked having another teacher in my room. We have become friends!"

Initially, teachers often are fearful about being observed by a peer. They worry about the overt or covert criticism they may receive. Thus it is important to introduce peer observation in a way that will allay these apprehensions. From the beginning, the confidential nature of the observations must be made clear. In the Stallings Effective Use of Time program, the confidentiality of the observation is made concrete by an oath stating that what was seen or heard in the classroom will not be spoken of outside of that classroom.

Critical to effective peer observation are the following procedures:

1. Introduce peer observation as a *confidential* observation.
2. The observation systems used should be *as objective as possible*. Subjective observations are open to differences of opinion and may cause problems when interpreting what has occurred. A record of the students spoken to during a class period is not disputed. Neither are the students' off-task records disputed. The appropriate amount of off-task time, given the grade level and subject matter, is often open to discussion, but the data themselves are not questioned.
3. The observations should be focused on *single behaviors*—for example, number of students off-task, number and types of questions asked, feedback given, time spent on activities, grouping arrangements, teachers' monitoring patterns. It is best to focus first on the students. Teachers find it easiest to begin by looking at students' behavior first, and then at their own.
4. The administrator must make time available for teachers to conduct peer observations. Secondary-school teachers may observe each other

during their preparation periods—for example, teacher A observes teacher B during A's first-hour preparation period; B observes A during B's second-hour preparation period. Another possibility is for the administrator to take teacher A's class so that A can observe B. Yet another solution is to hire a substitute teacher who could stand in for five or six teachers, allowing them to observe each other during one day.

5. For the observations described here, teachers must prepare a seating chart with students' names and give it to the observing teacher. Teachers should call on students by name to help the observer identify who is being spoken to.

6. The administrator must make time available for teachers to analyze and discuss their observation records. Teachers can effectively analyze their own data if they have access to a set of guiding questions and time to reflect on them.

7. When meetings are called to discuss the program they should be kept small (two to six participants) so that each teacher can have ample opportunity to discuss problems and solutions.

8. The meeting environment should be conducive to growth. People grow and change best when they feel secure and supported. If the meeting takes place after school, suggest that participants take turns in bringing snacks (fruit, coffee, sweets). Sharing helps people feel a part of the group.

9. Make it fun! Applaud and give gold stars or prizes when people show improvement—say, when student on-task rate increases from 69 percent to 83 percent, or a teacher is found to ask more thought-provoking questions or make more checks for understanding or provides more positive corrective guides for students.

OBSERVING ONE TO FOUR STUDENTS

Time-sample observation procedures may also be used to observe individual students. For example, Ms. Burns and Mr. Kesey want their students to work in cooperative learning groups, but they are not certain whether shy students will really be involved in a group effort. Careful observations of specific students during cooperative activities can help to guide instructional decisions. Other reasons for observing individual students include understanding the attention patterns of low achievers during independent seatwork and understanding the socialization of students. Observations of a sample of low achievers during independent seatwork or of special education students during play periods can help to inform us more about the behaviors of certain students.

The following procedures can be used when observing individual students:

1. State clearly the question being asked about children's behavior.
2. Identify the instructional activity to be observed—say, math, reading, social studies.
3. Identify the kind of students you want to observe—for example, shy students, low achievers, or high achievers.

Table 1. Example of Individual Student Observation Form.

TIME _____

Student Behaviors	STUDENT 1 OBSERVATION PERIOD*					STUDENT 2 OBSERVATION PERIOD					STUDENT 3 OBSERVATION PERIOD					STUDENT 4 OBSERVATION PERIOD				
	1	2	3	4	5	1	2	3	4	5	1	2	3	4	5	1	2	3	4	5
Initiates a task-related comment—other students listen																				
Asks another student for help—other student responds		✓							✓										✓	
Asks another student a question—other student ignores												✓								
Responds to another student's question or comment																				
Ignores another student's question																				
Listens to other students talking			✓					✓									✓			
Makes a negative comment																				
Is involved in completing the task																				
Seems uninvolved in the task																				

* Each observation period represents 1 minute of observation.

141

4. Select four or five students to represent the kind of students who are to be the focus of observation.

5. Identify the student behaviors to be observed. These behaviors should be carefully defined so that an observer can easily recognize and record the behavior as it occurs. Be certain to identify the *range* of behaviors that are of interest. For example, if shy students are observed during cooperative learning groups, the frequency with which those students initiate task-related comments, ask questions, or respond to other students' questions may be noted. These data can be compared with the frequency of other students' participation. Change in student participation over time can be measured. Suggestions for behaviors to record are presented in Table 1. This form allows four students to be observed during each time interval. The observers look at these children and determine whether the specified variables are occurring; if yes, a check is made in the appropriate column. Table 1 suggests that the shy students did not initiate comments. However, they did listen to others and asked for help from other students.

6. Students may be observed for as long or brief a period needed to provide useful information. For the shy children in cooperative groups, the observation may last as long as the group is expected to work together.

Modifications for Different Questions

The Individual Student Observation Form can be modified to observe different students in different situations. In each case, a grid like the one shown in Table 1 is developed, and the items are modified to fit the situation. Three examples are given below: low-achieving students in discussions, special education students, and girls' participation during mathematics instruction.

Question. To what degree do low-achieving students participate in class discussions? Variables include:

Group question is asked, student raises hand to respond.
Group question is asked, student calls out response.
Group question is asked, student does not raise hand.
Another student speaks, student appears to be listening.
Student is asked a question, student does not respond.
Student is asked a question, student responds.
Student initiates a question or comment.
Student raises hand to initiate a question or comment, student not called
    upon.
Teacher is talking, student appears to be listening.
Student does not appear to be listening to class discussion.

Question. What level of success is experienced by special education students who are mainstreamed into my class? Variables include:

Student responds correctly to teacher question.
Student responds incorrectly to teacher question.
Student declines to respond to teacher question.
Student does not appear to be attending to instruction.
Student appears to be attending to instruction.
Student appears to be working on independent seatwork successfully.
Student shows avoidance behavior when working on independent seatwork.

Question. What is the quality and quantity of girls' participation during mathematics instruction? Variables include:

Group factual or computational question is asked, student raises hand to respond.
Group factual or computational question is asked, student does not raise hand to respond.
Group inferential question is asked, student raises hand to respond.
Student is asked a factual or computation question, does not respond or gives incorrect answer.
Student is asked a factual or computation question, responds correctly.
Student is asked an inferential question, does not respond or responds incorrectly.
Student is asked an inferential question, responds correctly.
Student initiates a comment about lesson content.
Student initiates a request for clarification of lesson content.
Student volunteers to clarify a problem for another student.

The teacher and student observations described thus far are very objective: the observer counts behaviors or activities that occur. The numbers resulting from these observations provide classroom-level data that can be easily summarized and analyzed. The off-task data can identify children who should be studied in greater depth. These objective, quantitative types of observations are limited in their ability to provide in-depth contextual descriptions of children, however. For example, individual children identified as having problems may require more focused observations or comprehensive case studies in order to understand their problems and needs better.

CASE-STUDY APPROACH TO OBSERVING ONE CHILD

Having reorganized their lesson plans, activities, and grouping arrangements, Ms. Burns and Mr. Kesey each picked one child to study in depth. Ms. Burns chose Joe because, in spite of all the reorganization and attention to appropriate lessons and attention span, Joe continued to bother other students and to waste most of his time. The classroom off-task scans indicated that Joe was distracted even during group instruction from Ms. Burns. Once he fell off his chair, making everyone laugh. Most often he did not even begin his assigned work. He was frequently out of his seat, sharpening his already sharpened pencil and disrupting other children.

Mr. Kesey felt empathetic to Joe; he had once encountered a similar student. Mr. Kesey had found it impossible to watch one student and reprimand him all of the time. To learn more about his own problem child, Billy, Mr. Kesey had requested an assistant to observe Billy and write everything Billy said or did for two days. From that narrative record, Mr. Kesey received 60 handwritten pages of valuable information. Mr. Kesey learned that:

On the first day, Billy had wandered about the room 57 times. Since the school day was 5 hours long, this was about 10 times an hour. Billy had fallen off his chair 14 times, picked his nose 17 times, rubbed his eyes 23 times, received 13 smiles and 27 reprimands—mostly to stop falling off his chair and pay attention. Billy had initiated conversations with other children 44 times, but the interactions were only 1 or 2 sentences long. Billy spoke to everyone who passed his seat, tried to trip 3 people, succeeding twice. Billy was rejected 15 times by other children who were involved in some activity and was physically pushed away from a group of 3 who were working on a mural. During recess, he put a blanket over his desk, took his reading workbook and disappeared underneath. He stayed there for 5 minutes. The second day's observations were similar, and the picture that emerged was one of a hyperactive, highly distractible child who needed help in screening out the myriad distractions in the classroom.

Supported by these specific descriptions, Mr. Kesey requested conferences with Billy's parents, a reading specialist, and a school psychologist. The written account of Billy's behavior enabled Mr. Kesey to present factual information with a minimum of inference. The parents reported similar behavior at home. They felt impatient and tried to force Billy to calm down through threats of punishment and withdrawal of privileges. As a result of these meetings, an educational program was planned that helped Billy progress in his learning.

A reading specialist was assigned to work with him three times a week outside the classroom. In class, Mr. Kesey carried out the reading program the specialist prescribed. Billy's parents were advised by the school psychologist to plan for quiet times with Billy and to exert as much calming influence at home as possible. They were encouraged to have realistic expectations about his progress toward more controlled behavior.

The evaluation team decided that Billy needed help in screening out distracting influences in the classroom environment. Since Mr. Kesey had a large room, he decided to build three learning booths. He made these booths by placing three 4- x 5-foot fiberboard sheets in deep grooves cut into three 4-foot long, 2- x 4-inch runners. These dividers were then bracketed into the wall, starting at the corner of the room, with just enough space between them for a child's desk.

The entrances to the booths were curtained with fireproof cloth. Introducing the booths as special places where children could learn better allowed Billy to use them without appearing to have been singled out or sentenced to isolation. In fact, the learning booths became so popular with the children that there soon was a sign-up sheet to use them. The popularity of the learning booths did present a slight problem, in fact, in making certain that Billy received as much isolated learning time as he needed.

Ms. Burns decided to try to find someone to make a narrative record of Joe, but in the meantime, she made notes about Joe on an hourly basis, recording as much as she could see and remember. She could check out his distractibility and the appropriateness of lessons.

The narrative type of observation is useful for in-depth case studies such as Billy's. Jean Piaget (1966) used narrative to describe his continuous observations of his own children. Recorded daily for several years, these observations provided him with in-depth case studies on which he based his theory of intelligence. Other researchers, including Roger Barker (1963) and Pauline Sears and Vivian Sherman (1964), have organized and directed narrative observations that are excellent in-depth studies of individual children.

In anthropological studies, a method called ethnographic observation is used to record narratively everything about a family or a tribe. Tikunoff, Berliner, and Rist (1975) adapted this technique to large-scale studies of teaching processes. Key words, phrases, and ideas are counted and summarized for use in statistical analysis.

Narrative observations, valuable as they may be, do have some limitations, however. First, new observers may find it difficult to decide what to record, and, if they keep a running account of the entire day, the quality and quantity of the written material are likely to decline as the day progresses and fatigue sets in. Also, it is sometimes hard to analyze what has been recorded. Among other things, it takes a long time to read through 30 pages and count, for example, how many times Billy left his seat or talked to someone. Finally, although this is a good method for compiling information on just one child, it is difficult to use when observing groups of children or when describing a total classroom environment.

Observation of Intrusions

As the year progressed, Ms. Burns and Mr. Kesey found that they were better able to plan appropriate lessons and that students were more productive. More lessons were completed, and student reading-test scores were higher than was predicted from earlier results; the low achievers especially were making progress. Once the teachers became time-conscious, they began to examine other periods of the day. Both were concerned about the constant interruptions and the amount of

Table 2.   Time Spent on Organizing and on Classroom Interruptions.

TEACHER NAME_____ FOCUS ID# _____ DATE _____

SCHOOL _____ OBSERVER _____

	TIME STARTED	TIME STOPPED
Observation of Classroom Time *Spent in Organizing*		
Taking attendance		
Collecting lunch money		
Collecting homework or seatwork		
Making assignments for seatwork		
Making assignments for homework		
Distributing books and materials		
Explaining activities and procedures		
Organizing groups		
Shifting from one activity to another		
Disciplining students		
Observation of Classroom Interruptions		
Students enter late		
Students leave early		
Parents enter		
Administrator enters		
Other visitors enter		
Loud speaker announcements		
Special sales		
School events		
Outside noise		

time it took to get the day started. There were so many required procedures! A form developed for the Tennessee Department of Education's study of teaching time was made available to the two teachers (Table 2). Both teachers estimated the time the activities listed in Table 2 required. They also had an observer record exactly how long their managerial activities took. Using the form shown in Table 2 they gathered one week's data to show to Ms. Style. This type of observation is a checklist showing time started and time stopped. It is easily completed and easily summarized. It provides instant information about events that are for the most part out of the teacher's control but that affect the classroom. Fortunately, Ms. Style was attempting to improve school-wide use of time and found their report of school-level interruptions informative and helpful.

SUMMARY

Observations take many forms. We have described charts, checklists, and narratives. The type of observation must be determined by the type of questions to be asked. Observations can be conducted by principals, peers, assistants, or, in some cases, students. To be useful, observations must be reliable and credible. We believe that teachers should examine their own data and discuss with peers the implications of their findings. These discussions raise awareness of what occurs in classrooms; problems can be identified; solutions born of common experiences can be shared.

APPENDIX A

Off-Task Seating Charts

The Off-Task Seating Chart is designed to record (1) the nature of students' off-task behavior; (2) the activities in which students are most off-task; and (3) the period of time when students are most off-task. Teachers need this type of specific information to plan lessons appropriate for each student. The Off-Task Seating Chart provides teachers with exact information about each student's engaged rate. By analyzing the chart, teachers can better understand such things as which students are uninvolved, whether some activities are too long, and whether assigned independent work is appropriate.

Look at Off-Task Seating Chart 1. There are 31 students in this sixth-grade classroom. The off-task behavior record is a time sample. Ten records are made during one class period. They are spaced evenly across the period of time. The observer scans the classroom, going clockwise, and focuses on each child momentarily. We refer to this as a "sweep." If the student is doing what the teacher expects, no entry is made. If the student is not doing what is expected, then a code of the off-task behavior is made. The teacher's location is marked each time a sweep is made (for example, "T1" denotes the teacher's placement in the first sweep).

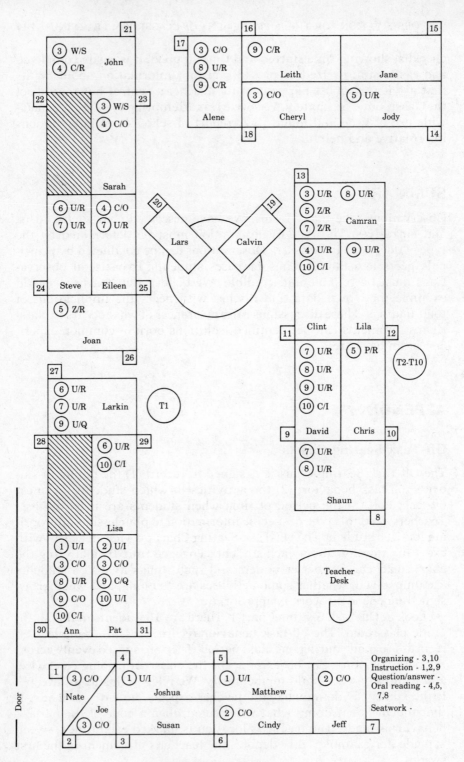

Off-Task Seating Chart 1

Organizing - 3,10
Instruction - 1,2,9
Question/answer -
Oral reading - 4,5, 7,8
Seatwork -

The coding system used here objectively and systematically describes students' off-task behavior. It includes six possible student behaviors that indicate that the students are not doing what the teacher expects:

C = chatting: low talking or whispering, passing notes between students

D = disruptive: bothering a number of students—for example, loud talking, throwing things, pushing, or fighting

P = personal needs: sharpening pencils, going to the toilet, getting a drink, getting papers or books

U = uninvolved: staring out window, doing something other than assigned tasks but not bothering anyone else—say, reading a comic book in math class

W = waiting: waiting with hand up for teacher's attention, waiting for materials to be passed

Z = sleeping

These behaviors are identified specifically because a teacher may want to respond differently to students who are uninvolved than to students who are chatting or disruptive. The off-task code is entered above the slash: C/ or D/, for instance.

The activity codes define *when* the students are off-task. If more students are off-task during organizing activities, this suggests one plan of action; if more students are off-task during instruction or seatwork, then another plan may be needed. The activity codes are as follows:

O = organizing: listening to the teacher make assignments or organizing; getting out paper and books

I = instruction: listening to the teacher's explanation of content or subject matter

Q = question/answer: teacher asks question of students, as in drill and practice. This also includes students computing math problems on the blackboard

S = seatwork: students are working at their seats on silent reading or written assignments

R = oral reading: student is a member of a reading group that is reading aloud

C = cooperative group work: working on a cooperative group task

G = games: playing academic games

The activity code is placed under the slash mark as follows:

C/O =   chatting during organizing

Z/I =   sleeping during instruction

To identify the time frame of the off-task behavior, the ten sweeps of the classroom are identified by entering an encircled numeral by

Summary Chart 1.

Sweeps	1	2	3	4	5	6	7	8	9	10	
Observation 1	3	1	11	3	4	3	6	5	8	5	= 49

Behaviors	Chatting	Disruptive	Personal needs	Uninvolved	Waiting	Sleeping	
Observation 1	19	0	1	24	2	3	= 49

Activities	Organizing	Instruction	Question/ answer discussion	Oral reading	Seat-work	Games	Cooperative groups	
Observation 1	10	9	3	25	2	0	0	= 49

Grade 3
Reading class

each off-task entry on the chart. For example, ④ C/I means that the student was chatting during instruction when the fourth sweep was made. This helps teachers to analyze whether their proximity to students functions to help students stay on task.

Examine Off-Task Seating Chart 1 and Summary Chart 1. The sweep entries at the lower right corner of the seating chart indicate that:

> I = instruction occurred during the first, second, and third sweeps
> O = organizing during the third sweep
> R = oral reading during the second, fifth, sixth, seventh, and eighth sweeps
> Q = question/answer discussion in the ninth sweep

Most of the time, the teacher was functioning near the chalkboard. Of the 31 students, 4 were on-task throughout all of the sweeps.

To learn as much as possible from an off-task seating chart, it is best to analyze the overall picture as well as to look at specific individuals. Look at Off-Task Seating Chart 1, and count the number of chattings, disruptives, personal needs, uninvolveds, waitings, and sleepings. The number for each type of off-task behavior is entered on Summary Chart 1. The total number is 49. Now count the times anyone was off-task during organizing, instruction, and so on; this figure also totals 49, as it should. Next, find the part of the period when the students were most off-task. This information is determined by the sweeps made. Consider the seating chart and the summary chart, and speculate about what you could do to improve the engaged rate for specific students if this were your class.

The off-task rate for the class can be computed using the following formula:

Number of off-task activities ÷ number of students × sweeps
= percentage off-task

49 off-task activities ÷ (31 students × 10 sweeps) = 16% off-task
100% − 16% = 84% engaged

Now look at Off-Task Seating Chart 2, and analyze it for problem areas. Enter your data on Summary Chart 2. Think carefully. How would you reorganize the lesson in terms of length of time spent on each activity? How would you rearrange the classroom furniture? Would you change students' seating arrangements or change where you place yourself when teaching? How would you decide whether the lessons assigned for seatwork are appropriate or not? See the list of questions in the form called Analyzing Off-Task Behavior and write down your answers.

Coding Off-Task Behavior Using an Alphabetical List

In classrooms where the students move from one seating arrangement to another, such as for reading groups or for laboratory work, it may be necessary to record students' off-task behavior by using a numbering system based on alphabetical order. Each student is given a stick-on number or a numbered arm band according to his or her number on the alphabetical list (see Summary Chart 3). Displaying numbers on the arms or shoulders allows the observer to follow the students as they move from one group to another. If students 3, 7, and 13 are whispering during the organizing time at the first sweep, then the observer finds numbers 3, 7, and 13 on the alphabetical list and enters C/O next to each of their numbers and names. Students' on-task and off-task patterns can be examined across all of the sweeps.

APPENDIX B

Preparing for the Interaction Observation by Peers

For this observation, you need to prepare a seating chart with your students' names. When you are being observed, it is important to say

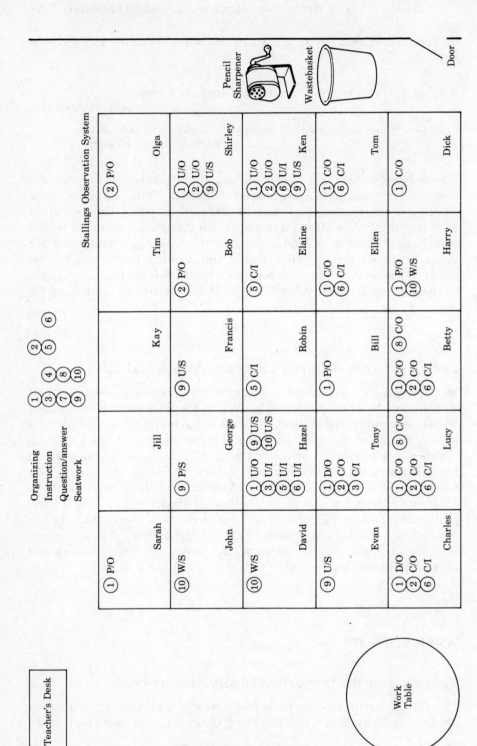

Off-Task Seating Chart 2.

Summary Chart 2.

Sweeps	1	2	3	4	5	6	7	8	9	10
Observation 2										

Behaviors	Chatting	Disruptive	Personal needs	Uninvolved	Waiting	Sleeping
Observation 2						

Activities	Organizing	Instruction	Question/ answer discussion	Oral reading	Seat-work	Games	Cooperative groups
Observation 2							

Analyzing off-task behavior.

What was most off-task behavior? _____

What might be the cause?

Recommendations to improve?

During which activity did most off-task behavior occur? _____

What might be the cause?

Recommendations to improve?

During which sweeps were most students off-task? _____

What might be the cause?

Recommendations to improve?

Which students were off-task most often? _____

Possible reasons

Possible solutions?

Overall recommendations:

Summary Chart 3. Stallings Time-Off-Task Observation Sheet.

OBSERVER NAME: _____ TEACHER NAME: _____ TEACHER NUMBER: _____

DATE: _____ SCHOOL NAME: _____ TOTAL NUMBER OF SWEEPS: _____ READING: _____ MATH: _____
(TIME) (TIME) (TIME)

Student Number	Student Name (alphabetized)	Time 9:15 Activity	Time 9:20 Activity	Time 9:25 Activity	Time 9:30 Activity	Time 9:35 Activity	Time 9:40 Activity	Time 9:45 Activity	Time 9:50 Activity	Time 9:55 Activity	Time 10:00 Activity	(A) Off-Task Total
1	Sally Allen											
2	Martin Brown											
3	Nancy Carter											
4	Eva Dowel											
5	Dolores Evertson											
6	Bruce Finn											
7	John Gage											
8	David Ginn											
9	Ethel Howey											
10	Ruth Irving											
11	Sammy Jones											
12	Jonathan Kent											
13	Henry Lowey											
14	Kirstan Murphy											
15	Ann Riley											

Off-Task: C = Chatting   U = Uninvolved   Activity: S = Seatwork   R = Reading aloud
           D = Disruptive   W = Waiting   O = Organizing   Q = Question/answer
           P = Personal needs Z = Sleeping   I = Instruction   G = Game
                                                                             C = Cooperative group

154

the students' names when you speak to them. Otherwise, the observer may have trouble correctly coding the student to whom you are speaking. Arrange a time to observe another teacher and a time to be observed. You study the seating-chart interaction record of your classroom, and the teacher you observed studies his or her chart. This exercise is meant as a self-analysis for each teacher; it is not peer coaching.

Using the codes and definitions shown in the Interaction Code System, you will enter a code in the box with the appropriate student's name each time the teacher you observe speaks to him or her. The code tells whether the interaction was a simple direct question, a check for understanding, or a higher cognitive question. Rather than asking teacher-observers to discriminate among the several types of higher cognitive questions, such as synthesis, analysis, or evaluation, we will code all of these questions as higher cognitive questions.

Interaction Code System.

? = Knowledge-level questions (direct questions): require a right answer, simple recall of facts; include review questions.

> EXAMPLE: What is the capital of Tennessee?
> How many degrees are in a right angle?

⑦ = Higher cognitive questions: require students to think, apply, interpret, analyze, synthesize, create, or evaluate.

> EXAMPLE: What is another way the story could end?
> What conclusion can you draw from this article?

⫲ = Checks for understanding: require students to show they understand the content or procedures of the lesson; call for summarizing, explaining, comparing. Students may respond orally, in writing, or by using hand signals, flash cards, or slates. Checks for understanding or comprehension can be given to the total group or individuals.

> EXAMPLE: State in your own words what "ratio" means.
> What is wrong with problem #3?
> If you agree with Cora's answer, hold up your blue card;
> if you disagree, hold up your red card.

+ = Praise or acknowledgment: students' academic responses, actions, or products are praised or acknowledged.

> EXAMPLE: Thank you for your contribution. That helps solve the problem.
> What an interesting bear! How did you make it so furry?

C = Correction: students' academic responses or products are wrong, and teacher corrects them.

> EXAMPLE: No, Barbara, the answer is 42.
> Betty, tell Richard the answer.

G = Guided correction: student's academic response is wrong or incomplete, and the teacher guides, probes, restates.

EXAMPLE: Your answer is almost right. Let's go through the steps
again. You are very close.
Let me ask the question another way.

√ = Social comments: teacher makes a social comment to a student. Even though stated as a question, a social comment is coded.

EXAMPLE: Well, how was your weekend?
Who won the basketball game?
That is a pretty dress.

− = Reprimand: teacher reprimands *behavior*. This code always refers to behavior.

EXAMPLE: Joe, sit down and be quiet!
Class, you will all have to make up time!

* = Student initiates: students sometimes initiate remarks or questions to the teacher. These are all coded *. Be sure to code the teacher's response if there is one.

EXAMPLE: Joe asks, "What do we do next?" Code *.
Teacher replies, "Joe, don't shout out questions." Code −
Note: Both codes are entered in Joe's seat box.

Teachers often address questions to the entire class. To code these whole-group interactions, use the large box designated "Class" at the top of the seating chart, as shown in Off-Task Seating Chart 1.

Analyzing Seating-Chart Interactions

Looking at the Interaction Seating Chart, we see that George was asked a knowledge-level question; he was corrected; he was asked another

Teacher's desk		Chalkboard		
		Class ⟩		
? + ? G + * ? + *	? +⟨?⟩+ * ⟩ G	√ ? C ? + *	√ * +	* +
Sarah	Jill	Kay	Tim	Olga
? + ? + * +	? C ? C * +	√⟨?⟩+	⟨?⟩	
John	George	Francis	Bob	Shirl
? C ? +		* +	⟩	− −
David	Hazel	Robin	Elaine	Ken
? C −	* − ? +	− ? C	? C	− −
Evan	Tony	Bill	Ellen	Tom

Interaction Seating Chart to analyze a 50-minute period.

Summary of interaction observation.

How many students were in the class? ___25___
How many students were spoken to? ___23___
Where was the most spoken-to student sitting? _____
Where were the students not spoken to sitting? _____
Was there any pattern? _____

	CLASS	INDIVIDUALS	TOTAL
Number of direct questions asked?	_____	_____	_____
Number of checks for understanding asked?	_____	_____	_____
Number of open-ended questions asked?	_____	_____	_____
Number of guides?	_____	_____	_____
Number of corrections?	_____	_____	_____
Number of praises?	_____	_____	_____
Number of reprimands?	_____	_____	_____

Recommendations for this teacher might include:

1. Rotating students from the back of the room to the front.
2. Moving the desks to form a horseshoe.
3. Moving the teacher's desk.
4. Moving the teacher up and down the rows periodically.

question and was corrected again. Then George initiated a question and was praised. This teacher spoke to 23 of the 25 students. Some students were spoken to 9 times while others were not spoken to even once. This teacher actually was trying to distribute the interactions evenly and was surprised to learn that some children were missed. Think: if all of the interactions weighed 1 pound, which way would the room tilt? Complete the form called the Summary of Interaction Observation. Always look for patterns and think how interaction patterns and levels of questions could be improved. Use forms like this to record interactions with your class. You will find out some things you did not know about yourself.

REFERENCES

Barker, R. (Ed.). (1963). *The stream of behavior.* New York: Appleton-Century-Crofts.

Emmer, E., Evertson, C., & Anderson, L. (1980). Effective management at the beginning of the school year. *Elementary School Journal, 80,* 219–231.

Madden, N. A., Stevens, R. J., & Slavin, R. L. (1986, April). A comprehensive cooperative learning approach to elementary reading and writing: Effects on student achievement. Paper presented at the meeting of the American Educational Research Association, San Francisco, CA.

Mohlman, G. (1982). Assessing the impact of three inservice teacher training models. Paper presented to the American Educational Research Association. New York.

Morine-Dershimer, G. (1983). Instructional strategy and the "creation" of classroom status. *American Educational Research Journal, 20* (4), 645–661.

Piaget, J. (1966). *The origin of intelligence in children.* Trans. by Margaret Cook. New York: International Universities Press.

Sears, P., & Sherman, V. (1964). *In pursuit of self-esteem.* Belmont, CA: Wadsworth.

Stallings, J. (1985). How effective is an analytic approach to staff development on teacher and student behavior? Paper presented to the American Educational Research Association. Chicago.

Stallings, J., Goodman, J., & Johnson, R. (1986). Engaged rates: Does grade level make a difference? *Journal of Research in Childhood Education, 1* (1), 22–27.

Stallings, J., Needels, M., & Stayrook, N. (1979). *How to change the process of teaching basic reading skills in secondary schools.* Final report to National Institute of Education. Menlo Park, CA: SRI International.

Tikunoff, W. J., Berliner, D. C., & Rist, R. C. (1975). *An ethnographic study of the forty classrooms of the Beginning Teacher Evaluation Study known sample. Technical report no. 75–10–5; special study A.* San Francisco: Far West Laboratory for Educational Research and Development.

CHAPTER 8

THOMAS L. GOOD

TEACHER EXPECTATIONS

The relationship of teacher expectations to student performance has been an area of active research over the past 20 years. Interest in teachers' expectations was stimulated by the publication of *Pygmalion in the Classroom* (Rosenthal & Jacobson, 1968). In that study, teachers were told that, on the basis of a written examination, several of their students had shown a remarkable potential for academic growth. In actuality, these students had been chosen at random; hence, there was no basis—other than an expectational one—for believing that they would perform better than other students. At the end of the school year, an intelligence test revealed that students in the early grades for whom teachers held artificially high expectations showed greater gains in intelligence than did their classmates.

Rosenthal and Jacobson's study stirred a great deal of interest in the study of teacher expectations. Although social scientists had been studying the phenomena of expectation and self-fulfilling prophecy for some time, this report focused educators' attention on the possible role of teacher expectations in explaining student performance in classrooms. Unfortunately, secondary sources describing the study made exaggerated claims that went far beyond those that Rosenthal and Jacobson made themselves. For example, an ad in *Reader's Digest* read: "Actual experiments prove this mysterious force can heighten your intelligence, your competitive ability, and your will to succeed. The secret: just make a prediction! Read how it works."

Almost two decades have passed, and a great deal of research and theoretical development have since taken place. In the past few years, many investigators, using a variety of methods, have established unequivocally that teachers' expectations can and do affect their classroom

159

behavior and Rosenthal and Jacobson's hypothesis has been supported, although the process underlying the communication of teacher expectations appears to be much more complicated than originally proposed (Brophy, 1982; Cooper & Good, 1983; Dusek, 1985; Marshall & Weinstein, 1984).

DEFINITIONS OF EXPECTATIONS

Several definitions have been used by various investigators who have studied expectations in the classroom. As Cooper and Tom (1984) note, these definitions fit into three general categories. First, teachers have been asked to describe students in terms of their present achievement, and teacher behavior is then examined to see if teachers treat students whom they believe to be higher achievers differently than they treat students whom they believe to be lower achievers. As we will note below, this type of achievement measure is more closely related to a sustaining prophecy than to a self-fulfilling one because it focuses on present performance and differential behavior rather than on expected degree of improvement and future performance.

A second type of expectation involves a teacher's prediction about how much academic progress a student will make during a specific period of time. As has been noted elsewhere (Cooper, Findley, & Good, 1982), expected improvement is weakly associated with a teacher's present assessment of a student's achievement. Thus teachers' beliefs about a student's present competence appear to be relatively independent of their predictions about his or her future achievement gains.

The third type of expectation that Cooper and Tom discuss is the degree to which a teacher over- or underestimates a student's present performance. This type of expectation is measured by comparing teachers' estimates of student ability (the first type of expectation that we described) with standardized test scores or some other "objective" performance measure. The discrepancy (an over- or underestimate) between measured teacher expectations and student performance on a standardized measure is used to predict the direction of change in a student's future performance.

When one reads the literature and considers the communication of expectation effects in the classroom, it is important to understand which definition the writer uses. In organizing this chapter, I view teacher expectations as inferences that teachers make about students' future academic achievement and about the types of classroom assignments students need in relation to teachers' perceptions of their abilities.

Teacher expectations may concern either the entire class, groups of students, or individual students. General expectations include teachers' beliefs about the changeability versus the inflexibility of students' abilities, the students' potential to benefit from instruction, the appropriate difficulty level of material for students in general or for a particular subgroup, whether the class should be taught as a group or individually, and whether students should memorize material or interpret and apply key concepts. I will return to other possible distinctions later in this chapter.

EXPECTATION EFFECTS

Researchers have examined two types of expectation effects. The first, and the more controversial, is called the *self-fulfilling prophecy*. A self-fulfilling prophecy occurs when an erroneous belief leads to behavior that makes the originally erroneous belief become true. Self-fulfilling prophecies are the most dramatic example of teacher expectations because they involve changes in a student's behavior. *Sustaining expectations* are also important. Cooper and Good (1983) use this term to refer to situations in which teachers fail to see student potential and hence do not respond to some students in a way that encourages them to fulfill their potential. Thus self-fulfilling prophecies bring about changes in student performance, whereas sustaining expectations prevent change. Teachers need to be concerned about the effects of both types of expectations on students.

TEACHER EXPECTATIONS AND STUDENT PERFORMANCE

It must be recognized that teacher expectations come from numerous sources and can be expressed to students in many ways. Figure 1 provides a picture of some of the general variables involved in communication of teacher expectations. The figure provides a general overview of possible relationships between teacher beliefs about student performance and actual student performance.

There are countless ways in which teacher beliefs, apart from teacher expectations, may affect student performance. Teachers hold many beliefs about teaching, and it is likely that these beliefs ultimately affect how teachers behave toward individual students. For example, some teachers believe that it is important for students to discover knowledge on their own and assume a great deal of independence. In contrast, other teachers believe that students should internalize information that teachers model and present. Some teachers believe that students should work individually, and other teachers prefer the use of student teams for learning activities. These different beliefs affect the way in which teachers use classroom resources and the range of peers that a given student comes into contact with.

Teachers' beliefs about subject matter may also have important

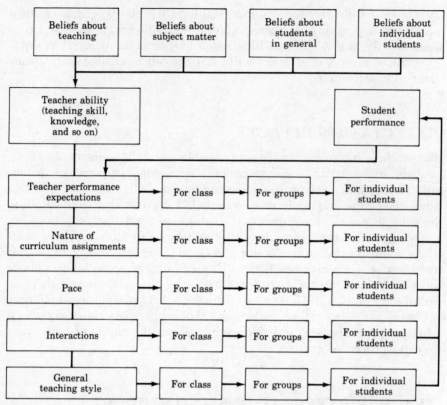

Figure 1. **The relationship between teachers' expectations and students' performance.**

TEACHER EXPECTATIONS / **163**

effects. For example, depending on whether teachers believe that reading instruction basically involves teaching phonics and comprehension skills (being able to determine what the author of a written passage means) or challenging students to develop their own interpretation and to read to achieve self-determined goals, the presentation of the curriculum and the students' opportunities will be quite different. Similarly, the importance that teachers attach to social studies will determine how much time they devote to this subject.

It may even be possible to predict student achievement in part from the emphasis teachers place on various subjects. For example, some elementary-school teachers clearly feel uncomfortable teaching geometry and spend little time presenting this subject. Not surprisingly, their students often do not do well in this area. This is an example of a self-fulfilling prophecy: the teacher erroneously believes that students will not profit from instruction in geometry, there is no instruction in geometry, and thus there is no growth in students' understanding of geometry, despite their potential.

In addition to teachers' beliefs about the relative importance of particular subject-matter concepts—how those concepts should be presented and how much emphasis should be placed on them—beliefs about other kinds of goals may influence teacher classroom behavior. For example, Prawat (1985) and Prawat and Nickerson (1985) note that although elementary-school teachers tend to emphasize affective goals, some have a primarily cognitive orientation and others strike a balance between affective and cognitive goals. Prawat and Nickerson (1985) illustrate that teachers' orientation does affect the way in which they structure classrooms and how students interact with one another and feel about one another. Thus, in complicated ways, teachers' orientation may influence the ways in which they communicate their beliefs about individual students. Teachers with strong affective and/or cognitive orientations may deal with individual students for whom they hold high or low expectations in quite different ways.

It is also clear that teachers' beliefs about students ultimately may affect how students learn. For example, some teachers may know a great deal about the developmental level of the students they teach (attention span, degree to which students can understand abstract information, and so on), while other teachers may not. Teachers also hold perceptions about what students find interesting and the way in which students will learn most effectively. These ideas affect how teachers structure their classroom environments. Similarly, beliefs about individual students will influence teachers' interactions with those students and may even affect the pace at which the entire class moves through the curriculum. If teachers think that a student is capable of learning, they may respond differently to an initial failure than to a similar failure by a student they believe has little potential for learning.

I have discussed only a few of the teachers' beliefs that may affect their classroom behavior. Ultimately, as Figure 1 suggests, these beliefs are mediated by teachers' abilities, their teaching skills, and their knowledge of the subject matter and of teaching. A teacher who knows several alternative ways to present a particular concept may be less likely to impede student performance than a teacher who has only a limited repertoire. That is, if a teacher has relatively low expectations for a student or group of students and knows only one or two ways to present a particular skill or concept, then that expectation may be more likely to lead to low student performance—the teacher may give up on the student(s) more quickly—than when a teacher has several alternative instructional methods at his or her disposal. The best teachers have high but realistic expectations for student performance in addition to a well-developed knowledge of students and teaching techniques. My point here is that teachers' beliefs do not relate to student performance in any simple fashion, and that teachers' competence and general motivation will mediate many of the beliefs that they hold for students.

As Figure 1 suggests, teachers ultimately develop performance expectations for entire classes, for groups of students in a class, and for individual students. Having formed these expectations, teachers then communicate them through curriculum assignments, the pace of instruction, and the way they interact with students. For example, teachers who hold low performance expectations are more likely to assign curriculum tasks that are drill-like and that involve less student decision making and control and less focus on conceptual meaning and understanding. These teachers also tend to go through the curriculum at a slower pace, and their interactions with their students are more likely to emphasize teacher control (Cooper, 1983). Furthermore, such teachers are less likely to involve low-achieving students centrally in classroom activities and are less likely to sustain academic response opportunities with those students (Brophy & Good, 1974; Weinstein et al., 1982).

Teachers' general instructional style also affects student learning. For example, the degree to which teachers present information enthusiastically and clearly affects the extent to which students are willing to listen and learn the material. Hines, Cruickshank, and Kennedy (1985) demonstrated that, at least under certain circumstances, teacher clarity is related positively to both student achievement and student satisfaction. Thus not only the content of instruction but also the general way in which teachers present information and assignments affects students. For example, some teachers may fail to provide conceptual explanations for laboratory phenomena, either to all students or to certain groups of students, reducing a potentially meaningful assignment to a rote, mechanical one.

I now turn to an examination of students' interpretive role in the expectation process. The communication of expectations by teachers is important; however, the way in which students interpret and act on teachers' cues is a critical determinant of student performance. For example, a student may perceive an assignment as gratuitous or as meaningful, depending on the way in which the teacher explains or presents it. Indeed, as I argue below, students' behavior and their reactions to classroom assignments can change teacher expectations as well as confirm or sustain them.

STUDENTS' PERFORMANCE EXPECTATIONS

Figure 2 shows that students also form expectations and that these expectations are related to students' effort and ultimately to their classroom performance. Like teachers, students are affected by a variety of influences. For example, they have spent a number of years in a home environment, interacting with parents and siblings who have helped them to develop some relatively stable expectations about their competency in various areas. Furthermore, students in the upper elementary (and higher) grades have developed school-related performance expectations that, while not immutable, at least affect students' interpretation of classroom events and activities. Furthermore, students are influenced by peers who have seen them perform over several consecutive years and by their out-of-school social contacts and employment. Students who hold a meaningful job outside school and who receive positive work-related feedback may view themselves somewhat differently than students who do not have this means to demonstrate their competency.

Teachers communicate their expectations to students in diverse ways. Equally important, different students may interpret the same teacher action quite differently because of their individual experiences and beliefs. These influences on students, including teachers' expectations, are ultimately mediated by students' abilities and interests. Students who, for whatever reason, are genuinely interested in doing well in school may be less affected by low expectations that others hold for them than students who begin school with little interest in performing. Students' abilities obviously are an important component of their success, and students with high ability may be relatively unaffected by low teacher expectations. However, students who continuously receive limited curriculum assignments and fragmented feedback are unlikely to do as well as students of comparable ability who receive more challenging assignments that require them to integrate and understand material.

Figure 2 shows that students ultimately interpret the various performance cues in a classroom (as mediated by background experiences) and form role expectations each year. Students who interpret the classroom environment as interesting and challenging are likely to expend more effort and to achieve more than are students who view the classroom differently. Students' interpretation of classroom events is a continuous process in which students constantly make judgments. That

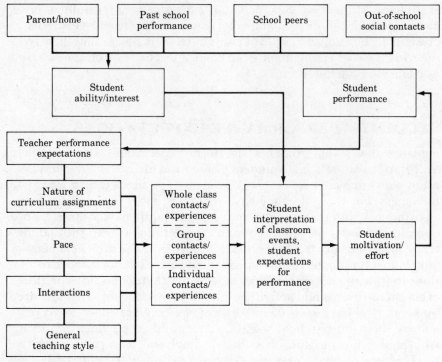

Figure 2.   Individual students' performance expectations.

is, students do not automatically conclude that the classroom is either important or unimportant and then continue to expend high or low effort throughout the year. Rather, they frequently judge the importance of a particular assignment and the extent to which they want to work on it in order to be successful.

A FOCUS ON TEACHERS' ACHIEVEMENT EXPECTATIONS

We have seen that the communication of expectations in a classroom is a complex issue. Indeed, at times, beliefs other than teachers' performance expectations may be the best predictors of certain student outcomes, as noted above in our example of the elementary-school teacher who is uncomfortable teaching geometry. Thus, although teachers' beliefs about student performance are extremely important, these are only one of many types of teacher beliefs. All of these beliefs interact in complex ways to determine teacher and student behavior.

In the remainder of this chapter, I want to discuss some of the practical, concrete ways in which teachers might communicate expectations to students. Hence, this chapter concentrates on only a small part of the relationship presented in Figures 1 and 2—namely, the communication of teacher expectations to individuals, groups, and the class as a whole. My discussion is organized around teachers' beliefs about students' academic ability. Many other performance-related expectations are beyond the scope of this chapter. For example, teachers hold performance beliefs about students who differ in race and gender as well as ability (for recent discussions of how students' gender and race affect their interactions with teachers, see Grant, 1985; Haller, 1985; Wilkinson & Marrett, 1985).

Research shows that teachers' performance expectations vary in terms of student characteristics other than achievement potential per se. For example, Brophy and Good (1974) noted that low-achieving girls tend to have especially impoverished academic classroom environments, whereas high-achieving boys tend to be afforded productive and responsive intellectual environments, despite the fact that when general measures of classroom interaction were used, teachers were more critical of boys than of girls.

Having discussed the complexity of relating beliefs to classroom behavior, I want to address specifically teacher expectations for students believed to have high and low potential. It must be understood that classrooms differ in important ways, as do individual students in the same classroom. Still, it is possible to explore research findings in order to understand some of the ways in which beliefs about achievement potential may inhibit effective classroom communication.

The concepts and findings associated with expectation research provide guidelines or frames of reference that allow teachers to think about, and attempt to alter, their classroom environments. These theories or concepts can help teachers to increase the number of dimensions they use in thinking about classroom performance and the number (and range) of hypotheses or alternative strategies available. The concepts also encourage teachers to consider the possible consequences of selected actions on various students (Good & Power, 1976).

In presenting these patterns, I shall first discuss teacher communication with individual students, then how teachers interact with groups of students who differ in perceived ability, and next teacher interactions and the communication of performance expectations to entire classes. Finally, I want to examine some of the implications of this research for classroom practice and to suggest a few general guidelines that teachers might consider in conceptualizing and monitoring their interactions with students who differ in ability.

HOW TEACHERS COMMUNICATE THEIR EXPECTATIONS

The Brophy-Good Model

Various models describe how teacher performance expectations influence student behavior (see, for example, Brophy & Good, 1974; Cooper, 1979; Cooper & Good, 1983; Marshall & Weinstein, 1984; Rosenthal, 1974). Perhaps the earliest explicit model for studying the expectation communication chain in the classroom was described by Brophy and Good (1970a). Stimulated by the earlier Rosenthal and Jacobson study, Brophy and Good proposed the following model:

1. The teacher expects different types of behavior and achievement from different students.
2. Because of these varied expectations, the teacher behaves differently toward different students.
3. This treatment communicates to the students what behavior and achievement the teacher expects from them and affects their self-concepts, achievement motivation, and levels of aspiration.
4. If this treatment is consistent over time, and if the students do not resist or change it in some way, it will shape their achievement and behavior. High-expectation students will be led to achieve at high levels, whereas the achievement of low-expectation students will decline.
5. With time, students' achievement and behavior will conform more and more closely to the behavior originally expected of them.

The model is broadly conceived, and such a general conceptualization has both advantages and disadvantages. However, as more data have been collected and as the diversity of classroom life has become more evident (especially the various ways in which high- and low-achieving students are treated), the breadth and general abstraction of the model seem appropriate.

The model focuses on the behavior and achievement of individual students (not classes or subgroups of students) and on overt differences in teacher behaviors. By far, the most extensive literature exists on step 2—teachers' expectations and behavior for individual students. Step 3 suggests the possibility of both direct effects of teacher behavior (that is, pupils will have less work to do) and indirect effects (student motivation). In retrospect, it is now clear that most of the research on teacher expectations has examined direct effects of differential teacher behavior, rather than indirect effects (students' perceptions of or their inferences about teacher behavior).

Step 4 suggests that some students will be more affected by classroom process than others. This occurs sometimes because of the reactive effects of students on teachers, such as how some students communicate their resistance to teacher influence and how some students proactively influence teachers. Unfortunately, little research has focused specifically on how students can alter or control teacher expectations. Similarly, few studies have addressed step 5, the effects of teacher expectations and behavior on student achievement.

Despite the number of questions that we could raise about the effects of teacher expectations, few have been examined carefully. A decade after teacher-expectation research began, most research has studied step 2 (do teachers treat high- and low-achieving students differently?). Also, most studies have examined only differential verbal teacher behavior; other important variables have not been analyzed. Although the coding system developed for our own work emphasizes verbal behavior (Brophy & Good, 1970b), the model does not exclude other forms of differential behavior, such as grading.

Research on the Model

Research based on the Brophy-Good model clearly shows that many teachers vary sharply in their interaction with high- and low-achieving students. Good and Brophy (1986) summarized some of the common ways in which teachers have been found to differ in their behavior toward students believed to be high or low achievers:

1. Waiting less time for lows to answer
2. Giving lows answers or calling on someone else, rather than trying to improve lows' responses by giving clues or additional opportunities to respond
3. Giving inappropriate reinforcement: rewarding inappropriate behavior or incorrect answers by lows

 4. Criticizing lows for failure more often
 5. Praising lows less frequently for success
 6. Failing to give feedback to the public responses of lows
 7. Paying less attention to lows generally or interacting with them less frequently
 8. Calling on lows less often to answer questions
 9. Seating lows farther from the teacher
10. Demanding less from lows
11. Interacting with lows more privately than publicly and monitoring and structuring their activities more closely
12. Administrating or grading tests and assignments differently in which highs but not lows are given the benefit of the doubt in borderline cases
13. Having fewer friendly interactions with lows, including less smiling and fewer other nonverbal indicators of support
14. Giving briefer and less informative feedback to lows' questions
15. Using less eye contact and other nonverbal communication of attention and responsiveness with lows
16. Using effective but time-consuming methods with lows when time is limited
17. Interrupting lows more often when they make reading mistakes

These behaviors do not necessarily characterize ineffective teaching; rather, they should be used as guidelines by supervisors and teachers as they analyze their own behavior and how it affects particular students. There is no reason to assume that teachers should treat all students alike. However, some teachers overreact to relatively small differences among students by teaching them in sharply divergent ways or by providing different levels of assignments.

It is important to state that not all teachers show a consistent pattern of sharply differentiated interaction toward high- and low-potential students. Also, the type of problem behavior varies from class to class; hence, no simple presumptions are possible. One estimate, based on several studies that were conducted over a number of years, suggested that about one-third of the observed teachers acted in a way that appeared to exaggerate the initial deficiencies of low achievers (Good & Brophy, 1980). That is, these teachers appeared to "cause" the students to decline by providing them with fewer educational opportunities and by teaching them less. We must examine the implications of such teacher behaviors for low achievers. It seems that it would be unwise for slow students who face such conditions to volunteer or to respond when called on, because such an instructional system discourages these students from taking risks. To the extent that students are motivated to reduce risk and ambiguity—and many argue that students are strongly motivated to do so (see Doyle, 1986)—it seems that students would become more passive in order to diminish the risk of public failure.

The pattern of teacher behavior described above was reported in one of the earliest classroom studies of teacher expectations (Brophy & Good, 1970a). This pattern involves teacher rejection of low achievers and attempts to minimize contact with these students. However, it is clear that there are other models of teacher behavior and different ways in which teachers can communicate low expectations to students.

Different Patterns of Teacher Behavior. As stated, studies show that some teachers criticize low achievers more frequently than highs per incorrect response, and praise lows less than highs per correct answer. In contrast, other teachers praise marginal or incorrect responses given by low achievers. These findings reflect two different types of teachers. Teachers who criticize lows for incorrect responses seem to be less tolerant of these pupils. In contrast, teachers who reward marginal or even wrong answers are excessively sympathetic and unnecessarily protective of lows. Both types of teacher behavior illustrate to students that effort and classroom performance are not related (Good & Brophy, 1977).

Over time, such differences in the way teachers treat low achievers— for example, in the third grade a student is praised or wins teacher acceptance for virtually any verbalization, but in the fourth grade he or she is seldom praised and is criticized more—may reduce these students' efforts and contribute to a passive learning style. Other teacher behaviors may also contribute to this problem. Low-achieving students who are called on frequently one year (the teacher believes that they need to be active if they are to learn) but who are called on infrequently the following year (the teacher doesn't want to embarrass them) may find it confusing to adjust to such different role definitions. Ironically, those students who have the least adaptive capacity may be asked to make the most adjustment as they move from classroom to classroom. The greater variation in how different teachers interact with lows (in contrast to the more similar patterns of behavior that high-achieving students receive from different teachers) may exist because teachers agree less about how to respond to students who do *not* learn readily.

GROUPING EFFECTS

We have seen that some teachers behave quite differently toward high- and low-achieving students. Other studies suggest that teachers behave differently and have varied effects on the performance of students who are assigned to different ability groups in the same classroom.

In American classrooms, students are usually grouped by ability for reading instruction. Most reading groups are small so that the teacher can easily maintain active engagement of students, and reading groups are composed of students of "comparable" ability in order to allow the teacher to adapt the pace of instruction to students. The theory, simply put, is that ability grouping allows teachers to pace instruction at a more nearly optimal level for all children than would be possible if the teacher tried to set a uniform pace for an entire class. However, research suggests that ability grouping improves the reading achievement of faster readers but impedes the reading achievement of students who have more difficulty learning to read or who are assigned to low-ability reading groups (Commission on Reading, 1984; Kulik & Kulik, 1982).

The Commission on Reading (1984) summarized the problem for low-ability students as follows:

> There are qualitative differences in the experience of children in high and low reading groups that would be expected to place children in low groups at a disadvantage. Children in low groups do relatively more reading aloud and relatively less silent reading. They more often read words without a meaningful context on lists or flashcards, and less often read words in stories. Teachers correct a higher proportion of oral reading mistakes of children in low groups than children in high groups. When a mistake is corrected, teachers are more often likely to furnish a clue about pronunciation and less likely to furnish a clue about meaning for children in low groups. Teachers ask relatively more simple, factual questions of children in low groups and relatively fewer questions that require reasoning. (pp. 89–90)

In essence, then, students in low-ability groups receive less interesting and less demanding reading instruction.

Classroom Studies

In a study of three first-grade classrooms, Weinstein (1976) noted that the reading group to which students were assigned predicted midyear achievement better than predictions based just on students' initial readiness scores. Weinstein did not, however, find differences in teaching behavior that would account for the differential effects of reading-group assignment. Still, it appears that group placement may represent an expectation effect that influences student achievement directly (by decreasing or increasing motivation) or indirectly (by exposing students to poor or good reading models).

Eder (1981) also studied reading groups in one first-grade class and found that students who were likely to have difficulty in learning to read were generally assigned to groups whose social context was not conducive to learning. In part, this was because assignments to first-grade reading groups were based on kindergarten teachers' recommendations, and major criteria of placement were the students' maturity and their perceived ability.

Most of the students in Eder's study had similar academic abilities and came from similar middle-class backgrounds. None of the students could read prior to entering first grade; however, there were probably some important differences with respect to various reading-readiness skills. Still, the students' progress in reading could plausibly be related to the reading instruction they received in first grade. Despite the relative homogeneity of these pupils, the teacher nevertheless grouped them for reading instruction.

Because the most immature, inattentive students were assigned to low groups, it was almost certain that these groups would cause more managerial problems than others, especially early in the year. Indeed, because the teacher was often distracted by the need to manage other students in the group while a student reader in the low group was responding, other students often provided the correct word for the reader. Readers in the low group were not allowed time to ascertain words on their own, even though less than a third of the students interviewed reported that they liked to be helped and most thought that this "help" interfered with their learning. Eder's work indicates that low students had less time than highs to correct their mistakes before other students or the teacher intervened.

Eder also found that students in the low group spent 40 percent of their listening time not attending to the lesson (as opposed to 22 percent in the high group). Low students frequently read out of turn, adding to the general confusion. Eder reported twice as many teacher "managerial acts" in the low group as in the high group (157 vs. 61) and found that interruptions in the low group increased over the course of the year. Due to management problems, frequent interruptions, and less serious teaching, low students may inadvertently have been encouraged to respond to social and procedural aspects of the reading group rather than to academic tasks.

Alloway (1984) found that favorable expectations expressed toward individual students in the classroom may have been undermined by low-expectancy-related comments made to *groups* of students. Following the advice of earlier researchers, she made a systematic record of expressed expectation comments that occurred outside of the teacher-pupil dyad. Some of these remarks follow; they illustrate some of the *low-group* expectations that teachers communicated: (1) "You children [low-expectancy group] are slower, so please get on with your work now"; (2) "I'll be over to help you slow ones in a moment. This [high] group can go on by itself"; (3) "You [lows] need this extra time, so pay attention to me, please"; (4) "The blue group will find this hard." Alloway also pointed out low expectations in the form of labels teachers gave to individual students: "Hurry up, Robyn. Even you can get this right"; "Michelle, you're slow as it is. You haven't got time to look around the classroom." Alloway used an existing coding system to examine and interpret classroom behavior (Brophy & Good, 1970b). However, using an expectation framework, she found other ways in which teachers communicated inappropriate expectations to individual students and groups of students.

As Hiebert (1983) and Borko and Eisenhart (in press) noted, reading lessons for high- and low-ability students often show marked contrasts. For highs, the reading lesson is loosely structured, with opportunities to read aloud or silently, give multiple answers, interpret reading passages, and answer meaningful questions. In contrast, low-ability students experience a more highly structured format in which decoding skills, short, specific answers, and appropriate behavior are stressed. In a study of one elementary school, Hart (1982) noted that reading for low-ability students was a group experience in which these students met at an earlier time, were part of a smaller group, had more special arrangements, and more extra helpers. With lows, teachers emphasized decoding rather than understanding language. In general, low-ability students were kept busy during the reading group, while highs had more fun and more often attempted to understand what they read.

Allington (1983) reported data from 21 first-grade classrooms and noted that readers in the top groups read about three times as many words per day during reading group as did poor readers. The difference is explained in part by the fact that 70 percent of poor readers' reading was oral; good readers spent more time reading silently. Obviously, students can read more material if they read silently at the same time rather than orally in turn, and continuous reading is more enjoyable than waiting one's turn.

Although there are sometimes good reasons for oral reading (for example, it can give the teacher a chance to diagnose a child's difficulties), there is evidence that the amount of silent reading correlates more positively with comprehension than does oral reading time. Indeed, some studies show amount of oral reading to be *negatively* correlated with student achievement. Allington (1983), for instance, contends that a focus on either oral or silent reading exerts subtle pressure on the teacher to behave in a particular way. Since reading in low-ability groups tends to be primarily oral, many teachers emphasize correct pronunciation, proper word sequence, and so on. In contrast, teachers' questioning of high-ability students who read silently is more likely to focus on text meaning. Durkin (1981) makes similar arguments and suggests that an emphasis on oral reading leads both teachers and students to view reading as a "performing art." The format of silent reading, on the other hand, promotes the concept of reading as a "meaning-getting process."

Obviously, some students make more mistakes than others, and the type of mistake varies as well. Research consistently suggests, however, that teachers interrupt poor readers more often after a mistake than they interrupt good readers (Allington, 1980; Eder, 1982). Allington (1983) believes that more frequent interruptions encourage slow readers to rely on the teacher and imply to students that one reads to please someone else. Excessive teacher control may eventually inhibit students' development of self-monitoring skills and may also distract readers from the immediate task of attempting to understand material. Frequent teacher interruptions may also result in the general tentativeness that some poor readers show in their behavior (frequent need for teacher approval). The implications of this work are similar to Good's (1980) passivity model.

Stability of Group Membership

One critical aspect of ability grouping is that membership in groups tends to remain quite stable over time, with the work of upper- and lower-ability groups becoming more sharply differentiated as time passes. By the fourth grade, children in the top and bottom groups often differ in achievement-test scores by as much as four grades (Heathers, 1969). Furthermore, research by Alexander and Cook (1982) shows that relevant prior coursework and grades in junior high school are important determinants of students' high-school track placements. These studies, in combination with recent research showing the significant effects of curriculum tracks on high-school pupils' achievement (for example, Coleman, Hoffer & Kilgore, 1982; Goodlad, 1984; Morgan, 1983a; 1983b), indicate that track placements in secondary school are largely determined by students' ability-group membership in elementary school.

Mackler (1969) conducted a longitudinal study of a Harlem school and concluded that placement in a low-ability group had permanent effects on students. Mackler's data indicate that no student originally placed in a lower group made it to the top reading group after third grade.

IMPLICATIONS OF DIFFERENTIAL BEHAVIOR DURING GROUP INSTRUCTION

In general, the implications for students from an expectational standpoint are similar to the conclusions derived from the review of teachers' differential communication with individual students. In brief, the assignments extended to lows often are practice/review-oriented and, in a word, dull. Those extended to high-ability groups involve more abstraction and conceptualization and are more likely to involve students actively in constructing knowledge meaningfully. Students in low-ability groups are more likely encouraged to endure; students in high-ability groups, to think and to understand. Good and Weinstein (1986) have summarized some of the major ways in which different classroom environments are afforded to students of high and low potential.

The set of behaviors reflected in Table 1, if consistently expressed over time, would be sufficient to sustain student performance at

Table 1. General Dimensions of Teachers' Communication of Differential Expectations and Selected Examples.

	Students Believed to Be More Capable Have:	Students Believed to Be Less Capable Have:
Task environment (Curriculum, procedures, task definition, pacing, qualities of environment)	More variety in assignments, more complex tasks, and more conceptual work.	Less variety (simple task structure), less conceptualization, more practice.
	More opportunity to perform publicly on meaningful tasks.	Less opportunity to perform publicly, especially on meaningful tasks (supplying alternate endings to a story vs. learning to pronounce a word correctly).
	More opportunity to think.	Less opportunity to think, analyze (since much work is aimed at practice).
	More rapid pace.	Less rapid pace.
	More assignments that deal with comprehension, understanding (in higher-ability groups).	Less choice on curriculum assignments—more opportunity to work on drill-like assignments.
Grouping practices	More opportunity to work with other students of high ability and motivation.	Less opportunity to work with other students of high ability and motivation.

Locus of responsibility for learning	More autonomy (more choice in assignments, fewer interruptions).	Less autonomy (frequent teacher monitoring of work, frequent interruptions).
Feedback and evaluation practices	More opportunity for self-evaluation.	Less opportunity for self-evaluation.
	More honest/contingent feedback.	Less honest/more gratuitous/less contingent feedback.
Motivational strategies	More new content.	Less new content, more review.
Quality of teacher relationships	More respect for the learner as an individual with unique interests and needs.	Less respect for the learner as an individual with unique interests and needs.

This expanded table is based on material presented in T. Good & R. Weinstein (1986). Teacher Expectations: A Framework for Exploring Classrooms. In K. Zumwalt (Ed.) *Improving Teaching, 1986 ASCD Yearbook*, Alexandria, VA: Association for Supervision and Curriculum Development.

unnecessarily low levels. These same teacher attitudes of low expectations (slower pace, and so on) may be expressed to entire classes of students as well.

TEACHER EXPECTATIONS TOWARD THE CLASS

In the past decade, there has been considerable interest in studying how teachers who obtain high levels of mean student achievement differ from teachers who teach students of comparable backgrounds under similar circumstances but who obtain less achievement. For example, Good, Grouws, and Beckerman (1978) found that teachers who obtained higher average achievement from their classes taught at a more rapid pace than did teachers who stimulated less achievement. In a study of 41 fourth-grade mathematics classes, these investigators found that pace was related to student performance on a standardized achievement test. However, studies of teacher effectiveness that compare teaching process among classrooms have not, in general, attempted to study teacher expectations about entire classes per se. Hence, although a great deal of process data examine teacher behavior toward the class per se, these studies have not, as a rule, studied teacher expectations. Hence, it is not possible in most cases to relate dimensions of "effectiveness" to particular teacher beliefs (is a slower classroom pace associated with low teacher expectations about the class?).

Some literature on tracking suggests that teachers are more active and more demanding when teaching high-track subjects (see, for example, Metz, 1978). Some have contended that little teaching occurs in low-track subjects (say, eighth-grade math vs. algebra) and that teachers of these classes focus more on review and practice than on helping students to think about and to understand the subject matter.

As a formal research area, the relationship between teacher expectations for the class as a whole and behavior toward the class has been ignored. However, it is clear that teachers can hold low expectations for a class as well as for individual students and groups of students. As a case in point, Rhona Weinstein and I had the opportunity to visit a school, and although our purpose was to examine teaching for differential behavior toward students believed to be of high vs. low ability, our most striking observation was the teachers' communication of low expectations to *all students* (Good & Weinstein, 1986).

For example, in one combined fifth- and sixth-grade language arts class we observed, even the physical environment helped to communicate low performance expectations. We were struck by the barren nature of the room. The wall clock was broken, there were few books around, there was virtually nothing on the walls, and little student work was visible.

The lesson we observed emphasized rules and procedures. The

teacher dominated, quizzing the students about the meaning of topic sentences, main ideas, and the instructions for the class assignment. The task was narrowly defined. It seems inappropriate that students who had studied paragraphing and had been reviewing related material for several days were not required to write a paragraph or at least to read several selections and identify which groups of sentences were paragraphs. Even the latter activity would have allowed active involvement and discussion about why some groups of sentences were not paragraphs. To us, this close monitoring of student behavior, attention to minor details (demanding procedural exactness—the precise words of the text in the precise order), and the lack of any discussion of the value or meaningfulness of the subject matter communicated low performance expectations to this class.

Furthermore, the pace was so painfully slow that the students (and observers) either became restless or sleepy. Although the teacher was aware of these symptoms, she attributed them to the students' lack of control ("I don't show being tired") and to students' lack of ability ("We've been on this a week," "What am I fighting, City Hall?"). Only once did the teacher express an awareness that perhaps she was not making herself clear.

In addition, the teacher expected students at both grade levels to cover the same material. From an inspection of the curriculum, we learned that both fifth- and sixth-graders completed the same task with similar instructions (although procedures were much clearer in the fifth-grade text) in their textbooks. The teacher also pointed out that if the fifth-grade students did not learn the material now, they would have a second opportunity in sixth grade. This redundancy in curriculum, accompanied by a teacher-directed, highly passive mode of delivery, virtually assured that students would not be interested in the lesson, and they were not. Their boredom was obvious, and it caused their failure to give the teacher the answers she wanted. Sadly, the teacher probably explained the students' inadequate performance by assuming they lacked ability.

More studies of the effects of the *composition of students* in individual classrooms need to be done. Certain combinations of students may make it more or less difficult for particular teachers to interact with individual low achievers and/or influence how teachers perceive the potential of individual students or the class as a whole (Beckerman & Good, 1981). Teachers commonly report that some classes are much more difficult or enjoyable to teach than others, yet we have comparatively little information about characteristics of classes that lead teachers to respond in these ways or about how teachers' expectations for an entire class subsequently influence their classroom behavior or expectations for individual students. More research emphasis needs to be placed on how different distributions of students influence teacher expectations and behavior.

STUDENT EXPECTATIONS ABOUT THE CLASS

It has been argued that teachers necessarily develop expectations for the class as a whole, for groups of students, and for individual students. Some teachers appear to offer limited environments for students who appear to have less potential and/or interest in schoolwork. Teachers' communication and actions (such as asking only factual questions or assigning boring tasks to be completed in isolation) appear to be sufficient to sustain unnecessarily low student achievement. However, teacher messages have to be perceived, interpreted, and acted on by students if they are to have impact. Although an analysis of student expectations is beyond the goals of this chapter, some discussion is necessary to place the suggestions for practice, which follow, in appropriate context.

There is growing evidence that students are aware of differential teacher behavior and that certain practices have negative effects on students' beliefs and achievement (see, for example, Weinstein, 1983). Weinstein and Middlestadt (1979) report that students in some classes believe that teachers give students perceived as more capable more special privileges, more opportunities to choose and define their academic projects, and more freedom to complete work in the ways they prefer. Students also report that teachers are less likely to expect low-achieving students to complete assigned work and that teachers monitor and supervise lows more closely when working with them than with students believed to be more capable. (For additional information about how students' thoughts may mediate classroom instructional behaviors, see Marshall & Weinstein, 1984; Wittrock, 1986.)

An analysis of the student perspective further helps us to realize that classrooms are complex environments that involve a great deal of interpretation of ambiguous behavior by *both* teachers and students. In some classes, students can, with much agreement, identify differential patterns in teachers' interactions with different students. This awareness can be informative for students and suggests what the teacher expects from them. Students can also learn about relative ability differences among students from such differential interactions. In other classes, various students interpret similar teacher behaviors differently. For example, some students may perceive a teacher question during class discussion primarily as a chance to perform; others may view the same question more negatively, emphasizing the teacher's evaluation of their response.

Furthermore, in a single class, students' interpretations of what is meaningful and important can vary considerably, especially when students' social backgrounds are diverse. For example, students from some cultures have difficulty understanding that one can ask a question to evaluate understanding; in their cultures, one asks a question only to obtain an answer. Similarly, in some cultures it is disrespectful to maintain eye contact with an authority figure, whereas in other cultures *not* maintaining eye contact is a sign of disrespect. Although many classroom behaviors do not involve such divergent meanings, teachers and students often interpret the same behavior quite differently.

EXPLANATIONS FOR DIFFERENTIAL TEACHER BEHAVIOR

Although there is strong evidence that teachers' assessments of the general achievement levels of students are accurate (see, for example, Brophy & Good, 1974; Egan & Archer, 1985), clinical evidence suggests that teachers' reactions to students with less potential are limited to a small repertoire of teaching strategies (say, drill). Thus factors other than poor diagnosis account for much of the inappropriate differential behavior that occurs in the classroom. We briefly discuss some of these factors here.

One basic cause of differential behavior is that classrooms are busy and complex environments, and it is difficult for teachers to assess accurately the frequency and quality of their interactions with individual students. A second explanation involves the fact that much classroom behavior must be interpreted before it is assigned meaning. Research suggests that once a teacher develops an expectation about a student (for example, that the student is not capable of learning), the teacher interprets subsequent ambiguous classroom events in a way consistent with his or her original expectation (see, for instance, Anderson-Levitt, 1984). Good (1980) maintains that most classroom behavior is ambiguous and subject to multiple interpretations.

A third reason why some teachers differentiate their behavior toward high- and low-achieving students is related to the issue of causality. Some teachers believe that they can and will influence student learning (see, for example, Brophy & Evertson, 1976). Such teachers usually interpret student failure as the need for more instruction, more clarification, and eventually increased opportunity to learn. Other teachers, because they assign blame rather than assume partial responsibility for student failure, often interpret failure as a cue to provide less challenge and fewer opportunities to learn. Teachers who do not have a strong sense that they can influence student learning are therefore more likely to overreact to student error and failure (perhaps by subsequently assigning work that is too easy) than are teachers who believe that they can influence student learning and that they are partially responsible for student failure when it occurs. Along these lines, Marshall and Weinstein (1984) argue that some teachers see intelligence as fixed; others see it as changeable. Differences in views of stability of intelligence can have important effects on teacher behavior.

Another explanation for differential teacher behavior is *student self-presentation.* Students present themselves in varied ways to teachers, and these styles may influence teachers' responses. Dee Spencer-Hall (1981) notes that some students are able to time their misbehavior in such a way as to escape teacher attention, whereas other students who misbehave no more often receive considerably more reprimands because the timing of their misbehavior is inappropriate. Carrasco (1979) suggests that some students demonstrate competence in a style that escapes teacher attention. This happens, say Green and Smith (1983), when the language a student uses makes it likely that teachers will underestimate the student's potential.

BASIC DESIRABLE TEACHER EXPECTATIONS

Having discussed some of the problems associated with expectation effects, I now turn to a discussion of some of the attitudes and technical skills that may prevent the communication of low expectations in the classroom. Elsewhere, Brophy and Good (1974) have specified some basic expectations that teachers would be wise to hold and convey to the class as a whole. These expectations are briefly summarized here.

The Teacher's Main Responsibility Is to Teach

Teaching involves many roles other than instructing students. At times, the teacher will serve as a surrogate parent, an entertainer, an authority figure, a recordkeeper, a counselor, and so on. All of these duties are necessary aspects of the teacher's role. However, important as they are, they must not be allowed to overshadow the teacher's basic instructional role. Thus the majority of teachers' time in the classroom should be spent on instructional activities.

Unfortunately, teachers often do not basically like to teach the curriculum and feel that they must apologize to or bribe the students when lessons are conducted. This type of teacher is meeting his or her own needs, not the students'. In such classrooms, too much of the instructional day is spent on arts-and-crafts projects, singing and listening to records, and completing show-and-tell activities.

At higher grade levels, failure to teach is sometimes a problem of teachers who have low expectations about their own classroom management abilities or about their class's learning ability. Where homogeneous achievement grouping is practiced—in a junior high or high school, for example—teachers assigned to a period with a low-achieving class may sometimes abandon serious attempts to teach. They may, perhaps, attempt to entertain the class or else merely act as a sort of proctor who sees that the noise does not get out of hand. Such behavior represents a total surrender to failure expectations, in which emphasis has been switched from teaching the class to merely keeping the class happy or, in some instances, busy.

Diagnosis, Remediation, and Enrichment

The teacher is in the classroom to instruct. This involves more than just giving demonstrations or presenting learning experiences. Unfortunately, some teachers act as if students are expected to learn entirely on their own, with no instructional guidance. If a student does not catch on immediately after one demonstration, the teacher reacts with impatience and frustration.

Teachers must expect students to have some difficulty and thus to expect that instruction also means giving additional help to those who are having trouble, diagnosing the source of their problem, and providing remedial assistance to correct it. It means conducting evaluations with an eye toward identifying and correcting difficulties and not merely as a prelude to passing out praise, criticism, or additional worksheets to be completed in a mindless fashion. It means keeping track of each student's individual progress, so that he or she can be instructed in terms of what was learned yesterday and what should be learned tomorrow.

The Teacher Should Expect Some Difficulties

Although positive teacher expectations may help to prevent problems, they will not avert or solve all classroom difficulties. Expectations are not automatically self-fulfilling. But even though appropriate positive attitudes and expectations are not automatically or totally effective by themselves, they are necessary and important teacher qualities. Teachers will not always succeed with them, but they will not get very far at all without them. Furthermore, by expecting students to encounter some difficulties, teachers will avoid the possibility of blaming students for failing to learn. Unfortunately, some teachers think that failure to learn means either a lack of ability, lack of attention, or a lack of effort on the part of students. Good instruction involves consistent efforts at communication, however, and many intelligent, motivated students need two or three attempts to learn material. Thus teachers should expect some difficulty but should be willing and able to deal with it and to expect that appropriate follow-up instruction will be more successful.

Minimum Specified Objectives

Teachers should expect all students to meet at least the minimum specified objectives in the curriculum. Although most students will be capable of going considerably beyond these minimum objectives—and the teacher should try to stimulate this development as far as students' interest and abilities allow—teachers must not lose sight of basic priorities. Students who need remedial work should receive it through carefully conceived and interestingly presented instruction.

Teachers with appropriate attitudes will spend extra time working with students who experience difficulty. Their behavior when interacting with these students will be characterized by supportiveness, patience, and confidence. In contrast, teachers with inappropriate attitudes will often spend less time with students who most need the extra help. When they do work with these students, they will tend to do so in a half-hearted way that communicates disappointment and frustration. Such teachers are often overly anxious to achieve easy success and to solicit many right answers. They will need to change this attitude if they are to develop the patience and confidence needed to provide slower students effective remedial instruction.

Dealing with Individual Students

In general, teachers should expect to deal with individual students, not groups or stereotypes, in thinking and planning for instruction. This does not mean that they should not practice grouping or that terms such as "low achievers" should not be used. It does mean that teachers must keep a proper perspective about priorities. Grouping must be practiced as a means toward the goal of meeting the individual needs of each student. Similarly, labels and stereotypes are often helpful in thinking about ways to teach individuals better. Ultimately, however, the teacher is teaching John Smith and Mary Haden, not group A or "low achievers." The way teachers talk about students in their classes is an indication of how they think about them. If there is a continual mentioning of groups to the exclusion of individuals, the teacher may well have begun to lose sight of individual differences within groups and to overemphasize the differences among groups.

Building a Stimulating Environment

As shown in Table 1, students, groups, or classes perceived as less talented are more likely to receive less stimulating assignments, more frequent monitoring, and less opportunity for choice and self-evaluation. Marshall and Weinstein (1984) discuss a number of variables associated with the complex task of trying to build an appropriate classroom environment. Good and Weinstein (1986) discuss three of the variables presented in Marshall and Weinstein's analysis: the role of student choice, self-evaluation, and motivational strategies that are related to positive communication and performance in the classroom.

Student Choice.   Teachers control the locus of responsibility for learning and evaluation in the classroom, and they can share this responsibility to varying degrees with individual students. Marshall and Weinstein argue that the amount of responsibility students have may affect their susceptibility to teachers' expectations. Previous research has shown that students perceive that teachers offer more choices to high achievers than to low achievers and that teachers give more directions to low achievers. It appears that, in some classrooms, high achievers benefit from this situation. First, their work is less open to comparison with others in their group (Rosenholtz & Simpson, 1984). Second, the freedom to pursue to some extent *their own* learning activities may motivate high achievers to work harder than they would if they had to follow a simple set of directions, as low-achieving students must often do.

Self-Evaluation.   Shared responsibility for evaluation is not practiced in many classrooms. Teachers generally do most of the evaluation, and when students do have the opportunity to check answers, it is usually against an answer sheet that the teacher has prepared. When the teacher is the evaluator, students are dependent on him or her for judgments about their ability, and their performance is more susceptible to teacher expectations. In contrast, when the teacher encourages students to evaluate their own performance and to develop their own standards and criteria, evaluation may be more private and may be based on more varied criteria, which are more realistic and understandable to students. Thus students may be less vulnerable to external evaluation pressures. For example, being called on as frequently as other students to make public responses may be less important in a classroom in which students spend considerable time setting their own learning goals and engaging in self-evaluation. Clearly, the locus of responsibility for learning and evaluation will mediate grouping effects and individual students' response opportunities.

It seems ironic that in some sixth-grade classrooms there are fewer opportunities for learners to make choices and to evaluate their own work than in most first-grade classrooms. I suspect that if teachers placed more emphasis on helping learners to develop the capacity for self-direction and self-evaluation, many students' invidious comparisons of their work to the work of others would disappear. I believe that one important outcome of schooling should be to help students develop greater capacity for self-direction and independent learning. Though they should be able to do what their teachers ask and feel some pride when they accomplish goals, in time they should learn to determine when and how well they have completed a task without feedback from anyone else. Further, I believe that students must also learn to determine task direction, to engage in task evaluation, and to integrate self- and other-directed work.

Motivational Strategies. Nicholls (in press) distinguishes among three types of motivation: extrinsic involvement, ego involvement, and task involvement. Under conditions of extrinsic involvement, learning is seen as a means to gain a reward or to please the teacher. Under ego involvement, learning is a means to look smart or to avoid looking stupid in comparison to peers. Under conditions of task involvement, learning is perceived as innately important, and individuals enjoy mastering the task itself; they are not concerned with how well they do on the task in relation to others. Marshall and Weinstein (1984) argue that when motivation is self-focused, opportunities for displaying competence in multiple areas are available, or rewards are unlimited, the fact that students are working on the same task, regardless of other dimensions, may not be as detrimental as it would be under competitive conditions for external reward. Furthermore, classrooms with a multi-task structure (students are working on different tasks at the same time, perhaps tasks that they have selected themselves) or with task-involved motivation, especially if emphasis is on multiple areas of competence, may overcome possible negative effects of comparison, public evaluation, and limited rewards on low achievers. Thus, in some classrooms, students may have the opportunity to be rewarded in public for various areas of task mastery. In contrast, even in multitask structures, particularly if the tasks are completed by all students at some point, an emphasis on single abilities or ego involvement may decrease the otherwise positive effects of multiple tasks on self-evaluation.

PRACTICAL SKILLS FOR WORKING WITH STUDENTS

It has been argued that teachers need to understand that a degree of failure will be present in any teaching situation and that teachers need to develop strategies for responding to student failure. Teachers are in classrooms to teach actively, and they must realize that student failure calls for reteaching rather than rationalization. Many teachers need to develop greater tolerance and skills for dealing with students when they do not achieve immediate success. But how can teachers work with students who fail in a public setting, and how can one assess student understanding in a class of 30?

Calling on Students to Answer Questions

As Brophy and Good (1986) note, research findings on this issue vary according to grade level, student background, and aptitude, as well as whether questions are being asked to whole classes or small groups. In the early grades, and especially during small-group lessons, it is important that all students participate overtly (and roughly equally).

In small-group reading lessons, this can be accomplished by using the "patterned turns" method, training the students not to call out answers or reading words, and calling on nonvolunteers as well as volunteers. In these grades, it is important to prevent assertive students from seizing other students' response opportunities and to ensure that reticent students participate regularly, even though they seldom volunteer. Similarly, it is important to call on students who may not know the answer as well as students whom the teacher is sure will know the correct answer.

All this suggests the following principle: when most students are eager to respond, teachers have to suppress their call-outs and train them to respect one another's response opportunities; however, when most students are reticent, teachers will have to encourage them to participate, which may include accepting relevant call-outs. But there is a danger in accepting call-outs in some classes because student call-outs usually correlate positively with achievement in classes with low-income students but negatively in classes with high-income students.

It is seldom feasible for all students to participate overtly in whole-class lessons, let alone to ensure that all take part equally (Brophy & Good, 1986). Even in the lower grades, this need not present a problem in subjects such as spelling or arithmetic, in which practice and assessment can be accomplished through written exercises. It may pose difficulties, however, for primary-grade teachers who are working on objectives that call for overt verbal practice and for teachers at any level whose assignments call for students to make oral presentations (speeches, research reports). Here, it may be necessary to divide the class into groups or to schedule only a few presentations per day and use the rest of the period for faster-paced activities.

In general, overt verbal participation in lessons does not seem to be an important achievement correlate in the *upper grades*. Still, rather than interact with the same few students most of the time, teachers in these grades should probably do more to encourage volunteering (pausing after asking questions, to give students time to think and raise their hands, will help here).

Questioning Students

A great deal of research relates general teacher behaviors (such as clarity, enthusiasm, amount of information presented to students) to student achievement. However, it is also important to note that teachers may communicate differently to individual students within the classroom. How teachers manage public response opportunities that occur during discussions is thus important because such responses affect not only students' opportunity to learn but also their motivation to learn. The emphasis here is on possible differences that teachers may communicate to students whom they perceive as high- vs. low-achieving students.

Difficulty Level of Questions

Studies of the difficulty level of questions have yielded mixed results. It seems clear that most questions (approximately 70 percent) should elicit correct student answers and most of the rest should elicit overt, substantive responses rather than failures to respond at all. However, these guidelines are of limited usefulness because they are generalized across instructional contexts, and optimal question difficulty varies with context in significant ways. For example, basic skills instruction requires a great deal of drill and practice, which means frequent, fast-paced drill/review lessons in which most questions should be answered rapidly and correctly. However, when teaching complex cognitive content, or when trying to stimulate students to generalize from, evaluate, or apply what they are learning, teachers will need to raise questions that few students can answer correctly (or that have no single correct answer). Similarly, relatively frequent errors may be expected early in the unit when new learning is occurring, but there should be few mistakes later in the unit, as mastery levels are supposed to have been achieved.

It is vital that teachers consider the *quality* of errors as well. Some errors occur because students understand the general idea correctly but make a minor miscalculation, or because they use sound logic but base it on assumptions that are plausible but faulty. Such "high-quality" errors are relatively acceptable and may even provide helpful guidance to the teacher. However, student mistakes that suggest inattention, hopeless confusion, or alienation from the material are undesirable.

In terms of dealing with low-achieving students, it seems critical to stay with these students when they make a high-quality mistake. Given their relatively lower base rates of attending and responding in the classroom, if their thinking is close or on target in trying to deal with a particular issue, then it seems essential that the teacher provide them with additional response opportunities. Furthermore, these students also benefit from a degree of challenge, and unfortunately some teachers appear to ask them only very simple questions. Although it may be useful to modify the types of questions that are asked of low-achieving students to some degree (easier questions than other students, on a percentage basis), it is imperative to realize that if they are not asked some challenging questions, they are going to remain at their present level of achievement. Hence, teachers must be sure to ask low-achieving students a reasonable number of questions of sufficient difficulty to challenge them to think, rather than simply to report facts that they have memorized.

Cognitive Level of Questions

Data on the cognitive level of questions (as distinct from the difficulty level) have produced conflicting results. However, they do clearly refute the simplistic, but frequently cited, notion that higher-level questions are categorically "better" than lower-level questions. That is, some investigators have indicated that categories of questions higher on Bloom's taxonomy (application, analysis, synthesis, evaluation) are superior to those types lower on this scale (knowledge, comprehension). Indeed, several studies indicate that lower-level questions facilitate learning, even learning of higher-order objectives (Brophy & Good, 1986).

For the teacher who has to confront a class of students who represent a range of ability levels, perhaps the key caveat here is that the desirability of the cognitive level of questions cannot be reduced to frequency norms. To develop more useful information, researchers will have to devise more complex methods of coding that take into consideration the teacher's goals and the quality, timing, and appropriateness of the questions. This will require shifting from the individual question to the question sequence as a unit of analysis. The important advice here for teachers would be to organize plans for instruction around logical, important goals. For example, if you want students to attend to relevant facts and then integrate the facts and draw an important conclusion from them, you would probably want to use a series of lower-level questions followed by higher-level questions. The key point is to think about the sequence of questions, rather than to ask a high number of higher-level questions per se.

In this context, it is extremely important that low-achieving students have the opportunity to apply ideas and evaluate conclusions. In some classrooms, only high-ability students have the opportunity to respond to higher-order questions. Thus, although it is impossible to provide a prescription that specifies a number of higher- and lower-order questions that should be asked, it is imperative that low-achieving students have the opportunity to participate in analysis and synthesis activities and not have their work limited to "drill and skill" activities (Good & Brophy, in press).

Sequences of Questions

Logical thinking about sequences of questions indicates that researchers' emphasis on the cognitive level of questions is misplaced. At a certain point in a class discussion, factual questions are important. At other times, questions of value and priority are essential and factual questions are inappropriate. For example, in Table 2 it is clear that a sequence of questions—even of relatively "low-level," factual questions—can lead to a meaningful exchange of information and insight. In this sequence, the teacher is helping students to understand the historical events that preceded the Boston Tea Party and is trying to illustrate that different events can be seen in different ways, depending on one's perspective. Here, key information is being tied to the concept of monopoly and

Table 2. A Reasonable Questioning Sequence.

1. What was the Boston Tea Party?
2. What events preceded the Boston Tea Party?
3. What is a monopoly?
4. Under what conditions might a monopoly be justified?
5. Do we provide favorable conditions for certain industries in this country that make it more difficult for foreign industries to compete?
6. What did the Boston Tea Party represent to British citizens? to American citizens?
7. Who participated in the Boston Tea Party?
8. How much was the tea worth?

SOURCE: T. Good & J. Brophy (in press). *Looking in Classrooms* (4th ed.). New York: Harper & Row.

representative taxation, and the factual questions that are being raised are helping students to understand the historical significance of activities. For example, the question "How much was the tea worth?" is a simple fact question, but it should help students to realize that in colonial times, tea was extraordinarily valuable. The fact that the colonists were willing to dump the tea into the harbor rather than take it home indicated how outraged they were. Similarly, the question "Who participated in the Boston Tea Party?" is trying to get at the fact that a wide range of citizens took part in the action.

In an unreasonable sequence, the factual questions that are asked would be trivial and would not really be used to develop any logical examination of what the Boston Tea Party represented. For example, questions about the number of ships that were in the harbor and what the colonists were wearing during the tea party seem to represent teachers' interest in whether or not the students had read the book carefully. Although such questions may be of occasional benefit and value, overemphasizing trivial details is counterproductive in most circumstances. Although students' knowledge of Townshend Duties and Coercive Acts might be important if the knowledge were being used to understand the causes and effects of the Boston Tea Party, the sequence in which

Table 3. An Unreasonable Questioning Sequence.

1. What was the Boston Tea Party?
2. How many ships in the harbor contained tea?
3. How did the colonials dress when they boarded the ships to destroy the tea?
4. Define Townshend Duties.
5. Define Coercive Acts.
6. Who was Thomas Hutchinson?
7. On what date did the Boston Tea Party occur?

SOURCE: T. Good & J. Brophy (in press). *Looking in Classrooms* (4th ed.). New York: Harper & Row.

the questions appear in Table 3 seems to be designed to determine whether the students had read the material rather than to play an instrumental role in an important sequence of thought. Hence, I believe that too much emphasis is placed on the apparent cognitive level of questions, rather than on the role that a particular question plays in stimulating discussion and debate. Unfortunately, when low-expectation students are called on, it is often at a point in the sequence where factual information is being sought. To reiterate, all students need to be challenged in the classroom.

Waiting for and Reacting to Student Responses

Once teachers do call on students (especially nonvolunteers), they should usually wait until the students offer a substantive response, ask for help or clarification, or actually say "I don't know." Sometimes, however, especially in whole-class lessons in which lengthy pauses threaten continuity or momentum, the teacher will have to curtail the pause by making one of the reacting moves discussed below.

As Brophy and Good (1986) note, once a teacher has asked a question and called on a student to answer, he or she then must monitor the student's response (or lack of it) and react to it. Simply expressed, there are four basic types of student responses that call for a teacher response.

Reactions to Correct Responses. Correct responses should be acknowledged as such, because even if the respondent knows that the answer is correct, some of the other students may not. Ordinarily (perhaps 90 percent of the time) this acknowledgment should take the form of overt feedback, which may range from brief nods through short affirmation statements ("Right," "Yes") or repetition of the answer, to more extensive praise or elaboration. Such overt affirmation can be omitted on occasion, such as during fast-paced drills in which the students understand that the teacher will simply move on to the next question if the previous question is answered correctly.

Although it is important for teachers to give feedback so that everyone knows that an answer is correct, it is not usually important to praise the student who answered. Such praise is often intrusive and distracting, and it may even embarrass the recipient, especially if the accomplishment was not especially praiseworthy in the first place. (Graham, 1984, for instance, has argued that praise of an obvious answer may "cue" students that the teacher expects little from the respondent.) In any case, teachers who maximize achievement are sparing rather than effusive in praising correct answers. To the extent that such praise is beneficial, it is more likely to be effective when specific rather than global, and when used with low-income or dependent/anxious students rather than with high-income or assertive/confident students.

Reacting to Partly Correct Responses. If a response is incomplete or only partly correct, teachers ordinarily should affirm the correct part and then follow up by giving clues or rephrasing the question. If this does not succeed, the teacher can give the answer or call on another student.

Reacting to Incorrect Responses. If an answer is incorrect, teachers should indicate that this is the case. Almost all (99 percent) of the time, this negative feedback should be simple negation rather than personal criticism, although criticism may be appropriate for students who have been persistently inattentive or unprepared.

Stating that the answer is incorrect, teachers should usually try to elicit an improved response by rephrasing the question or giving clues. But teachers should avoid "pointless pumping" when questions cannot be broken down or the student is too confused or anxious to profit from further questioning.

Sometimes the feedback following an incorrect answer should include not only the correct answer but a more extended explanation of why the answer is correct or how it can be determined from the information given. Such extended explanation should be offered whenever the respondent (or others in the class) might not "get the point" from the answer alone, as well as at times when a review or summary of part of the lesson is needed.

Reacting to "No Response." Teachers should train their students to respond overtly to questions, even if only to say "I don't know." Thus, if waiting has not produced an overt response, teachers should probe ("Do you know?"), elicit an overt response, and then follow up by giving feedback, supplying the answer, or calling on someone else (depending on the student's response to the probe).

Reacting to Student Questions and Comments. Teachers should answer relevant student questions or redirect them to the class, and incorporate relevant student comments into the lesson. Such use of student ideas appears to become more important in each succeeding grade level, as students become both more able to contribute useful ideas and more sensitive to whether teachers treat their ideas with interest and respect.

Seriously Attending to Students' Level of Understanding

Teachers who hold appropriately high performance expectations (even for students who are making, in a relative sense, the least amount of progress in class) will actively attempt to see whether or not students have mastered the material (Good, Grouws & Ebmeier, 1983; Emmer et al., 1982). Rosenshine and Stevens (1986) have summarized suggestions for finding out whether students have done this. Rosenshine and

Stevens (1986) note that some methods of checking for understanding include:

- Prepare a large number of oral questions beforehand.
- Ask many brief questions on main points, supplementary points, and on the process being taught.
- Call on students whose hands aren't raised in addition to those who volunteer.
- Ask students to summarize the rule or process in their own words.
- Have all students write the answers (on paper or blackboard) while the teacher circulates.
- Have all students write the answers and check them with a neighbor (frequently used with older students).
- At the end of a lecture/discussion (especially with older students), write the main points on the board and have the class meet in groups and summarize the main points to each other.

As Rosenshine and Stevens (1986) point out, the wrong way to check for understanding is to ask only a few questions, call on volunteers for their (usually correct) answers, and then assume that all of the class has now learned from hearing these responses. Another error is to ask, "Are there any questions?" and when no one raises a question to assume that everybody understands. Another error (particularly with older children) is to assume that it is not necessary to check for understanding and that simply repeating the points will be sufficient.

PRACTICAL SUGGESTIONS FOR IMPROVING PERFORMANCE OF LOW ACHIEVERS

Allington (1983) has offered a number of suggestions for improving the performance of students in low groups. Since these suggestions seem generally applicable to all subject areas, these recommendations are presented here.

1. *Add a second reading session with the low reading group.* If achievement differences are to be narrowed, teachers must allow more time for students who need to practice reading, although time alone is not an answer.
2. *Increase the amount of silent reading time for the low group.* Much of the additional reading time for the low group should be spent in silent reading. However, if this time is to be successful, teachers will have to instruct some readers in effective silent reading behaviors (determine the general purpose before reading the story, skip unknown words, try to understand the story, and so on).
3. *Provide an opportunity to reread easy material, and emphasize improving fluency.* Allington suggests that if poor readers are to become better readers, they need help to develop fluency skills. For example, a fourth-grade teacher might continue to work with poor readers until they can read a second-grade text orally as well as a good second-grade reader can.

4. *Focus instruction on developing readers who monitor their own performance.*
Perhaps the best way that teachers can do this is to emphasize the meaning
of a story for students. Furthermore, to the extent possible, teachers
should give students the chance to self-correct errors, because teacher
interruptions and student call-outs likely make students dependent on
others for correct words and for answers to comprehension questions.
Providing easier materials for slow readers, especially when they work
independently, might also help these students to self-correct.

5. *Decrease worksheet and workbook assignments.* Allington believes that poor
readers spend too much time in drill activities and suggests that they
need more contextual reading activities. Such activities are unlikely to
be helpful, however, unless teachers discuss the work with students and
encourage them to make brief reports and to tell or summarize the
material to other students.

6. *Assess the instructional environment afforded to poor readers.* Before
teachers make major changes in their behavior, they should tape-record
themselves on several occasions and carefully identify aspects of their
instructional behavior that they wish to alter. Teachers' goals should
be to change classroom practices and to determine whether or not changes
in practice are linked to improved student performance. (For detailed
information about strategies for describing teacher behavior, see *Looking
in Classrooms*, by Good & Brophy, 1984.) As a measure of success, Allington
suggests that teachers ask at the end of the year, "How many members
of my lower reading groups did I move into higher groups?"

Other Recommendations for Practice

To these six recommendations, Robinson and Good (in press) have added
three more. First, "poorer" readers should be taught for part of the
day in groups with "better" students, rather than receiving instruction
only with other slow readers. Second, teachers need to assign low achievers work that is meaningful and motivating. Third, teachers need to
become more aware of their classroom behavior and to work more
closely with other teachers and supervisors.

Alternate Instructional Formats.   Because serious problems are associated with ability-grouped reading instruction, the Commission on Reading (1984) urges exploration of other options for reading instruction.
One option is the use of whole-class instruction more frequently. This
format has been used successfully for certain topics in mathematics
(see Good, Grouws & Ebmeier, 1983), and seems feasible for instruction
in topics such as phonics, spelling, study skills, as well as for comprehension instruction. As the Commission notes, other alternatives to the
conventional arrangement of teacher-led instruction of ability-grouped
children are peer tutoring and cooperative work on assignments.

Another format involves students working together in mixed-ability
groups; reading groups do not have to be formed on the basis of ability.
Although small-group instruction is often advantageous (for example,

because some students do not pay attention during whole-class instruction), students can often be grouped, for example, on the basis of common interest in a topic. There is some evidence that children read more proficiently when they read material that is valuable or interesting to them (see, for example, Anderson, Shirey, Wilson & Fielding, in press). Thus, although students may need to receive some differential instruction related to their abilities (such as oral reading for slower readers), poor readers can benefit from occasional instruction with more competent readers.

Meaningful and Varied Assignments.   Although teachers need to be especially careful that assignments for low-ability students are meaningful and varied, many teachers react to skill deficiencies of slower readers by having them do practice drills. Students often do drill activities apart from any reading context, however, and come to view such work as arbitrary and boring.

Sometimes the lowest-ability groups read material that three or four other reading groups in a class have already read. Under these conditions, it is difficult for the teacher, as well as the students, to be interested in the story. Questions such as, "What do you think will happen at the circus?" are a bit flat the fourth time a story is read. Hence, students in low-ability groups need different but appropriate material and different sets of questions if they are to maintain motivation and interest in reading.

Working with Colleagues.   As we pointed out earlier, when teachers treat low-ability students inappropriately, they do so because of mistaken assumptions (for instance, they believe that more drillwork is needed) or because they are unaware of their own classroom behavior. Opportunities to be observed by other teachers, to observe other teachers, and to share information with teachers are excellent ways for teachers to increase their awareness of instructional strategies.

Unfortunately, teachers are too often isolated from contact with other professionals and are thus denied the opportunity to receive relevant feedback about their classroom behavior. The most important aspect of solving any problem is becoming aware of it and wanting to correct it. We believe that teachers need to be observed by other teachers and supervisors and that they should visit the classrooms of many other teachers who teach the same grade levels. Such observation provides an excellent way to learn how other teachers handle diversity, open and close lessons, find time to examine students' seatwork, and so on.

Teaching is both a science and an art (Gage, 1978), and accordingly every teacher must develop a style that suits his or her skills and interests, as well as students' needs. Differences in teaching styles are not only inevitable, but in many circumstances have positive effects on students. Thus there is no need for teachers in the same building or the same school system to use similar styles and practices. The idea of working with peers is to exchange ideas and to improve instruction, not to match or to model someone else's behavior.

Teachers should also be cognizant of the management and instructional styles of their colleagues who teach in the next lowest grades. For example, how do these teachers handle interruptions of groups (that is, what circumstances permit students to interrupt when the teacher is working with a small group?), when can students use classmates as resources, and what free choices are students allowed? Most students adjust easily to differences in teacher styles; however, important variations in expectations ("If you have trouble in seatwork, see me before you practice mistakes" vs. "Try to do the assignment before you ask questions") can be profitably explained at the beginning of the school year in order to prevent misunderstandings that can lead students to view teachers as indifferent and arbitrary. Teachers should give such explanations matter-of-factly so that they do not undermine the credibility of a previous teacher.

Knowledge of other teachers' behavior is helpful because it allows teachers to convey consistent academic and procedural expectations. This clarity seems especially useful to primary-school-age pupils, who may occasionally have difficulty understanding conflicting teacher behaviors or expectations. It also allows teachers to structure their own classrooms more meaningfully and to consider the continuity of curriculum and instruction that students receive from year to year. For example, a teacher who finds that students' previous teachers emphasized one form of seatwork 85 percent of the time may want to plan alternative types of assignments, especially early in the school year, so that students receive suitable but novel work.

It is not uncommon to visit schools in which seatwork assignments for fifth-grade students (such as copying sentences, answering factual questions) are less demanding than work that third-grade students receive (say, writing their own questions about a story). Furthermore, students in lower grades often have more choices in books that they read, more freedom to work with other students, and more opportunities to plan work assignments than do students in higher grades. Such discrepancies not only fail to challenge students to become progressively more independent and self-reliant, but may lower older students' motivation for and interest in schoolwork. Unfortunately, many teachers fail to provide enjoyable and appropriately challenging classroom assignments because they are unaware of what practices other teachers in the same school use.

Working with other teachers can help a teacher develop seatwork assignments that allow for successful, relatively independent work, are appropriate and meaningful, and reasonably varied. Considering the widespread criticism of the seatwork assignments in textbooks, teachers of the future will have to develop many of these materials themselves. Although producing an effective seatwork assignment takes considerable time and thought, by working together teachers can save time and use a wider variety of ideas. Such professional collaboration and discussion are valuable for all teachers, but especially for beginners. Teacher-training programs prepare students for a general role; however, a newly qualified teacher may be assigned to a sixth-grade class in an inner-city school or a first-grade class in a suburb. There is often no way to prepare in advance for the curriculum demands of a particular teaching context. Thus a beginning teacher must draw on the talents and ideas of teachers in the same school or other schools, particularly those who teach at the same grade level. Unfortunately, such contacts among teachers are relatively rare.

CONCLUSION

The research on teachers' and students' expectations leads me to some practical suggestions about the improvement of teaching. I recommend that the suggestions I make here (and those made in other chapters of this book) be shared with colleagues and that some peer observations be started. Collegial relationships that are critical and yet respectful can ensure against perpetuating negative expectations. This kind of relationship can help a teacher learn to communicate, through so many different ways, expectations that are positively motivating for students.

ACKNOWLEDGMENT: The author acknowledges the support of the Center for Research in Social Behavior at the University of Missouri-Columbia and especially wishes to thank Diane Chappell for her help in preparing this chapter.

REFERENCES

Alexander, K., & Cook, M. (1982). Curricula and coursework: A surprise ending to a familiar story. *American Sociological Review, 47,* 626–640.

Allington, R. (1980). Teacher interruption behaviors during primary grade oral reading. *Journal of Educational Psychology, 72,* 371–377.

———. (1983). The reading instruction provided readers of differing reading abilities. *Elementary School Journal, 83,* 548–559.

Alloway, N. (1984). Teacher expectations. Paper presented at the Australian Association for Research in Education Annual Conference, Perth, Australia.

Anderson, R., Shirey, L., Wilson, P., & Fielding, L. (in press). Interestingness of children's reading material. In R. Snow & M. Farr (Eds.), *Aptitude, learning, and instruction: Conative and affective process analyses.* Hillsdale, NJ: Erlbaum.

Anderson-Levitt, K. (1984). Teacher interpretation of student behavior: Cognitive and social processes. *Elementary School Journal, 84,* 315–337.

Beckerman, T., & Good, T. (1981). The classroom ratio of high- and low-aptitude students and its effect on achievement. *American Educational Research Journal, 18*, 317–327.

Borko, H., & Eisenhart, M. (in press). Students' conceptions of reading and their reading experiences in school. *Elementary School Journal.*

Brophy, J. (1982). Research on the self-fulfilling prophecy and teacher expectations. Paper presented at the annual meeting of the American Educational Research Association.

Brophy, J., & Evertson, C. (1976). *Learning from teaching: A developmental perspective.* Boston: Allyn & Bacon.

Brophy, J., & Good, T. (1970a). Teachers' communication of differential expectations for children's classroom performance: Some behavioral data. *Journal of Educational Psychology, 61*, 365–374.

———. (1970b). The Brophy-Good dyadic interaction system. In *Mirrors for behavior: An anthology of observation instruments continued.* 1970 supplement (Vols. A and B). Philadelphia: Research for Better Schools.

———. (1974). *Teacher-student relationships.* New York: Holt, Rinehart & Winston.

———. (1986). Teacher behavior and student achievement. In M. Wittrock (Ed.), *Third handbook of research on teaching.* New York: Macmillan.

Carrasco, R. (1979). Expanded awareness of student performance: A case study in applied ethnographic monitoring in a bilingual classroom. Social Linguistic Working Paper No. 60. Austin, TX: Southwest Educational Development Laboratory.

Coleman, J., Hoffer, T., & Kilgore, S. (1982). *High school achievement.* New York: Basic Books.

Commission on Reading. (1984). *Becoming a nation of readers.* Sponsored by the National Academy of Education. Washington, DC: National Institute of Education.

Cooper, H. (1979). Pygmalion grows up: A model for teacher expectation communication and performance influence. *Review of Educational Research, 49*, 389–410.

———. (1983). Teacher expectation effects. In L. Bickman (Ed.), *Applied social psychology annual 4.* San Francisco: Sage.

Cooper, H., Findley, M., & Good, T. (1982). The relations between student achievement and various indices of teacher expectations. *Journal of Educational Psychology, 74*, 577–579.

Cooper, H., & Good, T. (1983). *Pygmalion grows up. Studies in the expectation communication process.* New York: Longman.

Cooper, H., & Tom, D. (1984). Teacher expectation research: A review with implications for classroom instruction. *Elementary School Journal, 85*, 77–89.

Doyle, W. (1986). Classroom organization and management. In M. Wittrock (Ed.), *Third handbook of research on teaching.* New York: Macmillan.

Durkin, D. (1981). Reading comprehension instruction in five basal reader series. *Reading Research Quarterly, 16*, 515–544.

Dusek, J. (Ed.). (1985). *Teacher expectancies.* Hillsdale, NJ: Erlbaum.

Eder, D. (1981). Ability grouping as a self-fulfilling prophecy: A microanalysis of teacher-student interaction. *Sociology of Education, 54*, 151–162.

———. (1982). Differences in communicative styles across ability groups. In L. C. Wilkinson (Ed.), *Communicating in the classroom.* New York: Academic.

Egan, O., & Archer, P. (1985). The accuracy of teachers' ratings of ability: A regression model. *American Educational Research Journal, 22,* 25–34.

Emmer, E., Evertson, C., Sanford, J., & Clements, B. (1982). *Improving classroom management: An experimental study in junior high classes.* Austin, TX: Research and Development Center for Teacher Education.

Gage, N. (1978). *The scientific basis of the art of teaching.* New York: Teachers College Press.

Good, T. (1980). Classroom expectations: Teacher-pupil interactions. In J. McMillan (Ed.), *The social psychology of school learning.* New York: Academic.

Good, T., & Brophy, J. (1977). *Educational psychology: A realistic approach,* 1st ed. New York: Holt, Rinehart & Winston.

———. (1980). *Educational psychology: A realistic approach,* 2nd ed. New York: Holt, Rinehart & Winston.

———. (1984). *Looking in classrooms,* 3rd ed. New York: Harper & Row.

———. (1986). Teacher behavior and student achievement. In M. Wittrock (Ed.), *Third handbook of research on teaching.* New York: Macmillan.

———. (in press). *Looking in classrooms,* 4th ed. New York: Harper & Row.

Good, T., Grouws, D., & Beckerman, T. (1978). Curriculum pacing: Some empirical data in mathematics. *Journal of Curriculum Studies, 10,* 75–81.

Good, T., Grouws, D., & Ebmeier, H. (1983). *Active mathematics teaching: Empirical research in elementary and secondary classrooms.* New York: Longman.

Good, T., & Power, C. (1976). Designing successful classroom environments for different types of students. *Journal of Curriculum Studies, 8,* 1–16.

Good, T., & Weinstein, R. (1986). Classroom expectations: One framework for exploring classrooms. In K. Kepler Zumwalt (Ed.), *1986 ASCD Yearbook: Improving teaching.* Alexandria, VA: Association for Supervision and Curriculum Development.

Goodlad, J. I. (1984). *A place called school: Prospects for the future.* New York: McGraw-Hill.

Grant, L. (1985). Race-gender status, classroom interaction, and children's socialization in elementary school. In L. Wilkinson & C. Marrett (Eds.), *Gender influences in classroom interaction.* New York: Academic.

Green, J., & Smith, D. (1983). Teaching and learning: A linguistic perspective. *Elementary School Journal, 83,* 353–391.

Haller, E. (1985). Pupil race and elementary school ability grouping: Are teachers biased against black children? *American Educational Research Journal, 22,* 465–483.

Hart, S. (1982). Analyzing the social organization for reading in one elementary school. In G. Spindler (Ed.), *Doing the ethnography of schooling.* New York: Holt, Rinehart & Winston.

Heathers, G. (1969). Grouping. In R. Ebel (Ed.), *Encyclopedia of educational research.* 4th ed. New York: Macmillan.

Hiebert, E. (1983). An examination of ability grouping for reading instruction. *Reading Research Quarterly, 18,* 231–250.

Hines, C., Cruickshank, D., & Kennedy, J. (1985). Teacher clarity and its relationship to student achievement and satisfaction. *American Educational Research Journal, 22,* 87–99.

Kulik, C., & Kulik, J. (1982). Effects of ability grouping on secondary school students: A meta-analysis of evaluation findings. *American Educational Research Journal, 19,* 379–384.

Mackler, B. (1969). Grouping in the ghetto. *Education and Urban Society, 2,* 80–95.

Marshall, S., & Weinstein, R. (1984). Classrooms where students perceive high and low amounts of differential teacher treatment. Paper presented at the annual meeting of the American Educational Research Association, New Orleans.

Metz, M. (1978). *Classrooms and corridors: The crisis of authority in desegregated secondary schools.* Berkeley, CA: University of California Press.

Morgan, W. (1983a). Learning and student life quality of public and private school youth. *Sociology of Education, 56,* 187–202.

———. (1983b). School effects on youth from public, Catholic, and other private high schools. In M. Borus (Ed.), *Pathways to the future* (Vol. 3). Final report on the National Longitudinal Youth Market Experience in 1981 (pp. 88–138). Columbus, OH: Ohio State University, Center for Human Resources Research.

Nicholls, J. (in press). Conceptions of ability and achievement motivation: A theory and its implications for education. In S. Paris, G. Olson, & H. Stevenson (Eds.), *Learning and motivation in the classroom.* Hillsdale, NJ: Erlbaum.

Prawat, R. (1985). Affective versus cognitive goal orientations in elementary teachers. *American Educational Research Journal, 22,* 587–604.

Prawat, R., & Nickerson, J. (1985). The relationship between teacher thought and action and student affective outcomes. *Elementary School Journal, 85,* 529–540.

Robinson, R., & Good, T. (in press). *An introduction to elementary reading instruction.* New York: Harper & Row.

Rosenholtz, S., & Simpson, C. (1984). Classroom organization and student stratification. *Elementary School Journal, 85,* 21–38.

Rosenshine, B., & Stevens, R. (1986). Teaching functions. In M. Wittrock (Ed.), *Third handbook of research on teaching.* New York: Macmillan.

Rosenthal, R. (1974). *On the social psychology of the self-fulfilling prophecy: Further evidence for Pygmalion effects and their mediating mechanisms.* New York: MSS Modular Publications.

Rosenthal, R., & Jacobson, L. (1968). *Pygmalion in the classroom: Teacher expectation and pupil's intellectual development.* New York: Holt, Rinehart & Winston.

Spencer-Hall, D. (1981). Looking behind the teacher's back. *Elementary School Journal, 81,* 281–289.

Weinstein, R. (1976). Reading group membership in first grade: Teacher behaviors and pupil experience over time. *Journal of Educational Psychology, 68,* 103–116.

———. (1983). Student perceptions of schooling. *Elementary School Journal, 83,* 287–312.

Weinstein, R., Marshall, H., Brattesani, K., & Middlestadt, S. (1982). Student perceptions of differential teacher treatment in open and traditional classrooms. *Journal of Educational Psychology, 74,* 678–692.

Weinstein, R., & Middlestadt, S. (1979). Student perceptions of teacher interactions with male high and low achievers. *Journal of Educational Psychology, 71,* 421–431.

Wilkinson, L., & Marrett, C. (1985). *Gender influences in classroom interaction.* New York: Academic.

Wittrock, M. (1986). Students' thought processes. In M. Wittrock (Ed.), *Third handbook of research on teaching.* Chicago: Rand McNally.

CHAPTER 9

JERE BROPHY

ON MOTIVATING STUDENTS

"I don't know what it means, but I did it." This is what a first-grader was observed to say to himself as he finished a worksheet (Anderson et al., 1984, p. 20). Unusual only in that it was verbalized spontaneously, this remark typifies a problem noted frequently by Anderson et al. (1984) in their research, in which they observed first-grade students working on seatwork assignments and then interviewed them about what they had done, why they did it, and how. The data indicated that many students (especially low achievers) did not understand how to do the assignments. Rather than ask the teacher or seek help in other ways, however, these students often were content to respond randomly or rely on response sets (such as alternating or using geometrical patterns to select multiple-choice answers, or picking one new word from a list to fill a blank in a sentence without reading the sentence itself). Low achievers in particular tended to be more concerned about finishing their assignments than about understanding the content they were supposed to be learning.

High achievers completed most assignments successfully and showed less concern about finishing on time, but even they gave little evidence of understanding the content-related purposes of the assignments. No student consistently explained assignments in terms of their curricular content. Instead, most responses were vague generalities ("It's just our work," or "We learn to read"). In general, assignments were virtually meaningless rituals for many of the low achievers in these first-grade classes, and even the high achievers seemed only dimly aware of the purposes of the assignments or skills they were practicing.

Such findings are not rare. Rohrkemper and Bershon (1984) interviewed elementary-school students about what was on their minds when they worked on assignments. They found that of 49 students who gave codable responses, 45 were concerned about getting the answers correct, 2 were concerned only about finishing, but only 2 mentioned trying to understand what was being taught. Corno and Mandinach (1983) and Blumenfeld, Hamilton, Bossert, Wessels, and Meece (1983) have also expressed concern about the low quality of students' engagement in classroom activities. Doyle (1983) suggests that most students are preoccupied with meeting requirements and getting acceptable grades, rather than with learning what they are supposed to, to the point that they will avoid asking questions or probing deeper into the content; they want to stick with safe, familiar routines. Other research (Brophy, Rohrkemper, Rashid, & Goldberger, 1983; Harter, 1981; Lepper, 1983) suggests that students begin school with enthusiasm but gradually settle into a dull routine that centers on minimizing the ambiguity (about precisely what must be done) and risk (of failure) involved in meeting teachers' demands.

Given the nature of schooling, these student attitudes are understandable, at least to a degree. First, though schools are set up to benefit students themselves (as well as society at large, of course), the facts that attendance is compulsory and that performance will be graded tend to focus students' attention on the problem of meeting externally imposed demands, rather than on the personal benefits that they might derive from education. Second, teachers confronted with classes of 20–40 students cannot meet each individual student's needs optimally, so many students are frequently bored and many others are frequently confused or frustrated. Third, classrooms are public settings, so failure often means not only personal disappointment but public embarrassment before the peer group. Finally, even in classrooms where fear of failure, test anxiety, and concern about avoiding ambiguity and risk are minimized, both teachers and students can easily settle into familiar routines that become "the daily grind" as the school year progresses. That is, classroom activities designed as means tend to become ends in themselves, with attention focused on what must be done to complete the activities, rather than on the knowledge or skills that the activities were designed to teach.

This last factor leads to the main point of this chapter: even though we can expect students to be concerned about meeting requirements and earning acceptable grades, it is also reasonable to expect students to be aware and appreciative of the educational objectives of classroom activities and the potential of these activities for enhancing personal growth and quality of life, *if teachers consistently draw attention to these objectives and potentials*. Unfortunately, classroom research suggests that few teachers do this systematically.

Anderson et al. (1984) found that teachers' presentations of assignments typically included procedural directions or special hints (say, "Pay attention to the underlined words"), but seldom called attention to the purposes and meanings of the assignments. Only 5 percent of the teachers' presentations explicitly described the purpose of the assignment in terms of the content being taught, and only 1.5 percent included explicit descriptions of the cognitive strategies to be used when doing the assignment.

Brophy et al. (1983) reported similar results from their study of six fourth-, fifth-, and sixth-grade classrooms observed eight to fifteen times during reading and mathematics instruction. During these observations, not one of the six teachers ever mentioned that students could derive personal satisfaction from developing their knowledge or skills. Only about a third of the teachers' task-introduction statements included comments judged likely to have positive effects on student motivation, and most of these were brief general predictions that students would enjoy the task or do well on it. In about 100 hours of classroom observation, only nine task introductions were noted that included substantive information about motivation to learn the content or skills that the task was designed to develop:

These are not elementary, high-school, or college-level words; these are living-level words. You'll use them every day in life. If you plan to be a writer or enjoy reading, you will need these words.

Remember: the essential thing is to do them correctly, not to be the first to finish.

I think you will like this book. Someone picked it out for me, and it's really good.

This is really a strange story. It's written in the first person, so that the person talking is the one who wrote the story about his experience. It has some pretty interesting words in it. They are on the board.

The stories in this book are more interesting than the ones in the earlier-level books. They are more challenging because the stories and vocabulary are more difficult. Reading improves with practice, just like basketball. If you never shoot baskets except when you are in the game, you are not going to be very good. Same with reading. You can't do without it.

Answer the comprehension questions with complete sentences. All these stories are very interesting. You'll enjoy them.

You girls should like this story because it is a feminist story. You boys will enjoy yours, too. Your story is especially interesting. I want you to be sure to read it. It's a mystery, and you'll enjoy it.

Percent is very important. Banks use it for interest loans, and so on. So it is important that you pay attention.

You're going to need to know fractions for math next year. You will need fractions in the world to come.

Notice how minimal and essentially barren most of these remarks are. They do not go into enough detail to be very meaningful or memorable for most students, and many of the statements have a perfunctory quality, suggesting that the teacher was going through the motions without much enthusiasm or conviction. Furthermore, whatever positive effect these remarks may have had was probably undercut by the facts that: (1) most of the teachers' remarks concerned procedural demands and evaluations of work quality or progress rather than descriptions of the task itself or what the students might get out of it; and (2) the other remarks included the following:

Today's lesson is nothing new if you've been here.

If you get done by 10 o'clock, you can go outside.

Your scores will tell me whether we need to stay with multiplication for another week. If you are talking, I will deduct 10 points from your scores.

This penmanship assignment means that sometimes in life you just can't do what you want to do. The next time you have to do something you don't want to do, just think, "Well, that's part of life."

Get your nose in the book; otherwise I'll give you a writing assignment.

You don't expect me to give you baby work every day, do you?

You've been working real hard today, so let's stop early.

You'll have to work real quietly, otherwise you'll have to do more assignments.

My talkers are going to get a third page to do during lunch.

We don't have a huge amount to do, but it will be time-consuming.

This test is to see who the really smart ones are.

Such findings appear to be typical, although not universal. Our own subsequent research, conducted in junior-high-school social studies classes, identified several teachers who routinely say and do things that appear likely to motivate their students to be aware of and want to gain the knowledge and skill benefits that classroom activities are designed to develop, and who avoid potentially destructive comments such as those listed above. Marshall (1986) has also identified a few such teachers in the elementary grades. In general, however, it appears that most teachers, even those who are effective in other respects, do not systematically say and do things likely to stimulate their students' motivation to learn academic content and skills. In attempting to discover why this is so, I have concluded that it is because most teachers have not received much systematic information about strategies for motivating students to learn, and much of the information that they have received is limited or distorted.

Much of the advice given to teachers about motivation flows from either of two contradictory yet frequently expressed views that are both incorrect, at least in their extreme form. The first view is that learning should be fun and that, when classroom motivation problems appear, it is because the teacher somehow has converted an inherently enjoyable activity into drudgery. I believe that students should find academic activities meaningful and worthwhile, but not that they typically should find such activities to be "fun" in the same sense as recreational games and pastimes. The other extreme view is that school activities are necessarily boring, unrewarding, and even aversive, so that one must rely on extrinsic rewards and punishments in order to force students to engage in these unpleasant tasks. I believe that although extrinsic incentives have their place in the classroom, they should be only one among several sets of factors that influence student motivation. With proper instruction and socialization from teachers, students should find academic activities meaningful and worthwhile for reasons involving intrinsic motivation and personal self-actualization, not just because successful performance will earn extrinsic rewards.

Recent theory and research on student motivation have led to rejection of both of these extreme views in favor of a more balanced and sophisticated approach, and have suggested a rich range of motivational strategies. This chapter presents a list of such strategies developed from review and integration of this research literature. I place emphasis on strategies for motivating students to want to learn the academic content and skills that classroom activities were designed to develop. For more information about motivation in the classroom, see Chapter 10, this volume, and Ames and Ames (1984; 1985), Brophy (1983), Corno and Mandinach (1983), Corno and Rohrkemper (1985), Deci and Ryan (1985), Good and Brophy (1986; in press), Keller (1983), Kolesnik (1978), Lepper and Greene (1978), Maehr (1984), Malone and Lepper (in press), McCombs (1984), Nicholls (1984), and Wlodkowski (1978).

BASIC MOTIVATIONAL CONCEPTS

To place the subsequent discussion of teachers' strategies for motivating students into context, let us introduce several basic motivational concepts. These include the concept of student motivation to learn and the expectancy × value theory of motivation, which underlies and organizes my approach to the topic.

Definition of Motivation to Learn

Student motivation to learn is a student tendency to find academic activities meaningful and worthwhile and to try to derive the intended academic benefits from them. Motivation to learn can be construed as both a general trait and a situation-specific state. As a general trait, motivation to learn refers to an enduring disposition to strive for knowledge and mastery in learning situations. This trait is most characteristic of individuals who find learning intrinsically rewarding, who value it as a worthwhile and satisfying activity and enjoy expanding their store of information, increasing their understanding of concepts or processes, or mastering skills. However, similar levels of effort and persistence in learning situations may also be seen in individuals who are motivated by a sense of duty ("If you are going to do something at all, do it right") or a desire to make the most of their time ("If you are going to have to put in the time on something anyway, you may as well do your best and get the most from the experience").

In specific situations, a *state* of motivation to learn exists when the student engagement in an academic activity is guided by the goal or intention of acquiring the knowledge or mastering the skill that the activity is designed to teach. In classrooms, students reveal motivation to learn when they try to master the information, concepts, or skills being taught as they attend to lessons, read text, or work on assignments. Whether or not they find a particular activity interesting or enjoyable, students who are motivated to learn will try to get the intended benefits from the activity by striving to make sure that they understand and remember what they are supposed to be learning. In contrast, students who are not motivated to learn will do only as much as they believe they need to do in order to meet performance standards that will ensure reward or avoidance of punishment.

Implied in this definition of student motivation to learn is a basic distinction between learning and performance: *learning* refers to the information-processing, sense-making, and comprehension or mastery advances that occur during the acquisition of knowledge or skill; *performance* refers to the demonstration of such knowledge or skill after it has been acquired. Many approaches to the study of the relationships between motivation and behavior ignore this distinction or deal only with performance. Such approaches are inappropriate for studying student motivation to learn, however, because of the heavily cognitive nature of classroom learning. With a few exceptions, such as penmanship or zoology dissection skills, school learning is primarily covert and conceptual rather than overt and behavioral. Thus the term "motivation to learn" refers primarily to the motivation underlying these covert processes that occur during learning, rather than to the motivation that drives later performance. Similarly, the motivational strategies to be described apply not only to performance (work on tests or assignments), but also to the information-processing activities (attending to lessons, reading for understanding, comprehending instructions, putting things into one's own words) that are involved in learning content or skills in the first place. The emphasis here is on stimulating students to use thoughtful and effective information-processing and skill-building strategies when they are learning. This is quite different from merely offering them incentives to perform well.

A related implication is that the concept of student motivation to learn emphasizes the *cognitive* aspects of student motivation, not just the affective (emotional) aspects. The emphasis is not so much on whether students enjoy an activity as on whether they take it seriously and try to derive the intended benefits from it. Similarly, the emphasis is not on the intensity of physical effort devoted to an activity or the time spent on it, but on the *quality* of students' cognitive engagement in the activity—the degree to which they approach the activity purposefully and respond to it thoughtfully. Being motivated to learn implies such high-quality cognitive engagement in the activity, not mere enjoyment of it.

Expectancy × Value Theory

Most approaches to motivation, including this one, fit within general social learning theory and in particular within *expectancy × value theory* (Feather, 1982). This theory posits that the effort that people will be willing to expend on a task will be a product of: (1) the degree to which they *expect* to be able to perform the task successfully if they apply themselves (and thus the degree to which they expect to receive the rewards that successful performance of the task will bring); and (2) the degree to which they *value* those rewards. Investment of effort is viewed as the product rather than the sum of the expectancy and value factors, because it is assumed that no effort at all will be invested in a task if either factor is missing entirely, no matter how strongly the other factor may be present. People do not invest effort on tasks that do not lead to valued outcomes even if they know that they can perform the task successfully, and they do not invest effort on even highly valued tasks if they are convinced that they cannot succeed on these tasks no matter how hard they try.

Expectancy × value theories of motivation imply that, in order to motivate their students to learn, teachers need both to help their students appreciate the value of academic activities and to make sure that the students can succeed in these activities if they apply reasonable effort. The rest of the chapter is organized according to these expectancy × value theory ideas. We will first discuss some basic preconditions that must exist if teachers are to motivate their students successfully, then discuss strategies that involve establishing and maintaining success expectations in the students, and then describe strategies designed to enhance the subjective value that students place on school tasks. The latter strategies are subdivided into strategies that involve extrinsic incentives, those that involve taking advantage of existing intrinsic motivation, and those that involve stimulating student motivation to learn.

ESSENTIAL PRECONDITIONS FOR MOTIVATING STUDENTS

The following assumptions and preconditions underlie the effective use of the motivational strategies to be described. *The strategies cannot work effectively if these assumptions and preconditions are not in effect.*

Supportive Environment

Anxious or alienated students are unlikely to develop motivation to learn academic content. Nor is such motivation likely to develop in a chaotic classroom. Thus we assume that: (1) the teacher uses classroom organization and management skills that successfully establish the classroom as an effective learning environment (see Chapter 3); and (2) the teacher is a patient, encouraging person who makes students feel comfortable during academic activities and supports their learning efforts. The classroom atmosphere is businesslike but relaxed and supportive. Students feel comfortable in taking intellectual risks, because they know that the teacher will not embarrass or criticize them if they make a mistake.

Appropriate Level of Challenge/Difficulty

Activities must be of an appropriate level of difficulty for the students. If the task is so familiar or easy that it constitutes nothing more than busywork or, worse, if it is so unfamiliar or difficult that the students cannot succeed on it even if they apply reasonable effort, no strategies for inducing student motivation to learn are likely to succeed. Tasks are of appropriate difficulty when students are clear enough about what to do and how to do it that they can achieve high levels of success if they apply reasonable effort. When students encounter such tasks routinely, they will expect to succeed at them and thus will be able to concentrate on learning the tasks without worrying about failure.

Meaningful Learning Objectives

We cannot expect students to be motivated to learn if we present them with pointless or meaningless activities. Therefore, we assume that activities have been selected with worthwhile academic objectives in mind. That is, they *teach some knowledge or skill that is worth learning,* either in its own right or as a step toward some greater objective. The following activities will *not* meet this criterion: continued practice on skills that have already been mastered thoroughly; memorizing lists for no good reason; looking up and copying definitions of terms that are never used meaningfully in readings or assignments; reading vague or sketchy prose that contains many isolated facts but lacks integrative concepts and sufficient detail to allow the students to develop a concrete understanding of the content; reading about things that are completely foreign to their experience or described in such technical or abstract language as to make the material essentially meaningless; and working on tasks assigned merely to fill time rather than to attain some worthwhile instructional objective.

Moderation/Optimal Use

We assume that there is an optimal level for effective use of each motivational strategy. Strategies used too often or too routinely may lose their effectiveness, and any particular use of a strategy can become counterproductive if it goes on too long or is carried to extremes. Also, different activities will call for different numbers and kinds of motivational strategies. Where content is relatively unfamiliar and its value or meaningfulness is not obvious to students, significant motivational effort involving several of the strategies described in this chapter may be needed. In contrast, little or no special motivational effort may be needed when the task involves something that students are already eager to learn.

With these four preconditions in mind, let us consider the motivational strategies that various writers have suggested. We begin with strategies that address the expectancy factor (within the larger expectancy × value theory approach).

STRATEGIES FOR HELPING STUDENTS TO EXPECT ACADEMIC SUCCESS

Several strategies have been suggested for helping students to maintain expectations for success and the various desirable goal-setting behaviors, efficacy perceptions, and causal attributions that are associated with such expectations. All of these strategies assume that students are given tasks of appropriate difficulty and receive timely and informative feedback that is specific about the correctness of their responses and about the progress they are making toward ultimate objectives. In short, these strategies involve helping students to make and recognize genuine progress, rather than misleading them or offering them only empty reassurances.

Program for Success

The simplest way to ensure that students expect success is to make sure that they achieve success consistently by beginning at their level, moving in small steps, and preparing them sufficiently for each new step so that they can adjust to it without much confusion or frustration. Two points need to be made about this strategy to clarify that it does not mean that teachers should mostly assign unchallenging busywork.

First, we speak here of success achieved through reasonable effort that leads to gradual mastery of appropriately challenging objectives, not to success achieved through quick, easy application of overlearned skills to overly familiar tasks. It is true that certain basic knowledge and skills must be practiced until mastered to a level of smooth, error-free performance, but it is also true that students should be paced through the curriculum as briskly as they can progress without undue frustration. Thus programming for success must be seen as a means toward the end of maximizing students' achievement progress, and not as an end in itself.

Second, keep the role of the teacher in mind. Levels of success that students can achieve on a particular task depend not only on the difficulty of the task itself, but on the degree to which the teacher prepares them for the task through advance instruction and assists their learning efforts through guidance and feedback. A task that would be too difficult for the students if they were left to their own devices might be just right when learned through active instruction by the teacher, followed by supervised practice. In short, your help in making sure that students know what to do and how to do it is an important factor in determining whether they will succeed in classroom tasks.

It can be difficult to program low achievers for success, especially in heterogeneous classrooms. You can help by providing extra instruction and assistance to slower students, and by monitoring their progress more continuously. Give them briefer or easier assignments if they cannot succeed even with extra help and support, but continue to demand that they put forth reasonable effort and that they progress as briskly as their abilities will allow. If necessary, divide the class into subgroups that receive differentiated instruction and assignments, and grade according to Mastery Learning procedures that do not penalize slower students for the extra time that they take to achieve mastery (Levine, 1985) or according to criteria specified in individualized performance contracts (see Good & Brophy, in press, concerning providing differentiated instruction in heterogeneous classrooms).

Low achievers may need strong teacher statements of confidence in their abilities or willingness to accept slow progress (so long as the students consistently put forth reasonable effort), especially when grades must be assigned according to fixed common standards or comparisons with peers or norms, rather than according to degree of effort expended or degree of success achieved in meeting individually prescribed goals. You may need to help low achievers learn to take satisfaction in receiving Bs or even Cs when such grades represent successful performance based on reasonable effort. For some low achievers, achieving a grade of C is an occasion for taking pride in a job well done. When this is the case, teachers should express to these students (and to the parents, as well) their recognition of the accomplishment and their appreciation of the effort that it represents.

Regardless of the range of student ability or achievement levels represented in the class, conditions should be arranged so that every student who consistently puts forth reasonable effort can earn at least a grade of C. Where this is not the case, neither motivation nor achievement will be fostered effectively.

Goal Setting, Performance Appraisal, and Self-Reinforcement

Help your students to identify and use appropriate standards for judging their progress. This begins with *goal setting*. Research indicates that setting goals and making a commitment to trying to reach these goals increase performance (Bandura & Schunk, 1981; Tollefson et al., 1984). Goal setting is especially effective: (1) when the goals are *proximal* rather than distal (they refer to performance on a task to be attempted here and now, rather than to attainment of some ultimate goal in the distant future); (2) when they are *specific* (for example, to complete a page of math problems with no more than one error) rather than global ("Work carefully and do a good job"); and (3) when they are *challenging* (difficult but reachable) rather than too easy or too hard.

For particular brief tasks or assignments, the appropriate goal is to meet the instructional objective. Teachers who state the objectives when introducing activities help their students to be aware of the objectives and to use them as guides to their responses. If the objectives have been phrased in terms of specific, observable behaviors, students can use them as criteria for assessing their performance.

For more comprehensive assignments or tests, perfect performance will not be a realistic goal for many students. These students may need help in formulating challenging but reachable goals that represent what they can expect to achieve if they consistently put forth reasonable effort. In the case of a long series of activities that ultimately lead to some distal goal, it is important to establish specific goals for each intervening activity and to make sure that students are aware of the links between each of these activities and the ultimate goal (Bandura & Schunk, 1981; Morgan, 1985).

Goal setting by itself is not enough; there must also be *goal commitment*. Students must take the goals seriously and must commit themselves to trying to reach them. It may be necessary to negotiate such goal setting with some students, or at least to provide them with guidance and to stimulate them to think about their performance potential. Where an ultimate or cumulative level of performance that would earn a grade of A is not a realistic goal, help students to identify and commit themselves to realistic goals that, if reached, will yield a grade of B or C (rather than to have them verbalize unrealistically high goals that they are not really committed to). One way to do this is to provide a menu of potential goals (graduated in terms of the levels of effort that will be required to meet them and the grades or other rewards that will be earned if success is achieved), and ask students to commit themselves to particular goals and associated levels of effort. Another approach is to use performance contracting, in which students formally contract for a certain level of effort or performance in exchange for specified grades or rewards (Tollefson et al., 1984). Performance contracting can be time-consuming and may call more attention to the rewards than is desirable, but it has the advantages of ensuring active teacher-student negotiation about goal setting and formalizing of students' commitment to goals.

Finally, students may need help in assessing progress toward established goals by using *appropriate standards for judging levels of success*. In particular, they may need to learn to compare their work with absolute standards (progress toward achieving an objectively specified level of success) or with their own previous performance levels (improvement over time), rather than to judge only by comparing their work with that of peers. You can help here by providing accurate but encouraging feedback. That is, you must label errors as such if they are to be recognized and corrected, but your more general evaluative comments should provide encouragement by noting levels of success achieved in meeting established goals or by judging accomplishments with reference to what is reasonable to expect (rather than with reference to absolute perfection or to the performance of peers). Where performance is unsatisfactory, provide remedial instruction and additional opportunities for improvement, along with continued encouragement that the student will achieve realistic goals if he or she continues to put forth reasonable effort.

Some students will need *specific, detailed feedback* concerning both the strengths and weaknesses of their performance (Elawar & Corno, 1985). Such students may have only vague appreciation of when and why they have done well or poorly, so they may need not only general evaluative feedback but concepts and terms that they can use to describe their performance and evaluate it with precision. This is especially true for assignments such as compositions, research projects, laboratory experiments, and other complex activities that are evaluated using general qualitative criteria, rather than by scoring answers to specific questions as correct or incorrect. Rather than just assigning letter grades, provide your students with detailed feedback about their performance in such activities (for example, comment on the relevance, accuracy, and completeness of the content of a composition; its general organization and structuring with a coherent beginning, middle, and end; its sequencing and subdivision into appropriate paragraphs; the structuring of paragraphs to feature main ideas; the variety and appropriateness of sentence structures and vocabulary for communicating the content; and the mechanics of grammar, spelling, and punctuation).

Students who have been working toward specific proximal goals and who have the necessary concepts and language with which to evaluate their performance accurately will be in position to *reinforce themselves* for the successes that they achieve. Many students will do this habitually, but others will need encouragement to check their work and take credit for their successes (that is, to attribute their successes to the fact that they were willing and able to make the effort required to attain success). If necessary, you can focus students' attention on their progress more directly by comparing their current accomplishments with performance samples from earlier points in time, or by having the students keep scrapbooks, graphs, or other records to document their progress.

Remedial Work with Discouraged Students

Some students with long histories of failure will tend to give up at the first sign of difficulty or frustration, and will need more intensive and individualized motivational encouragement than the rest of the class will. These students are likely to benefit from the strategies used in Mastery Learning approaches: program for success by giving them tasks that they should be able to handle, provide them not only with the usual group instruction but also with individualized tutoring as needed, and allow them to contract for particular levels of performance and to continue to study, practice, and take tests until they achieve that level of performance. By virtually guaranteeing success, this approach builds confidence and increases discouraged students' willingness to take the risks involved in seriously committing themselves to challenging goals (Grabe, 1985).

You can also help by working on these students' beliefs, attitudes, and expectations. One way is to *portray effort as an investment rather than a risk.* Help discouraged students to appreciate that learning may take time and may involve confusion or mistakes, but that persistence and careful work should eventually yield knowledge or skill mastery. Furthermore, such mastery not only represents success in the particular task involved, but "empowers" students by providing them with knowledge or skills that will make them more capable of handling higher-level tasks in the future. If they give up on tasks that they could master if they persisted, they cheat themselves out of such growth potential.

It also helps to *portray skill development as incremental and domain-specific.* Make sure that your students realize that their intellectual abilities are open to improvement, rather than fixed and limited, and that they possess a great many such abilities, rather than just a few. Usually, difficulties in learning particular tasks occur not because the student lacks ability or does not make an effort, but because he or she lacks experience with the particular type of task involved. With patience, persistence, and help from the teacher, students can acquire the knowledge and skills specific to the domain that the task represents, and this domain-specific knowledge and skill development will enable them to succeed on that task and on others like it. In short, help discouraged students to realize that their success depends not just on general ability but on possession and use of a great range of specific knowledge and strategies built up gradually through a great many experiences in each domain. Difficulty in learning mathematics does not necessarily imply difficulty in learning other subjects, and even within mathematics, difficulty in learning to graph coordinates does not necessarily mean difficulty in learning to solve differential equations or understand geometric relationships. Even within a problem area (say, graphing coordinates), knowledge and skills can be built up gradually through mastery of each successive step toward the ultimate objectives, if the student persists in putting forth reasonable effort, accepts teacher help, and does not lose patience or give up whenever success does not come easily.

In this connection, it is helpful if you *focus on mastery* when monitoring the performance of discouraged students and giving them feedback. Stress the quality of the students' task engagement and the degree to which they are making continuous progress, rather than comparing their performance with their peers' (McColskey & Leary, 1985). Treat errors as learning opportunities rather than as failures: errors should lead to remedial or additional instruction, followed by additional practice opportunities. Make-up exams, credit for effort, or extra-credit assignments should be used to provide struggling students with opportunities to overcome initial failures through persistent effort.

Discouraged students may also benefit from *attribution retraining* (Craske, 1985; Dweck & Elliott, 1983; Fowler & Peterson, 1981; Medway & Venino, 1982). Attribution retraining involves modeling, socialization, and practice exercises designed to help students learn to concentrate on the task at hand, rather than to become distracted by fear of failure; to cope with frustrations by retracing their steps to see where they went wrong or by finding another way to approach the problem (rather than to give up); and to attribute their failures to insufficient effort, lack of information, or reliance on ineffective strategies, rather than to lack of ability. Instead of giving students this advice in third-person (lecture) language or even in second-person (direction-giving) language, you are likely to communicate these cognitive strategies most successfully if you model them for the students in first-person (thinking-out-loud) language, demonstrating how to do the task yourself while verbalizing the thinking ("self-talk") that guides your actions. Discouraged students are especially likely to benefit from this type of modeling, which focuses on developing solutions to the problem when confronted with frustration or failure (as opposed to modeling of smooth, successful performance unfettered by confusion or difficulty). In other words, your modeling should not only convince discouraged students that *you* can do the task (they know that already anyway), but should convince these students that *they* can do the task (because they already possess, or can reasonably expect to learn, the necessary knowledge and skills). Such modeling demystifies the task for the students and arms them with coping strategies that they can use instead of giving up when they become confused or frustrated.

Finally, some students may suffer from severe *test anxiety*. Such students may succeed well enough in informal, pressure-free situations, but become highly anxious and perform at considerably below their potential on tests or during any testlike situation in which they are aware of being monitored and evaluated. You can minimize such problems by avoiding time pressures unless they are truly central to the skill being taught; stressing the feedback functions rather than the evaluation or grading function when discussing tests with students; portraying tests as opportunities to assess progress in developing knowledge or skill rather than as measures of ability; telling students, where appropriate, that some problems are beyond their present achievement level so that they should not be concerned about missing them; giving pretests to accustom the students to "failure" and to provide base rates for comparison when post-tests are administered later; and teaching stress management skills and effective test-taking skills and attitudes (see Hill & Wigfield, 1984; McCombs, 1984; Plass & Hill, 1986).

Concluding Comments About Maintaining Students' Success Expectations

Bear in mind that the expectancy aspects of student motivation depend less on the degree of objective success that students achieve than on how they view their performance: what they see as possible for them to achieve with reasonable effort, whether they define their level of achievement as successful or not, and whether they attribute their performance to controllable factors (effort, learning effective strategies) or to uncontrollable factors (fixed general ability, luck). Therefore, whatever their ability levels, the motivation levels of all students, even the most discouraged, are open to reshaping by their teachers. Empty reassurances or a few words of encouragement will not do the job. Instead, a combination of appropriately challenging demands with systematic socialization, designed to make the student see that success can be achieved with reasonable effort, should be effective.

STRATEGIES FOR INDUCING STUDENTS TO VALUE ACADEMIC ACTIVITIES

The previous section of this chapter focused on the expectancy factor of the expectancy × value approach to motivation. It discussed strategies for helping students to develop and maintain the expectation that they can achieve success in academic activities if they put forth reasonable effort. The remaining sections of the chapter concern the value factor. They describe strategies for helping students to see good reasons for engaging in the activities in the first place—good enough reasons to motivate them to take the activities seriously and expend the necessary efforts. These include strategies for supplying extrinsic motivation, for capitalizing on existing intrinsic motivation, and for stimulating student motivation to learn.

Strategies for Supplying Extrinsic Motivation

Strategies for supplying extrinsic motivation do not attempt to increase the value that students place on the task itself. Instead, they link successful task performance with consequences that the students do value. These consequences typically include grades, but they may also include: (1) material rewards (money, prizes, trinkets, food); (2) activity rewards and special privileges (opportunity to play games, use special equipment, or engage in self-selected activities); (3) symbolic rewards (honor rolls, posting good papers on the wall); (4) praise and social rewards; and (5) teacher rewards (opportunities to go places or do things with the teacher).

Offer Rewards or Incentives. Rewards will motivate students to put forth effort, especially if they are offered in advance as incentives for striving to reach specified levels of performance. However, rewards are more effective for stimulating intensity of effort than thoughtfulness or quality of performance, and they guide behavior more effectively when students must follow a familiar path to a clear goal than when they must discover or invent strategies for responding to a new task. Therefore, rewards are better used with routine tasks than with novel ones, better with tasks intended to produce mastery of specific skills than with tasks designed to encourage incidental learning or discovery, and better with tasks where speed of performance or quantity of output is of more concern than creativity, artistry, or craftsmanship. It is more appropriate, for example, to offer rewards as incentives for meeting performance standards on skills that require a great deal of drill and practice (arithmetic computation, typing, spelling) than it is for work on a major research or demonstration project.

It is helpful if rewards are delivered in ways that support attempts to develop motivation to learn, so that students are encouraged to appreciate their developing knowledge and skills, rather than just to think about the rewards. Guidelines for accomplishing this are listed in Table 1. They are phrased in terms of delivering verbal praise, but they can be applied to other types of reward as well.

Rewards will be effective as motivators only for those students who believe that they have a chance to get the rewards if they put forth reasonable effort. If students lack such perceptions, rewards will not be effective and may even backfire by causing depression or resentment. Therefore, to ensure that rewards act as incentives for everyone and not just the high-ability students, everyone must have equal (or at least reasonably equal) access to the rewards.

Structure Appropriate Competition. The opportunity to compete for prizes or recognition can add incentive and excitement to classroom activities. Students may compete either as individuals or as teams. In addition to structuring competition based on test scores or other performance measures, it is possible to build competitive elements into ordinary instruction by including activities such as argumentative essays, debates, or simulation games that involve competition (Keller, 1983).

Two important qualifications need to be kept in mind by teachers who consider using competition as a motivational strategy. First, competition is even more salient and distracting than rewards for many students, so it will be important to depersonalize the competition and emphasize the content being learned rather than who won and who lost. Second, competition will motivate only students who have a good (or at least an equal) chance of winning. In team competition, therefore, teams must be balanced by ability profiles, and individual competition will require a handicapping system to equalize everyone's opportunity to win. Team approaches are more desirable because they can be structured so that students cooperate in addition to competing (members of the same team help one another learn in preparation for competing against other teams). See Slavin (1983) for more information about such team-learning approaches.

Call Attention to the Instrumental Value of Academic Activities. Because much has been written about rewards and competition as extrinsic incentives, and because most teachers are familiar with these techniques, no more will be said about them here. However, we do wish to mention a third strategy for supplying extrinsic motivation: making students aware of the applications of knowledge and skills taught in school to their lives outside of school. Where possible, note that the knowledge or skills developed by a task will be useful in enabling students to meet their own current needs, in easing their social advancement, or in preparing them for occupational success or success in life generally. Better yet, cite concrete examples by relating personal experiences or telling anecdotes about individuals with whom the students

Table 1. Guidelines for Effective Praise.

EFFECTIVE PRAISE	INEFFECTIVE PRAISE
1. Is delivered contingently.	1. Is delivered randomly or unsystematically.
2. Specifies the particulars of the accomplishment.	2. Is restricted to global positive reactions.
3. Shows spontaneity, variety, and other signs of credibility; suggests clear attention to the student's accomplishment.	3. Shows a bland uniformity that suggests a conditioned response made with minimal attention to the student's accomplishment.
4. Rewards attainment of specified performance criteria (which can include effort criteria, however).	4. Rewards mere participation, without consideration of performance processes or outcomes.
5. Provides information to students about their competence or the value of their accomplishments.	5. Provides no information at all or gives students information about their status.
6. Orients students toward better appreciation of their own task-related behavior and thinking about problem solving.	6. Orients students toward comparing themselves with others and thinking about competing.
7. Uses students' own prior accomplishments as the context for describing present accomplishments.	7. Uses the accomplishments of peers as the context for describing students' present accomplishments.
8. Is given in recognition of noteworthy effort or success at difficult (for *this* student) tasks.	8. Is given without regard to the effort expended or the meaning of the accomplishment.
9. Attributes success to effort and ability, implying that similar successes can be expected in the future.	9. Attributes success to ability alone or to external factors such as luck or (easy) task difficulty.
10. Fosters endogenous attributions (students believe that they expend effort on the task because they enjoy the task and/or want to develop task-relevant skills).	10. Fosters exogenous attributions (students believe that they expend effort on the task for external reasons—to please the teacher, win a competition or reward, etc.).
11. Focuses students' attention on their own task-relevant behavior.	11. Focuses students' attention on the teacher as an external authority figure who is manipulating them.
12. Fosters appreciation of, and desirable attributions about, task-relevant behavior after the process is completed.	12. Intrudes into the ongoing process, distracting attention from task-relevant behavior.

SOURCE: From J. Brophy, "Teacher Praise: A Functional Analysis," *Review of Educational Research, 51* (1981), pp. 5–32. Copyright 1981 by American Educational Research Association, Washington, DC. Reprinted with permission.

can identify (famous people that they look up to, former students from the same school, or individuals with whom they are already familiar).

This strategy is probably not used as often as it could be, and when it is used, it is often used in self-defeating ways. Rather than stress the positive by identifying the present or future application of what is being learned, many teachers stress personal embarrassment ("You don't want people to think that you are ignorant") or future educational or occupational disasters ("You'll never get through sixth grade," "How are you going to get a job if you can't do basic math?"). Other teachers use variations that cast the student in a more positive light but portray society as hostile ("Learn to count so that merchants don't cheat you," "Learn to read so that you don't get taken when signing a contract").

Therefore, besides forewarning your students that they will need certain knowledge and skills in the future and making them aware that most desirable occupations require at least a high-school diploma, help them to appreciate the more specific applications of what they are learning. Basic language arts and mathematics skills are used daily when shopping, banking, driving, reading instructions for using products, paying bills and carrying on business correspondence, and planning home-maintenance projects or family vacations. General knowledge is useful for everything from coping effectively with minor everyday challenges to making sound decisions in emergency situations. Knowledge of history and related social studies topics is useful for everything from voting on local issues to determining national policy (as several United States presidents have acknowledged). In general, a good working knowledge of the information, principles, and skills taught in school prepares people to make well-informed decisions that result in savings of time, trouble, expense, or even lives, and it readies them to recognize and take advantage of the opportunities that society offers. These benefits of schooling are well recognized and highly prized in societies where education is still a privilege rather than a right, but they tend to go unrecognized or be taken for granted in societies like ours where mass education is not only available but required. Do what you can to rekindle this appreciation in your students by helping them to see academic activities as enabling opportunities to be valued, rather than as imposed demands to be resisted.

Concluding Comments About Extrinsic Motivational Strategies. Extrinsic motivational strategies can be effective under certain circumstances, but teachers should not rely on them too heavily. If students are preoccupied with rewards or competition, they may not pay as much attention as they should to what they are supposed to be learning, and they may not appreciate its value. The quality of task engagement, and ultimately the quality of achievement, is higher when students perceive themselves to be engaged in tasks for their own reasons (intrinsic motivation) than when they perceive themselves to be engaged in order to please an authority figure, obtain a reward, escape punishment, or respond to some other extrinsic pressure (Deci & Ryan, 1985; Lepper, 1983). More specifically, if students perceive themselves as performing at tasks solely to obtain a reward, they will tend to adopt a "piecework mentality" or "minimax strategy," in which they concentrate on maximizing rewards by meeting minimum standards for performance (and then moving on to something else), rather than on doing a high-quality job (Condry & Chambers, 1978; Kruglanski, 1978). As a result, they may write 300-word essays containing exactly 300 words or read only those parts of a text that they need to read in order to answer the questions on an assignment. You can reduce the risk of encouraging students to develop such undesirable attitudes by following the guidelines in Table 1, but bear in mind that even effective use of motivational strategies will not help students to value academic activities. This will require strategies that capitalize on existing intrinsic motivation or that stimulate students' motivation to learn.

Strategies for Capitalizing on Existing Intrinsic Motivation

The intrinsic motivation approach calls for teachers to select or design academic activities that students will engage in willingly because these activities incorporate content that the students are already interested in or activities that the students enjoy. However, teachers' opportunities to capitalize on students' existing intrinsic motivation are limited by several features inherent to the nature of schooling, which were described at the beginning of the chapter (attendance is compulsory, the curriculum is prescribed externally rather than chosen by the student, mistakes may lead to public embarrassment, and teachers must assign grades and enforce school rules in addition to promoting learning). Furthermore, different students find different topics interesting and different activities enjoyable. Even so, teachers can sometimes take advantage of students' existing intrinsic motivation by selecting or designing classroom activities that incorporate elements that most if not all students will find rewarding. Such elements include the following.

Adapt Tasks to Students' Interests. Whenever particular curriculum objectives can be accomplished using a variety of examples or activities, take advantage of the opportunity to *incorporate content that the students find interesting or activities that they enjoy.* For example, people, fads, or events that are currently prominent in the news or the youth culture can be worked into everyday lessons when giving examples or applications of the concepts being learned. One history teacher we observed, for example, pointed out that the Ark of the Covenant mentioned in his class's ancient history text was the same ark featured in the movie *Raiders of the Lost Ark.* Similarly, a geography teacher sparked student interest in studying latitude and longitude by pointing out that the sunken remains of the *Titanic* were found, even though they lie hundreds of miles out to sea, because the discoverers fixed the location precisely with the coordinates.

Another way to adapt school activities to student interest is to *offer the students a range of tasks so that they can exercise some autonomy in choosing among alternative ways to meet requirements.* Most written composition assignments and many research projects, for example, can be adapted to student interests by allowing students to choose topics or at least by taking their known interests into account when assigning topics. If you think that students might make undesirable choices if left completely on their own, provide them with alternatives to select from, or require them to get your approval of their choice before they proceed.

Finally, you can incorporate student interests into your activities by making it clear that you *encourage student comments and questions* about the topic and by asking questions or making assignments that invite the students to state opinions, make evaluations, or to respond personally to the content in some other way. Relevant student-initiated questions and comments provide "teachable moments" that wise teachers take advantage of, temporarily suspending the planned syllabus in order to pursue the issue that the student raised. The very fact that the question was asked or the comment was made guarantees interest on the part of the student who voiced it, and the chances are that many other students will share this interest as well. Furthermore, classroom research indicates that this teacher behavior is associated both with higher achievement gains by the students and with higher scores on measures of student liking for the subject matter, the class, and the teacher.

It is also helpful, from both an instructional and a motivational point of view, to ensure that your questions and assignments not only cover basic factual knowledge but also *include divergent questions and opportunities for students to express opinions or make other personal responses to the content.* For example, after reviewing the basic facts about the Christians and the lions, the gladiators, and other excesses of the Roman circuses, a history teacher we observed asked the students why they thought such practices had developed in Roman society, how otherwise cultured people could take pleasure in such cruelty, and so on. This led to a very productive discussion in which students made contributions and developed insights on such issues as violence in sports and in society generally in modern times, the role of peer pressure in escalating aggression once a conflict flares up, and the difference between desirable enjoyment of pleasures and undesirable indulgence in excesses. The same teacher, after reviewing differences between Athens and Sparta, asked the students which city they would rather live in, and why. Again, this led to a lively discussion that contrasted modern nations that place heavy priority on building up military strength at a cost in quality of civilian life and those with more balanced priorities.

Plan for Novelty and Variety.   Students faced with the same routines and the same types of tasks each day will soon become bored. Therefore, try to make sure that something about each task (its form, its content, the media involved, or the nature of the responses that it demands) is new to the students or at least different from what they have been doing recently. When introducing an activity to your students, call attention to its new or different elements, and take the opportunity to state that you expect them to find the activity particularly interesting, challenging, or enjoyable.

Provide Opportunities for Students to Respond and to Get Feedback.   Most students prefer activities to allow them to respond actively—to interact with the teacher or with one another, to manipulate materials, or to respond more actively than by just listening or reading. This is one function of drill, recitation, discussion, boardwork, and seatwork activities. Ideally, however, students will often get *active response opportunities* that go beyond the simple question-answer formats seen in typical recitation and seatwork activities. These opportunities include projects, experiments, role play, simulations, educational games, and creative applications of subject matter. For example, language arts instruction should include dramatic readings and prose and poetry composition; mathematics instruction should include problem-solving exercises and realistic application opportunities; science instruction should include experiments, laboratory work, and other applications; and social studies instruction should include debates, research projects, and simulation exercises. Such activities allow students to feel that school learning involves *doing* something, not just having something done to them.

Students particularly enjoy tasks that allow them not only to respond actively, but to get *immediate feedback* that can be used to guide subsequent responses. This is one of the reasons why computer games and other pastimes featured in arcades are so popular (Malone & Lepper, in press). Automatic feedback features are built into many educational toys and Montessori materials used in preschools and kindergartens, and into programmed learning materials and other "self-correcting" materials used in elementary- and secondary-school classrooms. And many computerized learning programs allow students to respond actively and then get immediate feedback.

You can also provide feedback personally for more typical classroom activities. You can do this when going through an activity with the class or a small group or when circulating to supervise progress during seatwork. When you are less available for immediate response (such as when you are teaching a small group and the rest of the students are working at their seats), you can still arrange for students to get feedback by having them check answer keys, follow instructions about how to check their work, consult with an adult volunteer or appointed student helper, or review and discuss the work in pairs or small groups.

Feedback motivates students by giving their activities immediacy and impact. It can be quite boring for students to work through long seatwork assignments without getting feedback from their responses, and they may even be reinforcing errors without realizing it. Even if the work is carefully corrected and good feedback is received a day or two later, the immediacy of the feedback will be lacking.

Psychologically, most students find it much more difficult and less rewarding to try to relearn something that "we did already" than to respond to immediate feedback when learning something for the first time. Therefore, you should avoid putting your students in the position of having to respond for lengthy periods of time without knowing whether or not their responses are correct. There are three basic ways to accomplish this: (1) where possible, design or select activities that enable students to respond and get immediate feedback; (2) for other activities, give thorough enough instructions and work through enough practice examples to enable the students to evaluate the correctness of their responses on their own for the most part; and (3) rather than leaving students on their own, circulate during seatwork to supervise progress and provide immediate feedback and help to those who need it.

Among activities that do allow for active response with immediate feedback, students are likely to especially enjoy activities that allow them to *create a finished product*. Industrial psychologists have shown that workers enjoy jobs that allow them to create a product that they can point to as their own more than they enjoy jobs that do not yield such tangible evidence of their labor. It seems likely that students will respond similarly to academic tasks. That is, they are likely to prefer tasks that have meaning or integrity in their own right to tasks that are mere subparts of some larger entity, and they are likely to experience a satisfying sense of completion or accomplishment when they finish such tasks. Ideally, the finished product will be one that the students can use or display (a map, diagram, or some other illustration; an essay or report; a scale model; a completed puzzle; or something other than just another ditto or workbook page).

Incorporate "Fun" Features.   Most academic activities can be planned to incorporate certain features that most students find enjoyable. Three of these are fantasy or simulation features, gamelike features, and opportunities to interact with peers.

Where more direct applications of what is being learned are not feasible, you can *introduce fantasy or imagination elements that will engage students' interest or allow them to experience events vicariously.* In studying poems or stories, you can tell students about why the authors wrote the poems or stories or about formative experiences in the authors' lives that led to these works. In studying scientific or mathematical principles and methods, you can tell students about the practical problems that needed to be solved or the personal motives of the thinkers that led to the development of the knowledge or skills being taught. Or you can set up role-play or simulation activities that allow students to identify with real or fictional characters or to deal with academic content in direct, personal ways. Rather than just assigning your students to read history, for example, you can make the subject matter come alive by arranging for them to role-play Columbus and his crew after 30 days at sea or to take the roles of different Americans as they learned that Geraldine Ferraro is a candidate for vice president.

Simulation exercises include, but are not confined to, full-scale dramatic productions, role playing, and simulation games. Briefer, more modest simulation exercises can be incorporated into everyday instruction, inviting students to bring fantasy or imagination to bear in thinking about the content they are learning. In teaching a particular mathematical procedure, for example, you might ask students to name problems that come up in everyday living that the procedure might help to solve (and then list these on the board). We observed a history teacher bring ancient history alive by having students describe what facilities they would expect to find in an ancient Roman bath, and a geography teacher "brought home" material on the Soviet Union by asking students to imagine and talk about what it would be like to seek housing in a country where the government owned all of the property, and to get accurate information about world events in a country where the government controlled all of the media. Such fantasy or simulation exercises do not take much time or require special preparations, and they can quite successfully encourage students to relate to the content more personally and to take greater interest in it.

Practice and application activities for almost any kind of content can be presented as games or can be structured to include *features typically associated with games or recreational pastimes* (Keller, 1983; Malone & Lepper, in press). With a bit of imagination, ordinary seatwork assignments can be transformed into "test yourself" challenges, puzzles, or brain teasers. Some of these activities require the students to solve problems, avoid traps, or overcome obstacles in order to reach clearly defined goals (such as exercises that ask students to suggest possible solutions to science or engineering problems or to find a shortcut to use instead of a tedious mathematical procedure). Other such activities challenge the students to "find the problem" by identifying the goal itself and by developing a method for reaching it (many "explore and discover" activities follow this model). Some gamelike activities involve elements of suspense or hidden information that emerges as the activity is completed (puzzles that convey some message or provide the answer to some question once they are filled in). Other such activities involve a degree of randomness or some method of inducing uncertainty about what the outcome of one's performance is likely to be on any given trial (knowledge games that cover a variety of topics at various levels of difficulty that are assigned according to card draws or dice rolls—Trivial Pursuit is an example).

Note that most of these gamelike features involve presenting intellectual challenges appropriate for individual students or groups who work cooperatively. This is mentioned to call attention to the fact that the term "gamelike features" is intended to have a much broader meaning than the typical meaning of the term "games," which most teachers associate specifically with team competitions. There is reason to believe that the gamelike features described here are likely to be both less distracting from curriculum objectives and more effective in promoting student motivation to learn than are competitive games, especially competitive games that emphasize speed in recalling memorized facts rather than integration or application of knowledge.

Most students enjoy activities that allow them to interact with their peers. You can easily build such *peer-interaction opportunities* into classroom activities such as discussion, debate, role playing, or simulation. In addition, you can plan follow-up activities that allow students to work together in pairs or small groups to tutor one another, discuss issues, develop suggested solutions to problems, or work as a team in a competition, a simulation game, or some group project (a report or display, for instance).

Peer-interaction activities are likely to be most effective if: (1) they are sufficiently structured around curriculum objectives to make them worthwhile learning experiences rather than mere occasions for socializing; and (2) conditions are arranged so that every student has a significant role to play and must participate actively in carrying out the group's mission, rather than so that one or two assertive students can dominate the interaction while others just watch. See Slavin, 1983, and Slavin et al., 1985, for more information about peer-interaction and cooperative learning activities.

Concluding Comments About Intrinsic Motivational Strategies. Schooling should be as enjoyable as it can be for both teachers and students. Therefore, whenever curriculum objectives can be met through various activities, wise teachers will emphasize activities that students find rewarding and avoid those that they find boring or aversive. However, two important limitations on what can be accomplished through intrinsic motivational strategies should be kept in mind.

First, your opportunities to use intrinsic motivational strategies in the classroom are limited. You must teach the whole curriculum, not just the parts that appeal to the students, and you must teach factual knowledge and basic skills in addition to higher-level objectives. Opportunities to provide student choices, gamelike features, and so on are restricted. Thus, even if you use these intrinsic motivational strategies optimally, your students will still be in a school, not in a recreational setting, and all of the constraints that are built into the teacher and student roles will still be in place. Learning will often be enjoyable, but it will still require concentration and effort. It will not be the same sort of "fun" as a visit to an arcade or an amusement park.

Second, although intrinsic motivational strategies should increase students' enjoyment of classroom activities, they will not in any direct way increase the students' motivation to learn the content or skills being taught. Therefore, as is the case with extrinsic motivational strategies, these strategies will need to be supplemented with strategies for stimulating motivation to learn (described in the next section). Otherwise, the students may enjoy classroom activities but fail to derive the intended knowledge or skills from them.

In this connection, it is worth noting that our colloquial language for discussing intrinsic motivation is misleading. We commonly describe certain topics or tasks as "intrinsically interesting" and speak of engaging in activities "for their own sake." Taken literally, such language implies that motivation resides in activities rather than in people. In reality, though, *people* generate intrinsic motivation. We study or do something not for *its* sake, but for *ours*—because it brings us pleasure, meets our needs, or in some other way stimulates or satisfies us. We each have our own degrees and patterns of intrinsic motivation, which develop in response to our experiences and to the socialization we receive from significant others in our lives. In the case of motivation to learn academic knowledge and skills, teachers are key "significant others." Therefore, rather than just confining themselves to accommodating classroom activities to students' existing motivational patterns, teachers can try to shape those motivational patterns through systematic socialization efforts designed to stimulate student motivation to learn.

Strategies for Stimulating Student Motivation to Learn

The following strategies are recommended methods of going beyond both manipulation of student performance through extrinsic reward and punishment and intrinsic motivational strategies to promote student engagement in classroom activities to the point of stimulating students' motivation to learn (for example, to take academic activities seriously and attempt to acquire the knowledge or skills that these activities were designed to develop). The first three strategies discussed below are general ones that describe pervasive features of the learning environment that should be established in the classroom. They involve teaching students to understand that the classroom is primarily a place for learning and that acquiring and applying knowledge and skills will affect their overall quality of life, not just their grades.

General Modeling of Motivation to Learn. In all of your interactions with your students, routinely model interest in learning: *let the students see that you value learning as a rewarding, self-actualizing activity that produces personal satisfaction and enriches your life.* In addition to teaching what is in the textbooks, share your interests in current events and items of general knowledge (especially as they relate to aspects of the subject matter that you teach). Call attention to current books, articles, television programs, or movies on the subject. Also, refer to examples or applications of subject matter in everyday living, in the local environment, or in current events.

"Modeling" here means more than just directing attention to examples or applications of concepts taught in school. It also means acting as a model—sharing your thinking about such examples or applications so that your students can see how educated people use information and concepts learned in school to understand and respond to their own everyday experiences and to current events in the news. Without being preachy, you can relate personal experiences that illustrate how language arts knowledge enables you to communicate or express yourself effectively in important situations, how mathematical or scientific know-how enables you to solve everyday household engineering or repair problems, or how social studies knowledge helps you to appreciate what you see in your travels and to understand the significance of events in other parts of the world. You can also voice insights or opinions about current events or how current crises will be resolved. In general, let the students see that it is both stimulating and satisfying to understand (or even just to think or wonder about) what is happening in the world around them (see Good & Brophy, in press, for more information about modeling).

One teacher we observed used modeling effectively in connection with an assignment involving reading about current events in the newspaper. He began by noting that he reads the editorial page of the newspaper regularly and finds that he sometimes agrees and sometimes disagrees with the editorials but that, in either case, they are always informative and thought-provoking. He went on to discuss the newspaper's and his own positions on a forthcoming international summit meeting. He noted that at first he was relatively uninformed about, uninterested in, and pessimistic about the likely outcome of this summit, but that he had become more interested and more optimistic about it as he learned more about it by reading the newspaper and watching the news on television. This led to a stimulating discussion of the positions of the United States, the Soviet Union, the editorial writer, and the teacher on major issues to be discussed at the summit. The teacher generated additional interest and curiosity in the students by noting that although he was sharing his own views on the issues being discussed that day, he often deliberately withheld his positions on issues discussed in class so as to encourage the students to think for themselves and to avoid inhibiting students who might disagree with him. Throughout the discussion, he referred to aspects of the history and geography of the United States and the Soviet Union that helped shape their present rivalry and their positions on the issues to be discussed at the summit meeting. In addition, he communicated the pride and satisfaction he took in "feeling like an expert in world affairs" when he read articles or watched television programs on the summit meeting and realized that he had a good understanding of the issues and events involved. It is likely that this modeling increased his students' interest in and appreciation of the importance and usefulness of social studies concepts and information. In addition, it probably increased their interest in newspaper articles and television programs about current events, as well as providing them with a model to follow in responding to those articles or programs in active, thoughtful ways.

Communicate Desirable Expectations and Attributions. In all of your interactions with students, routinely project attitudes, beliefs, expectations, and attributions (statements about the reasons for students' behavior) that imply that your students share your own enthusiasm for learning. To the extent that you *treat your students as if they already are eager learners*, they will be more likely to become eager learners. Let your students know that you expect them to be curious, to want to learn facts and understand principles clearly, to master skills, and to see their learning as meaningful and applicable to their everyday lives.

At minimum, this means avoiding suggestions that students will dislike working on academic activities or will work on them only in order to get good grades. Better yet, it means treating students as active, motivated learners who care about their learning and are trying to understand (Good & Brophy, 1986, in press). One teacher we observed communicated positive expectations routinely by announcing at the beginning of the year that her class was intended to turn her students into "social scientists," and by referring back to this idea throughout the year through such comments as, "Since you are social scientists, you will recognize that the description of this area as a tropical rain forest has implications about what kinds of crops will grow there," or "Thinking as social scientists, what conclusions might we draw from this information?" Another teacher frequently encouraged his students to "read the material carefully and put it into your own words as you go along so that you will make sure that you understand it. Then answer the questions that follow. Remember, if you really understand the material, you should not only be able to answer the questions correctly but also be able to explain why your answers are correct."

Minimize Students' Performance Anxiety. Motivation is likely to develop most fully in classrooms in which the students are goal-oriented but relaxed enough to be able to concentrate on the task at hand without worrying about whether or not they can meet performance expectations. You can strike this balance by making clear separations between instruction or practice activities designed to promote learning and tests designed to evaluate performance. *Most classroom activities should be structured as learning experiences rather than as tests.*

Where instruction or practice activities include testlike items (recitation questions, practice exercises), treat these as opportunities for the students to work with and apply the material, rather than as attempts to find out who knows the material and who does not. If you expect students to engage in academic activities with motivation to learn (which implies a willingness to take risks and make mistakes), you will need to protect them from anxiety or premature concern about adequate performance.

You must, of course, evaluate student performance and assign grades using tests or other assessment devices. Until that point in the unit, however, the emphasis should be on teaching and learning rather than on evaluation, and students should be encouraged to respond to questions and performance demands in terms of "Let's assess our progress and learn from our mistakes," rather than "Let's see who knows it and who doesn't." Where possible, give students opportunities to correct their mistakes or improve their responses by rephrasing the question or giving them a clue; do not just give the answer or move on to someone else. If you have to give the answer or elicit it from another student, be sure to include any explanation that may be needed to make sure that the first student understands what the correct answer is and why. Have students correct their mistakes on seatwork and homework assignments as well. In general, encourage your students to treat each question and performance demand as an opportunity to check their own understanding or apply what they are learning, and not merely as an opportunity to gain or lose points toward their grades. Where necessary, you may also want to make statements such as, "We're here to learn, and you can't do that without making mistakes," to caution students against laughing at the mistakes their peers make, or to use the strategies for minimizing students' test anxiety that were described earlier in this chapter.

If you consistently implement these three general strategies, you will establish a learning environment in which student motivation to learn can flourish and become a general trait. Then, when implementing particular academic activities, you can supplement these general strategies by using one or more of the following specific strategies for motivating students to learn the content or skills that a particular activity is designed to develop.

Project Intensity. Whenever you instruct, but especially when you present key explanations, you can use timing, nonverbal expressions and gestures, and cueing and other verbal techniques to project a level of intensity that tells students that the material is important and deserves close scrutiny. Such a presentation might begin with a direct statement of the importance of the message ("I'm going to show you how to invert fractions. Now pay close attention and make sure that you understand these procedures"). Then you would present the message itself using verbal and nonverbal public speaking techniques that convey intensity and command attention: a slow-paced, step-by-step presentation during which you emphasize or underline key words, use dramatic voice modulations or gestures to focus attention on key terms or procedural steps, and scan the group intensely after presenting each step to look for signs of understanding or confusion (and to allow anyone with a question to be able to ask it immediately). In addition to what you are saying, everything about *your tone and manner should communicate to the students that what is being said is important* and that they should give it full attention and be prepared to ask questions about anything they do not understand.

Projecting intensity through slower pacing, exaggerated cueing, and related rhetorical techniques is especially useful when demonstrating procedures or problem-solving strategies (as opposed to when merely presenting or reviewing information). Such demonstrations have built-in step-by-step structures that lend themselves to this type of delivery, and the first- or second-person language that is used in modeling or demonstrating procedures lends itself more naturally to a high-intensity communication style than does the third-person language typically used to communicate information.

You cannot be intense all the time. Even if you could, students would adjust to the style so that it would lose much of its effectiveness. Therefore, reserve special intensity for times when you want to communicate "This is important; pay especially close attention." Likely occasions for such communication would include: introduction of important new terms or definitions, especially those likely to be confusing to the students; demonstration of procedures and problem-solving techniques, including instructions for how to do seatwork or homework assignments; instruction in concepts that the students are likely to find confusing or difficult; and instruction that must eliminate currently held misconceptions in addition to teaching new conceptions (thus requiring students to become aware that, even though they think they already understand the point in question, their "knowledge" is in fact incorrect). Dramatic intensity is less appropriate for more routine instructional situations, although teachers are well advised to slow down the pace and be particularly alert for signs of confusion or student desire to ask a question whenever they are covering new or complex material (Gambrell, 1983; Good & Brophy, 1986; Rowe, 1974; Swift & Gooding, 1983; Tobin & Capie, 1982).

Project Enthusiasm. Unless they are already quite familiar with the topic or assignment, students will look to you for cues about how to respond to academic activities. Consciously or not, you model attitudes and beliefs about topics and assignments, and students pick up on these cues. If you convey that a topic or assignment is interesting, important, or worthwhile, your students are likely to adopt this same attitude (Bettencourt et al., 1983). In suggesting that you project enthusiasm, we do not mean that you resort to pep talks or unnecessary theatrics. Instead, we mean that you should identify your own reasons for being interested in a topic or for finding it meaningful or important, and should project these reasons to the students when teaching the topic. Use dramatics or forceful salesmanship if you are comfortable with these techniques, but if not, low-key but sincere statements of the value that you place on a topic or activity will be just as effective. Thus a brief comment showing that a topic is provocative, interesting, unique, or different from previously studied topics may be sufficient. In short, the primary objective of projecting enthusiasm as a strategy for motivating students to learn is to induce the students to value the topic or activity, rather than to amuse, entertain, or excite them.

One history teacher we observed generated a great deal of enthusiasm (as well as pulled together a great many concepts) by eagerly explaining to his students that during the Middle Ages, the Mediterranean was in effect the center of the world, while England was an outpost of civilization. Then, he went on, all of this changed drastically when the New World was discovered and new centers of trade and culture emerged. The teacher used references to maps, reminders about the primary modes of transportation at the time, characterizations of the attitudes of the people in the Middle Ages and Renaissance and their knowledge about other countries and trade routes, and so on. Similarly, another teacher brought ancient Israel alive by elaborating enthusiastically on the textbook in order to tell his students about David as the slayer of Goliath and ancestor of Jesus, Abraham leading his people to the Promised Land, Solomon as a wise man and builder of the Temple, and Moses as the individual who received the Ten Commandments from God and led his people from the wilderness. This discussion also featured use of a map, as well as speculation about whether the temple might be rebuilt in modern Jerusalem (noting that a major Muslim temple is located immediately next to the site of Solomon's Temple). In both of the above cases, the teacher was able to parlay personal interest in a topic, along with detailed knowledge, into a very effective presentation that sparked interest and drew many questions and comments from the students.

Induce Interest in or Appreciation of the Task. You can also induce students' interest in or appreciation of a topic or activity by verbalizing reasons why the students should value it. If the topic or activity is related to something that the students already recognize as interesting or important, this connection should be noted (such as the link between the Ark of the Covenant and *Raiders of the Lost Ark* mentioned earlier). When the knowledge or skills to be taught are relevant to everyday living, their applications should be mentioned (especially those that will allow the students to solve problems or accomplish goals that are important to them). You can also note new, challenging, or especially interesting or exotic aspects of the activities the students can look forward to.

For example, we observed a history teacher motivate students to read about the ancient Greek legal system by noting that it was similar to ours in many ways, except that it called for 501 jurors. And a geography teacher motivated his students to study the map of Greece by explaining that no place in Greece is more than 40 miles from the sea and that the country's jagged contours give it far more coastline than most other countries, including much larger ones.

Induce Curiosity or Suspense.   You can stimulate curiosity or suspense in your students by posing questions or doing "set-ups" that make them feel the need to resolve some ambiguity or obtain more information about a topic. To prepare them to read about the Soviet Union, for example, you could ask your students if they know that Russia is only one part of the Soviet Union, what the term "Iron Curtain" means, how many time zones there are in the Soviet Union, or how the United States acquired Alaska. Such questions help transform just another reading assignment into an interesting experience by encouraging the students to make connections between what they will learn and what they already know (or think they know). Furthermore, by inducing curiosity or suspense, such questions make the new information food for thought rather than merely more material to be memorized. Most students will think that Russia is just another name for the Soviet Union and will be curious to find out the difference once they have been alerted to the fact that a difference exists. Most students will have heard the term "Iron Curtain" but will not have thought much about it, and will want to learn more about it when stimulated to think about it in interesting ways (is there an actual curtain? is it made of iron? if not, why is the term used?). Similarly, most students will be amazed to discover that the Soviet Union encompasses 11 time zones and that the United States purchased Alaska from Russia. Whether or not students find such facts interesting and will think actively about them, rather than merely try to memorize them, will depend largely on the degree to which their teachers stimulate curiosity and provide a context for thinking about associations between these facts and existing knowledge or beliefs. This is another illustration of the point made earlier that interest value does not reside in topics or activities—it resides in people.

You can encourage your students to generate such interest by: (1) asking them to speculate or make predictions about what they will be learning; (2) raising questions that successful completion of the activity will enable them to answer; (3) showing them, where relevant, that their existing knowledge is not complete enough to enable them to accomplish some valued objective, perhaps because the knowledge they hold is logically inconsistent or inconsistent with new information, or that their present knowledge exists in scattered form but could be organized around certain general principles or powerful ideas (Malone & Lepper, in press). More generally, you can put your students into an active information-processing or problem-solving mode by posing interesting questions or problems that the activity will address (Keller, 1983).

Induce Dissonance or Cognitive Conflict. If the topic of a text is already familiar, students may think that they already know everything that there is to know about it, and thus they may read the material with little conscious attention or thought. You can counter this tendency by pointing out unexpected, incongruous, or paradoxical aspects of the content, by calling attention to unusual or exotic elements, by noting exceptions to general rules, or by challenging students to solve the "mystery" that underlies a paradox.

The school curriculum includes a great many "strange but true" phenomena, especially in mathematics and science. You can call attention to such phenomena and get students to begin asking themselves, "How can that be?" Otherwise, students may treat the input as just more information to be absorbed, perhaps without even noticing that it seems to contradict previously learned information. For example, you might introduce the topic of photosynthesis by noting that although animals get their food from the environment, plants make their own food. You might introduce free verse by noting that "some poetry doesn't rhyme." Or you might tell students that "with fractions, we multiply in order to divide."

We have observed several teachers who use these strategies effectively. One introduced a unit on the Middle Ages by telling the students that they would learn about "our ancestors," who chose to remain illiterate and ignorant and who persecuted people who did not share their religion. Later, he noted the Muslim advances in mathematics, medicine, and the construction of libraries, and contrasted these achievements with the illiteracy of most Christians of the time. Another teacher stimulated curiosity about the Persian Empire by noting that Darius was popular with the people he conquered, and by asking the students to speculate reasons why this may have been so. A third teacher introduced a selection on the Trojan War by telling the students that they would read about "how just one horse enabled the Greeks to win a major battle against the Trojans." A fourth introduced a film on the fall of the Roman Empire by saying, "Some say that the factors that led to the decay of the Roman Empire are presently at work in the United States. As you watch the film, see if you notice parallels."

Make Abstract Content More Personal, Concrete, or Familiar. Definitions, principles, and other general or abstract inputs may have little meaning for students unless you discuss them in concrete terms. One way to accomplish this is to promote personal identification with the content by relating experiences or anecdotes that illustrate how the content applies to the lives of particular individuals (especially individuals whom the students are interested in and likely to identify with). For example, we observed a history teacher who read the students a brief passage about Spartacus in order to personalize a selection that they were to read about slavery in ancient times. When covering the Crusades, this teacher put particular emphasis on the Children's Crusade, noting that the children involved were "your age and younger" and that most of them died before this crusade eventually failed. He also made poignant connections with modern Iran, where fundamentalist Islamic zeal is also causing preadolescents to volunteer to go to war. Another teacher brought the medieval guilds alive for her students by asking their reactions to the fact that, had they lived at the time, they would have had to leave their homes as children and spend seven years apprenticed to a master craftsman in order to become journeymen.

You can also make abstractions concrete by showing your class objects or pictures or by conducting demonstrations. You can also help students to relate new or strange content to their existing knowledge by using examples or analogies that refer to familiar concepts, objects, or events. For example, we have observed teachers make the following connections:

1. The Nile River flooding and its effects on Egyptian customs compared to spring flooding in Michigan rivers and its effect on local customs
2. The Washington Monument as a modern example of an obelisk
3. "Three times the size of the Pontiac Silverdome" to describe the size of the largest Roman colosseum
4. Identification of students in the class (or failing that, famous personalities) descended from the ancient peoples or the geographical areas being studied
5. Linking of students' family names to the medieval guilds (Smith, Tanner, Miller, Baker, and so on)
6. Similarities in climate and potential for flower raising and dairy farming as reasons why the Dutch were drawn to the Holland, Michigan, area
7. Similarities in the customs associated with the Roman Saturn Festival compared to those associated with modern Christmas celebrations
8. Explanation of how the medieval social and political system worked by

describing the local (rural central Michigan) area as part of the outlying
lands surrounding a manor based in Lansing, which in turn was protected
by and paid taxes to "the King of Detroit"

Sometimes the content is not too abstract or unfamiliar for the
students to understand, but the text simply does not provide enough
explanation. For example, it is not enough to say that Russia backed
out of World War I because "the revolution came and a new government
was established." This brief statement does not supply enough details
to enable students to comprehend and visualize the events surrounding
the Russian Revolution. To make these events more understandable
to the students, you would have to elaborate on the text by explaining
why and (especially) how the Communists and others organized political
and eventually military resistance to the czar's regime, killed or expelled
the imperial family and key officials, and established a new government.
Such elaboration on the text transforms the relatively meaningless statement that "the revolution came and a new government was established"
into a meaningful statement that students can explain in their own
words because they can relate it to their prior knowledge and visualize
the events to which it refers. This will enable them to actively process
the content instead of just trying to memorize it. As one teacher recently
explained in an interview, good teachers look on texts as outlines to
be elaborated, not as the entire curriculum.

Induce Students to Generate Their Own Motivation to Learn.   You can
induce your students to generate their own motivation to learn by asking
them to think about topics or activities in relation to their own interests
and preconceptions. For example, you can ask the students to note
questions about the topic that they would like to have answered, to
list their particular interests in the topic, or to note things that they
find surprising as they read. Besides generating motivation in a particular situation, such exercises help students to understand that motivation
to learn must come from within—that it is a property of the learner
rather than of the task to be learned (Ortiz, 1983).

State Learning Objectives and Provide Advance Organizers.   Instructional
theorists have shown that learners retain more information when their
learning is goal-directed and when they can structure the information
to be learned around key concepts (Alexander, Frankiewicz, & Williams,
1979; Ausubel, Novak, & Hanesian, 1978; Mayer, 1979). Such theorists
commonly advise teachers to introduce activities by stating learning
objectives (the knowledge or skills that the students should be able to
display when they complete the activities successfully) and by providing
advance organizers (statements or illustrations that characterize the
activity in general terms so that the students will know what to expect
and will be prepared to apply relevant background knowledge or learn-

ing strategies as they engage in it). Stating learning objectives and providing advance organizers are desirable strategies for motivational reasons as well. By calling attention to the nature of the task and the academic benefits that students should get from engaging in it, these techniques help students to establish a learning set to use in guiding their responses to the task.

You can prepare your students to get more out of lectures, films, or reading assignments by clarifying what you want them to concentrate on or think about as they process the information. You may want to distribute a partially filled in outline or study guide, for example, or to give specific guidelines about note taking (Carrier & Titus, 1979; Kierwa, 1985; Ladas, 1980). If particular structuring devices have been built into the content (lists, generalizations followed by elaborations, comparison or contrast structures, historical narratives or other sequential descriptions, or presentations of rules followed by examples, questions followed by answers, or concept definitions followed by examples of the concept), you could call the students' attention to these structural elements so as to increase the likelihood that the students will be able to use them to help them organize and remember what they learn (Armbruster & Anderson, 1984). In general, to the extent that you can be clear about exactly how you want your students to approach an activity (memorizing verbatim vs. getting the gist and being able to explain it in their own words; degree of emphasis on specific facts vs. more general principles or applications; use of particular main ideas for organizing vs. interpreting the larger body of information), your students will be more likely to adopt the appropriate learning set and get what you want them to get out of the activity.

Provide Informative Feedback. Feedback was discussed previously in connection with other aspects of student motivation, but we mention it again briefly here to underscore its importance as part of a systematic attempt to encourage students to engage in academic activities with motivation to learn. If students are to function as active learners, they need opportunities to assess their progress in understanding content or mastering skills—in short, opportunities to make responses and get feedback. Therefore, as soon as possible after exposing them to information, you should give your students questions or assignments that will require them to restate the information in their own words, to show that they understand the input and can apply it successfully, or to summarize, integrate, or evaluate what they have learned. Such response opportunities and the feedback associated with them will motivate students' learning by reinforcing their sense of competence or efficacy (when learning has been successful) or by underscoring the need for further efforts (when it has not).

Model Task-Related Thinking and Problem Solving. The information-processing and problem-solving strategies that you use when thinking about curricular content and responding to academic tasks will be unknown to your students unless you make these strategies overt and observable by modeling them. Therefore, when teaching particular content, and especially when demonstrating skills or problem-solving strategies, do not just tell the students what to do in second- or third-person language. In addition, model the process by showing the students what to do, and think out loud as you demonstrate. Include the thinking that goes into selecting the general approach to use, deciding on options to take, checking progress as you go along, and satisfying yourself that you are on the right track. Model recovery from false starts and from occasional use of inappropriate strategies as well, so that students can see how one can develop a successful strategy even when one is not sure about what to do at first (Diener & Dweck, 1978).

This kind of *cognitive modeling* (thinking out loud so that students can observe one's information-processing and problem-solving strategies) can be powerful not only as an instructional device but as a way to socialize student motivation to learn (see Chapter 10). That is, in addition to modeling the particular strategies needed for the task at hand, it is a way to show students what it means to approach a task with motivation to learn by modeling some of the general beliefs and attitudes associated with such motivation (patience, confidence, persistence in seeking solutions through information processing and rational decision making, benefiting from the information supplied by mistakes rather than giving up in frustration).

Modeling opportunities arise whenever an academic activity calls for use of some cognitive process or strategy. Among other things, this includes demonstrations of how to conduct scientific experiments, understand and develop ways to solve mathematics problems, identify the main ideas in paragraphs, develop a plan for conducting a research project or an outline for writing a composition, identify the moral of a story, induce general principles from collections of facts, deduce applications of general principles to specific situations, check your own understanding of content by trying to answer questions about it or paraphrase it into your own words, or find and correct your own errors. (For more information on modeling as a motivational technique, see Good and Brophy, 1986, in press.)

Concluding Comments About Strategies for Motivating Students to Learn.
Contemporary learning theorists have shown that learning, and most especially the kind of cognitive learning emphasized in school, is not mere response to stimulation. Nor is teaching mere infusion of knowledge into a vacuum. Learning involves active processing of input and making sense of it by relating it to existing knowledge, ideally in ways that involve transformation of the input into the student's own words and retention in a form that makes it easily accessible for retrieval or application. Similarly, ideal teaching involves not only presenting input to students but helping them to be able to process the input using

generative learning strategies (Weinstein & Mayer, 1986) for processing the input actively, relating it to their existing knowledge, putting it into their own words, making sure that they understand it, and so on. In the classroom context, motivating students to learn means not only stimulating them to take an interest in and see the value of what they are learning, but also providing them with guidance about how to go about learning it. Although strategies for effectively motivating students to learn can be discussed separately for purposes of analysis, in practice they are closely intertwined with strategies for planning and implementing effective instruction generally.

Consequently, the motivational strategies described in this chapter will be most effective if they are used in conjunction with instructional strategies designed to teach students to be aware of their goals during task engagement, to monitor the strategies that they use to pursue these goals, to note the effects of these strategies as they are used, and to monitor their subjective responses to these unfolding events. Ideally, then, students not only will be motivated to learn and armed with cognitive strategies for doing so, but also will be able to maintain metacognitive awareness of what they are doing as they do it, in order to monitor their progress and adjust their strategies if necessary. (For information about cognitive and metacognitive strategy training with students, see Baker & Brown, 1984; Book et al., 1985; Good & Brophy, 1986; McCombs, 1984; Palincsar & Brown, 1984; Paris, Cross, & Lipson, 1984; Roehler & Duffy, 1984; and Weinstein & Mayer, 1986.)

BUILDING MOTIVATIONAL STRATEGIES INTO YOUR INSTRUCTIONAL PLANS

When planning courses from scratch, you can study the strategies discussed in this chapter and list ways that they can be implemented in the process of reaching the objectives to be included in the curriculum. More typically, however, you will be working with given curricula and materials and will need to incorporate the strategies into your instructional plans or adjust these plans as needed. Thinking about the following questions may be helpful for this purpose.

For All Activities

Consider the following questions when planning any academic activity.

Objectives. What are the curricular and instructional goals of the activity? How do these translate into specific objectives for the students? (What will the students be able to do when they complete the activity? Why are they learning this information or skill? When and how will they use it?) Convey this information to the students through the learning objectives that you state when introducing the activity to them.

Advance Organizers. Before getting into the activity itself, how can you characterize it for the students in familiar, general terms that indicate the nature of the activity and provide organizing concepts that encompass the more specific information to be presented? Communicate such advance organizers to the students (typically right before mentioning the learning objectives).

Interest/Application/Curiosity/Suspense/Dissonance. Does the activity produce information that the students are likely to find interesting or build skills that they are eager to develop? Does it contain unusual or surprising input? Can the content be related to current events or events in the students' lives? Can you create dissonance by telling students about something surprising that they will learn through this activity and inviting them to speculate about how it could be true? Are there ways to stimulate curiosity or create suspense by posing interesting questions? Where the answer to one or more of these questions is yes, capitalize on the opportunity to induce student motivation to learn by creating interest, appreciation, curiosity, suspense, or dissonance when you introduce the activity.

Listening and Reading Activities

Consider the following questions when planning activities that require students to attend to an oral presentation, watch a visual presentation, or learn by reading.

Enthusiasm. What is your personal response to the content? What do you find interesting or noteworthy about it? What aspects are particularly important, and why? Your answers to these questions represent your own enthusiasm about the subject, and this should be communicated to the students during your presentation.

Personalization. Are there any personal experiences that you can share or objects that you can display that are related to the content? Are you aware of content-related anecdotes about the experiences of others or about how the knowledge was discovered? Including such stories should spice up the presentation.

Variety in Cognitive Level. Does your presentation contain sufficient variety in the cognitive levels of information communicated and the types of response demanded? Ordinarily, the presentation should not be confined to facts and terms for students to memorize. It should include attention to skills or applications as well as analysis, synthesis, or evaluation of the content.

Provision for Active Response. What is the anticipated length of the presentation? If it appears that there will be too much uninterrupted lecture, plan to break up the presentation by asking questions, initiating discussion, or allowing time for students to take notes or respond to a study guide or brief assignment.

Preparing the Students to Process the Information. How should the students respond to the presentation or text? Should they take notes or underline key ideas? Should they keep particular issues or questions in mind as they listen or read? Should they be given a set of questions, a partially filled-in outline, or a study guide to respond to while listening or reading? Are there particular organizational structures that the students can recognize and use in learning (lists, generalizations followed by elaborations, compare/contrast structures, historical narratives or other sequential descriptions, description of wholes followed by descriptions of each of the parts, presentations of rules followed by examples, questions followed by answers, or concept definitions followed by examples and nonexamples of the concept)? To the extent that you want students to do something more specific than just pay attention and try to get the most they can out of the experience, tell them specifically what you want them to do. If necessary, help them by supplying questions, outlines, study guides, or information about how the material is organized.

Problem Prevention. Is there some key point that the students might easily miss if not forewarned? Does the presentation or text contain abstractions that will not be meaningful to the students without additional explanation or concrete examples? Are there concepts that the students may have trouble with because they are subtle or difficult, because they are not well explained in the text, or because they conflict with the students' personal experiences or expectations? If so, you may want to adjust your presentation to allow for extra attention to these trouble spots, or to prepare students by making sure that they have the prerequisite knowledge they will need to get the intended benefit from the presentation or text.

For Activities Requiring Active Response

Consider the following questions when planning activities or assignments that require students to do something more active than listen or read (answer questions, prepare a report, work on a project, and so on).

A Learning Experience, Not a Test. How can you make sure that the students see the activity as an opportunity to apply knowledge or develop skill rather than as a test (unless it *is* a test)? When and how might you encourage students to ask questions and seek whatever information or help they may need to clear up confusion and perform well?

Modeling. Does the activity demand new or complex responses that should be modeled for the students? If so, work through several examples by thinking out loud as you perform each step, explaining any information gathering or decision making that is involved and the rationales for actions and demonstrating the actions themselves. In addition to modeling ideal performance (making all the right decisions and moving through the task smoothly), model hypothesis-testing strategies (considering two or more alternatives at a choice point and selecting the correct one after reasoning or brief experimentation) and troubleshooting or repair strategies (discovering that you have selected an inappropriate strategy or made some other mistake and rechecking or using logical reasoning to identify and correct the problem). In general, to the extent that successful performance depends on effective planning, thinking, decision making, and covert problem solving, make sure that you model these mental processes for the students in addition to demonstrating the more overt responses.

Feedback. When, how, and from whom will the students receive feedback on their performance? What should they do if they do not understand a question or are not sure about how to respond? What should they do when they think they are finished? Try to arrange activities so that students can get the feedback they need when they need it.

Metacognitive Awareness. What can you do to ensure that the students will monitor and correct the strategies that they use to respond to the activity? Good modeling is probably the most important factor here. In addition, though, it is helpful (when you are giving your initial instructions) to remind students to pay attention to the strategies they use, as well as to ask questions about these strategies (when you are providing help or giving feedback). It is also helpful if your instructions and feedback reinforce what you have told the students about learning objectives (to help them keep in mind that the point of the activity is to help them understand or apply knowledge or skill, and not merely to produce correct responses to a particular set of questions).

CONCLUSION

Although it cannot be taught directly like a concept or skill, student motivation to learn academic content and skills can be developed by teachers who systematically socialize their students using the strategies discussed above as part of a larger package of curriculum and instruction that is also effective with respect to other criteria. The list of strategies presented here is not complete; undoubtedly further research will identify new tactics and additional qualifications on the use of strategies we have described. Nevertheless, the present list makes a good "starter set" of strategies to select from in planning to motivate your students to learn. In particular, it serves as a reminder that students need not only to be given incentives for good performance and activities that they will enjoy as much as possible, but also to be motivated to learn the knowledge and skills being taught.

ACKNOWLEDGMENTS: This work is sponsored in part by the Institute for Research on Teaching, College of Education, Michigan State University. The Institute for Research on Teaching is funded primarily by the Program for Teaching and Instruction of the National Institute of Education, United States Department of Education. The opinions expressed in this publication do not necessarily reflect the position, policy, or endorsement of the National Institute of Education. (Contract No. 400–81–0014)

The author wishes to thank June Smith for her assistance in preparation of this chapter.

REFERENCES

Alexander, L., Frankiewicz, R., & Williams, R. (1979). Facilitation of learning and retention of oral instruction using advance and post organizers. *Journal of Educational Psychology, 71,* 701–707.

Ames, C., & Ames, R. (Eds.). (1985). *Research on motivation in education, volume II: The classroom milieu.* Orlando, FL: Academic.

Ames, R., & Ames, C. (Eds.). (1984). *Research on motivation in education, volume I: Student motivation.* New York: Academic.

Anderson, L., Brubaker, N., Alleman-Brooks, J., & Duffy, G. (1984). *Making seatwork work.* (Research Series No. 142). East Lansing, MI: Institute for Research on Teaching, Michigan State University.

Armbruster, B., & Anderson, T. (1984). Structures of explanations in history textbooks, or so what if Governor Stanford missed the spike and hit the rail? *Journal of Curriculum Studies, 16,* 181–194.

Ausubel, D., Novak, J., & Hanesian, H. (1978). *Educational psychology: A cognitive view.* New York: Holt, Rinehart & Winston.

Baker, F., & Brown, A. (1984). Metacognitive skills and reading. In P. Pearson, M. Kamil, R. Barr, & P. Mosenthal (Eds.), *Handbook of reading research.* New York: Longman.

Bandura, A., & Schunk, D. (1981). Cultivating competence, self-efficacy, and intrinsic interest through proximal self-motivation. *Journal of Personality and Social Psychology, 41,* 586–598.

Bettencourt, E., Gillett, M., Gall, M., & Hull, R. (1983). Effects of teacher enthusiasm training on student on-task behavior and achievement. *American Educational Research Journal, 20,* 435–450.

Blumenfeld, P., Hamilton, V., Bossert, S., Wessels, K., & Meece, J. (1983). Teacher talk and student thought: Socialization into the student role. In J. Levine & M. Wang (Eds.), *Teacher and student perceptions: Implications for learning.* Hillsdale, NJ: Erlbaum.

Book, C., Duffy, G., Roehler, L., Meloth, M., & Vavrus, L. (1985). A study of the relationships between teacher explanation and student metacognitive awareness during reading instruction. *Communication Education, 34,* 29–36.

Brophy, J. (1983). Conceptualizing student motivation. *Educational Psychologist, 18,* 200–215.

Brophy, J., Rohrkemper, M., Rashid, H., & Goldberger, M. (1983). Relationships between teachers' presentations of classroom tasks and students' engagement in those tasks. *Journal of Educational Psychology, 75,* 544–552.

Carrier, C., & Titus, A. (1979). The effects of notetaking: A review of studies. *Contemporary Educational Psychology, 4,* 299–314.

Condry, J., & Chambers, J. (1978). Intrinsic motivation and the process of learning. In M. Lepper & D. Greene (Eds.), *The hidden costs of reward: New perspectives on the psychology of human motivation.* Hillsdale, NJ: Erlbaum.

Corno, L., & Mandinach, E. (1983). The role of cognitive engagement in classroom learning and motivation. *Educational Psychologist, 18,* 88–108.

Corno, L., & Rohrkemper, M. (1985). The intrinsic motivation to learn in classrooms. In C. Ames & R. Ames (Eds.), *Research on motivation in education, volume II: The classroom milieu.* Orlando, FL: Academic.

Craske, M. L. (1985). Improving persistence through observational learning and attribution retraining. *British Journal of Educational Psychology, 55,* 138–147.

Deci, E., & Ryan, R. (1985). *Intrinsic motivation and self-determination in human behavior.* New York: Plenum.

Diener, D., & Dweck, C. (1978). An analysis of learned helplessness: Continuous changes in performance, strategy, and achievement cognitions following failure. *Journal of Personality and Social Psychology, 36,* 451–462.

Doyle, W. (1983). Academic work. *Review of Educational Research, 53,* 159–199.

Dweck, C., & Elliott, E. (1983). Achievement motivation. In P. Mussen (Ed.), *Handbook of child psychology, 4th ed., Vol. IV: Socialization, personality, and social development.* New York: Wiley.

Elawar, M. C., & Corno, L. (1985). A factorial experiment in teachers' written feedback on student homework: Changing teacher behavior a little rather than a lot. *Journal of Educational Psychology, 77,* 162–173.

Feather, N. (Ed.). (1982). *Expectations and actions.* Hillsdale, NJ: Erlbaum.

Fowler, J. W., & Peterson, P. L. (1981). Increasing reading persistence and altering attributional style of learned helpless children. *Journal of Educational Psychology, 73,* 251–260.

Gambrell, L. (1983). The occurrence of think-time during reading comprehension instruction. *Journal of Educational Research, 77,* 77–80.

Good, T., & Brophy, J. (1986). *Educational psychology: A realistic approach,* 3rd ed. New York: Longman.

———. (in press). *Looking in classrooms,* 4th ed. New York: Harper & Row.

Grabe, M. (1985). Attributions in a Mastery instructional system: Is an emphasis on effort harmful? *Contemporary Educational Psychology, 10,* 113–126.

Harter, S. (1981). A new self-report scale of intrinsic versus extrinsic orientation in the classroom: Motivational and informational components. *Developmental Psychology, 17,* 300–317.

Hill, K. T., & Wigfield, A. (1984). Test anxiety: A major educational problem and what can be done about it. *Elementary School Journal, 85,* 105–126.

Keller, J. (1983). Motivational design of instruction. In C. Reigeluth (Ed.), *Instructional-design theories and models: An overview of their current status.* Hillsdale, NJ: Erlbaum.

Kierwa, K. (1985). Investigating notetaking and review: A depth of processing alternative. *Educational Psychologist, 20,* 23–32.

Kolesnik, W. (1978). *Motivation: Understanding and influencing human behavior.* Boston: Allyn & Bacon.

Kruglanski, A. (1978). Endogenous attribution and intrinsic motivation. In M. Lepper & D. Greene (Eds.), *The hidden costs of reward: New perspectives on the psychology of human motivation.* Hillsdale, NJ: Erlbaum.

Ladas, H. (1980). Summarizing research: A case study. *Review of Educational Research, 50,* 597–624.

Lepper, M. (1983). Extrinsic reward and intrinsic motivation: Implications for the classroom. In J. Levine & M. Wang (Eds.), *Teacher and student perspectives: Implications for learning.* Hillsdale, NJ: Erlbaum.

Lepper, M., & Greene, D. (Eds.). (1978). *The hidden costs of reward: New perspectives on the psychology of human motivation.* Hillsdale, NJ: Erlbaum.

Levine, D. (Ed.). (1985). *Improving student achievement through Mastery Learning programs.* San Francisco: Jossey-Bass.

Maehr, M. (1984). Meaning and motivation: Toward a theory of personal investment. In R. Ames & C. Ames (Eds.), *Research on motivation in education, Volume I: Student motivation.* Orlando, FL: Academic.

Malone, T., & Lepper, M. (in press). Making learning fun: A taxonomy of intrinsic motivation for learning. In R. Snow & M. Farr (Eds.), *Aptitude, learning, and instruction: III. Conative and affective process analysis.* Hillsdale, NJ: Erlbaum.

Marshall, H. (1986). Games teachers and students play: An analysis of motivation in three fifth-grade classrooms. Paper presented at the annual meeting of the American Educational Research Association, San Francisco, April 1986.

Mayer, R. (1979). Can advance organizers influence meaningful learning? *Review of Educational Research, 49,* 371–383.

McColskey, W., & Leary, M. R. (1985). Differential effects of norm-referenced and self-referenced feedback on performance expectancies, attributions, and motivation. *Contemporary Educational Psychology, 10,* 275–284.

McCombs, B. (1984). Processes and skills underlying continuing intrinsic motivation to learn: Toward a definition of motivational skills training and interventions. *Educational Psychologist, 19,* 199–218.

Medway, F. M., & Venino, G. R. (1982). The effects of effort feedback and performance patterns on children's attribution and task persistence. *Contemporary Educational Psychology, 7,* 26–34.

Morgan, M. (1985). Self-monitoring of attained subgoals in private study. *Journal of Educational Psychology, 77,* 623–630.

Nicholls, J. (1984). Conceptions of ability and achievement motivation. In R. Ames & C. Ames (Eds.), *Research on motivation in education, Volume I: Student motivation.* Orlando, FL: Academic.

Ortiz, R. (1983). Generating interest in reading. *Journal of Reading, 27*, 113–119.

Palincsar, A., & Brown, A. (1984). Reciprocal teaching of comprehension-fostering and comprehension-monitoring activities. *Cognition and Instruction, 1*, 117–175.

Paris, S., Cross, D., & Lipson, M. (1984). Informed strategies for learning: A program to improve children's reading awareness and comprehension. *Journal of Educational Psychology, 76*, 1239–1252.

Plass, J. A., & Hill, K. T. (1986). Children's achievement strategies and test performance: The role of time pressure, evaluation anxiety, and sex. *Developmental Psychology, 22*, 31–36.

Roehler, L., & Duffy, G. (1984). Direct explanation of comprehension processes. In G. Duffy, L. Roehler, & J. Mason (Eds.), *Comprehension instruction: Perspectives and suggestions*. New York: Longman.

Rohrkemper, M., & Bershon, B. (1984). Elementary school students' reports of the causes and effects of problem difficulty in mathematics. *Elementary School Journal, 85*, 127–147.

Rowe, M. (1974). Pausing phenomena: Influence on quality of instruction. *Journal of Psycholinguistic Research, 3*, 203–224.

Schunk, D. H. (1983). Self-efficacy and classroom learning. *Psychology in the Schools, 22*, 208–223.

Slavin, R. (1983). *Cooperative learning*. New York: Longman.

Slavin, R., Sharan, S., Kagan, S., Lazarowitz, R., Webb, C., & Schmuck, R. (Eds.). (1985). *Learning to cooperate, cooperating to learn*. New York: Plenum.

Swift, N., & Gooding, C. (1983). Interaction of wait-time feedback and questioning instruction on middle school science teaching. *Journal of Research in Science Teaching, 20*, 721–730.

Tobin, K., & Capie, W. (1982). Relationships between classroom process variables and middle-school science achievement. *Journal of Educational Psychology, 74*, 441–454.

Tollefson, N., Tracy, D., Johnsen, E., Farmer, W., & Buenning, M. (1984). Goal setting and personal responsibility for LD adolescents. *Psychology in the Schools, 21*, 224–233.

Weinstein, C., & Mayer, R. (1986). The teaching of learning strategies. In M. Wittrock (Ed.), *Handbook of research on teaching*, 3rd ed. New York: Macmillan.

Wlodkowski, R. J. (1978). *Motivation and teaching: A practical guide*. Washington, DC: National Education Association.

STUDENT COGNITIONS

PART IV

STUDENT COGNITIONS

CHAPTER 10

LYN CORNO

TEACHING AND SELF-REGULATED LEARNING

Do every day or two something for no other reason than that you would rather not do it, so that when the hour of dire need draws nigh, it may find you not unnerved and untrained to stand the test.
—WILLIAM JAMES, *Principles of Psychology* (1890)

Most teachers are grateful for their few students who are self-starters—students who really seem to know what to do and who do it almost without being asked. Those of us who study teaching are interested in these self-starters as well. There is a body of work currently addressing the issue called theory and research on *self-regulated learning*. Self-regulated learners are said to be *enactive*, rather than reactive or merely active. They apply themselves in a way that makes learning easier. They have, as one theorist said, "tools of personal agency" (Bandura, 1983, p. 754)—academic learning skills and a kind of self-control—that create a facility for learning that in turn sustains the desire to learn. Again, while most teachers know some students like this, self-regulated learners are not, unfortunately, the norm. Even the benefits of advanced cognitive development fail to guarantee self-regulation; enactive involvement with learning is in part, but not entirely, a function of cognitive competence, and it can also be used to develop cognitive competence in students. The position I would like to advance here is that we can promote self-regulated learning through teaching. The argument rests on some key ideas about self-regulation and how it develops naturally, as well as on some recent research on teaching.

SELF-REGULATED LEARNING AND HOW IT DEVELOPS

One of the most important outcomes of modern research on human learning has been a better understanding of an old idea that dates back to Plato: that people use what they already know as a kind of

249

framework or template for interpreting the new and unfamiliar (see, for example, Resnick, 1983; Phillips & Soltis, 1985). The knowledge and attitudes that students already hold about a subject will color and filter what I, as a teacher, might have them learn on a given day. So in teaching new material, I must accept—and perhaps plan for— the fact that each student, no matter what I do, will come to understand the subject on his or her own terms.

In teaching something about self-regulated learning here, for example, I can engineer my presentation to promote your interest in and further your knowledge of the subject, but I also must ask for your assistance in this process. That is, when I give a talk in which I hope to teach something, I design it to maximize your role. Being considerate of my audience's information-processing limitations, I use a logical sequence and plenty of examples to which I hope people can relate. I attempt, as John Dewey said, to "lay bare the skeleton of the subject" as a simplified whole. Also, when I give a talk, I implicitly, if not explicitly, convey the message that the audience should use a number of conventional techniques for learning from lectures—such as note taking, repeating phrases to oneself, and paraphrasing—which I assume have become second nature over the years.

Here is where self-regulated learners separate from the rest. They will want to learn from my talk, and so they will do things to make that happen. They will ponder my anecdotes and examples. They may take notes or make mental notes to validate things I have said. They might even ask me to clarify something confusing or explain something further. They might, like my graduate students have begun doing, audiotape the talk and analyze it later. In this way, students can even make up for deficiencies in my talk. They can force me to give better or more examples, or to extend and apply ideas in different ways. If others in the room hear what the self-regulated learners say, they can benefit as well. In short, these learners direct the educational experience to ensure that learning occurs.

The extent to which any individual does any of these things when listening to a talk depends, however, on a number of conditions that may or may not exist. We need to understand these conditions in order to foster them in school, so let me discuss them here briefly. They fall broadly into three important areas: motivation, volition, and cognitive competency.

Motivation

I have already said that enactive engagement in academic tasks depends in part on an *intent* to learn. Motivation theory and research say that intent is influenced, first, by the "carrot" or incentive—what knowing more about a subject will gain someone and how much that outcome means (see, for instance, Weiner, 1980). If ideas I am discussing here were to give teachers the means to instill an enthusiasm for learning in unruly high-school students, these ideas might well be worth more than if they were only to be learned for continuing education credits at a local university. Both these goals may be meaningful for teachers, but the former has an immediate impact on daily experience that probably outweighs the latter. It is also important to realize that the values we place on such anticipated outcomes differ from person to person and change over our lifetimes. In any case, our valued goals act as incentives.

Other factors that influence the intent or commitment to learn are *perceived blocks* to valued goals. These include perceptions that a task is difficult or boring, or that there are too many factors over which one has no control. If a student's willingness to try is jeopardized when any of these motivational factors reaches a critical point, it should not surprise us that he or she will resist school. School tasks often *are* difficult; they may be *designed* so that only some will succeed, and they typically require students to use a particular approach that is not of their own choosing. In the possible event that we change the situation—that we permit students to select their own approach to classroom tasks, and we design tasks that are more relevant to students' interests or more "meaningful" (Ryan et al., 1985)—students might intend to learn and try in school. But that would still address only part of the story. Besides motivation, we need to consider what is known about volition or self-discipline.

Volition

According to theories of volition, a student may well intend to learn in school but be unable to protect that intent from competing intentions or distractions. He or she may be unable to mobilize the strategies for ensuring learning at the appropriate time (Kuhl & Beckmann, 1985). In this instance, the student is said to have a *self-management* problem; there is a failure to plan and control learning. This may be happening because other more interesting thoughts captivate the student; or it may be because the student is distracted by something else, or anxious about the task, or feeling lazy, or some combination of these. Here there is a failure to produce the desired behavior, despite adequate capabilities and intent, and this can be traced to a lack of self-discipline or a failure to apply appropriate control strategies (Corno, 1986b).

Cognitive Competency

Students may both intend to learn and be able to control their intention but still fail to accomplish tasks because they do not have effective learning strategies or do not know how to use them when situations demand. Here the problem is one of competence. When knowing how to learn in school is outside a student's repertoire, poor performance is not surprising. Research has shown that people who score high on standardized ability tests characteristically use effective *learning strategies*—strategies that allow them to grasp the essence of subject matter and to commit it to long-term memory (Snow & Lohman, 1984). The consistent and deliberate application of such strategies at appropriate times is in fact the trademark of excellent performance. Among psychologists, the extreme view is that the tendency for an individual to readily call up self-regulatory mechanisms (such as learning and self-management strategies) when learning and solving problems is a major ingredient of general intelligence (Sternberg, 1982). What is important for us here is that, without knowing effective learning strategies, students are likely to think learning is hard work, as well as something they are not good at, and that this situation will never change—that it will follow them through life, limiting their future choices and chances.

In the jargon of motivation theory, we say that patterns of motivation, whether constructive or destructive, develop a kind of functional autonomy (Allport, 1963). A destructive pattern leads the student into a downward spiral with respect to schoolwork from which he or she may never recover. The combination of failures and public records or knowledge of them, coupled with a tendency to interpret failure in ways that reflect badly on oneself, results in low expectations for success and a belief that one's own efforts will do little to compensate for past poor performance (Weiner, 1980). This self-limiting belief has been called *learned helplessness* (Seligman, 1975). Students who have learned to be helpless will tend to withdraw from performance situations when given a choice (and often even when not given a choice)—they will simply refuse to try to study and learn. Many school dropouts have been shown to exhibit this syndrome, particularly lower-class minority students, whose perceptions actually have some basis in social realities (Nicholls, 1983).

On the other hand, when students begin to learn how to learn—including how to adapt tasks in ways that remove perceived blocks—and how to manage and control their concentration in school, they generally find that learning becomes easier (Corno & Rohrkemper, 1985; Novak & Gowin, 1984; Palincsar & Brown, 1984). *Effective* strategies for the different learning situations we encounter in school—whether they be lectures, classroom recitation, textbooks, group work, or independent problem solving—steer learning along. They reduce the information-processing burden of schoolwork, and while they may not make learning fun for all of us, they do allow us to build a storehouse of knowledge that leads to the kinds of success experiences in school that, in turn, relate to positive feelings about oneself as a learner and a competent person.

There is growing knowledge that self-regulation is an aspect of intelligence that develops through experience and example (Brown, 1978;

Flavell, 1970; Meichenbaum, 1977). It seems we can teach students to become self-regulated learners (Corno & Mandinach, 1983; Mandinach & Corno, 1985). And at a time when most states are including the teaching of thinking and learning skills among their objectives for public education, this news should appeal. But we also need to appreciate the synergistic connection between a student's cognitive competence and his or her academic motivation and volition.

Whenever I talk to teachers, I sense an almost desperate concern about how to motivate students to learn. Many of us seem to view motivation as our biggest problem; it is both elusive and complex. Clearly, teachers wonder how it develops. But what I find interesting is the fact that, while there is no shortage of available techniques for motivating students in school, these lists of techniques often quickly wear thin. They do not always seem sensible, and they usually imply that the teacher has to be designing lessons that constantly grab and hold student attention. That is tough. Also, most of us have already tried many of the techniques in the books and have found that sometimes they work and sometimes they do not. When they fail it is not always clear what to try next. If this strikes a familiar chord, it may help to know that many teachers' intuitions on this subject seem to reflect what the research has shown to be true: that one of the best things we can do to help motivate students for school learning is to teach them how to *self-motivate, and then to require this in school tasks.* Once a student knows how to manage and control his own learning and begins to apply that knowledge to assigned tasks, there is no more powerful or reliable motivator.

Significantly, the evidence seems to suggest that the route to self-motivation—a sort of reflective awareness of how and why one performs—is through learning how to learn in those situations we define as school tasks and through learning how to manage and control the learning process. Again, the combination of techniques for maintaining concentration, simplifying and reducing material to be learned, and making it one's own has been termed self-regulated learning. The self-management aspect of self-regulation is believed to direct and control concentration during school tasks; the use of appropriate learning strategies plays an important role in retention and transfer (Corno & Rohrkemper, 1985).

Let us now turn to the evidence that supports this view. The key research question being addressed is; What aspects of self-regulation are most relevant for academic work, and how can these be taught to students who might benefit from them? To answer the first part of this question, we can draw from research on the self-management and learning strategies students use naturally on academic tasks. We can also cite research that has trained students to use particular strategies and assessed effects on performance. The second part of our question suggests an exploration of the way in which students come to acquire self-regulatory capabilities in the natural environments to which they are exposed. And finally, we should consider research attempting to develop self-regulation along similar naturalistic lines.

THE RESEARCH BASE OF SELF-REGULATION AND TEACHING

The research base of self-regulation and teaching is still young; the earliest studies were published in the 1970s. Most of these studies were conducted in situations in which students completed academic tasks individually and away from the distractions of the natural classroom. The results are difficult to generalize to the situations that interest us here. While we can draw on such research for promising leads, studies conducted in actual classrooms where students learn real school material are more relevant. Again, there have been few such investigations to date (most published since 1983), but we have enough to provide some important examples.

One study by Peterson et al. (1983) asked sixth-graders to describe what they thought about in class. To help students remember their thoughts, the researchers videotaped lessons and played them back for students, stopping the tape at various points. Here is what one student said he was thinking about during a lesson in mathematics:

> When he [the teacher] was saying, you know, like he was asking people like, "What would number seven be?" I'm saying it. Like he says . . . I'm saying [it] . . . in my head. And I know they're saying [it]. . . . And he [the teacher] would say if it was right so I would see if I'm doing it right. (p. 28)

This student paid attention to the teacher's question, tried to answer it mentally, assumed other kids were doing the same, and listened to the teacher's reaction as a way of gaining evaluative feedback. Put differently, he used the self-management strategies of self-regulated learning: alertness, timely execution, monitoring and control, and evaluative feedback (Corno & Mandinach, 1983). The authors considered this student "relatively sophisticated" among their sample of sixth-graders.

Such descriptive studies find that students differ considerably in their tendency to use such enactive mental strategies in class. Other studies have shown that among students equally willing or intending to learn, older students (sixth grade and above) use them more often than younger students do. Theories of cognitive development argue that self-regulatory capabilities develop between the ages of five and fifteen (Flavell, 1970; Henderson, 1982). Also, within grades, there appear big differences in the quality of self-regulatory statements that different learners make. Weaker students often fail to learn these skills by middle to late childhood, or at least fail to use them fluidly. While self-regulated learning relates positively to measures of general ability, our own research—work by Ellen Mandinach (see Mandinach & Corno, 1985) and Barry Schimmel (1986) —suggests that cognitive ability and self-regulation are not the same thing. Among uniformly able students in the Mandinach study, and uniformly less able subjects in Schimmel's, we still observed wide variation in the active self-management strategies that mark self-regulation. Ease of application (or mobility and flexibility) seems to depend on having had opportunities for learning in home and school environments where strategies were brought into consciousness and applied. Shirley Heath (1983), for example, has traced early academic accomplishments to homes in which language is used to train children in routines and to expose them to varied levels of questions and responses.

Donald Meichenbaum (1977), a psychologist who has written extensively about self-regulation, tells a story about how his young son, David, learned to control his early tendency to leave a trail of peels and cores behind him when he ate apples. While David watched, Daddy modeled (with words and actions) how the "dirty old core" must get picked up and put in the trash can, not left on the floor. On another occasion, Mommy did the same thing. Soon little David was picking up the refuse absentmindedly dropped by some unsuspecting individual in a store, who was embarrassed to hear David say, as he pitched the litter into a nearby receptacle, that garbage belonged in the trash can. In much the same way that they acquire language or values, children seem to acquire the higher-level mental skills of self-regulation *from an environment that provides multiple models (explained examples) of self-regulatory behavior and encourages emulating them when appropriate.* The earlier and more frequently such explanations and encouragements occur, the better, for experiences with intellectual operations build on one another over time (Piaget, 1970; Perkins, 1985).

A critical point in this argument is the significance of teaching the child the context in which self-regulatory strategies are appropriate. It has been said before that education aims at transfer (Snow, 1982). Some students will transfer learning to an appropriate situation without adult prompting, but not all will do this. Many will require adult intervention or mediation; that is, an adult will have to assist the child in making the connection between the prior experience and a present appropriate context. David was able to transfer his learning without prompting, but a different child might have needed to be told to follow his or her parents' lead and that the rule for picking up garbage holds for anything, not just apple cores. Direct mediation helps to ensure transfer when it fails to occur spontaneously. Again, since students of all ages differ in natural abilities, mediation will be important if many youngsters are to develop self-regulation. Such mediation is an important aspect of the teacher's role in promoting self-regulatory skills in a heterogeneous class. Thus it is widely believed that examples and encouragement from significant adults induce children to set their own goals and to evaluate their own performance accordingly (Bower & Hilgard, 1980).

One point on which researchers still disagree is the extent to which self-regulation can be taught with special programs that stand apart from the larger academic curriculum. There are thinking-skills programs that have students work out puzzles and problems that do not appear to resemble school subject-matter tasks. It is also unclear whether self-regulated learning benefits from examples offered without explanation or from working on tasks that either demand self-regulatory skills or afford opportunities for applying them with little or no teacher mediation or assistance (see, for example, Papert, 1980).

The evidence at hand supports the teaching of self-regulatory skills and strategies in the context of regular school curricula and highlights the importance of teachers and other students as models and mediators of this knowledge (Perkins, 1985; Ryan et al., 1985). The theoretical explanation is that acquiring the higher-order skills of self-regulation demands a coconstructive or social learning process in which students first observe the procedures at work in a variety of appropriate situations (including the results or consequences incurred). Later, students must be encouraged or prompted to apply the procedures themselves, with evaluative feedback along the way. This is a natural form of teaching— one made focal in the powerful theory of the Soviet psychologist Lev Vygotsky (1962). It occurs in many informal teaching or tutoring contexts. Albert Bandura (1977) has given it the most descriptive label: *participant modeling instruction.* But descriptions of essentially the same approach have also been called mediated learning (Feuerstein, 1980), expert scaffolding, and proleptic teaching (Bruner, 1978; Wertsch, 1979; after Vygotsky, 1962). Whatever term we use, this approach involves modeling plus explanation and instruction and is marked by a gradual press for student independence in the context of supportive coaching (see also Corno & Snow, 1986).

Variations on participant modeling instruction have been used successfully to teach the self-management aspects of self-regulated learning to students who have trouble with behavioral self-control (Kendall & Hollon, 1979) and to students who tend to be impulsive or anxious in school (Meichenbaum, 1977). Students can be taught to call forth self-statements and questions such as those presented in Figure 1 to help themselves prepare to learn and to monitor and control their concentration during the process. Donald Meichenbaum's (1977) research, for example, has demonstrated the utility of teaching internal self-speech to children in school settings. Often questions and statements such as, "What are the different ways I can do this?" or "Where did I go wrong?" are intended to replace the negative self-statements that weaker

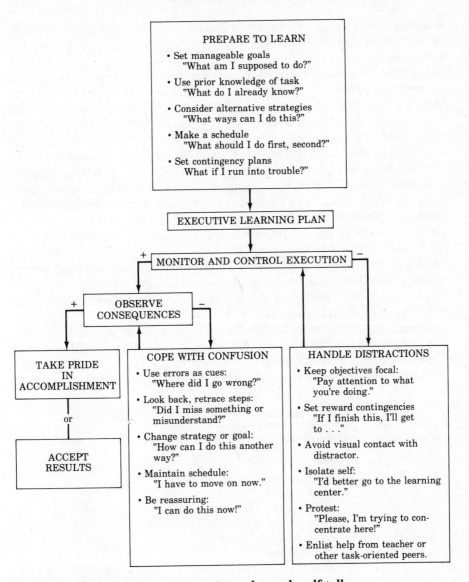

Figure 1. Self-management strategies and sample self-talk.

students tend to make naturally—"I can't do this," "I'm just not good at it." As was mentioned earlier, internal statements that are negative— such as dismissing one's own role in one's success—have a way of crystallizing into pervasive, self-limiting beliefs that impede the flow of effective information processing during school tasks. Classroom studies indicate this is particularly the case with statements that draw attention to perceived weaknesses in ability (see, for instance, Rohrkemper & Bershon, 1984.)

In addition to its usefulness for teaching self-management, participant modeling instruction has also proved effective in teaching general and subject-matter-specific learning strategies to both elementary- and high-school students (see, for example, Bereiter & Bird, 1985; Schunk, 1984; Palincsar & Brown, 1984; Weinstein & Mayer, 1986; Corno, 1986a.) Strongest effects (retention and transfer) are found when students learn strategies specific to the subject matter in question—such as strategies for solving mathematics problems or for comprehending written text. General learning strategies—those that cut across subject matter and task domains—may be used to learn in history as well as in science, and from textbooks as well as oral lessons. Take, for example, the general strategy of selecting the most important points from any reading material or oral lesson. These are obtained by identifying and attending to information in places like summaries and marginal notes. There are also general strategies for committing important material

Table 1.   Strategies for Finding Key Points.

INSPECT MATERIAL (TEXTS, ORAL LESSONS) FOR

1. *Common Structural Features*

> Outlines (table of contents, topic headings)
> Statements of purpose; objectives
> Rules, key concepts, and examples
> Conclusions
> Summaries
> Questions on the material

2. *Clues Within the Structure*

> Important points are often

>> Said once and repeated later
>> Underlined or otherwise highlighted
>> Noted in margins
>> In conclusions
>> In summaries
>> The focus of questions on the material

Short paragraphs or discussions may contain as much important material as long ones.

Figure 2. Strategies for committing key points to memory.

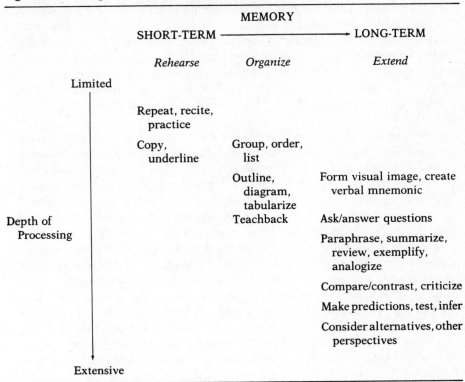

SOURCE: After Weinstein & Mayer (1986).

to memory. "Extension" strategies, such as summarizing and predicting, are believed to be more powerful facilitators of retention and transfer than are "rehearsal" strategies, such as repetition and copying. "Organizing" strategies, such as grouping and diagramming, fall somewhere between the two. Examples of strategies that cut across subject matter are presented in Table 1 and Figure 2. Research on teaching general strategies shows that students will use them in school if they are learned and practiced in several subject areas and if the situations in which they will be useful are taught as well (Pressley, Borkowski & O'Sullivan, 1983). Students seem to need time and varied exposure to formulate clear general strategies for learning in school (Snow, 1982).

TEACHING TO ENHANCE SELF-REGULATED LEARNING

We now believe that teachers can provide such opportunities by designing activities that incorporate specific and general learning and self-management strategies into regular lessons as additional instructional goals. That is, students can be taught to take "extension" notes from lectures (rather than copying verbatim what is said). They can be taught to highlight the important points in texts; to monitor comprehension as they read; to use memory-support devices such as metaphors, imagery, and mnemonics; and to diagram, tabularize, or otherwise organize complex academic material. These strategies must also be seen by students for what they are—tools that good learners use to make schoolwork easier and to increase the likelihood of success (Corno, 1980; Flavell, 1981).

A series of experimental studies by Palincsar and Brown (1984) used a variation on participant modeling called *reciprocal teaching* to teach some key strategies of good readers to students who fail to use them on their own. The researchers trained teachers to demonstrate comprehension strategies such as summarizing, composing questions about content, and making predictions about future content. They then asked the teachers to involve students gradually in the process until they were able to use these strategies themselves to monitor and understand what they read. A section of dialogue from one of the actual sessions in this study is presented below. This session included one teacher and a small group of students. The dialogue is preceded by a silent reading of a short passage of expository text on how salt is made. Students and teacher together then use the strategies they have learned by demonstration and example to comprehend the text. Students are identified by letters other than T, which represents the teacher. I have annotated the dialogue to make events clear.

TEXT: . . . Table salt is made by the third method—artificial evaporation. Pumping water into an underground salt bed dissolves the salt to make a brine that is brought to the surface. After purification at high temperatures, the salt is ready for our tables.

K: After purification at high temperatures, the salt is ready for what? [A designated student asks the first question about content to the group—"as a teacher would."]

C: Our tables. [Response to K's question.]

K: That's correct. To summarize: After its purification, the salt is put on our tables. [Confirmation and summary—note that K is *teaching* C.]

T: That was a fine job, Ken, and I appreciate all that work, but I think there might be something else to add to our summary. There is more important information that I think we need to include. This paragraph is mostly about what? [Constructive feedback, prompting for elaboration, modeling a more challenging kind of question to ask when summarizing.]

A: The third method of artificial evaporation. [Another student answers.]

B: It mainly tells about pumping water from an underground salt bed that dissolves the salt to make a brine that is brought to the surface. [Another student elaborates.]

T: Angela hit it right on the money. This paragraph is mostly about the method of artificial evaporation, and then everything else in the paragraph is telling us about that process. O.K. Next teacher. [Confirmation, restatement of correct answer, transition to next segment of passage to be led by next designated "teacher."] (pp. 162–163)

This research illustrates how a teacher can, through guided practice in applying learning strategies, build the capabilities for better reading comprehension. Note that the students also learned something about *teaching* in the process because they were taught to raise potential test questions. The expectation is that when students engage in reflective activity after reading many different types of passages and genres, they will ultimately gain the higher-level knowledge that these strategies will be of use in learning written material *of any kind*. Students should also begin to mobilize the strategies automatically when confronted with written material. Palincsar and Brown's experiments confirmed this hypothesis; the junior-high-school students tested used the strategies on reading tasks included in the experiments and continued to use them on similar tasks up to eight weeks after instruction. In addition, use of the strategies resulted in improved performance on school achievement tests as well.

We can use well-designed studies like this to develop general recommendations for teaching that promotes self-regulated learning, which may then be tested in other experiments. These recommendations are presented in Table 2. The steps in this type of instruction reflect the features of participant modeling. The self-management strategies of goal setting, execution, monitoring, control, and evaluative feedback are always included in the lessons. These are aspects of teaching that the teacher first discusses with students as they carry them out. Eventually, the management of learning is taken over by the students themselves, so the learning becomes self- rather than teacher-regulated. That is, the teacher may start out a lesson with goals he or she has chosen, but this fact is pointed out to the students and the goals are made clear. Ultimately, the teacher involves the students in the task of setting additional lesson goals. The procedure is similar for monitoring, control, and evaluative feedback. Again, one way to think about this approach is that it is teaching students about teaching as well as learning, and it is emphasizing the process of transfer so that learning becomes a kind of self-teaching.

In research we are conducting at Teachers College, we have developed lessons using this approach in different subject areas, and are testing them in high-school and junior college classrooms. We identified learning strategies that appear specific to social studies and mathematics and have asked teachers to make these specific strategies and general self-management skills additional goals of their regular lessons. Some of the domain-specific social studies strategies we are emphasizing include debating, conflict resolution, and constructing mental "maps" of different cultures. To construct a mental map, for example, the teacher

Table 2. Teaching for Self-Regulated Learning.

The following are recommendations for teaching *learning and self-management strategies* in the context of regular subject-matter instruction:

GOALS
1. Define lesson goals. Discuss subject matter and strategy goals with students, soliciting their input when appropriate.

PRIOR KNOWLEDGE
2. Conduct activities that clarify what students already know about the subject and target strategies (reviews, small-group listing of ideas, writing out and answering questions a teacher might ask, and so on).

MODEL/EXPLANATION
3. Demonstrate by examples/activities how the strategies are used to learn the material. Verbalize self-management strategies at the same time. Give students time to ask questions.

GUIDED PRACTICE
4. Have students work through different examples/activities that require strategy use (see below). Provide assistance and coaching as indicated. Raise questions about strategies for deriving answers and solving problems, such as asking students why they used a particular approach. Have students describe aloud how the strategy is working for them. Prompt self-monitoring, self-reward statements as indicated. Gradually withdraw prompts.

INDEPENDENT ASSIGNMENT
5. Assign an exercise/activity in which students, on their own or in small groups, must use the knowledge and strategies learned. Require a self-check and self-reward. Gradually remove requirements, but evaluate use of self-management.

FEEDBACK
6. Give critical feedback on student assignments (from #5 above) that coaches on improved strategy use and self-management.

Note: These steps may be streamlined if students grasp the learning strategies easily and are able to display self-management.

The following are examples of some creative *classroom activities* teachers have used to help teach self-regulated learning:

Projects requiring students to produce some product and use or explain it, or to inquire into some puzzle or paradox. These may be group as well as independent projects.

Face-to-face discussions of issues that prompt dialogue, debate, speculation, and explanation.

Table 2   (Continued)

Real-life simulations of past or current situations or events that involve students in identification and role playing.

Metaphor/analogy hunts through written material; creating metaphors for new concepts, ideas.

Discussions of common errors in subject-matter learning, how to circumvent them or use them as cues to a second try.

Discussions of how to study from books in different subject areas.

—How to find key points, supporting facts, and concepts.
—How to commit key points to long-term memory.

For example:

—History textbook: Look for periods of history, recurring causes of events.
—Science textbook: Look for taxonomies, theories, and ways of testing them.
—Literature: Look for author's purpose, sequence of events, character development; examine writing style; and so on.

Teaching note taking (*not* copying, but getting the gist and extending it).

Reinforce this as follows:

—Stop lesson and ask students to take notes periodically.
—Ask students to share notes/discuss good and bad note taking with class.
—Have students integrate class notes with notes on textbooks; set a due date.

Discuss the "inner voice" of learning—what students tell themselves about schoolwork and how they manage to learn school material—and how to alter negative self-statements.

asks students to visualize themselves on a train that travels from one period of a country's history into another. With teacher prompting and support, the students envision the country's cultural and social characteristics as well as the changing economic and political climate. These visualizations then become data from which the class traces the array of political, economic, and social causes for key historical events. In each case, the strategy is named, defined, modeled, and transferred to students through participant modeling. The strategies are also formally tested. We feel strongly that if you do not test process, it will not be seen as legitimate learning to students. So we design exercises that require students to use these skills, and they are graded like other skills in which students are expected to display competence.

In pilot tests we are running in preparation for a larger study, high-school students used such strategies in large and small groups. The small groups were taught to use peer reciprocal teaching (after Palincsar & Brown, 1984) to prompt one another "as a teacher would" to evaluate and clarify answers, ask questions, and provide encouraging feedback. Again, the students learn about teaching as well as self-regulated learning. Scores on subject-matter tests are higher for experimental than for control students, and teachers leverage their own skills by sharing the teaching with students. In addition, students tell us they wish they had been taught earlier how to monitor and control their own learning.

While the rudiments of self-management are generally learned early, at home as well as in school, our own and other studies seem to indicate that these strategies need to be made conscious for many students and need constant reinforcement when the subject matter is not of a student's own choosing or is not inherently interesting. This is often the case with academic work. But if we can equip our students with a rich sampling of learning and self-management strategies, as well as subject-matter knowledge, they should be in a good position *and* predisposed to deepen and extend that knowledge base throughout their lifetimes, whether in a classroom or not.

REFERENCES

Allport, G. W. (1963). *Pattern and growth in personality*. New York: Holt, Rinehart & Winston.

Bandura, A. (1977). Self-efficacy: Toward a unifying theory of behavioral change. *Psychological Review, 84,* 191–215.

———. (1983). The psychology of chance encounters and life paths. *American Psychologist, 37,* 747–756.

Bereiter, C., & Bird, M. (1985). Use of thinking aloud in identification and teaching of reading comprehension strategies. *Cognition and Instruction, 2,* 131–156.

Bower, G., & Hilgard, E. (1980). *Theories of learning.* Englewood Cliffs, NJ: Prentice-Hall.

Brown, A. L. (1978). Knowing when, where, and how to remember: A problem of metacognition. In R. Glaser (Ed.), *Advances in instructional psychology, Vol. 1.* Hillsdale, NJ: Erlbaum.

Bruner, J. (1978). The role of dialogue in language acquisition. In A. Sinclair, R. J. Jarvella, & W. J. M. Levelt (Eds.), *The child's conception of language.* Berlin: Springer-Verlag.

Corno, L. (1980). Individual and class level effects of parent-assisted instruction in classroom memory support strategies. *Journal of Educational Psychology, 74,* 278–292.

———. (1986a, in press). The study of teaching for mathematics learning: Views through two lenses. *Educational Psychologist.*

———. (1986b, in press). The metacognitive control components of self-regulated learning. *Contemporary Educational Psychology.*

Corno, L., & Mandinach, E. B. (1983). The role of cognitive engagement in classroom learning and motivation. *Educational Psychologist, 18,* 88–108.

Corno, L., & Rohrkemper, M. M. (1985). The intrinsic motivation to learn in classrooms. In C. Ames & R. Ames (Eds.), *Research on motivation in education: The classroom milieu.* Orlando, FL: Academic.

Corno, L., & Snow, R. E. (1986). Adapting teaching to individual differences among learners. In M. C. Wittrock (Ed.), *Third handbook of research on teaching.* New York: Macmillan.

Feuerstein, R. (1980). *Instrumental enrichment.* Baltimore, MD: University Park Press.

Flavell, J. H. (1970). Developmental studies in mediated memory. In H. W. Reese & L. P. Lipsett (Eds.), *Advances in child development and behavior, Vol. 5.* New York: Academic.

———. (1981). Cognitive monitoring. In P. Dickson (Ed.), *Children's oral communication skills.* New York: Academic.

Heath, S. B. (1983). *Ways with words: Language, life and work in communities and classrooms.* Cambridge, England: Cambridge University Press.

Henderson, R. W. (1982). Personal and social causation in the school context. In T. Worell (Ed.), *Psychological development in the elementary years.* New York: Academic.

Kendall, P. C., & Hollon, S. D. (Eds.) (1979). *Cognitive-behavioral interventions: Theory, research, and procedures.* New York: Academic.

Kuhl, J., & Beckmann, J. (Eds.) (1985). *Action control: From cognition to behavior.* Berlin: Springer-Verlag.

Mandinach, E. B., & Corno, L. (1985). Cognitive engagement variations among students of different ability level and sex in a computer problem solving game. *Sex Roles, 13,* 241–251.

Meichenbaum, D. (1977). *Cognitive behavior modification.* New York: Plenum.

Nicholls, J. G. (1983). Conceptions of ability and achievement motivation: A theory and its implications for education. In S. G. Paris, G. M. Olson, & H. W. Stevensen (Eds.), *Learning and motivation in the classroom.* Hillsdale, NJ: Erlbaum.

Novak, J. D., & Gowin, D. B. (1984). *Learning how to learn.* Cambridge, England: Cambridge University Press.

Palincsar, A. S., & Brown, A. L. (1984). Reciprocal teaching of comprehension-fostering and comprehension-monitoring activities. *Cognition and Instruction, 1,* 117–175.

Papert, S. (1980). *Mindstorms.* New York: Basic Books.

Perkins, D. N. (1985). The fingertip effect: How information-processing technology shapes thinking. *Educational Researcher, 14,* 11–17.

Peterson, P. L., Swing, S. R., Stark, D. D., & Waass, G. A. (1983, April). Students' reports of their cognitive processes and affective thoughts during classroom instruction. Paper presented at the meeting of the American Educational Research Association, Montreal, Canada.

Phillips, D. C., & Soltis, J. F. (1985). *Perspectives on learning.* New York: Teachers College Press.

Piaget, J. (1970). Piaget's theory. In P. Mussen (Ed.), *Carmichael's manual of child psychology.* New York: Wiley.

Pressley, M., Borkowski, J. G., & O'Sullivan, J. T. (1983). Memory strategy instruction is made of this: Metamemory and durable strategy use. *Educational Psychologist, 19,* 94–107.

Resnick, L. B. (1983). Mathematics and science learning: A new conception. *Science, 220,* 477–478.

Rohrkemper, M. M., & Bershon, B. L. (1984). The quality of student task engagement: Elementary school students' reports of the causes and effects of problem difficulty. *Elementary School Journal, 85,* 127–147.

Ryan, R. M., Connell, J. P., & Deci, E. L. (1985). A motivational analysis of self-determination and self-regulation in education. In C. Ames & R. Ames

(Eds.), *Research on motivation in education, Vol. 2: The classroom milieu.* Orlando, FL: Academic.

Schimmel, B. J. (1986). *Feedback use by low ability students in computer-based education.* Doctoral dissertation, Teachers College, Columbia University, New York.

Schunk, D. (1984). Self-efficacy perspective on achievement behavior. *Educational Psychologist, 19,* 48–58.

Seligman, M. E. P. (1975). *Helplessness.* San Francisco: Freeman.

Snow, R. E., with the assistance of E. Yalow. (1982). Education and intelligence. In R. J. Sternberg (Ed.), *Handbook of human intelligence.* Cambridge, England: Cambridge University Press.

Snow, R. E., & Lohman, D. F. (1984). Toward a theory of cognitive aptitude for learning from instruction. *Journal of Educational Psychology, 76,* 347–377.

Sternberg, R. J. (Ed.). (1982). *Handbook of human intelligence.* Cambridge, England: Cambridge University Press.

Vygotsky, L. S. (1962). *Thought and language.* (E. Hanfman & G. Vakar, Eds.). Cambridge, MA: MIT Press.

Weiner, B. (1980). *Human motivation.* New York: Holt, Rinehart & Winston.

Weinstein, C. E., & Mayer, R. E. (1986). The teaching of learning strategies. In M. C. Wittrock (Ed.), *Third handbook of research on teaching.* New York: Macmillan.

Wertsch, J. (1979). From social interaction to higher psychological processes. *Human Development, 22,* 1–22.

CHAPTER 11

RONALD W. MARX

PHILIP H. WINNE

THE BEST TOOL TEACHERS HAVE—THEIR STUDENTS' THINKING

"Here's a tricky one. *Think* before you try to answer it."

"That's right, Pat. Now, do you *understand* why?"

"Who *remembers* what we do next?"

"What's your *strategy* for answering problems like this?"

"OK, now pay *attention* to this next part."

"Where did you *get* that idea?"

"You'll just have to *memorize* it."

"Well, just *forget* that this line is here for now."

"Can you *invent* some concepts that might relate the two parts?"

"Make sure you *know* this."

These sentences have two things in common. First, sentences like these can be heard every few minutes in practically any classroom. Second, the italicized word in each of these sentences refers to an aspect of cognition. More specifically, these words refer to a cognitive operation or plan that students are being guided to use in order to help them reach an instructional objective. This chapter is about the nature of these cognitions and how teachers can use knowledge of them to enhance their instructional activities.

Teaching involves many activities, most of which directly support the educational goals of schools, although many concern social, administrative, and clerical functions. Many of these activities and functions are described in the various chapters of this book. We are concerned exclusively in this chapter with educational activities of teaching. Even more narrowly, our concern is with instructional tasks in which teachers and students engage in classrooms. In our view, discussions about classroom instruction must attend to the ways that teachers influence students to think about subject matter. Teaching is effective when the cognitive operations and plans that students use successfully lead to increased knowledge and positive affect. When teachers are able to teach effectively without having to backtrack often or repair false starts, their teaching is also efficient. Efficiency is important because much research has shown that there is a clear relationship between the amount of time students are engaged in productive educational activities and their chances of achieving the goals of teaching. Thus it is important for teachers to be able to design and present instruction that is both effective and efficient. The former helps accomplish the educational goals of schooling; the latter supports the former.

We use this conception of teaching and instruction here as a basis for reporting what research has found out about teaching and instruction and about how teachers can help students to learn in classrooms. As we review these findings, we will also put forward principles for making teaching effective and efficient whenever the research justifies them.

The first section of this chapter begins with a brief comparison of two predominant approaches to the study of teaching, followed by an argument for "a contract for teaching and learning" that forms the basis for the cognitive mediational approach to teaching. Cognitive mediation is a psychologist's way of saying that between an instructional act and a measure of learning are a lot of students' thoughts (cognitions). These thoughts link instruction and learning, that is, they mediate between them. Thus, these kinds of thoughts are worth studying. The next section presents a discussion of difficulties that students have as they try to learn from teaching and includes procedures for overcoming these difficulties. The third section of the chapter outlines cognitive plans students use in school, and the fourth section discusses how to use these suggestions in your classroom.

TWO MODELS FOR TEACHING

The Performance-Based Model of Teaching Effectiveness

About 20 years ago, a movement called performance-based teacher education swept schools of education. Performance-based teaching was predicated on the view that teaching could be analyzed as a set of discrete behaviors or skills. Examples of such behaviors are stating objectives, posing higher cognitive questions, praising correct or commendable performance, and summarizing content at logical breaks in a lesson. Each teaching behavior was assumed to increase students' achievement. By practicing these behaviors, student-teachers would master component skills for teaching. By linking together these skills, effective strategies for teaching would develop.

The reasoning behind research studies that adopt a performance-based view of teaching is that a simple cause-and-effect chain exists between teaching behavior and student learning. A teacher's behavior that was used one or several times during a lesson played the role of cause. After the lesson, the effect of this cause was assessed by the scores students received on an achievement test or an attitude scale. In a typical experimental study of this genre, one group of students would be taught by a teacher using a particular behavior. A second group would be taught the same subject matter by a teacher who did not use that particular behavior (or by a teacher using a related, but presumably less effective, behavior). When the test or attitude scores of students whose lesson included the teacher behavior were higher than those of students whose lesson did not include the behavior, the teacher behavior was declared "effective." In this research tradition, the cause occurred during lessons when teachers used the behavior being investigated. The effect occurred after the lesson was over when students took tests or responded to attitude questionnaires.

This model of performance-based teaching had two noteworthy results. First, the view that effective teaching was based on teacher behaviors became a great stimulus for research. Researchers took advantage of the descriptive precision offered by a language of teacher behaviors to sharpen their studies of teaching effectiveness. The important and useful results of this work are synthesized in several other chapters of this book, especially Chapter 4. Second, this model had a major impact on teacher education. As a result of the research it fostered, student-teachers and their supervisors had available to them concepts and associated procedures that enabled them to address teaching in fairly specific terms—namely, teacher behaviors. This approach fostered a clearer descriptive language for planning and analyzing teaching.

Despite the gains that were made by adopting a performance-based model of teaching, experience with it also indicated some shortcomings. These were revealed when the model was used as a tool for trying to think about what makes teaching effective. As you might surmise from the conception of teaching and instruction that we offered earlier, the most critical problem with the performance-based model is that it does not include a formal description of how students actually learn from teaching.

From our perspective, the achievements and attitudes that students display after lessons are not caused directly by how teachers behave during lessons. Instead, we believe that the causes of these effects—that is, the knowledge, concepts, and skills that students acquire and the attitudes toward school, learning, and self that they develop—rest with the cognitive activities that students pursue as they work through their lessons. From this perspective, teacher behaviors are signals that can provide guidance to students about effective ways to think about the content of lessons. Also, a teacher's behavior reflects his or her intentions about what students are to learn and how students are to think as they attempt to complete classroom tasks. Correspondingly, students come to class with their own intentions and understandings of the ways in which classrooms operate. Thus teacher and student behavior in classrooms is an overt reflection of both parties' intentions and understandings. This reasoning provides a basis for important revisions to the simple cause-and-effect model that underlies a performance-based view of teaching. We call our model the cognitive mediational model.

The Cognitive Mediational Model of Teaching and Learning from Teaching

After many studies of performance-based teaching effectiveness had been carried out, reviews of studies that investigated a particular teaching behavior were conducted. One of us (Winne) wrote such a review of the research about the effectiveness of teachers' use of higher cognitive questions. Upon surveying the studies carefully, it became apparent that not one of them had documented with data what particular cognitive operations or plans higher cognitive questions were supposed to signal. Instead, researchers used students' scores on tests administered after lessons were over to speculate about the kinds of cognition students had used while learning. These researchers' speculations were not entirely justified, because the results from many studies suggested that higher cognitive questions were not much more effective than other kinds of questions. On the basis of both logical analysis and laboratory research about human learning, one would have expected higher cognitive questions to have a much stronger track record if students really had used the cognitions presumed to be signaled by higher-order questions.

In trying to explain why findings from this and many other reviews were neither as consistent nor as supportive as they should have been according to the performance-based model, we and other researchers proposed a modification of this model. Put simply, between the teacher behavior and students' accomplishments assessed after teaching, we inserted an explicit place for students' cognition to occur. Researchers and educational theorists suggest that there are a variety of cognitive operations and plans from which students can select. Thus it also was necessary to propose a mechanism by which students select the cognitions they use on particular occasions. Hence, the cognitive mediational model was born.

The cognitive mediational model adds two intervening elements to the performance-based model. One is a "cognitive" element, reflecting the belief that students can use any of a number of different cognitions in trying to achieve instructional objectives. The other is a "mediational" element, reflecting the belief that teacher behaviors have to be interpreted by students. In other words, a teacher behavior does not unequivocally dictate to students that they use specific cognitive operations or plans at particular points in a lesson. Rather, students' perceptions of teachers' behaviors mediated between what the teacher overtly intended students to think about and how students covertly carried out cognitive operations and plans. Furthermore, as much research on cognition has shown, human perception is not simply a process of perceiving everything in the environment. Instead, it is a constructive event. The person's experience, knowledge, and expectations influence the products of perception, particularly the perception of ambiguous events. As we will document later, many classroom activities are ambiguous. The perceptions that a student constructs for these aspects of teaching inevitably are a result of an interaction between the event and his or her particular background.

The cognitive mediational model also recast the locus of causation in the performance-based model. Instead of teacher behaviors serving as causes of students' learning, teacher behaviors in the cognitive mediational model became signals for students to use certain cognitions to learn content. The students' cognitions were considered the causes for learning. Theoretically, students' selection of which cognitions to use is a result of their constructive perception of the teacher's signals. Thus the previous and simpler two-part chain of teacher behavior as cause for the effect observed as students' test scores was transformed and rendered more complex. Teacher behaviors now signaled students' cognition, and students' cognitive work on content caused the effects observed when students answered questions on tests or attitude questionnaires.

This new view led to two important developments. First, it seemed to explain the inconsistencies of effectiveness that were reported in the reviews of research on performance-based teaching. None of the research designed according to the performance-based model had taken steps to validate that students' cognitive mediations and behavior matched teachers' and researchers' intentions for cognitions. Therefore, teaching behaviors could have been ineffective because students mediated teachers' signals in ways that did not support learning. Second, a theoretical stance was taken that explicitly represented teachers and students as thinking agents. This stance requires both research and practice to acknowledge that teachers and students come to classrooms as purposeful, intentional people. Of course, it is reasonable to expect a considerable amount of variation among teachers and students in their purposes and intentions as they navigate the social and academic waters of the classroom. Indeed, one of the unique attributes of the teaching profession is the teachers' need to harness students' individual purposes and intentions to the goals of education.

A CONTRACT FOR TEACHING AND LEARNING FROM TEACHING

Students and teachers make a social contract in order to carry out lessons. This contract is rarely negotiated openly and explicitly in the way that a business contract is negotiated. Rather, many of the responsibilities that bind each party to act in a particular manner while engaged in classroom learning tasks are not spelled out. Sometimes these responsibilities are simply assumed to be included in the contract, and sometimes they are just not thought of by one or both parties. Moreover, we do not mean to imply that teachers and students always interact as if they were conforming to this implicit contract. But many of the interactions between teachers and students can be viewed as if such a contract existed. Were such an implicit contract not operating in classrooms, it is unlikely that much learning would take place, given additional ethical principles that constrain the possible educational activities in a liberal democracy. The point here is that for schooling to result in education rather than indoctrination, teachers cannot use coercion and subterfuge.

On the teacher's side of the contract, two responsibilities are paramount: (1) to present to students or make available to them opportunities to interact with the content that they are expected to learn; and (2) to provide students with guidance about how to think about this content so that it can be learned effectively and efficiently. On the student's side of the contract, there also are two responsibilities: (1) to seek out the guidance teachers offer about the cognitions that best promote learning; and (2) to provide the teacher with feedback about how well learning is progressing.

When the terms of this contract are fulfilled, we predict that teaching and learning in classrooms will be enhanced. Teachers will have presented either directly or indirectly the content that students should acquire in order to achieve the objectives of instruction. Students will be taking advantage of the teacher's superior knowledge about the kinds of cognitions that are best suited to learning content, and when they are having difficulty with this task, they will make sure that the teacher is aware of it. Then the teacher can adapt instruction to provide students with what they need to learn. Let us look at how teachers and students act in classes to see if what they do supports the notion of an implicit contract.

Do Teachers Present Content?

The answer to this question is a simple yes. Research on teachers' planning for lessons (see Chapter 14) and observations of thousands of lessons confirm that, in general, teachers cover in one way or another most of the content that they specify in objectives for instruction. In fact, most teacher behaviors that were found to be effective addressed means for presenting content. For our purposes, we assume that this aspect of the contract between teacher and students is fulfilled and that it is highly characteristic of lessons.

Do Teachers Signal Students About Cognition?

There are two ways to answer this question. One way is to ask teachers if they signal students about cognitive strategies in their teaching, or to ask researchers whether the teaching they observe includes signals for students to use particular cognitive operations or plans. The second approach to answering this question is to ask students if they perceive that teachers signal them to use cognitive operations while they are trying to learn. We consider teachers' and researchers' answers first, then turn to students' views.

Teachers' Views of Their Signals. If teachers believe the reasons that are offered for using behaviors such as higher cognitive questions and praise, they must also believe that something about these behaviors indicates to students that particular cognitions are called for at that time. For instance, higher cognitive questions are supposed to signal students to carry out particular kinds of cognitive operations. These operations are different from those involved in answering questions that call for simple recall. In order for students to discriminate between these two types of questions, some feature of the wording of a question would have to cue the student about which cognitive operations are being signaled.

As another example, consider praise. If one function of praise is to draw students' attention to their successes at learning, then something about the way a teacher praises has to cue students to focus their attention on their previous accomplishment, rather than prompt them to engage in some other cognition. In general, reasons for most of the instructional behaviors that teachers use refer to particular cognitive operations that it is believed students ought to apply to content as the students respond to those behaviors. Therefore, in order for students to be able to use the particular cognitive operation that the teacher intends, the teacher's behavior must contain a cue that pinpoints the right cognition for the student.

What about teachers' analyses of their own teaching? In addition to the preceding argument that teachers signal students about cognitions, do teachers say that they actually do this while teaching? The answer is a clear yes. Evidence for this comes from a study that we conducted, in which we videotaped lessons and then interviewed teachers about their teaching. In the interviews, we replayed the videotapes. While the teachers watched the replay, we asked them to stop the tape whenever they saw themselves trying to influence their students to use particular cognitive operations to promote learning.

The teachers in our study stopped their videotapes often. Not only did they report many occasions in every lesson at which they cued particular student cognitions, but they also described a fairly wide range of cognitive operations that they were trying to cue. For example, these teachers signaled their students to focus on details, to create different systems for cataloguing information, and to monitor the mental techniques they used for answering questions. Thus these teachers' reports of their reasons for using certain teaching behaviors support the logical argument presented earlier about cuing students' cognitions. Everyday teaching is ripe with cues that teachers deliver to guide students' thinking.

Students' Views of Teachers' Signals.   Now, given that researchers and teachers find cues are commonly used, do students concur? Yes, they do. Our evidence for this comes from several studies, including the one just mentioned. In that study, we also interviewed students as they watched videotape replays of the lessons in which they had participated. When we asked them at preselected points in the lesson, "Do you think the teacher wanted you to be thinking in some particular way that would help you learn?" students often replied yes. When students responded affirmatively, we followed up with questions to find out whether they also could describe which feature of their teacher's behavior cued them about which cognitive operations they were supposed to use. Often they could provide this information. For example, students were able to tell us that they had to pay particular attention to lesson content that the teacher wrote on the chalkboard, because it invariably would be included on a test. We conclude, therefore, that students also notice that teaching contains cues for operating cognitively on content in order to learn it.

Do Students Seek Out Signals About Cognitions?

Our answer to the last question showed that students notice cues for cognition that their teachers use during instruction. However, this does not necessarily demonstrate that students actively look for cues. One way to show that students seek out cues is to locate places in lessons where teachers do not claim that a cue was used. Then, if students tell us that they observed a cue there nonetheless, we have evidence that they actively look for cues.

The same study we have been describing also provided data that fits this situation. Occasionally, we stopped the replay of a lesson for a teacher because we thought a cue had been given but had not been identified. On some of these occasions, the teachers said that they were not sure that they really used a cue at that point. On others, they were sure a cue had been used but they gave ambiguous descriptions about the cognitions that they were trying to guide students to apply.

Since teachers were vague in describing these situations to us, we inferred that they also could not have communicated a clear intention to students. At other times when we stopped the replay to ask the teacher if a cue had been skipped, the teacher said no. At these points in the lesson, the teacher was sure that there was no clear signal for students to engage in particular cognitive activities.

When we interviewed students, we replayed the videotape, stopping it at all these types of situations. The evidence supporting our contention that students are active seekers of cues comes from their responses to the incidents where their teacher either was ambiguous about whether a cue was delivered or was certain that no cue had been used. At these points, students sometimes claimed that the teacher had indeed behaved in a way that signaled them to use a particular cognitive strategy to respond to teaching. For the ambiguous incidents, they could often provide a clear description of what their teacher did to signal this intention. In some instances, they also provided elaborate descriptions of the cognitions signaled. For incidents where teachers had told us that there was no cue, students occasionally responded in the same way as they had for the ambiguous incidents. That is, they identified a cue and described cognitions associated with it. Since students were able to find cues for guiding cognitions in places where the teacher was ambiguous or was certain there was no cue, we believe they may have been actively searching for them in the first place.

Research exists to show that students interpret a wide range of instructional activities as signals for cognitive operations. Few teachers would fail to understand the meaning implied by student questions such as "Will this be on the test?" or "Will the questions be multiple choice or essay?" These questions reveal that students are aware of teachers' intentions for their cognitive operations and that they look for signals from teachers to help them allocate their cognitive resources. Also, some studies have shown that when students' expectations are violated regarding the ways in which they should be thinking, considerable disquiet results. When a teacher says that only multiple-choice items will appear on a test and then includes essay questions, he or she should expect a roar of protest. Indeed, such violations are frequently viewed as breaches in the moral code of the classroom. We interpret these breaches as failures to live up to the terms of the implicit classroom contract.

Do Students Provide Feedback About Their Cognition to Teachers?

There are at least three ways in which we can address this question. First, we could ask students. Second, we could record the kinds of things students say in class to identify whether any of their comments refer to their cognition. Third, we could infer that teachers receive and act on such feedback during lessons when they adapt instruction to redirect it toward optimum learning.

Insofar as we know, no research bears directly on the first line of inquiry. It seems odd that no one has asked students whether or how they provide feedback to the teacher concerning how well their cognition is succeeding in promoting learning. Nonetheless, this seems to be the case.

More data about what students say during lessons have been gathered in studies that recorded and classified classroom discourse. Overall, students supply about one-fifth to one-third of all the talk in lessons. Unfortunately, these data shed little light on our question. Instead, this research focused mainly on whether students correctly answered questions, whether the content of their answers was of a high or low cognitive level, or whether students' talk initiated a change of topic, asked a question, or was a response to a question.

Finally, we do know that teachers make decisions to change instruction during lessons. To the extent that teachers try to guide students' cognitions, as we noted earlier, some of these changes may be aimed at redirecting students' cognitions. We believe that what students say and do may provide feedback to the teacher about how well the students' cognition is supporting learning. However, we do not know whether students provide this feedback deliberately, thoughtfully, or frequently. We can only reason that such feedback must be available to the teacher sometimes.

Thus we do not know much about whether students provide their teacher with feedback about how well instruction is guiding their cognitive efforts to learn the subject matter. We remain fairly ignorant about how often they do it and what they say. Perhaps this absence of research-based knowledge is due to the fact that the cognitive mediational model has only recently been introduced. Before this model gained favor and force, little data were gathered from students or about them, other than their scores on tests that were administered after lessons were over. Nevertheless, it does not seem logical that students could completely hide their cognitive processes from teachers when we have findings that show teachers do change their instructional practices during lessons. Thus we answer the question about whether students provide feedback with a yes, but we admit that this is more of a logical deduction than an empirically demonstrated fact.

Yes, the Contract Between Teachers and Students Is Real

Teachers do present content to students. They supplement their presentation of content with behaviors that can guide students to select appropriate cognitive operations and plans in order to learn more effectively. We know these cues exist because teachers and their students can find such cues in lessons they view. Also, students actively seek out cues during lessons to guide their cognitive processing of content. We know this because students find cues in teaching even when their teacher cannot or does not intend to deliver them. Moreover, we hypothesize that students use cues strategically to learn from teaching. Finally, we find that there is not much research to prove that students provide feedback to their teachers about how learning is progressing toward the objectives of instruction. We are forced to reason only indirectly that this feedback is provided, because teachers must use some information as a basis for adapting instruction on the spot to help students meet the objectives of teaching. This part of the contract seems to be real, but it is certainly not well understood.

Having established that this contract between teachers and students is one way to think about teaching, we now take up in more detail the issues that surround teachers' use of cues, students' cognitive mediations of cues, and teaching effectiveness. First, we return to the topic of difficulties that students can have in meeting the responsibilities specified for them by this contract. Then, in the following sections, we discuss two further topics: research that illuminates the cognitive operations and plans that students may use to increase the effectiveness of learning, and what we know and can suggest about how teachers can cue and support students' cognitions.

DIFFICULTIES STUDENTS CAN HAVE WITH CUES— AND HOW TO LESSEN THEM

Teaching would be easy and effective if students could easily understand the signals for thinking that their teachers use and if they were able to request from their teachers further information and guidance about what to do cognitively to learn. We know this is not as much the case as teachers would like. Our analysis suggests four main sources for student difficulties in this area. Knowing what these four sources are suggests remedies.

Difficulty #1: Attending to Signals

In order for students to take advantage of instructional cues, they first have to notice them. If a teacher uses a cue but a student does not notice it, the cue cannot guide the student's selection of cognitions. In turn, we would not expect the student to be as likely to reach the objectives for the lesson because he or she would likely not have used the particular cognitive operation referred to by this cue. This is not to say that there is only one way for students to think about particular content in order to learn it, but we do argue that the teacher's role is to guide the way in which students think about content. If the signals that teachers use to provide this guidance are not critical for teaching to be effective, then there is little justification for teaching to be anything more than simply presenting content. Surely this cannot be the case. Effective teachers do more than present content. They create situations in which students are guided to think about what they are learning in particular ways. This section and the next deal with the ways in which teachers make these situations clear to students.

Why would students fail to attend to cues? There are three general causes for inadequate attention. First, a student might not know that a cue is a cue. In this case, the cue would slip by even if the student were paying attention. For example, in one of our studies, a teacher would characteristically begin lessons with amusing activities that he intended to arouse students' interest. Some students, however, did not understand this intention and were merely confused by the activities. Second, a student might be busy with other work when a signal is used. Had the student been able to attend to the teacher, the cue might have been noticed. Third, even if the student understood what intention a cue signaled and was not otherwise occupied, the cue may have been too subtle or hidden within other messages. In this situation where the signal was not sufficiently obvious, the task of identifying the cue was too hard for the student.

Remedies for Inattention to Cues. For the first kind of inattention, in which students cannot recognize a cue, the remedy is to make sure that each student knows about the cues you use. To accomplish this, take time to teach students about cues. Describe what the cue "looks like." Demonstrate the various ways you will use it in lessons. Test students' abilities to identify a cue when it is embedded in lessons. Do this first in simple contexts and later during regular lessons. To keep students on their toes in lessons long after they have been taught to identify your cues, occasionally give a "pop quiz" about whether they noticed a cue you delivered in the last few minutes. These remedies are analogous to well-established principles regarding classroom management. Early in the school year effective classroom managers establish clear rules for decorum and regular procedures for work. The same should be done for signaling to students how they should be thinking.

If students miss cues because cues are "overworked," the remedy rests mostly with you. In this case, you must plan and then deliver lessons so that students do not have to do two things at once. Inevitably, some students will either lag behind or surge ahead of others. You should not speed up to accommodate the fast students, since that will hurt average and slower students. Nor can you wait for slower students to catch up, since doing so would likely lose the interest of average and faster students. We suggest that you strike a happy medium and deliver redundant cues spaced about 10 or 15 seconds apart. For instance, follow up an oral cue about the importance of a fact, such as changing your tone of voice, with one written on the blackboard, such as underlining the fact. Slower students can pick up the second cue, while faster students can check their previous work on the content to which it refers. This obviously implies some redundancy in the use of these signals. Using the same cues but delivering them by different means will help keep the redundancy from becoming intrusive. Specifically, you should speak, write, and repeat the signals you provide to guide students' thinking.

Overcoming students' inattention to cues that results from the cue being buried in content or other activities is also primarily your job. To accomplish this, follow the same remedies as mentioned for the two previous kinds of inattention. In addition, try to make your cues stand out. Use oral emphasis, special and consistent gestures, and symbols such as asterisks, colored chalk, and underlining on the blackboard. Also, try to surround oral cues with short pauses of just a second or two so that they are separated from other material. All these activities will highlight cues that students might otherwise have trouble locating.

If you follow these suggestions, students should rarely miss the cues you provide. Attending to cues, however, does not guarantee that students will profit from them. After cues have been noticed, students have to know which cognitions to use.

Difficulty #2: Perceiving the Meaning of Cues

Cues for students to perform a cognitive operation or use a cognitive plan are rarely complete. Instead, they usually are just abbreviated signals. Students have to learn what your cues signal about the cognitions you want them to use so that when you deliver a cue, their perception of what to do cognitively is accurate.

Research has documented very clearly that students can have trouble perceiving correctly the cognitions they are being signaled to carry out. For instance, statements of praise can be perceived in many ways. For example, when a student correctly solves a hard problem, a teacher might say, "Excellent work!" In reacting to this phrase, the student could perform a number of cognitive operations; for example, rehearse all the steps that were involved in solving this type of problem or prepare to do the next problem. The student could also anticipate that these problems are solvable if enough effort is put into them, or simply feel rewarded for a job well done.

An example of differences in the way students can interpret the meaning of cues comes from a study we conducted. One of the sixth-grade teachers we worked with always began lessons with an introduction that included a statement of that lesson's objectives. Two students in this teacher's class held very different perceptions about these cues. The following excerpt comes from our interviews after a lesson about using laws of trigonometry to calculate practical measurements. The first student used the cue to set up a plan for cognitively monitoring whether parts of the lesson made sense and for fitting these parts together.

RESEARCHER: Why do you think Mr. R. would want you to know what you were going to end up doing?

STUDENT: Well, it's easier to learn when you know what you're going to make—sort of like making a model, so you first put the pieces together if you know what you're going to make first.

The second student we interviewed about this same cue had a very different understanding of it. He perceived a signal that led to a potentially debilitating plan for attending to information in the rest of the lesson.

RESEARCHER: Was there anything, Mike, that was different for you?

MIKE: Yeah, he does it all the time, and I really don't like it because it kind of scares you at the start when he goes, "This is what you're gonna do, you're gonna learn how to measure a tree and how you do it outside," and I get scared because I don't think I'm gonna be able to do that . . . it sounds so complicated to me, and I'm scared. . . .

RESEARCHER: I see. So it has a different effect on you . . . and you think you'd be more relaxed and learn better if you didn't know [the objective].

MIKE: Yeah and then he'd say, "How about you guys go out and measure the tree," and I say, "Oh, okay, it's a challenge." But he says it at the start, and then I don't pay attention, I'm trying to catch everything he says and I get confused.

As a third example of problems students may face in correctly perceiving the cognitions that a cue signals, consider a situation in which a teacher has finished a brief explanation about a principle and then asks, almost rhetorically, "Okay, now is that clear?" Exactly what cognitive plan should a student follow when a teacher uses this cue? One perception of the cue implies that the student should quickly check to confirm that he or she could recall each part of the explanation should it be necessary. This is just a superficial check of whether the information was registered in memory in a rote manner. Alternatively, the student might actually retrieve the principle from memory, mentally go through it, and supplement each step with his or her own paraphrase of the teacher's explanation. This second plan actually tests whether the explanation makes sense and can be used to demonstrate true understanding. Research findings suggest that these two alternative plans have quite different effects on learning; the second one is much more likely to result in higher achievement.

Remedies for Students' Misperceptions of Cues. There are several explanations why students perceive the same cue differently. Some cues naturally are ambiguous, as our illustrations in this section and at the opening of the chapter show. Students may also be at different points along the dimensions of mastery of subject matter or of integrating parts of subject matter into a complete structure. How you should deal with students' different perceptions of the same cue depends on which of these two reasons is more applicable to a particular student or group of students.

Fortunately there are some tactics to follow in remedying misperceptions that arise because of ambiguity in cues. One tactic is to train students so that they learn which cognitions ought to be paired with which cues. This procedure is similar to teaching students a new vocabulary word. Cues, whether verbal, gestural, or written on the board, are the "new words" to learn. Cognitions correspond to the "definitions" of these new words. Competence in using the link between a cue and a cognition follows after a number of practice sessions in which the two are used during lessons. By following this tactic, you reduce the chances that students will misperceive your guidance about the cognitions that your cues signal. In other words, they will understand what you are "talking about" when you cue them about cognitions.

Another tactic you can use to reduce the ambiguity of cues is to change the way you use them. Make cues explicit, and be sure to provide clear directions about using cognitions. Along these lines, do not ask, "Is that clear?" Instead, ask, "Can you give a reason for each step in your own words? Do it mentally and then check your own versions with your partner." Do not implore students to "think." Tell them exactly what cognitive plan is appropriate for the content they are working on. For instance, remind them, "Search your memory for a word or phrase that you associate with each term in this question. Then use what you found to do the same kind of searching a second time. This will provide the information you need for your answer."

We noted that another reason why students might perceive cues differently is that they may be at different points in mastering or integrating content. In this case, it is entirely appropriate that students have different perceptions about what a cue suggests they do cognitively. Research is quite clear about the fact that differing degrees of expertise permit or require differing types of cognitive work.

Differences in the kind of mental work students need to do to perform a task can easily be seen in the classroom. Research shows that the kind of thinking used by a beginning reader who is just learning to decode is quite different from that used by a more advanced reader. The beginning reader is attending to literal features of the words in the story. An advanced reader is working out elaborations and "getting into" what the story says. A teacher would expect different answers to the question "What important event happened in the story?" from beginning readers than from those who are more advanced. These different answers reflect differences in the cognitive work required to create the answer. This is not to say that one task is intrinsically harder than the other. It is just that different kinds of cognitive work are enabled by the degree of skill that each student possesses. It may be necessary for you to remind students about the different kinds of cognitions they are capable of carrying out, depending on what they know about the content.

Now suppose that your students attend to instructional cues and correctly perceive which cognitions they should apply to the content being presented. These two conditions set the stage for students to think in ways that are likely to enhance their learning. Yet students still need to be able to perform the cognitive operations and plans that have been cued in order to succeed at learning.

Difficulty #3: Having the Capability to Carry Out Cognitions Needed to Perform Tasks

If you have taught in a way that has increased the chances that your students perceive cues correctly, they already have some experience with two important elements in the effective guidance of their thinking. First, they now know something about using cognitive plans to work with content. Second, they are familiar with the process of associating a particular cognitive plan with a particular set of cues. However, even though students may have learned how to carry out cognitive plans, they may not be able to use these plans in a facile way. Research shows that students, particularly in the elementary grades, need other information about the task that creates an opportunity to use these cognitions. Research also suggests that you can present tasks in ways that support students' cognitive work. Before offering suggestions along these lines, we first need to be clear about what tasks are.

What Are Tasks? Tasks are units of work that students perform in order to learn new content or demonstrate what they can do with old content. Every task has four parts: *conditions, operations, products,* and *evaluations of products.* Tasks provide the opportunities for students to think, to learn, and to refine thinking skills. Tasks are the activities during which students practice using the information and skills required in order to gain fluency. Fluency in this regard is what psychologists call *automaticity.* Automaticity refers to the development of a sufficiently high level of skill in using a set of cognitive operations such that each component of the set need not be thought of separately. When a student has achieved automaticity at a task, all the student needs to do is to recognize (perceive a cue) that an opportunity to apply the appropriate set of cognitive operations is presented. Once begun, the completion of the task unfolds in an automatic manner. For example, as you read this passage, you are able to decode the words and create meaning for yourself automatically. You do not deliberately focus on how to decode the words or on what they mean; you do it automatically. For most of the cognitive skills taught in classrooms, automaticity is the goal toward which teachers should strive.

Conditions under which students work on a task include the amount of content that they have to work with, the ways in which the individual parts of this content are interrelated and given structure, the time students have for carrying out their work, whether other resources such as books or peers can be consulted to help with the task, and how much latitude students are given in determining these conditions.

The importance of the conditions for enactment of a task can be seen when a teacher finishes off a long explanation with a question such as, "Now, are there any questions about that?" (Let us assume that this question is meant to be answered; it is not rhetorical.) The conditions under which students have to respond to this cognitive task make it quite difficult. First, because there was a large amount of content involved in the explanation, students have many things to check; the difficulty of a task is directly proportional to the amount of content it involves. Second, the format of the question, particularly the word "that," does not provide much structure for students to use in recalling the material that was presented. Research has found that the less structure there is, the harder it is to work with content. Third, research shows that many teachers do not wait very long for students to carry out the cognitive plans needed to re-examine the material. In fact, teachers commonly allow students only one or two seconds to think about their answers to a question. For many questions, this is not likely to be long enough for students to finish checking their understanding. Fourth, if little of the content referred to by "that" was on a chalkboard or taken down by students in their notes, students may be overburdened with having to recall this relatively new information from memory, where, because it is so new, it is only weakly represented. Or if the teacher dealt with old information differently from the way the book describes it, the student may have to focus on translating between the two versions of content. Finally, because the teacher's question is so open, students have considerable latitude in setting some of the conditions. For instance, they need to choose whether to look in their book. If they spent the first part of their one or two seconds determining what the conditions are for the task, less time is available for working directly on the job or checking their understanding. All of these difficulties might be lessened by asking this version of the question instead: "Now, that I've contrasted the two characters in terms of motives, take half a minute to check the ending of the story in the book to see if I've covered the categories listed on the board, and then ask a question about any I've missed."

The second part of any task is the set of cognitive *operations* students use to perform the task. This topic will be taken up in the section titled "Cognitive Plans for Your Classroom." We move now to examine the remaining components of tasks.

Products of tasks are the results of students' cognitive operations on content. From the students' point of view, products are mostly answers to questions posed by the teacher, a textbook, or a peer. For teachers, products are the heart of instructional objectives—the knowledge, skill, and attitudes that students are to gain as the result, or product, of participating in lessons. An extremely large range of events constitute the products of cognitive operations. Products can be students' behavior in the classroom, feelings about their performance, or answers on worksheets, essays, or oral presentations. Products are goals for both students and teachers.

Two features that describe the conditions of tasks are also appropriate for describing products—the amount of content that is contained in a product and the structure that this content should have. In addition, there are some other characteristics of products that should be examined. One is the difference or distance between information that is available in the initial conditions of the task and the information that should be in the product. The greater this difference, the harder the task is for students. For example, most students find it more difficult to solve word problems in mathematics than to solve equations that are already expressed clearly. No doubt, much of the difficulty in the word problems comes from the extra cognitive requirement of properly representing them mentally so that appropriate equations can be created. In other words, the more original thinking that is required of students in the product, the more difficult it will be for students to complete the task successfully. Another characteristic of the products is the criteria. Criteria are the dimensions you and your students will use to evaluate the product of a task.

We realize that all this analysis sounds very complex, but we believe that each of these features of products relates predictably to students' capabilities for carrying out tasks that your cues set for them. When the product of a task includes large amounts of new content, when the difference between the content at the start of a task and content in a product is great, and when students have trouble understanding the criteria that their products must satisfy, or when there are too few criteria to aim for, tasks are hard. Look again at the task posed by the teacher's question "Now, are there any questions about that?" Here, the criteria for judging a product of this task are vague. Does a student have a question about "that" when he or she: (1) cannot recall all the points the teacher made; (2) does not see how one of the points really describes one of the main characters; (3) feels uneasy about his or her ability to write a test question that compares the motives of the two main characters; and so on. In contrast, the second version of the teacher's question that we gave, above, provided clearer criteria for the student about what the product should be. These criteria were explicitly stated when the teacher requested that students check whether the examples in the explanation fit into the categories of motives written on the board. The second version of the question also provides an explicit structure for the information that comprises this product. It specifies that the teacher wants students to see if they can recognize the points from the lecture as examples of the abstract categories of motives listed on the board. Research has found that both providing criteria for products and describing the structure of content that makes up the product help students complete tasks successfully.

The final component of tasks is *evaluations* of products. Research documents that these evaluations are central in facilitating students' work on instructional tasks. Without evaluations of products, students are unsure as to whether they have finished a task or whether they are part way toward the final product of a large task. Evaluations provide information about the degree to which products meet criteria. Thus clearer and more specific criteria for products provide better information for students about the nature of your evaluations. When criteria are clear and specific, we predict that students will be able to generate their own evaluations without requiring feedback from other sources. Furthermore, it is very important that students be taught how to evaluate the quality of their own work, because abilities and dispositions regarding self-evaluation are important attributes of autonomous learners.

To summarize, instructional tasks that students carry out to learn from teaching can be analyzed into four components: conditions, operations, products, and evaluations. These four components are easy to remember if you form the word "cope" from the first letter of each component and then remember that students have to "cope" with tasks in order to learn.

Now that we have analyzed the components of tasks, we return to the difficulties that students experience while trying to accomplish tasks. These have been mentioned in passing as we described a task's conditions, operations, products, and evaluations. Let us discuss these features again to suggest ways that you can enhance students' capabilities to succeed at the tasks involved in learning.

Remedies for Low Capabilities to Perform Tasks. To say that a task contains features that make it more difficult is another way of saying that these features strain students' capabilities to perform them. In general, then, features of tasks that strain students' capabilities can be remedied by making tasks easier. This is not to say that tasks should not challenge students. In fact, tasks that are too simple are known to lower students' motivation. What we do mean is that tasks students need to perform in order to learn should not present difficulties that are irrelevant to what constitutes achievement of instructional objectives. In other words, the only source of difficulty in tasks should be intrinsic to content, rather than added to content.

Teachers can support students' capabilities to deal effectively with the conditions of tasks in several ways. First, teachers should make tasks manageable by including in them only the essential content. Second, they should make that content explicit by repeating it or giving it an informative label in the task, rather than using vague referents such as "that." This guideline requires teachers to use precise language and to be considerate of their audience. Research is clear that these features support students' learning.

Third, teachers should try to develop a structure for the content and provide students with access to it. Put graphics, tables, outlines and mnemonic aids on the blackboard or on worksheets. Think about allowing students to check with a neighbor when the focus of a task is on learning rather than testing, and remind them when it is appropriate to do this. Not only does the freedom to work with a peer give them access to necessary information, but it allows for some evaluation of their products earlier in time than is usual. Evaluation, then, becomes part of the learning rather than an activity added to the end of learning.

Finally, unless the task you pose is one that requires the student to create a new plan, try to restrict the alternatives for approaching the task. Such constraint might require you to make clear to students how you want them to think as they work on the task. You can provide this clarity by "thinking aloud" as you work out a set of examples. Make your stream of consciousness available to the students by verbalizing your own thoughts. Describe what you are thinking about and what you are planning to do as you work out the example. Also, talk about what you do *not* do and describe your reasons for *not* performing certain procedures. Remember that you want to influence the way your students think, not only their completion of the products of classroom tasks. We suggest here that you can influence the way they think by providing a model of how you think about the things worth thinking about. All of these steps will help to make tasks more manageable for students, by reducing unnecessary strain on their cognitive systems, while at the same time requiring them to work at learning.

Turning to features of the products of tasks, similar remedies can be suggested. Try to include only essential content in products. Make sure that the criteria for judging a product are available to students, that the set of criteria are clear, and that they are adequate for judging the product. These measures provide students with knowledge of the goal toward which they are working and allow them to work backward as well as forward in doing the task. In addition, do not unnecessarily lengthen the distance between the task's initial content and the product. Keep the number of steps or transformations needed to develop the product to a small number. Do this by dividing large tasks into smaller ones with two or three steps. Have students practice each of these two- or three-step parts until it functions like one unit. Then combine two or three of these units into a task, and so on. This procedure will increase the chances that students will be able to develop automaticity in their cognitive plans. It also decreases the chances that they will practice incorrect versions of plans.

Finally, enhance students' capabilities to perform tasks by making sure that their products are evaluated. We have already mentioned that it is important for students' products to be evaluated promptly. Having students work with a partner is one excellent technique for doing this. Creating an environment where learning from mistakes is prized also can contribute to ensuring that students seek out evaluations of their products.

We have one more remedy to offer. Frankly, we do not know of any research that supports us on this point. But it makes such good common sense that we do not think this is a drawback. Do the task yourself exactly like you want students to do it. Do not skip steps. Use this information to make the conditions of the task clear to your students. When you have to decide how to move from step 2 to step 3, write down the basis for your decision. The information about what is needed to proceed through a plan should also be part of the content that you teach in the task. Time yourself, and then estimate that students will need at least twice as much time. Also, by practicing the task in the same way you expect a student to do it, you generate the basis for making your "thinking aloud" presentations informative and useful to your students.

Assume for now that students avoid all of the three difficulties we have been discussing. They consistently attend to the instructional cues you provide, they clearly perceive the cognitions you intend them to apply to content, and you have arranged the tasks that they tackle so that their capabilities to carry out cognitive plans are not overly strained. Is there any remaining possibility that your teaching and your students' cognitive mediations of it might be interfered with? Yes, there is.

Difficulty #4: Motivation to Work at Tasks

As you surely remember from your days as a student and even now as you read this chapter, learning is hard work. No matter how successful students are at avoiding or overcoming the difficulties to learning, noted above, two important questions still remain: why bother? and what's in it for me? If students lack motivation to be actively involved in cognitively mediating your teaching and in applying cognition to content, both their immediate learning and their later motivation will suffer.

Chapters 9 and 10 address the topic of motivating students. In addition to the excellent information you can find there, we also have a few points to make about the cognitive mediational view of motivation for engaging in and completing tasks. To do this, we first introduce a very brief model of motivation, the AEIOU model. With this model in mind, we then suggest ways to avoid difficulties due to students' low motivation.

AEIOU—Five Aspects of Motivation. We begin with a premise that not everyone agrees with, but that is central to our argument: students decide whether to be motivated. That is, we do not view motivation for classroom learning as a swelling of desire or disgust that originates in some deeply personal place that only professionally trained psychologists can help a student to visit. Motivation is not that mystical. Instead, an explanation of motivation in a classroom is quite simple.

The main question students ask is this: will I enjoy learning from teaching? If they expect so, then, provided that the foregoing three difficulties do not impede their work, they will work hard to learn. In answering this main question, students are shrewd. They search for five kinds of information to predict whether the investment they will have to make in order to complete tasks is likely to return some enjoyment. Each of the letters in AEIOU stands for one type of information, and we present brief descriptions of these next. However, we present them out of alphabetical order to bring out the relations among them.

Letter O stands for the *outcomes* that students predict will follow if they do the work you signal with a cue. The question asked by the student is simple: what is the result of the work predicted to be—some new knowledge that resolves a puzzle, a chance to say something in class, a chance to take notes on material that is likely to appear on a test, or an opportunity to spend class time with a friend? These outcome expectations are affectively neutral. They are simply predictions about what will be the end products of working on the task you pose with the cue.

Letter E represents the students' *expectations* about whether they will be effective, whether they are capable of creating those outcomes or products successfully. Expectations about one's own efficacy are based on students' judgments about whether they possess the cognitions needed to perform tasks. They ask, "Do I have a good plan for working on this task, and can I make that plan work under these conditions?" In order to answer this question affirmatively, students must also believe that they can perceive what cues mean. If you doubt that the cues you are using in teaching are being interpreted correctly, then it is likely that students will not select the best plan to work on the task. Thus we believe that students' sense of efficacy for a task is related to their sense of control over their responses to the cognitive demands of the task. Our position is based on a considerable body of research showing that a sense of control is an extremely important determinant of a person's intrinsic motivation to complete a task.

Letter A corresponds to students' *attributions* for the expectation they have about efficacy. These attributions are judgments about why students believe they can or cannot accomplish a task. The source of information on which to base attributions is students' previous performance on similar tasks. Some attributions bolster or protect self-concept. "I can do this task because I'm good at problems like these," and "I may have trouble with this one because the teacher is really pressing on fast," illustrate such. Other attributions damage self-concept: "I'm just not smart enough to get these right," or "The teacher gave me an especially simple task just so I could succeed." Attributions for success or failure set the stage for how students will feel about their work—proud, shameful, lucky, or indifferent.

Letter I refers to *incentive.* Incentive reflects the value that will be gained or lost if the outcome expectation is or is not fulfilled. Values are idiosyncratic. Some students find considerable incentive in being able to answer questions in class, even if their replies are wrong. Other students find high incentive in reaching the end of a long intricate task. It is important for you to know which outcomes hold high or low incentives for your students. Find out by asking them directly and by observing carefully what they choose to do when given a free choice to select tasks to work on. (As an aside, if a student shows high motivation at tasks in free-choice settings, do not reward the student at a later time for doing the same task. One of the easiest ways of destroying intrinsic motivation for a task is to provide extrinsic rewards.)

The fifth letter, U, is for the relative *utility* of working on this particular task, as opposed to working on another one. Theoretically, the utility of a task is calculated by weighing the attributions and incentives that a student associates with working on it, and combining this result with the efficacy expectation. A task with only a moderate utility and a moderate efficacy expectation will not be as motivating as one with slightly lower utility but a very high expectation about efficacy.

Whether students really make decisions based on AEIOUs for every task and engage only in the most rational choice of tasks for them is not the issue. The point is that the AEIOU model provides a productive way for you to think about motivating students.

Remedies for Low Motivation. Consider the parts of the model of motivation in the order that we explained them: O, E, A, I, U. Students who cannot predict what the outcome of working on a task will be will lack too much of the information they need to choose whether to approach the task. First, notice that one kind of outcome students need to be clear about is the product of the task. Students need this information. Second, students need to be clear about the social outcomes of working on a task. This means they need to know whether their performance will be public or private, examined by you or self-checked, and so on. There are steps you can take to remedy low motivation that stems from students' difficulty in predicting what outcomes to expect.

First, early in the school year, set up a consistent social system within which instructional tasks are carried out. This provides students with some surety about the social outcomes of tasks. Second, always remind students about the outcomes of the tasks you set when you cue them to start work.

Students also need to predict whether they can accomplish the task effectively. Again, this expectation rests squarely on overcoming some prior difficulties—namely, reaching clear perceptions about the cognitive task to which a cue applies and having a well-practiced cognitive plan for working on the task. Using this information to remedy low motivation suggests that you should describe how new tasks are like old ones at which students have succeeded. Do this by referring back to a prior, similar task, and even reviewing or modeling the cognitive plan that is appropriate for working on it. These remedies not only cement prior achievements, but provide exactly the kind of information students need to generate positive expectations of efficacy. In brief, build on past accomplishments to enhance students' expectations about efficacy.

This remedy also helps to bolster students' attributions for successes at instructional tasks. If you point out that the cognitive strategies or plans they have mastered or are developing result in success, students' attributions for their successes and failures will focus on their own competencies for learning. Cognitive plans are adaptable, they can be controlled by a student, and students must learn this. Attributions to low ability, luck, or other debilitating causes are not appropriate when a lack of suitable cognitive tools is the problem. Also, when students succeed, they can take pride in the fact that they mastered and applied their cognitive tools productively to accomplish a task.

You should take care not to erode "productive attributions." You probably err when you introduce tasks by saying, "This one is so easy that everyone should get it." Present hard tasks as challenges that can be conquered, rather than as obviously insoluble problems. And remind students directly about attributions for their success and failure that are fruitful. These are as much a part of the curriculum as subject matter is, so review them.

There really are no remedies for the components of the AEIOU model that address incentives and utilities. Incentives are what students select as valuable, not what you say is valuable, although there is overlap. Personal incentives, however, are also partially arrived at on the basis of other information you can provide students about outcomes, their feelings of efficacy, and their attributions. The same is true of utilities. So, to address incentives and utilities, focus directly on remedying all the difficulties we have discussed. Provided that you offer incentives that students value, as we mentioned earlier, utilities will take care of themselves.

COGNITIVE PLANS FOR YOUR CLASSROOM

We will assume for now that you and your students are abiding by the conditions of the contract for work in classrooms, and that the four difficulties that students can experience when responding to your cues have been generally overcome. What remains is to discuss the cognitive plans that students can use to learn from teaching and the principles that teachers can use to teach these plans to students.

Children enter school with a wide range of individual differences. The attributes on which children differ are many, ranging from family background to personality traits to differences in ability. We are going to add to the already long list of differences among students noted by many researchers. Our addition, as you might well guess, is that students differ in the extent to which they possess and skillfully use various cognitive plans for learning in classrooms.

Consider the following example of individual differences in using cognitive plans for learning. A common task in the primary grades is to learn lists of information, which, from a student's point of view, are likely to be seen as arbitrary. Some examples of such lists are the letters of the alphabet, the four seasons, the primary colors, and the foods in the major food groups. When children in primary grades are given such lists to learn, some will use a *strategy* to make the task less difficult. Suppose the list is a series of nouns, say, a catalog of what you ate yesterday—hamburger, carrots, granola bars, yogurt, sausages, bran flakes, and so on. These foods can be grouped into different categories—namely, meats, fruits and vegetables, grains, and dairy products. If you should ask students to remember that catalog, some of them will try to learn the list by grouping the foods into their respective categories. They will apply this plan for organizing the words without being told. Other children will not try to organize the words in the food groups, but instead will use a "brute force" strategy of simply repeating the words over and over. Not surprisingly, the students who use the organizing strategy are much more likely to learn the list successfully and to be able to recall it more completely.

As children advance through the grades, most eventually acquire simple cognitive plans like the procedure for organizing terms into labeled categories. Fewer children, however, develop highly sophisticated plans that enable them to learn and retain much more. But a growing body of research is demonstrating that many of these plans, both simple and sophisticated, can be taught to children and, in turn, that children who use them improve their achievement. In this section, we describe what some of these plans are. We will discuss cognitive plans for rehearsing, elaborating, organizing, and monitoring. But before this discussion, we present some general principles to guide your thinking about these ideas.

Basic Principles About Cognitive Plans

Principle #1: Cognitive Plans Are Characteristic of How People Learn and Remember.   All people, except those with very serious mental handicaps, use plans for learning new information and for remembering information that they have learned; it is an attribute of being human. This is important to consider as a teacher, because you must be aware of your students' efforts to use the plans they have and to make sense of what they are doing. This is another way of saying what we have written previously about "students' purposes and intentions" and students' "strategic" perception of cues in the classroom. Children in classrooms are not simply passive agents waiting for you to fill them up with knowledge and competence. They have something to say about how they respond to your teaching. One of the most important aspects of their contribution is the plan *they* select to help learning along. The basis for their selection of a plan is whether it makes sense to them.

Principle #2: Most People Already Possess Successful Cognitive Plans.   We assume that all learning is influenced by the cognitive plans learners use. Recent research has shown that successful learners use a wide range of such plans to complete their work. Interviews with students of all ages substantiate this finding.

An intriguing aspect of this research is that teachers can inadvertently disrupt students' plans, and this leads to lowered achievement. We once did a study with university undergraduates who were taking our introductory course in educational psychology. We taught some of our students a sophisticated strategy for learning from our lectures. Specifically, we taught these students how to recognize key cues that we used in our lectures, plus a sophisticated plan for organizing and elaborating the content presented in concert with these cues. This cognitive plan was based on research that had shown that students who used the strategy learned much more than students who did not. Students in the control group were given some extra attention so they would not feel slighted, but they received none of the special training about perceiving cues or using the cognitive plan.

Much to our surprise and chagrin, our weekly quizzes showed that students in the control group were learning more than the students we had trained. Interviews with the students solved this mystery. Students we had trained sincerely tried to use the sophisticated plan we taught them. However, these university students could not do both that and what they normally did to learn in our lectures—they could not use their own well-developed strategies to help them learn. Although these students told us that they thought our plan was potentially useful, they liked their old, "less potent" ones better. They also told us that we did not provide them with sufficient practice with the new plan so that they could use it automatically and with skill. Other researchers have also found that interfering with learners' use of their own successful strategies can impair learning.

Principle #3: New Plans Must Be Practiced Extensively. The message from the study we conducted and other similar research is not that learning will be depressed if you put findings from research to use. Rather, it is that students need to reach skilled levels of performance in the plans they use to learn. Established, well-practiced, less powerful plans are more productive than new, shaky, but more powerful ones. The research shows very consistently, however, that when students do reach skilled levels in using potent cognitive plans, they learn much more effectively. The trick for the teacher is to replace incorrect or inefficient cognitive plans with better ones, and then to ensure that students get enough practice to use the better plan with ease and skill.

Principle #4: If Students Fail to Use a Plan, Do Not Assume They Cannot Use It. Many Studies have shown that students who have not used a strategy can use it when they recognize an occasion to use it. In a typical study—for example, one in which a simple rehearsal strategy is investigated—young children are divided into two groups, those who rehearse spontaneously and those who do not. Spontaneous rehearsers use their plan without any prompting, while the nonrehearsers simply work on their learning task. Nonrehearsers do not know about rehearsing. Spontaneous rehearsers also are observed to learn much more information than nonrehearsers in this first of three learning tasks.

Next, the children who do not know how to rehearse are taught a plan for rehearsing information. They are provided sufficient opportunity to practice this plan to reach skilled levels of use. Significantly, they also are asked if they believe the plan to be useful for learning and if they are motivated to use the plan. They say yes to both questions and support their answers by pointing out how much more they remember when they use the plan for rehearsing. A second learning task is then presented to both groups, and the previous nonrehearsers, who now know how to use the rehearsing plan, are reminded to use it. This time, their performance equals that of the spontaneous rehearsers.

Without much delay, a third learning task is presented. This time, the nonrehearsers are *not* reminded to use the new plan. The trained nonrehearsers fall back to their original level of lower performance. Moreover, they are not observed to use the rehearsing plan they were taught. When told to use it, however, they did, and they learned more.

Important implications are derived from this account. First, even when students know about a cognitive plan, are capable of using it productively, and are motivated to use it because they believe it is useful, they may not use it. It appears that they fail to use it because they do not realize that the occasion is right. Either there was no cue to use the plan, or a cue was offered but not attended to, or a cue was presented but not perceived to mean that a particular plan should be used. We have covered these issues before. For children with these difficulties, the teacher should make cues for cognitive plans more explicit and more meaningful.

The second implication is new. Some children have a plan available but do not use it. Other children have not acquired the plan at all, and still other children need to practice it to reach levels of skilled performance. Thorough assessment is needed to identify which students fall into which group before embarking on a program that either teaches children plans that they need to know or provides practice with plans they already know.

With these three principles in mind, we turn now to examining the kinds of cognitive plans that researchers have found to enhance students' participation in learning.

Four Families of Cognitive Plans

The four types of plans discussed here form a continuum. Each type actually represents a family of plans for which a wide range of instances exists. The first family of plans, *rehearsing plans,* is the simplest and the most limited in its range of application. Rehearsing plans focus mainly on collections of rather discrete items of information. The second family of plans is *elaborating plans.* These involve more complex forms of cognition, and, correspondingly, they result in more elaborate learning. *Organizing plans* form the third family. These involve activities in which the learner arranges material to be learned into a new structure. They are a step beyond elaborating plans. *Monitoring plans* comprise the fourth family, and they are at the highest level. Some researchers refer to these plans as "executive processes" in order to imply that monitoring plans are used by learners to control lower-level plans. Other researchers refer to them as "metacognitive" plans, suggesting that monitoring plans provide learners with a mechanism for thinking about thinking. We accept both alternative terms but will here use just one label—monitoring.

We need to make an important point explicitly at the beginning of this section: our and others' research shows that, for any particular learning activity, individual students probably differ in the plan they need to or should use. While a particular task may call for rehearsing by one learner, an elaborating strategy may be more appropriate for another student. Which plan is most appropriate depends on some characteristics of the student's knowledge; for example, the amount that the student knows or the kind and degree of organization the student has imposed on the knowledge.

In this discussion, we treat these types of plans as discrete. In reality, in classrooms, the boundaries that we draw here are likely to be much less sharp. Nonetheless, it is useful to consider the families of plans as separate at the start, because this simplifies your planning to teach these cognitive skills to students. Ultimately, however, your goal should be for students to achieve smooth, automatic, and integrated use of these plans under their own control. In effect, this will help students to become adept self-teachers and self-learners. When students have productive control of their plans for learning, they will be able to compensate for your teaching and accommodate instruction to their own individual differences. We believe that this is really the only practical way to address the inescapable fact that students' individual differences are so varied and so influential in learning.

Plans for Rehearsing. Everyone is familiar with these plans. We all have used them in one form or another for a variety of learning tasks. Simple rehearsal—repeating words over and over or looking at a diagram several times and trying to reproduce it in your "mind's eye"— is a common technique for absorbing information. Many mature learners, however, recognize the limits that such plans have. First, rehearsal plans are relatively less efficient than other types of plans. When only rehearsal plans are used, more time is usually needed to learn information completely than with other strategies. Second, information learned by applying only rehearsing plans is usually poorly integrated with the rest of our knowledge. Many high-school and college students who cram for tests are intimately familiar with what happens to knowledge they acquire by using only simple rehearsal strategies: it is quickly forgotten because it is memorized in chunks that are connected neither to one another nor to one's rich structures of prior knowledge. Until other plans are used to integrate it with our broader knowledge, rote information may have little influence on whatever else we know.

Most children know how to use plans for rehearsing simple material by the third or fourth grade. Younger children of 6 or 7 might be able to use these strategies, but they have less success than older children. Their lack of success might be related to less sophisticated monitoring plans. That is, these very young students might know how to use the strategy, but they might not know when to use it, how to adjust it to achieve different kinds of goals, or when to abandon it.

Rehearsing plans can be used with content such as simple paired associates, like symbols for the chemical elements; lists of items, such as countries in the Common Market; serial lists, such as letters of the alphabet; and diagrams, like the geometric construction of an angle bisector. But these plans can also be used for more complicated content. A common application is in taking notes from a lecture or from a book. Here, simply copying the complicated spoken or written material rehearses it. Another plan is to underline material in a text or on dittos. Compared to no rehearsal at all, these techniques usually boost learning and later recall. But it has the same drawbacks noted earlier. Additionally, these simple rehearsing plans will not be very productive when students have difficulty identifying the important points to be rehearsed. In such cases they may rehearse relatively less central information. This can be a serious limitation for younger students, especially those who have not yet reached sixth grade.

For all the negative things we have written about rehearsing plans, we should point out that they do have at least one important positive feature: they are useful simply because they can make information available for subsequent use. When students have trouble using another kind of cognitive plan, rehearsing plans do help to acquire the information. Sometimes, this is sufficient.

Plans for Elaborating. Elaborating means adding together different bits of information to construct a larger or more detailed unit. Many different theories of learning have emphasized the role of elaborating as a basic learning process. For example, a leading current theory of learning and memory is based on the metaphor that long-term memory acts as a large net. Concepts and larger units of meaning are the knots in this net, technically called nodes. Nodes are tied together by strings of different kinds, each kind expressing a relation. Some examples of different relations are: sodium IS AN element, elements HAVE PROPERTY of mass, isotopes RESEMBLE elements, and sodium IS PART OF salt. Each relationship elaborates the meaning of the nodes it connects. The more elaborations a node has to other nodes, the richer the network of meaning. The more meaningful a node, the easier it is to remember, because there are alternative ways to travel along the net of meaning to find any particular node and because the learner has extra information to call on in developing answers to questions. It follows that cognitive plans that build richer connections among bits of information—or elaborate this information—produce knowledge that is at once more available for recall and more useful. Plans for elaborating, then, are based on this theory of learning and memory.

Diverse elaboration strategies have been investigated. Perhaps the simplest plans for elaborating are ones like rhyming and making acronyms. Rhyming helps children learn the sequence of numbers: "One, two, buckle my shoe. Three, four, close the door." Acronyms like ROY G BIV for colors in the spectrum, Chief SOH-CAH-TOA for the formulas to compute sine, cosine, and tangent, and our AEIOU for components in motivation elaborate simple lists and procedures. These simple elaboration plans add little meaning, but they do add relations in the net of memory. They are useful but limited.

One elaborating plan that much research has validated as useful is making images. For example, to learn topographical features—say, the names of the Great Lakes and their positions on the map—a typical imagery plan would involve the learner in creating and labeling vivid mental pictures of the information to be remembered. Students might imagine Lake Superior as an old king dressed in regal robes and sitting atop a giant rabbit named Mitch (for Lake Michigan). It is possible to teach students to use imagery strategies in a number of different subject areas. What is important is that students learn to produce vivid images that have meaning for them.

A related cognitive plan is called the keyword method. In this plan, there are two types of elaboration—acoustic similarity and images. For instance, to learn the definition of the verb "persuade," students identify a "key" word that sounds like the word to be learned. "Purse" sounds like "persuade." The second step in this plan is to create an image that elaborates the key word with the meaning of the word to learn. Students might picture a woman being persuaded to buy a purse. On the vocabulary test, when they hear "persuade," students use the acoustic elaboration to remember "purse," then use "purse" to remember the picture, and finally use the picture to remember the definition.

The keyword plan has been successfully used to learn several subject areas, such as foreign-language vocabulary, geography, and the order of United States presidents. The critical features of the keyword and related plans are that learners use active and vivid images, and when they are capable, that they create their own images rather than use ones that the teacher provides. However, some evidence indicates that elementary-school children might have difficulty generating the images necessary for plans like the keyword method to be successful. Thus teachers might have to provide the images for younger students or, if possible, to devote time to teaching their students how to develop their own images.

The elaboration strategies discussed to this point are useful for relatively simple content. But many goals of classroom instruction involve more complex content. Plans like the keyword method are not particularly useful if students are trying to understand the differences in foreign policies that individual NATO nations advocate. Nor would the keyword method be useful if students were merely trying to remember these different foreign policies. In such instances, more complex plans for elaborating are required, such as paraphrasing, summarizing, creating analogies and examples, and note taking that involves abstraction and synthesis. The research literature shows that students who are taught how to use these strategies and who actually do use them perform better on achievement measures than students who do not receive or apply such instruction.

It is important to note that the effectiveness of elaborating strategies depends on which cognitive operations students actually use. Note taking is a good example, because the observable activity of writing notes can reflect either simple copying, as discussed earlier, or it can draw on a more complex elaborative cognitive plan. A teacher should not expect students who have taken notes from readings or lectures to achieve a fuller understanding of a topic if their notes constitute mere copying. If students do not use more complex cognitive activities during note taking, teachers should not expect more elaborate results than simple reproduction of the material.

Plans for Organizing.   To organize information involves three steps:

1. Putting separate items of information into groups based on a meaningful relationship linking the items together.
2. Labeling the group with the name of the relationship.
3. Identifying relations among the groups formed in the first step.

Our classification of cognitive plans that students use to enhance learning is an immediate example of organizing. We have clustered many different plans into four families based on a major kind of cognitive operation shared by each plan within a family. Then we labeled the group with the cognitive operation—rehearsing, elaborating, organizing, or monitoring. We have also imposed a relationship among the groups based on a continuum of the cognitive complexity that is involved in carrying out the plan.

There are many kinds of organizing plans. Students learning the products of a foreign country's economy can apply an organizing plan called *clustering* to good benefit. With this plan, they group goods like timber, computers, aluminum, beef, wheat, tractors, iron, and paper into the clusters: forest products, mining, farm products, and manufactured goods. There are distinct benefits of this kind of organizing. First, as was the case with elaborating, seeking out relations among initially separate items of information adds meaning to the material being studied. Second, by clustering several items together into one group whose name represents a feature that all the items share, the strain on memory when recalling items is reduced. Instead of having to recall tractors and computers separately, the student needs to remember just one item, manufactured goods. In addition, the name of this group provides a cue for searching the network of previously acquired information—namely, that these goods are manufactured.

When the material students are to learn contains many different kinds of relationships among items of information, simple clustering does not capture the richness of meaning. For these more complicated materials, other organizing plans are more effective. One of these is called *networking*. To apply this plan, students search through information in a book, on the chalkboard, or in their notes to identify basic types of relations. Then they draw a diagram of the information that includes the items and their relations.

We will not elaborate on other organizing plans, but many exist. They are powerful tools for promoting learning. They provide all the benefits of rehearsing because students must practice using information in order to prepare a diagram or to outline the material. Also, if students add to the new material other information that they know already by using IS LIKE and GO TOGETHER relations, they combine elaborating with organizing. Finally, because you can involve students in thinking about the material in a way that requires them to leave a record of what they thought, a network diagram or an outline, you can keep track of their progress much more readily than when thinking remains invisibly inside their minds.

Plans for Monitoring.   Cognitive plans for monitoring are the most general plans we discuss because they are the most abstract. The label *monitoring* in this context means "to keep track of and make corrections when things get off track." What do monitoring plans monitor? They monitor the status of how well other cognitive plans are working. In order to do this, students need to have readily available a set of criteria for judging how well a particular cognitive plan is working. With these criteria in mind, students then need to carry out periodic assessments of how well that plan is working. When the cognitive plan being monitored is not working well enough, students then need to have an idea about how to repair it.

While this may sound too complicated for students to do while they also are trying to learn material, it is not. Researchers have demonstrated repeatedly that students of all ages can be taught monitoring plans and can use them to enhance achievement substantially. What is also apparent from this research is that proper conditions have to be provided for students to use monitoring plans. We describe two different kinds of monitoring plans here. The first kind is for monitoring comprehension; the second kind is for coping with a task when motivation is not supporting a sustained focus on performance. Variations on the themes of these two plans abound in the literature. They also are relatively easy for you to design on your own. Just make sure that the content in any plan for monitoring you invent fits the general form: a list of criteria against which progress is monitored, rules for when to monitor, and strategies for repairing problems.

Plans for monitoring comprehension have been investigated in situations in which students read textbooks. Suppose the reading material is a story. The criteria used to keep track of how well the story is understood could be answers to two questions: (1) Who did what, where, when, and how? (2) Why does this fit into the plot of the story?

When should monitoring be carried out? A reasonable answer is at the end of every paragraph or page. What should a student do when answers to the questions are hard to come up with or are imprecise? There are several alternatives. One technique for repair is simply to read the passage again and mentally cross out the information that has already been used to answer one of the questions. What is left ought to contain information or at least a clue for one of the other answers. Another method is to postpone answering the question until another section of the text has been read. While reading that section, the student searches for the missing information. A third repairing strategy is to ask someone.

Suppose the text being read is expository—for example, a social studies or science chapter. Criteria for monitoring comprehension of this kind of material might include the following: what vocabulary words are new, and what does each mean? what is the one main idea in each paragraph? which type of information is this paragraph generally about—examples, a cause-effect relation, a list, a definition, or a compare-and-contrast relation? Asking these questions paragraph by paragraph is a good schedule for monitoring. To repair flaws revealed by monitoring, several strategies are available: using the glossary or a dictionary to obtain the meaning of new vocabulary words; checking the first sentence of the paragraph to see if it names the topic discussed in the paragraph; looking for words in the paragraph that are synonyms of important words.

Now, we turn to the second type of plan for monitoring performance, the type that focuses on coping with a task when motivation is not optimal. We have already described the main pieces of information that students need to have in order to make decisions about whether they will be motivated, the AEIOUs. These five kinds of information identify the first criterion in plans for coping—namely, that students need to be aware of how they view the AEIOUs associated with performing a task. Sometimes, simply being clear about one's motivational state is all that is needed to correct inappropriate levels of motivation. But, when this is not enough, the student must follow a plan to cope with the task.

Coping can mean many things. Reducing feelings of personal inadequacy, finding a reason to persist, and feeling good about what has been accomplished are probably the most common motivational problems students have to deal with. Most of the recent research in this area has focused on ways in which students can be taught to anticipate motivational problems before they occur. Then students are taught how to avoid the debilitating effects of barriers to achieving success at school such as anxiety, boredom, doubt about one's ability to learn, and peer pressure to conform to disruptive behavior.

Monitoring plans to improve motivation have much in common with similar plans used to monitor learning activities. They are based on the assumption that people can be aware of at least some of their own cognitive activities, and that this awareness can be used to achieve success at learning. Most plans for monitoring motivational states have focussed on the same elements. First, the learner must set goals toward which he or she works. Much research has shown that learners who set clear goals for themselves have a better chance to achieve success than learners who do not. Second, the learner must make an assessment of the progress he or she is making toward the goal. Self-assessment procedures can take on many forms, but they usually involve the self-observation of thoughts, feelings, and behavior. Some examples include analyzing one's own negative thoughts, noticing the situations that occur when boredom sets in, or thinking about one's physical reactions to test situations. Setting goals and assessing the extent to which one is progressing toward them are such useful devices that it is often sufficient for a student to perform only these elements of a motivation monitoring plan in order to achieve success.

Additional commonly found elements in motivation monitoring plans, coping and mastery, are concerned with strategies for implementation. Coping strategies involve teaching the student how to anticipate impediments to the achievement of goals, and how to live with some of the discomfort and frustration that is inevitably associated with striving for success at difficult tasks. Frequently, these strategies include teaching learners to use positive, facilitating self-talk, rather than negative, debilitating language. A second common feature is to teach learners to anticipate and be prepared for difficulties. One of the major goals of coping strategies is to help the learner avoid feelings of being overwhelmed and, consequently, becoming disengaged from the learning task.

Mastery strategies are designed to help learners succeed at tasks for which they otherwise would predict failure. Commonly, these strategies include teaching learners to attribute success or failure to modifiable personal characteristics, such as the amount of effort they expend, rather than to characteristics they can do nothing about, such as their innate ability. They are taught to master tasks by being persistent, rather than to fail at tasks by being passive. Other mastery strategies require the learner to proceed through tasks with graduated levels of difficulty, while helping the learner refocus self-talk from negative to positive expectations. These strategies, frequently referred to as expectancy retraining, have been shown to be effective in a wide range of educational activities.

Teaching Cognitive Plans

How can we teach cognitive plans to students who do not possess them? Three principles merit special mention. These are about meaningfulness, practice, and feedback.

The Principle of Meaning. The content to be learned about a cognitive plan has to be presented in such a way that students understand what they are doing. The teacher's presentation has to be clear and must help students develop meaning. Fundamentally, as we discussed in the section on elaborating plans, meaning results when different pieces of information are related to one another.

The primary source of meaning in classroom teaching is what students know already. The general principle, then, is this: Learn what students know already, and use that prior knowledge when developing new knowledge. For cognitive plans, this prior knowledge resides in the "tricks" that students have already developed to help them learn. Every student at every age will have something to tell you about how they learn. Ask them how they do it, and build on their answers.

The Principle of Practice. It is critical that students practice using the cognitive plans that you want them to learn. If you want students to learn how to use plans for elaborating or organizing information, then you must create instructional activities that require them to use these plans. First, ensure that the subject matter is appropriate to using these kinds of plans. Second, encourage students to practice.

If you, classmates, or the text does most of the hard work for them, students will not learn how to do these things themselves. For example, it is common for classroom tasks to be surreptitiously divided up among students so that each student works on only that part of a task at which he or she is already good. Teachers sometimes unwittingly keep students from learning certain plans by allowing some students to withdraw from a task because requirements for completing it seem too arduous. The cumulative effect of many individual occasions when students can avoid practicing complex cognitive plans is that they never learn them well.

The Principle of Feedback. Without feedback about the quality of the work in which students engage, the effects of instruction are diminished. The feedback you give should be specific about what is successful and what is not. It should relate directly to previously established criteria for the product of tasks. Feedback also should provide some guidance about how to correct errors, not just that there are errors. Finally, you must be truthful. Telling students that their work is adequate or "good enough" when it is not is neither instructionally sound nor honest.

How do you give feedback when the subject matter is cognitive plans? Every plan has steps. Turn the students' covert cognitive steps into something observable. Teachers do that whenever they say, "Show me how you got that." Students can think out loud about the cognitive plans they apply to learning. They can leave traces of those plans on worksheets by writing their elaborations, making diagrams of their organizations, and describing how they monitored their performance by stating things like, "This is right because. . . ." When students provide these kinds of information to you, you can provide clear, timely, and productive feedback to them.

SUMMARY

We have covered a great deal of information in this chapter. We now attempt to summarize it in a few concise paragraphs. Along the way, we repeat our main principles for teaching that we gleaned from the research that underlies our presentation.

Teachers and students each contribute to making instruction effective. We used the metaphor of a contract to characterize these contributions. Teachers are obliged to present subject matter and to guide students' cognitive treatment of that information. Students are responsible for seeking out their teacher's guidance and for providing feedback about how well they make use of it to learn.

Interference in communication about cognitive plans from the teacher to students can occur in four ways. First, students may not attend to cues that teachers provide about how to work on content. Teachers can correct this problem by making sure students know what form a cue takes, by making sure that they are not so overloaded that they do not have time to attend, and by making cues salient.

Second, students may misperceive which cognitive plans to apply to content when they attend to a cue. This problem can be remedied in two ways: by training students to know what a cue means, and by altering your cues so they describe explicitly which cognitive operations students should use.

The third form of interference is students' inability to perform the cognitive plan that you signal for a learning task. Here, you must consider the conditions, operations, products, and evaluations of each learning task. Concerning conditions, make sure that you do not present too much information, that the information is in a structured format, that you give students enough time to carry out the plan, and that the content is not unnecessarily complicated. Regarding cognitive operations, make sure that students have been taught about them, have practiced them extensively, and have received accurate feedback about their use of these plans. With respect to products, ensure that products do not require too much information, are not excessively different from the content that was presented in the conditions initially, and that students are clear about the criteria that determine whether a product is correct or good. Regarding evaluations, be sure that they identify errors precisely in terms of the criteria students expect to be applied to the products, ensure they contain some suggestion about how to correct errors, and make them honest.

Finally, motivation can be an important source of interference. Here, you have to consider five topics, the AEIOUs. Make outcome expectations easy by telling students what outcomes follow from using particular cognitive plans. Remind students of previous occasions when they have been successful on similar tasks. Encourage them to attribute performance to appropriate sources. Find out what serves as incentives for your students, and then provide real incentives for the work they do. Lastly, optimize the utility for doing the task well. Arrange the class so that doing the task you set is more productive and valued than doing something else.

SUGGESTED READINGS

Marx, R. W. (1983). Student perception in classrooms. *Educational Psychologist*, *18*, 145–164.

Weinstein, C. F., & Mayer, R. E. (1985). The teaching of learning strategies. In M. C. Wittrock (Ed.), *Handbook of research on teaching*, 3rd ed. New York: Macmillan.

Winne, P. H. (1985). Steps toward promoting cognitive achievements. *Elementary School Journal*, *85*, 673–693.

Wittrock, M. C. (1985). Students' thought processes. In M. C. Wittrock (Ed.), *Handbook of research on teaching*, 3rd ed. New York: Macmillan.

PART V

INSTRUCTIONAL GOALS, TESTING, AND PLANNING

CHAPTER 12

PHILIP W. JACKSON

ON THE PLACE OF NARRATION IN TEACHING

All people have an innate need to hear and tell stories and to have a story to live by.

HARVEY COX, *The Seduction of the Spirit*

Students of all ages spend a lot of time listening to stories in school. Except for the very youngest and the most severely retarded, they also spend a lot of time reading stories on their own, sometimes voluntarily but more often because they are required to do so. Moreover, these listening and reading activities are frequently only the beginning phases of a class's encounter with a particular narrative. Next come discussions, in which teacher and students scrutinize the story more carefully, dispelling ambiguities, analyzing plot and character, evaluating the story's worth, and so forth. Quizzes sometimes follow, as do writing assignments designed to find out how well the students understood and remembered what they have heard or read.

In what school subjects do these formal encounters with stories take place? Foremost in history and literature, certainly, whose content is essentially narrative in structure. But stories are prominent elsewhere in the curriculum as well. Teachers of reading, including those who teach the reading of foreign languages, rely on them, as do teachers of the social studies and the sciences and many, if not most, of the arts. In fact, there is probably not a single school subject in which stories play no part at all. For even when the subject matter is not itself a story, the lesson usually includes a number of narrative segments all the same. These take the form of jokes, recollections, testimony, anecdotes, illustrations, examples, and more. Indeed, it is hard to imagine a lesson being totally devoid of narrative in one form or another.

This state of affairs is not at all surprising, of course, given the prominence of stories in our lives. "Man lives surrounded by his stories and the stories of others," Sartre tells us. "He sees everything that happens to him through them, and he tries to live his life as if he were recounting it" (Sartre, 1965, p. 61).

What Sartre seems to mean by describing our lives as being "surrounded" by stories is that we rarely can get through a day, perhaps not even an hour, without either hearing, reading, or telling a story in whole or part. This condition may make the sheer abundance of stories in schools rather unexceptional after all. What makes their presence there special, however, is their presumed educational value. In brief, the chief reason for our requiring students to be exposed to many different kinds of stories in school is because we think that students will be better off for having had such experiences, that they will be changed in ways that are both beneficial and enduring.

We seldom expect the same of the stories we read, hear, or tell elsewhere. We only ask that these be entertaining and little more than that. This is certainly true of most of the stories on television, for example, and in the popular press. Of course, the stories studied in school can also be entertaining in addition to being educational—many obviously are—but, as a general rule, the primary reason for requiring students to study them is because someone believes some lasting good will come from their doing so.

How do stories educate? What "lasting goods" do they produce? Casual speculation appears to yield two quite different answers to these questions. One says that the educative function of stories is chiefly to equip students with knowledge that will later prove to be useful. The other points to the possibility of using stories to achieve purposes that might be characterized as "deeper" or "more profound" than those having to do with the acquisition of knowledge per se.

What might these "deeper" purposes be? It is not easy to answer this question precisely, but our response seems to involve *what we want students to be like as human beings,* above and beyond what we want them to *know.* This would include the values we want them to hold, the characteristic traits we want them to exhibit, the views of the world and of themselves we want them to cultivate, and so forth.

Of these two answers to why we pay so much attention to stories in school, the first requires little in the way of explanation, for it accords rather well with the popular view of school as a place where useful information is acquired. At the same time, this view is by no means free of controversy, doubt, and uncertainty, as we shall soon see. The second answer is more difficult to come to grips with than is the first, not because it is any harder to understand intellectually, but because the educational goals with which it supposedly deals are admittedly rather vague, as are the criteria for their attainment, the procedures by which they are most effectively sought, and so forth.

These two views of the educational value of stories comprise the chief topics of this chapter. After examining each view in as much detail as an essay of this kind allows, I shall introduce a concrete example of a teacher who uses a story in order to effect some kind of a change in attitude or character in one or more of his listeners. The teacher is Socrates, and the situation in which we find him is the closing scene of Plato's *Gorgias*. The episode is instructive in several ways. It prompts us to think about the uncertainty associated with the educational use of stories, particularly when they are used for what might be thought of as moral or ethical purposes. It also raises questions about how purposeful a teacher's use of stories must actually be.

A major reason for requiring students of all ages to study stories of one kind or another is because so many stories contain knowledge that is readily put to use in situations outside school. Indeed, in many instances the stories do not simply *contain* knowledge; rather, *they are themselves the knowledge we want students to possess.* Let us call this the *epistemological* function of narration. "To be a participant in a culture," the philosopher Richard Kuhns asserts, "is, by definition, to have experience of the community established by literary statements" (Kuhns, 1974, p. 5). What Kuhns seems to mean is that our sense of being part of a community is established, at least in part, by our shared *knowledge* of a set of well-known stories. Lacking that knowledge, a person is unable to participate fully in the social community to which he or she belongs.

To test Kuhns's claim, albeit crudely, all we need do is to name two or three of the best-known stories in our own culture, either fictional or true, and then try to imagine what it would be like for a person to be without that knowledge in today's world. Would an American adult who knew nothing, say, of the story of Adam and Eve, the story of Lincoln's life and assassination, and the story of World War II be in any way handicapped? I find it hard to imagine that this person would not be at least inconvenienced by such a deficiency. To begin with, he or she presumably would not know what people were talking about when they referred to these events, either directly or indirectly. How often might that happen? There is no way of telling for sure, and the answer would obviously vary, depending on the person, his or her acquaintances and occupation, and so forth. But the importance of each of these stories within the culture at large makes it improbable that anyone could manage to escape all mention of them for months or even weeks at a time.

More important, however, without knowledge of these three stories, this person would lack the understanding each of them gives to related events and to the encompassing stories in which each is embedded. For example, a person who knows nothing of Adam and Eve likely knows nothing of the other Biblical tales from the book of Genesis. Someone who has never heard of Abraham Lincoln is certain to have, at best, a very incomplete knowledge of the Civil War. A person whose knowledge of World War II is close to nil would certainly have difficulty understanding the state of the world today. Other unhappy consequences of such ignorance are easily imagined.

How many stories are like this? How many must we know to avoid suffering some kind of disadvantage? Scores certainly, hundreds perhaps. What portion of that number are first and perhaps only encountered in school? It is impossible to say for sure, but the percentage has to be large. Where else but in school do most people first hear of such well-known characters as Christopher Columbus, Huck Finn, Hamlet, Adolf Hitler, and Omar Khayyam—each embedded in its own story? And what of the story of how the earth was formed, how the Midwest was settled, how the atom bomb came to be dropped, and how the nation of Israel came into being? These tales, too, and countless others like them, are first made known to most of us during our days in school.

As commonsensical as it might appear, the epistomological explanation for there being so many stories in school is not free of controversy, as we have already noted. One source of difficulty arises from disagreements over which stories should be taught. Should every child in the United States be introduced to the story of Abraham Lincoln? What of Adam and Eve? And how about the stories of Shakespeare? Although all three options may sound quite suitable to most Americans, they likely would not be so to all. Schools in certain sections of the country might not look as kindly on the story of Lincoln as would schools elsewhere. Some people might object to the story of Adam and Eve on religious grounds. Even the stories of Shakespeare, some might insist, are only valuable for students who are going on to college.

When the broader question of what knowledge is of most worth is raised, stories, even ones as well known as those that have been mentioned, do not always fare well. The person who is unable to read or write or perform arithmetic calculations or who lacks what today are sometimes called "marketable skills" is looked on by many as being far worse off from the standpoint of getting by in our society than is one whose only deficiency is knowledge of our country's history, let us say, or the plot of some Shakespearean play.

What this means—as teachers of the humanities in many of our colleges and universities have known for some time, and as teachers in our public schools have recently been finding out—is that those school subjects in which narratives predominate are looked on by some people, perhaps even by the majority of our citizens, as less essential and hence less important than are some of the more skill-oriented subjects. Indeed, in many of our inner-city schools, especially those whose teachers and administrators have espoused the so-called back-to-basics movement, humanistically oriented studies, which is but another name for those that rely heavily on narration, are consciously de-emphasized, if not totally overlooked. As the Report of the Commission on the Humanities pointed out a few years back (1980, p. 28), "Wherever basic education concentrates exclusively on the three R's, or whenever academic achievement is reduced to what can be measured by standardized testing, the humanities are likely to be misunderstood as expendable frills."

The report's point about standardized testing brings us to yet a third difficulty confronting the defense of stories as knowledge. This one has to do with the amount of detail in which the stories taught in school are to be presented and remembered. One or two brief examples should suffice to convey a sense of the problem. Suppose all a person knew of the story of Adam and Eve was that the Bible presents them as being the first man and woman, that Eve was tempted by the serpent to eat of the forbidden fruit of the Tree of Knowledge, which she also gave to Adam, and that the two of them were expelled by God from the Garden of Eden. Would that not be enough to get by in most of life's situations that call for knowledge of this tale? Or take the story of Lincoln and his assassination. Suppose one knew that Lincoln was a Midwestern boy who became president, led the Northern states in a civil war against slavery, and was assassinated while attending the theater. What more need one know to earn at least a passing grade on whatever "tests" about Lincoln might come one's way in the course of a lifetime?

These two brief examples do not allow us to draw a firm conclusion, but they are at least suggestive. They seem to say that, in many situations, we can make do with very skimpy knowledge of even the best-known stories. The bare bones of plot and character, which are all most of us probably remember anyhow, are in all likelihood all we will need to know of the vast majority of the stories we have studied in school. The question that naturally follows from that is whether we should have been taught any more than those bare bones to start with.

Thus, to counterbalance the argument that many stories are useful to know—some of them close to essential—we have mentioned three objections that might be raised in opposition to their epistemological usefulness. These are: (1) the possibility of there being widespread disagreement over which stories are important enough to be taught in school and which are not; (2) the insistence that other educational objectives have a higher priority than those requiring students to hear and read stories; and (3) the observation that, from a purely pragmatic, utilitarian point of view, most of us probably do not need to remember much about the stories we have been taught. How badly do these objections weaken the epistemological argument on behalf of the place of stories in our schools' curriculum?

To begin with, they do not challenge the initial claim—that a person who lacks knowledge of a fair number of the stories thought to be important in a culture will be seriously inconvenienced, if not actually handicapped, in dealing with that culture and its people. The fact that there may be disagreement over which stories are important and which are not does highlight the importance of working out procedures for averting such disagreements or for resolving them harmoniously. But it certainly does not weaken the notion that most of us need to know a rather large collection of stories in order to get by in life. Nor does it contradict the subsidiary belief, which is that school is where most of us become acquainted with such stories.

The contention that there are more important things to learn in school than stories—the three R's, for instance—does constitute an attack on the educational worth of narration in general. But the assault is indirect, rather than direct. Unless accompanied by a claim that the so-called basics are *all* that should be learned in school, a position that few defenders of the back-to-basics movement seem willing to support, it leaves open the possibility of finding room for stories within the curriculum, perhaps even ample room, once the "more important" subjects have been taken care of.

The observation that plot summaries and outlines are all one needs to know about most stories sounds reasonable enough, if all we are thinking about is the epistemological function of narration. So long as we stay within the stories-as-knowledge framework, the notion of restricting our educational efforts to just such "necessities" seems to make perfectly good sense. Why teach anything but summaries, outlines, synopses, and so forth, if they are all that most people need to remember of the stories they have been taught? From a strictly utilitarian point of view, a kind of *Reader's Digest* version of the school curriculum— and not just its narrative portion, incidentally—would seem to do quite well.

There are, however, some difficulties with such an outlook, even if we stay within the epistemological perspective. For one thing, it is by no means certain that people actually do make use of only fragmentary knowledge of the stories they have heard and studied. To make certain that such abbreviated versions are all we really need know in most of life's situations, we would require a careful empirical investigation of that claim. Furthermore, there may well be "cognitive" or "psychological" reasons why students may need to study more than they will later need to know. Perhaps, for example, they most readily retain the "key points" of stories they have heard or read in full. Perhaps hearing or reading the whole story contributes crucially to the motivation required to undertake remembering it. Other possibilities of this kind would have to be investigated before we could say for certain that the study of detailed and complete stories is totally unnecessary from a purely epistemological point of view.

However, other considerations must be taken into account before conceding to proponents of the plots-and-summaries-only point of view. These considerations relate to what stories do for us *beyond* providing information that might later prove to be useful knowledge. What other purpose might stories have from an educational point of view?

A preliminary answer to this question has already been given, though it is not a very satisfying one. Stories, we noted, sometimes change us in ways that have relatively little to do with knowledge per se, or so we often credit them with doing. They leave us with altered states of consciousness, new perspectives, changed outlooks, and more. They make us wish for things we have not wished for before. They gladden and sadden, inspire and instruct, not by transmitting facts and principles, but by acquainting us with aspects of life that we heretofore had not experienced. By showing us, for instance, how others have lived, stories can influence the way we ourselves live.

Not all stories have such a powerful and enduring impact on us, of course, but some appear to do so. The changes they effect in our outlook on life and in other of our traits and dispositions I shall refer to as "transformations," in order to differentiate them from accumulations of knowledge per se, which are also a form of change, of course. But I also give them this name because the verb and its noun—"transform" and "transformation"—carry the suggestion of something profound and enduring. Once again, I am not suggesting that all transformations are necessarily of this character, but some of them seem to be, as will soon be apparent. The various forms these changes might take and the ways they might be accomplished are the topics to which we now turn.

The most rudimentary of all stories designed to "transform," not simply to "inform," the reader or listener must surely be the fable, with its tacked-on moral. Consider, for example, "The Tortoise and the Hare" or "The Fox and the Grapes." Why introduce either one to a classroom full of ten-year-olds? The chief reason, it would seem, is neither to entertain nor to inform, though the experience of listening to either tale may be both entertaining and informative. Rather, it is to convince the youthful listeners that one way of behaving is more prudent than another. The fable, in other words, is like a fancy piece of embroidery whose ornamental stitchery embellishes a simple moral message. The hope of the person relating the tale is that the message will not merely be heard and understood but will be taken to heart.

At the other extreme of complexity among stories intended to transform us are religious narratives, which purport to convey not simply an isolated moral message but something more akin to a total way of life. Here is how one modern theologian addresses the centrality of narrative within Christianity:

> The nature of Christian ethics is determined by the fact that Christian convictions take the form of a story, or perhaps better, a set of stories that constitutes a tradition, which in turn creates and forms a community. Christian ethics does not begin by emphasizing rules or principles, but by calling our

attention to a narrative that tells of God's dealing with creation. . . . My contention is that the narrative mode is neither incidental nor accidental to Christian belief. There is no more fundamental way to talk of God than in a story. (Hauerwas, 1983, pp. 24–25)

Whether or not we accept Hauerwas's claim about how crucial narration is within Christianity, it is certainly the case that most religions do indeed have one or more sacred texts that contain stories whose content is thought to be both morally and intellectually enlightening. The way these stories are to be taken, whether as literally true or as fictive constructions—albeit divinely inspired, perhaps—varies considerably from one religion to another and sometimes even from individual to individual. However, insofar as their transformative power is concerned, their importance has less to do with their literal truth than with their capacity to arouse allegiance and commitment among those whose religious beliefs they shape.

Hauerwas tells us that the set of stories within Christianity "constitutes a tradition, which in turn creates and forms a community." How does this happen? How does a set of stories constitute a tradition? It does so, one might imagine, by being passed along from generation to generation, by being pored over and studied with loving care, even to the point of memorization, perhaps. It does so by becoming so firmly embedded in the collective consciousness and way of life of a group of people that, as Hauerwas says, it actually molds them into a community. In short, religions and their stories transform us by becoming "ours" and we, by subscribing to what they tell us, become "theirs."

If a fable by Aesop represents the simplest example of a story used for transformative ends and a complete religious text, such as the Koran or the Bible, represents the most complex, what lies in between? A quick answer would include all forms of narration that convey a moral of any kind. Myths, fairy tales, and biographies come most readily to mind, even though not each and every one of these is moralistic in intent. So do stories that might have a corrupting influence on those who read or listen to them, for nothing about the concept of transformation limits it to having a positive effect. Nor need we limit our answer to stories in the conventional sense, whether fictional or true. Other narrative forms, such as histories and political treatises, may also be powerfully transformative as well. Consider, for instance, the testimony of William H. McNeill, a historian, who describes his encounter, some forty-five years earlier, with the writings of fellow historian Arnold J. Toynbee:

Only two or three times in my life have I been transported by reading a work of intellectual discourse. It often happens that imaginative literature can do this by inviting the reader to identify himself with characters in a poem, play or novel. My reading of Toynbee was that kind of experience. But on this occasion I identified with another person's ideas, expressed abstractly and without the mediation of imaginary human characters. Nevertheless, for a while his thoughts were my thoughts—or so it seemed. Afterward, letdown; more mundane experience flowed in; differences of outlook and sensibility obtruded; questions arose for me that Toynbee had not touched on. But the moment of transport left its mark, as rapture always does. Older ideas required readjustment in my mind to make room for Toynbee, and conversely, Toynbee's ideas had to be twisted about so as to fit in with what I already knew and believed. (McNeill, 1985, p. 24)

Here we have another instance of a story, or something akin to one, achieving transformative ends, but ends quite different from those having to do with either the fable or the religious tract. McNeill certainly sounds as though he has been changed unequivocally by his experience. He will never again be the same. Let us look a little more closely at the quality of his experience. Notice, McNeill says that for a time Toynbee's thoughts were his thoughts, "or so it seemed." It was as though he had replaced his own way of thinking with someone else's. But the replacement was only temporary, for "Afterward, letdown; more mundane experience flowed in; differences of outlook and sensibility obtruded; questions arose for me that Toynbee had not touched on." So the magic of transformation was only momentary. Yet, "the moment of transport left its mark," McNeill reports, adding almost incidentally, "as rapture always does." He goes on to describe this phenomenon in language that calls to mind Piaget's notions of "assimilation" and "accommodation": "Older ideas required readjustment in my mind to make room for Toynbee," he tells us, "and conversely, Toynbee's ideas had to be twisted about so as to fit with what I already knew and believed."

Yet a third conception of how stories transform us is provided by Arthur C. Danto in his presidential address to the Eastern Meeting of the American Philosophical Association in 1983. Danto's remarks are ostensibly concerned with the difference between literature and philosophy, but his thoughts inevitably turn to the question of how literary works affect us. Literature, he explains, "is about each reader who experiences it. . . . The work finds its subject only when read" (Danto, 1985, p. 79). To elaborate on this observation, he makes use of a well-known metaphor:

> . . . It is natural to think . . . of literature as a kind of mirror, not simply in the sense of rendering up an external reality, but as giving me to myself for each self peering into it, showing each of us something inaccessible without mirrors, namely that each has an external aspect and what that external aspect is. . . . It is a mirror less in passively returning an image than in transforming the self-consciousness of the reader who in virtue of identifying with the image recognizes what he is. Literature is in this sense transfigurative, and in a way which cuts across the distinction between fiction and truth. (Danto, 1985, pp. 78–79)

The exact meaning of Danto's observations is not easy to fathom under the best of circumstances. It is even more difficult to discern, I fear, when the reader has only a mere snippet of the full address to work with. However, even this brief fragment from Danto's remarks should suffice to convey the general direction of his thoughts. He seems to be saying that through identifying ourselves with characters in the texts we read or listen to (and perhaps with more than just the characters, perhaps with the constellation of meanings embodied in the text as a whole), we somehow become ourselves. Our encounters with texts change us, but according to Danto they do more than that. In his view, the stories we read and study, at least some of them, *actually make us what we are.* They constitute our personhood.

Here, then, is yet another conception of how stories can transform us. Danto's description of the process sounds akin to what McNeill experienced on reading Toynbee, though perhaps broader in scope. And it appears to fall somewhere between the extremes of simplicity and complexity of our first two examples. The kind of change Danto speaks of goes far beyond what one might expect would be the outcome of reading one of Aesop's fables, say, yet it is not quite as all-encompassing as the transformations thought to accompany our acceptance of a religious story that we have chosen to call our own.

Transformed and transfigured by stories. Transported by them. Stirring images of the power of narration, all right, but how common are such events? Let's suppose that some stories actually do change people in ways that almost deserve to be called miraculous. Testimonials like McNeill's, together with the observations of scholars like Hauerwas and Danto, would certainly support that supposition. But how many stories are like that? How many have that kind of an impact on us? Not very many, it would seem. For the kind of experience McNeill relates is surely not an everyday affair, as he himself points out, nor are the sorts of transformations that Hauerwas and Danto discuss.

But if such momentous events are relatively rare, what does that say about the place of the transformative function of narration within schools? If teachers cannot rely on stories to work their magic, so to speak, if such wonders only occur once in a blue moon, does that not suggest that teachers ought forsake all such ambitions and concentrate exclusively on what stories can do for their pupils from a purely epistemological point of view? Perhaps transformations of the kind we have been discussing are chiefly matters of luck and chance—as McNeill's seems to have been—and ought simply be treated as such by school personnel.

Earlier we spoke of fables as perhaps the simplest kinds of stories with transformative goals. We speculated that a teacher of young children might tell such a tale to his or her students not so they could pass a quiz on its contents but so they could take the story's "message" to heart. Now we seem to be asking whether it is worthwhile for teachers to relate such stories after all, except as entertainment, perhaps, or because they believe students need to know them for reasons having nothing to do with their moral or ethical significance. For it seems very unlikely that the few minutes it takes to tell a tale such as "The Fox and the Grapes" or "The Tortoise and the Hare" will yield much in the way of transformative change among those listening. Why bother, then?

The same reasoning applies, of course, not just to fables and other forms of children's literature but also to the stories teachers tell and assign to older students. Why should teachers seek to achieve transformative goals at all, if the chances of success are either remote or unpredictable?

To examine this question within the context of a particular teaching situation, we turn now to a famous Socratic dialogue: Plato's *Gorgias*. In this narrative, Socrates relates a mythical tale to his companions. He does so with what appears to be a transformative goal in mind. In preparation for our asking what the episode tells us, if anything, about the place of narration in schools and about other "chancy" maneuverings on the part of ordinary teachers, let us see how the situation comes about and what comes of it.

With four companions—Chaerephon, Polus, Gorgias, and Callicles—Socrates has been discussing the merits of oratory. This discussion has led to the question of whether it is better to suffer wrong or to do wrong, with Socrates taking the position that a wrongdoer is in the worst position possible. On this point he manages to convince or silence all but Callicles, who remains adamant in his conviction that a tyrant who does wrong is better off than the people who suffer under his rule. Perhaps realizing that he has reached the limits of Callicles' understanding or at least of his willingness to continue with the discussion, Socrates introduces a story as though to put a kind of finishing touch on his argument. He does so with these words: "Give ear then, as they say, to a very fine story, which will, I suppose, seem fiction to you but is fact to me; what I am going to tell you I tell you as the truth" (Plato, 1960, p. 142).

Socrates then goes on to relate a tale about man's fate after death. It seems that in the time of Cronus, a law was ordained that when righteous people died they would depart to the Isle of the Blessed, whereas the wicked and godless would instead be imprisoned in a place of retribution and punishment called Tartarus. However, at that time, people had foreknowledge of the date of their death, and they also appeared before living judges, who decreed their ultimate destination on the day they were fated to die. Socrates says:

This led to perversion of justice, so Pluto and the overseers of the isles of the blessed came to Zeus and complained that men were arriving at both destinations contrary to their deserts. Then Zeus said: "I will put an end to this. The cause of this miscarriage of justice is that men, being tried in their life-time are tried in their clothes. Many whose souls are wicked are dressed in the trappings of physical beauty and high birth and riches, and when their trial takes place they are supported by a crowd of witnesses, who come to testify to the righteousness of their lives. This causes confusion to the judges, who are also hampered by being clothed themselves, so that their soul's vision is clouded by the physical veil of eyes and ears and the rest of the body, and their own vesture as well as the accused's constitutes an obstacle between them and the truth. Our first task, then," said Zeus, "is to take from men the foreknowledge of the hour of their death which they at present enjoy. I have charged Prometheus to bring this to an end. Next, they must all be tried naked, that is, when they are dead, and to ensure complete justice the judge too must be naked and dead himself, viewing with bare soul the bare soul of every man as soon as he is dead, when he has no kinsmen to aid him and has left behind on earth all his former glory." (Plato, 1960, pp. 142–143)

To this end, Zeus appointed three of his sons—Minos, Rhadamanthus, and Aeacus—to become judges upon their death, thus assuring "that men's ultimate destiny is decided in accordance with perfect justice" (Plato, 1960, p. 144).

After relating this story in only slightly greater detail than is presented here, Socrates reiterates his belief in its truth. "This, Callicles, is what I have heard and believe to be true," he says (Plato, 1960, p. 144). He then goes on to draw a set of conclusions that seem to him to follow from the account he has related. These epitomize the line of argument that led up to his telling of the story. In essence, they highlight the importance of leading a good life and the value of punishment for those who are wrongdoers. He concludes by urging Callicles to join him in the practice of virtue; his final words deliver a stinging judgment: "[The way of life you defend] is quite worthless, Callicles," Socrates intones, and on that sober note the dialogue comes to a close (Plato, 1960, p. 149).

In using the fable as he does, Socrates certainly seems to be trying to achieve a transformative end, the goal being that of getting Callicles to "see the light," so to speak. Moreover, what Socrates is aiming to accomplish calls to mind Arthur Danto's remarks about how literature seems to work. In fact, Danto's exact words fit the situation quite well. Socrates seems to be using the fable "as a kind of mirror" for Callicles, "not simply in the sense of rendering up an external reality" but for showing him an aspect of himself that he "would not know was [his] without benefit of that mirror." The goal seems to be that of "transforming the self-consciousness of [Callicles] who in virtue of identifying with the image [of the man who after death is judged to be a wrongdoer]" will recognize what he is and what fate awaits him. Even Danto's description of literature as being "transfigurative, and in a way which cuts across the distinction between fiction and truth" is echoed in Socrates' insistence that the tale he is about to tell is "fact" and "the truth" as he himself sees it, though it might seem otherwise to Callicles.

Does Socrates believe in the literal truth of the story he tells? He certainly calls the story *true*, as we have seen, and he follows that by saying, "Personally, Callicles, I put faith in this story . . ." (Plato, 1960, p. 147). But how we should interpret his professed beliefs is by no means clear. One possibility is that Socrates is supremely confident of the moral truths embodied in the myth—that to do wrong is far worse than to suffer it, and that there is no happiness for the wrongdoer— and means nothing more than that by his profession of faith. Here is the way one interpreter of the dialogue puts it:

> When Socrates says, "Personally, I put faith in this story," we must remember the connection between belief and will here. "I put faith in this story" means "I hope that nothing will get me to depart from the path of justice, and nothing will ever persuade me to put considerations of justice and decency second." (Dilman, 1979, p. 174)

Further along in his argument, the same critic observes:

> Yet Socrates' faith in [the story's] truth does not rest on the kind of evidence with which one would support an ordinary prophesy. His desire to live a good life, his preferring to suffer rather than inflict wrong on others, is not conditional to what will happen to him in the future in the hands of his judges. (Dilman, 1979, p. 176)

Whatever we might believe about Socrates' acceptance or rejection of the literal truth of the story he tells, he clearly is deeply committed to its moral message and remains so throughout the dialogue. Indeed, the depth of his commitment calls to mind the attachment to religious narratives that we have discussed.

We earlier asked whether terms like "transforming," "transfiguring," and so on might not be a bit overblown when applied to what a teacher tries to do when he or she introduces a story or fable to a class. We offered the episode from the *Gorgias* as evidence that Socrates seems to have had just such a goal in mind when he told Callicles the story of the judgment of the dead, the inference being that if Socrates can legitimately use a story in this way, so can other teachers as well.

There is a difficulty, however, when we read the *Gorgias* example as legitimizing the use of narration for transformative ends: the dialogue closes with Socrates' anecdote, leaving the reader to guess what Callicles' reactions might be, both to the story and to the conclusions Socrates draws from it. Did the story work? Did Callicles come to his senses at last? Was he undergoing a change of heart even as Socrates spoke?

In one sense, these are idle questions, for all we can ever know about Callicles is what Plato has chosen to tell us. Indeed, it is generally supposed that, unlike the other characters in the *Gorgias*, Callicles is completely fictitious. So he has no real past or future for us to wonder about. But the fact that they can be asked at all leaves us free to believe that Socrates might not have accomplished much by telling the tale to Callicles. This possibility is disturbing, as we have already seen, for it suggests that stories may or may not "work" as intended, which in turn raises the question of whether they are sufficiently reliable as instruments of transformative change to warrant their widespread use in classrooms.

Let us assume that stories do not always have the effects teachers wish them to have and that sometimes they may seem to have no effect at all. What of it? The answer would seem to be that if they proved not to achieve transformative ends, teachers should discontinue using them for such purposes. But how unreliable must they become before such a decision is reached? Worded this way, the question calls for an empirical answer. It makes us want to administer "before" and "after" tests of transformative ends in order to find out whether the educational benefits of telling stories to students are sufficiently reliable to warrant continuing this practice. Is such testing feasible? Is that what Socrates should have done? To see why the answer to both questions is probably no, we need return to the puzzle created by Callicles' failure to respond during the closing moments of the dialogue and when Socrates' story-cum-speech had ended.

We first must ask how reasonable it is to expect a person of Callicles' disposition to experience a change of heart in response to a story whose telling, were the dialogue played out in real time, could not have taken more than five or ten minutes at most? Even without their knowing anything about the kind of person Callicles is depicted as being, most people would probably agree that such an outcome is quite unlikely. When informed that Callicles is portrayed as being very set in his ways, becoming so emotional and adamant in defending his position that he speaks abusively to Socrates, they likely would be even more firmly convinced that the telling of a brief story, even when followed by a Socratic moral, would probably not be sufficient to make a person like Callicles change his mind.

As a psychological portrait of a man set in his ways, the image of Callicles presented throughout the dialogue is all of a piece. His silence at the end is quite in character. He may be defeated in argument, but it seems unlikely that he is altered in spirit. It is much easier to imagine him continuing to sulk long after everyone has departed than it is to picture him a changed man, reacting gratefully to the lesson he has been taught and imploring Socrates to forgive him for his earlier rudeness.

But here we have a curious state of affairs. If Callicles is so set in his views that the telling of a brief story is unlikely to have much of an effect on him, and if his stubborn streak is obvious to even a casual reader, should Socrates not have come to that realization himself long before he introduced the fable? Should he not have known better than even to *try* to persuade the headstrong Callicles to change his attitudes?

We have already acknowledged that the character of Callicles throughout the dialogue is consistent and psychologically credible. But what of that of Socrates? Is Socrates behaving believably as a teacher when he chooses to tell the story, even though the likelihood of its having much of an impact on Callicles seems slim?

It seems to me possible to defend Socrates' action from a pedagogical point of view, though with what success remains to be seen. At least two lines of defense are open. One of them stays within the customary framework of viewing teachers as purposeful, goal-oriented "change agents" who have a reasonably clear view of what they are trying to accomplish and who go about their work as efficiently as possible. The other defensive posture moves beyond the set of assumptions and presuppositions that underlie some of our more conventional ways of thinking about teachers and teaching. It invites us to regard pedagogical affairs from a different perspective than usual, without abandoning today's heightened concern for the attainment of educational "outcomes" and "products."

Why might Socrates have told the story, even though he may have known or strongly suspected that Callicles, in all likelihood, would not heed its message? Of the two explanations to be considered, the easier one to start with opens by reminding us that three other characters—Chaerephon, Polus, and Gorgias—were within earshot when Socrates spoke to Callicles. Perhaps Socrates told the story as much for their benefit as for that of Callicles alone. We can easily imagine all who were present paying close attention to what was going on. Thus, if we want to know whether Socrates behaved sensibly, perhaps our proper worry ought not be the effect he thought the story would have on Callicles but, rather, what he anticipated its effect might be on the others present (including, perhaps, the readers of the dialogue, if we shift the locus of intentionality from Socrates to Plato).

The fact that Socrates' other companions remain as silent as Callicles does when the narrative has ended still leaves us in the dark with respect to its actual efficacy. However, the way Polus and Gorgias in particular respond to Socrates' argument earlier in the dialogue—their apparent willingness to bend to reason, for example—makes it at least plausible that they might be influenced by a well-told tale. This possibility casts a different light on Socrates' telling of the tale than if we look at it solely as an attempt to persuade Callicles of the error of his ways.

A second possible explanation of why Socrates might have gone ahead with his story, all misgivings about the efficacy of doing so notwithstanding, requires us to adopt a rather different slant on teaching than is customary these days, as we have already warned. It demands that we think of teachers not simply as persons in charge of helping students attain a specified set of educational goals, useful though such a outlook may be for certain purposes, but asks that we also think of them as persons engaged in a kind of "methodic groping," a term used by the philosopher Justus Buchler to refer to what he further describes as "a kind of comradeship with chance—a conditional alliance" (Buchler, 1961, p. 84). Buchler explains:

> To maintain the alliance, the methodic agent requires only alertness and strength of perception. In a sense, the profoundest of methods, those of the sciences, the arts, and philosophy, depend upon the alliance most heavily. . . . Each instance of practice contains an element of contingency and obscurity which only a desire for new insight can surmount. This element of contingency is a trait of the method, and not merely of the method's particular conditions.
>
> No inventive process can be said to obviate groping on the part of those who engage in it. For every direction is vague in some degree when it starts with the prospect of uniqueness and unknown value in the product. (Buchler, 1961, p. 85)

Teachers certainly are no less in the dark as they go about their work than are the scientists, the artists, and the philosophers that Buchler mentions, even though they may experience the darkness rather differently than do the others. They too must maintain "a kind of comradeship with chance—a conditional alliance." For them, as for the others, "[e]ach instance of practice contains an element of contingency and obscurity," which only desire combined with effort can surmount. Though teachers may not be reaching for the same kinds of insights as are research scientists, say, or writers of fiction, they are often called on to be inventive in their work. As Buchler points out, this means starting "with the prospect of uniqueness and unknown value in the product"—the latter, in the case of teachers, referring not to some law of nature or work of art but, rather, to the overall conduct of a specific encounter with a student or group of students.

What does such a "comradeship with chance" entail? The answer to this question must surely vary from one occupation to another. For teachers, it seems to mean doing what *feels* right from time to time, even when you cannot say for sure why you are doing it. Taking a cue from Socrates, it also seems to mean being true to your ethical principles and acting in accordance with them when all other guides fail, even when doing so promises to yield no benefit whatsoever insofar as a specific "learning outcome" is concerned.

Returning to the *Gorgias*, we should by now have no difficulty understanding the import of the second of our two explanations for why Socrates related the myth, even though Callicles may no longer have been paying attention. He told the story, in this view, simply because it occurred to him to do so. It seemed the right thing to do under the circumstances, right in a variety of ways, perhaps in more ways than either Socrates or Plato himself understood.

This point of view pictures Socrates as recollecting the story at some point during the discussion—perhaps only milliseconds before telling it—immediately sensing its relationship to all that he had been saying prior to that point, and finally deciding to use it as a capstone for his argument. He tells it not solely or even primarily because of the effect it likely will have on Callicles or anyone else. Instead, he does so for no better reason than that it seems right for him to do so. It "feels" right; it "fits."

A similar line of reasoning would seem to apply to Plato's decision to include the story in the dialogue. As author of the work—hence a storyteller himself—Plato, too, was probably feeling his way much of the time as he tried to figure out how best to portray Socrates in action, while perhaps hoping to accomplish a variety of additional goals as well, some pedagogical and others not. Why, then, did he add the myth at the end? Obviously, we cannot know for sure, but it seems at least plausible that his reasoning was not very different from what Socrates' might have been, had he himself been faced with the choice. Here is a story that seems to fit both the rhetorical and the dramatic requirements of the dialogue better than anything else he may have thought of at the time. It also happened to embody the fundamental moral truth that Socrates is portrayed as seeking to affirm—namely, that the virtuous life is the only one worth living. What better reasons could he have had for ending with the myth as he did?

What emerges from this line of reasoning is a view of pedagogy that may be discomforting to people who cling to the hope that teaching may someday become a science or something akin to one. For it seems to give teachers license to tell stories in class or assign them to be read outside school simply because it "feels right" or "seems like" a reasonable thing to do and not because they know for sure what such activities and assignments might accomplish. Such a policy could possibly work, some critics might concede, if all teachers were as talented as Plato or Socrates, for the intuitions of individuals of genius are often in accord with what later turns out to be true. But since most teachers are far from being geniuses, as the same critics are usually quick to point out, the ordinary teacher's rationale for using stories ought to be spelled out in considerable detail and should include a clear description of the goals of such activities.

There is something reasonable about this advice but something unsettling as well. What seems reasonable is for us to expect teachers to take their work seriously. This means, among other things, careful deliberation and choice when it comes to the materials they use and the assignments they make. The trouble with this advice when put into practice is that the rationality it advocates so often turns out to be of a particular kind, one that seeks to tie teachers' actions to observable outcomes of instruction and little else, thereby grossly constricting the range of reasons that might legitimately guide what a teacher does.

What seems needed, if we are to leave room for teachers not only to introduce stories at appropriate times but also to do so in a spontaneous and natural way, is a view of both teaching and narration that allows the complexity of each to become more fully understood and appreciated than either seems to be at present. Two aspects of that complexity merit mention here. One has mostly to do with teachers, the other with texts.

Like most other people, teachers sometimes behave enigmatically. They do things for reasons that are not immediately apparent. They give conflicting signals about what they think of their students and what they expect of them. They can be all smiles one minute and all frowns the next. Their words and actions are occasionally contradictory and inconsistent. In short, they behave in ways that are downright puzzling at times.

Again, like most people, teachers are sometimes puzzling not only to their students and others who might be watching them but also to themselves. They too may wonder why they behave in one way toward one student and in a different way toward another. They also may wonder why they teach as they do, why they prefer one set of activities or one pedagogical style to another. Of course to say that they *may* wonder about such things is not to say that they invariably do so, nor is it to say that they wonder about the same aspects of their behavior that baffle others. They may quite possibly have no good explanation for why they behave in a certain way yet not be particularly curious about their actions. Moreover, the fact that teachers (and the rest of us) sometimes behave in puzzling ways does not mean that all such puzzles are necessarily solved by either the teacher or those with whom he or she interacts. Some puzzles remain puzzles for a very long time. Others are never solved. We just learn to live with them.

Texts can sometimes be as puzzling as people—perhaps even more so, in fact. We commonly complain about not being able to understand them. We find them disappointing at times. They confuse us. They are difficult to follow. When the texts have characters, as stories commonly do, we sometimes find their actions to be even more bewildering than those of people in real life.

Now, when stories are told to us, assigned to be read by a teacher, or recommended by a friend, the complexities unique to texts and those unique to human beings sometimes have a way of becoming entangled with one another. It is then that certain questions suddenly become relevant: why is he telling this story? why was this assigned? what does she expect me to get out of it? which is the correct interpretation? These questions add to whatever complexity resides in the text alone. At such moments, our thoughts about texts and the persons who present them to us often get jumbled up in a way that produces a doubly enigmatic puzzle.

A provocative presentation of such a puzzle as it pertains to teachers and texts is offered by Angela S. Moger, who argues as follows:

> Actually, pedagogy and narrative are coincident in their reliance on the mechanism of desire as a modus operandi. Teaching and telling exist, endure, function, by means of perpetually renewed postponement of fulfillment. . . . Once the object of desire has been appropriated, it loses its status as desirable. Now, meaning is to narrative as fulfillment is to desire; possession means death. Stories work by going through the motions of imparting information which they only promise but never really deliver. A story is a question to be pursued; if there is no enigma, no space to be traversed, there is no story.
>
> Teaching is another such "optical" illusion; it functions by a similar sleight of hand. The pedagogical stance is a pretext that there is something substantive to be deciphered and appropriated. But wisdom, like love and the story, is not found in nature; it has no empirical status. Like the beloved or the narrative, it exists only in the eye of the beholder; I am a teacher only in the mind of one who thinks I might teach him something he does not know. But since I do not possess the knowledge he desires, to teach is only to continue to generate the desire for wisdom. Pedagogy, like narrative, functions by means of withholding rather than by means of transmission.
>
> . . .
>
> If the immediate goal of teaching is the satisfaction of the quest for knowledge, it can also be said that its fundamental goal is the denial of that satisfaction in favor of the renewal of questing itself. (Moger, 1982, pp. 135–136)

What shall we make of this perspective on narration and teaching? What light, if any, does it shed on the problems associated with a teacher's use of stories? Let us begin by summarizing its two main points.

Stories, we are told, work by promising to impart information that is never really delivered. They arouse desire but perpetually postpone its fulfillment. Similarly, to teach, we are given to understand, is to continue to generate the desire for wisdom, to deny satisfaction in favor of the renewal of questing itself. It would seem to follow, then, that when teachers use stories in their teaching, their students are being doubly tantalized by the promise of goods that are never delivered.

Is there any truth in this assertion? Do both stories and teaching arouse and sustain desires that are never fully satisfied? There is more than one sense in which this seems to be the case. Some stories certainly end before we want them to. They leave us wishing we could know more about the characters and events within them. Others, which may include many of the first type, whet our appetite for more books by the same author, perhaps, or more within the same literary genre. We develop a craving for detective stories or historical novels, for instance.

Teachers have been known to have similar effects on their students. Some teachers leave us wishing the class or the course had not ended. They make us want to take other courses they teach, and sometimes we go on to study the same subject with other teachers. A few teachers— Socrates, for instance—may even successfully heighten our love of knowledge in general.

At the same time, our encounters with both stories and teachers can be richly satisfying, as we all know. The completion of some stories leaves us buried in thought. We then do not want that same tale to continue or others to take its place; instead, we cling to the memory of what we have just read or listened to. In our reverie, we savor the pleasures that stories alone can bring. After the ensuing lull of appetite, the hunger for other stories commonly returns, but it does nothing to diminish the sense of fulfillment and completion that the best stories can engender.

And so it is, we might suspect, with the best of teaching as well. There, too, we commonly experience a sense of completion and fulfillment when a class or a course has finished. Yet, if the experience has been successful, we soon hunger for more. Is this what Moger means when she claims that teaching proceeds by continually renewing the desire for wisdom? I think it must be. But what about the business of denying satisfaction in the process? What about her assertion that "to teach is *only* to continue to generate the desire for wisdom" (italics added)? I have no trouble with the claim in general; it is the word "only" that I reject. Though many teachers may generate a desire for wisdom among their students (and sometimes do so without conscious intention, we might add), they certainly do other things as well—such as transmitting genuine knowledge and skill, for example. Furthermore, though a continuing desire for more knowledge or wisdom, or anything else for that matter, may never be completely fulfilled—this by definition—there is nothing to stop it from being partially fulfilled and, therefore, temporarily satisfied, which seems to be precisely what teaching at its best succeeds in doing.

Moger's view that "(p)edagogy, like narrative, functions by means of withholding rather than by means of transmission . . . ," which might be called her "double tease" theory of what happens when teachers become storytellers, seems to be only partially true, at best. It remains helpful, all the same, by reminding us that, within almost any teaching encounter, one may come upon layers of significance and meaning about which none of the participants, including the teacher, are fully aware. Why is it helpful to remember this? It is so because we often seem to forget that the full meaning of our actions often requires a kind of reflection that can occur only after we have acted. The significance of this fact for teaching is as follows.

When we think about what teachers normally do, we usually imagine a two-step sequence of events. First, we picture them making plans of some sort, and then we imagine them translating those plans into actions. During the planning stage, teachers are supposed to settle on both the means and the ends of instruction. This requires, first of all, deciding on goals and objectives, which presumably entails also being clear about *why* those goals and objectives have been chosen. Only then, the model seems to imply, is it legitimate for the teacher to move to the next stage of deciding upon means to achieve those ends, and only then is he or she in a position to act responsibly.

How essential is it for teachers to proceed in this fashion? The two-step sequence *seems* logical. It is certainly what many so-called experts in the field of teacher education have been recommending for some time. But is it absolutely necessary? If presented as a pedagogical dictum, seldom if ever to be violated, is it even good advice?

Moger's remarks about teachers promising more than they deliver comprise a kind of Freudian assault on the rationality implicit in a plans-into-action model of teaching. They announce to the world what a lot of teachers already know: that far more is going on in most teaching situations than one might guess, and that at least some of those goings-on may have a dark side to them from time to time. But there is a bright side to that same observation, allowing us to reverse Moger's language and still have it make sense. Many teachers, we might say, appear to deliver *more* than they have promised, in that their lessons are far richer and fuller of educational significance than a perusal of their plans or a conversation with them ahead of time would ever suggest. A lot of the time, it would seem, teachers come to *discover* at least a portion of the educational worth of what they are doing in the process of doing it. Perhaps most do.

Does something like this happen with the stories teachers read or assign to their students? I suspect it does. Do we not often find, as we seemed to do in the case of Socrates, that teachers frequently undertake such activities in the vague hope that something good—something transformative—might come of them and find out only later, if ever, whether their original hunch was right or wrong? Such is the way a lot of teachers seem to work. But here is a crucial question: can teachers and administrators and legislators and even the public at large continue to tolerate that kind of uncertainty in today's climate of educational reform, with its call for "accountability" and for ever more exacting measures of "outcomes"? The future place of narration in teaching—

and perhaps even the future of education—would seem to depend on the answer we give.

ACKNOWLEDGMENT: The preparation of this chapter was supported in part by a grant from the Benton Center for Curriculum and Instruction, located in the Department of Education of the University of Chicago. I wish to thank Sophie Haroutunian-Gordon and Barak Rosenshine for their careful reading and thoughtful critique of an earlier draft of the manuscript.

REFERENCES

Buchler, J. (1961). *The concept of method*. New York: Columbia University Press.

Cox, H. (1973). *The seduction of the spirit*. New York: Simon & Schuster.

Danto, A. C. (1985). Philosophy as/and/of literature. In J. Rajchman & C. West (Eds.), *Post-analytic philosophy* (pp. 63–83). New York: Columbia University Press.

Dilman, I. (1979). *Morality and the inner life*. New York: Harper & Row.

Hauerwas, S. (1983). *The peaceable kingdom*. Notre Dame, IN: University of Notre Dame Press.

Kuhns, R. (1974). *Structures of experience*. New York: Harper & Row.

McNeill, W. H. (1985, 29 December). Encounters with Toynbee. *New York Times Book Review*, pp. 1, 24.

Moger, A. S. (1982). That obscure object of narrative. In *The pedagogical imperative: Teaching as a literary genre*. *Yale French Studies, 63*, 129–138.

Plato (1960). *Gorgias*. New York: Penguin Books.

Report of the Commission on the Humanities (1980). *The humanities in American life*. Berkeley: University of California Press.

Sartre, J.P. (1965). *Nausea*. Harmondsworth, England: Penguin.

CHAPTER 13

ROBERT GLASER

THE INTEGRATION OF INSTRUCTION AND TESTING

Implications from the Study of Human Cognition

In this chapter, I consider the proposition that in the foreseeable future, testing, in relation to the educational process, will undergo significant redirection. The conditions necessitating this change have been accumulating over many years and now must be faced squarely. With each decade in the twentieth century, we have increased the proportion of children attending schools; we have expanded both the range of social groups and the amount and kinds of education offered. Today's and the next century's challenge is to teach successfully all of the diverse children and youth who have become the active concern of our educational systems. We have also, in the last half of this century, expanded our understanding of human cognition and now are able in better and better detail to specify the knowledge and skill that students require for various kinds of school performance. New approaches to testing and instruction are possible and will be necessary to make it possible for everyone to meet standards of educational performance that, only three or four decades ago, were expected from a smaller segment of the population. The then acceptable route to educational attainment in which high standards were achieved by selective means is no longer adequate. Dropping reluctant or difficult learners, or testing primarily to segregate them in programs that make few demands and offer few opportunities, will not be a viable alternative. Simultaneously, we will assure that our most talented and most difficult students optimize their learning.

At present, tests (with the exception of the important informal assessments of the good classroom teacher) typically are not designed to guide the specifics of instruction. We use them primarily as indicators to signal general rises or declines in school performance. They serve as an index to the standards of schools, but they are not designed to shape progress effectively toward these standards—and can do so only indirectly, if at all. In the future, tests and other forms of assessment will be valued for their ability to facilitate constructive adaptations of educational programs.

To accomplish this, students and teachers will need information that can inform instructional decisions rather than just predict academic success or offer a percentile or grade-level index of relative standing and global attainment. The information required will be analogous to that used by an opera teacher or a swimming coach to guide the development of further competence and proficiency. Testing and teaching will be integral events. A test that monitors access to education only and does not monitor the progress of education will not be tolerated for either the slow or the quick learner. Relationships between test score information and the nature of competence in school subject matters will be empirically studied and conceptually better understood.

In comparison to our current well-developed technology for aptitude measurement and our techniques for achievement test standardization, techniques for measuring the growth and development of human competence are not well developed; a strong theory of the design of achievement testing has not emerged. Lee Cronbach (1970) recognized this state of affairs 15 years ago when he wrote: "The design and construction of achievement test items has been given almost no scholarly attention. . . . Demands for content validity have suddenly become insistent, thanks to demands for genuine diagnosis and mastery testing, for national assessment and local accountability, for data that describe learners rather than rank them, [however,] the art of test construction has so far not coped very well with these demands" (pp. 509–511). Cronbach went on to say that some important ideas have been generated, such as criterion-referenced testing, items as samples of operationally defined content universes, and analysis of information-processing requirements of tasks, but that much work lies ahead to clarify these ideas and turn them into useful procedures.

In recent years, the general outline of theoretical grounds for forms of assessment that can assist educators in monitoring the characteristics of new learning and attained levels of ability has emerged. There is a wide recognition of the need to ascertain the critical differences between successful and unsuccessful student performance by appraising the structures of knowledge and cognitive processes that reveal degrees of competence in a field of study. More and more, the design of measurement techniques that can guide instruction will be based on the accumulating studies of learning that identify the performance components that facilitate or interfere with the eventual attainment of higher levels of achievement. In essence, this is the theme of this chapter: that the measurement of achievement should rely on our knowledge of learning and of the course of acquisition of competence in the subject matters that we teach. In the near future we should be able to develop assessments of learning that are more indicative of competence than tests with which we are now familiar.

The usual forms of achievement test scores do not provide the level of detail necessary for making appropriate instructional decisions. An array of subject-matter subtests differing in difficulty is not enough (Linn, 1983). Sources of difficulty need to be identified for specific problems in learning and performance. Tests also should permit learners to demonstrate the limits of their knowledge and the degree of their expertise. The construction of tests that are diagnostic of different levels of competence is a difficult task, but recent advances in the psychology of subject-matter competence and research on the functional differences between experts and novices in various fields are good starting points for framing the theories that should underlie achievement measurement.

From this perspective, consider our customary practices. Most of the technology of testing has been designed to occur after test items are constructed. The analysis of item difficulty, discrimination indices, scaling and norming procedures, and the analysis of test dimensions and factorial composition all take place once the item is written. In contrast, in the future, sustained attention to theory will be required before and during item design. We will rely on what we know about the cognitive properties of acquired proficiency and the structures and processes that develop as individuals move from beginning to advanced learners. The assessment of achievement will be integrally tied to the study of the nature of learning. Modern learning theory is taking on the characteristics of a developmental psychology of performance changes—the study of changes that occur as knowledge and complex cognitive strategies are acquired. In the future, achievement measurement will be designed to assess these performance changes. It will be cast in developmental terms to identify attainment at various levels of acquisition, emphasizing not only content considerations but structural and process considerations involved in sources of difficulty and in facilitators of the growth of competence (Messick, 1984).

This prediction about the future of achievement testing is encouraged because a marked change is taking place in our knowledge and theories of human learning and intelligence. In the course of this century, theories of psychological measurement have focused on the testing of general processes—general forms of intelligence (verbal, numerical, and spatial)—and on general aptitudes of various kinds that showed correlational relationships to overall success in school and in other forms of learning. Similarly, the study of learning also has sought for evidence of general processes and general conditions of learning—pervasive laws that influence all kinds of learning, such as forms of conditioning, the nature of reinforcement and feedback as a consequence of learning, and conditions of practice such as massed and spaced learning. Such broad-based analyses, although they helped in explicating important principles of learning, could only assist instruction in a general way on the basis of rather weak heuristics, such as categorizing classes of learning deficits that impede ability to learn.

In contrast, in recent years the study of human performance has become more oriented toward studying the specific types of knowledge and skill that people acquire in their lives. This change has led to considerable emphasis on learning in the knowledge-rich domains that correspond to the academic disciplines and the subject matters of schooling. This new emphasis will make it feasible to identify a student's strengths and weaknesses in performing academic tasks. Rather than attempting to identify a general underlying deficit, we will concentrate more precisely on helping the learner recognize incomplete or partial knowledge that can become a focus for more direct instructional attention (Brown & Campione, 1984, in press).

Two advances in the study of human cognition are particularly noteworthy here. One is the information-processing analyses of the performances that contribute to proficiency in academic tasks. The other is the increased understanding of the nature of competent performance that has resulted from study of experts and novices in various domains of human endeavor. In the analysis of school tasks, elementary arithmetic provides a good example. Progress has been made in mapping the development of children's grasp of the principles that underlie counting skill and their understanding of the concept of number and numerical reasoning (Gelman & Gallistel, 1978; Greeno, Riley, & Gelman, 1984), of the acquisition of arithmetic facts (Ashcraft, 1982; Siegler & Shrager, 1984), of knowledge and tactics for solving arithmetic word problems (Kintsch & Greeno, 1985; Riley, Greeno, & Heller, 1983), and of principles underlying place-value notation that is basic to computational skill (Resnick, 1982, 1984). These efforts and work on the diagnosis and categorization of error patterns in arithmetic performance (Brown & Burton, 1978; Brown & VanLehn, 1980) will provide a basis for informed diagnosis of a child's understanding or misunderstanding in early mathematics learning. It will become easier to identify the incomplete knowledge and procedures and the incomplete conceptual understanding (Resnick, 1984) that contribute to weak performance and can be remedied in the course of instruction. We will be able to appraise the knowledge that reveals degrees of competence and that determines functional differences between superficial and more lasting achievement.

Consider now several ideas for "learning assessments"—a term that may be more apt than "tests." These ideas are: the analysis of rules of performance, the assessment of prior knowledge, the coordination of basic and advanced performance, and analysis of the nature of competence and expertise.

ANALYSIS OF RULES OF PERFORMANCE

One technique of learning assessment will be the analysis of task performances in a way that mimics an important skill of teaching, that is, the ability to synthesize from a student's performance an accurate picture of misconceptions that lead to error and of attainment that can lead to new learning. This goes deeper than identifying incorrect or correct answers and pointing them out to the student and the teacher; it attempts to identify the nature of the concept of the rule that the student is employing in some systematic way. The assumption is that in most cases the student's behavior is not random or careless but is driven by some underlying misconception or by incomplete knowledge.

Such diagnostic procedures are based on the decomposition of a complex skill into component procedures that contain elements of the underlying ability. Misconceptions that result from incorrect implementation of the various component skills are identified through a student's patterns of error on a set of tasks. From an apparently confusing array of student responses, patterned scoring procedures have been able to identify systematic sources of error. Studies of errors in subtraction (Brown & Burton, 1978) illustrate the point well. In some cases the student subtracts the smaller digit in each column from the larger digit, regardless of which is on top; or when the student needs to borrow, he or she adds ten to the top digit of the current column without subtracting one from the next column on the left; or when borrowing from a column whose top digit is zero, the student writes nine but does not continue borrowing from the column to the left of the zero. Students' problems in working with fractions (Tatsuoka, 1981) show comparable systematicity. Often the student converts mixed numbers to the wrong improper fractions but uses the correct combination rule or omits the whole number after using the correct procedure on fraction parts.

Similarly, in writing, a student may put in a comma every time an *and* is used, rather than when the *and* introduces an independent clause; or a student may connect any relative clause that comes at the end of a sentence to the independent clause before it with the phrase *in which;* or the student may determine the boundaries of sentences by the erroneous rule "Put a period at long pauses" (Hull, 1985; Shaughnessy, 1977a, 1977b).

Scoring systems that identify systematic bugs of this kind have important implications for testing because students are evaluated not on the basis of the number of errors on their tests but rather on the basis of the misconceptions or incomplete rules that influence their performance. Diagnosing performance in this way links testing to instruction. It encourages the teacher to see that the apparently random, careless, or lazy behavior of a student is frequently rooted in a complex and logical process of thought toward which teaching can be directed. A diagnostic testing emphasis of this kind is useful and impressive to teachers; they view it as an important aspect of their own skills and as a way of respecting the systematic intelligence of their students.

ASSESSMENT OF PRIOR KNOWLEDGE

Consider another aspect of student performance that might be assessed to assist instruction. It is well known that comprehension and learning are based on current beliefs, and a student attempts to understand and think about new information in terms of what he or she already knows. This being the case, it seems best to base teaching on the forms of knowledge that a student currently holds. High levels of learning and understanding can be fostered by ensuring contact between new information and the student's prior knowledge, which then can be restructured through instruction. The possible benefits of assessment of this kind have been indicated by studies in various subject areas, particularly by research in science education.

In science, the information with which students enter classrooms is based upon intuitive theories derived from prior experiences, from the perspective of commonsense interpretations of scientific phenomena. Common misconceptions are prevalent in a student's beliefs about velocity and acceleration, free fall, electric circuits, photosynthesis, and so forth. These informal theories are not readily abandoned; they frequently come up against scientific principles that are the focus of instruction and are counterintuitive and therefore not easily assimilated to the student's current notions. As science education researchers point out, "When a student's naive beliefs are not addressed, instruction may only serve to provide the student . . . with new terminology for expressing his erroneous beliefs" (McCloskey, Caramazza, & Green, 1980, p. 1141). If learning entails restructuring or replacing these ideas, then it is not enough to assess whether or not the student knows the science information that is taught—we must also assess what the beginning student believes as a basis for instruction (Messick, 1984). Thus, we point to another important aspect of performance diagnosis that is relevant to the integration of learning and instruction.

COORDINATION OF BASIC AND ADVANCED SKILLS

Consider now the coordination of basic skills and advanced performance. Studies of competent performance have made it clear that human ability to carry out many attention-demanding tasks is rather limited. If the simultaneous processing of the many tasks that make up a complex activity requires conscious attention, then difficulties arise because attention must be switched from one task to the other. However, if performance of some of the tasks becomes sufficiently automated through practice and requires little conscious attention, then effort can be devoted to other, frequently higher level, tasks.

This orchestration of task components has been of special interest in the study of reading, particularly in investigations of the relationships between word-level reading skills and advanced processes of comprehension. A reader's attention may vacillate between the decoding skills of recognizing words and the skills of comprehension that integrate text ideas into memory. Shifts in attention are apparent in the beginning reader, who alternately concentrates on sounding out a word and on considering what the word means in the context of what is being read. Although these component processes may work well when tested separately, they may not be efficient enough to work together. Because attention to each process takes time, slowness of a component process in interaction with other processes can lead to a breakdown in overall proficiency (Perfetti & Lesgold, 1979). Low levels of reading performance often reflect the interfering effects of slow, inefficient word decoding on the execution of higher level comprehension tasks.

Such interference effects between the component processes of a complex performance have important implications for learning assessment. Certain processes need to attain a certain level of efficiency so that other processes can be carried out simultaneously and in a coordinated manner. Hence, to optimize the success of learning where such coordination is important, it would be useful to assess the level of basic skill efficiency that is required to minimize interfering effects with higher level processes. The important index of performance is not whether the two processes can be carried out independently, but whether proficiency has reached a level where one process facilitates another. This suggests devising methods for diagnosing competence in basic skills in ways that indicate their success in freeing attention for advanced levels of achievement.

THE NATURE OF COMPETENCE

Over the past 15 years, developments in cognitive psychology and artificial intelligence have spurred increasing investigations of the nature of proficiency and high levels of competence that could influence the design of learning assessment. The central questions are how knowledge becomes organized and how the processes that use this knowledge develop over long periods of learning and experience. Just what are the factors that enable expertise and the amazing efficiency, judgment, and problem-solving abilities shown by individuals who are very good at what they do?

A great deal of effort is now being devoted to understanding the cognitive structures and abilities of the skilled performer and to analyzing the processes involved in the transformation of novice learners into increasingly expert individuals. As we gain understanding of the nature of competence, we should begin to see possibilities for advances in techniques for assessing attainment at various levels of proficiency. One of the most salient and consistent findings of this research is that proficient individuals develop organizations of knowledge that enable them to rapidly perceive meaningful patterns in their memory. This allows them to form representations of problems that lead to appropriate, meaningful action. Novices, on the other hand, represent problems in qualitatively different and superficial ways that make problem situations more difficult to solve. Adept pattern recognition and problem representation are indices of competence that might be included in assessments of developing expertise.

There are many evidences of this phenomenon. The classic work was carried out in studies of skill in chess (Chase & Simon, 1973; de Groot, 1965, 1966; Simon & Chase, 1973). The striking difference between chess masters and weaker players is not the masters' superior general intelligence or their superior ability to keep all the moves of a game in memory, but their ability to recognize quickly patterns on the chessboard for their meaningful strategic implications. The estimated size of a chess master's pattern vocabulary is roughly 50,000 configurations in contrast to the thousand patterns of an average player and the very few patterns of a novice. The chess expert is a superior recognizer, rather than a deeper thinker. This explains how chess masters are able to play many individuals at one time; for the most part they rely on pattern recognition abilities (so-called chess intuition) to generate potentially good moves (Chase & Chi, 1981).

Analogous abilities are found in those who perform well in the subject-matter domains of schooling. Investigations of students solving problems of elementary physics have studied the phenomenon of physical intuition, which is much like the chess master's intuition (Chi, Feltovich, & Glaser, 1981; Chi, Glaser, & Rees, 1982; Larkin, McDermott, Simon, & Simon, 1980; Simon & Simon, 1978). Good solutions are associated with the perception of significant patterns. In contrasting novices and graduate students, it seems clear that the proficient performer rapidly perceives the deep central principles that underlie the problem. His or her knowledge is organized around central principles of physics that inform solution procedures, whereas the knowledge and perceptions of the novice are organized around the surface features and physical description of the entities in a problem. Upon looking at a problem, the proficient individual says, "That's a Newton's second law problem." The less proficient individual says, "It is a pulley problem, or an inclined plane problem." Both students may solve the problem, but the way the problem is initially perceived and represented determines the selection of problem-solving procedures, which results in differences in efficiency and the ability to handle difficult situations.

Similar results have been obtained in other subject-matter areas. For example, proficient students in high school and college algebra develop rapid perceptions of the semantic structure of algebra problems (Hinsley, Hayes, & Simon, 1978). After reading the first sentence or two of a problem and before carrying out steps toward a solution, they quickly categorize the problem as belonging to a class of problems— a triangle problem, or a ratio problem, or a river current problem. They say, "Oh, that's a triangle problem, and it's solved by using the Pythagorean theorem." For these students, problem categories rapidly trigger appropriate solutions in memory. This ability suggests a possibility for learning assessment. We should be able to develop procedures to test problem perception and to observe the forms in which it occurs in the course of developing competence.

TOWARD PRINCIPLES FOR THE MEASUREMENT OF ACHIEVEMENT

To summarize the ideas I have described, it may be useful to suggest a framework for the design of learning assessment instruments—instruments for determining levels of knowledge and skill that are attained in the course of instruction. These ideas should be considered as a basis for test-item construction that is coordinate with or prior to psychometric considerations. They assume that achievement measurement can be grounded by modern cognitive theory that describes learning as the acquisition of knowledge and competence. At various stages of acquisition, there exist different integrations of knowledge, different degrees of procedural skill, and differences in access to memory and in representations of the tasks one is to perform. These different indices signal assessment levels of advancing expertise or possible blockages in the course of learning (Glaser, Lesgold, & Lajoie, in press).

Achievement measurement theory based on this kind of knowledge is at an early stage. Many of the essential ideas are yet to be worked out, but enough work has been done to indicate the shape of a guiding framework. A tentative set of *dimensions* can be proposed in an effort to characterize components of developing proficiency that might underlie the assessment of achievement. Consider as a representative sample the following four dimensions: principled performance and active knowledge, theory change, problem representation, and automaticity to reduce attentional demands.

1. Principled Performance and Active Knowledge. As competence is attained, elements of knowledge and components of skill become increasingly interconnected and rule based, so that individuals access rules for their performance rather than fragmentary pieces of information. This is apparent in various subject-matter domains; a beginner's knowledge consists of incomplete definitions, erroneous rules, and superficial understandings, but from the pattern of a student's test responses, systematicities of performance can be determined to explain behavior. The diagnosis of these principles of performance becomes a candidate dimension for the assessment of achievement that can inform instruction.

A related point is that the course of acquisition of knowledge proceeds from an initial accumulation of information in declarative form to a form that is more active and useful. In essence, we can know a principle, or a rule, or an item of specialized vocabulary without knowing initially the conditions under which it is to be used effectively. Studies of the difference between experts and novices indicate that beginners may have requisite knowledge, but this knowledge is not bound to the conditions of applicability. When knowledge is accessed by experts, it is associated with indications of how and when it is to be appropriately used. Assessments of the development of achievement in an area of knowledge through this progression from declarative to active information can be a useful measure of competence. Test items can be comprised of two elements—requisite information and information about the conditions under which use of this knowledge is appropriate.

2. Theory Change. Learning takes place on the basis of existing mental models and theories held by students, which either enhance or retard learning. With appropriate instruction, students test, evaluate, and modify their current theories on the basis of new information, and, as a result, develop new schemata that facilitate more advanced thinking. However, as indicated, students can hold naive theories at the beginning of a course that make learning difficult. Even after instruction, these naive theories may persist. Although students have learned to solve problems in some mechanical fashion, they may have little understanding. Thus, theories of knowledge become targets for assessment. The characteristics of a student's theory might indicate whether it is amenable to change under certain instructional conditions, or whether the theory is more intractable and will result in learning difficulties that require more thorough instruction.

Students' theories add an important dimension to achievement assessment. They can be assessed to determine not only the task complexity that the student is capable of handling but also the level of thinking demanded by school curricula. The demands of school tasks may require levels of understanding less sophisticated than the teacher envisions. This discrepancy poses a dilemma because when proficiency is assessed, students will have acquired and retained the model required by actual performance, not the one envisioned by desired teaching objectives.

3. Problem Representation. It is now known that novices recognize the surface features of a problem or task situation and more proficient individuals go beyond surface features and identify inferences or principles that subsume the surface structure. This growing ability for fast recognition of underlying principles indicates developing achievement and could be assessed by appropriate pattern recognition tasks in verbal and graphic situations. Because certain forms of representation appear to be highly correlated with the ability to carry out the steps of a problem solution, test items might concentrate on assessing the initial understanding that is displayed by problem representation, as well as the details of arriving at the correct answer.

4. Automaticity to Reduce Attentional Demands. Investigations of competence make it evident that human ability to perform competing, attention-demanding tasks is limited. When the subtasks of a complex activity simultaneously require attention, the efficiency of the overall task is affected. This fact has particular implications for diagnostic assessment of the interaction between components of performance. Although component processes may work well when tested separately, they may not be efficient enough to work together. If a task demands an orchestration of skills, then measurement procedures should be able to diagnose inefficiencies. Criteria for assessment become the level of automaticity required for subprocesses to have minimal interference effects and the level required to facilitate total performance and new learning.

CONCLUSION

To conclude, achievement testing, as defined here, is a method of assessing competence through indicators of the development of knowledge, skill, and cognitive process. These indicators reveal stages of performance that have been attained and that provide a basis for further learning. They also show forms of error and misconception that result in inefficient and incomplete performances and require specific instructional attention. Achievement measurement defined in this way needs to be informed by theories of the acquisition of subject-matter knowledge and by a focus on various dimensions of proficiency, such as rules of performance, automaticity, forms of representation, and procedural efficiencies that can index the growth and development of competence.

I have speculated on some possible dimensions, and further research is required, but we have grounds for anticipating important advances. It is likely that new theoretical sophistication will be brought to achievement measurement. Our aspiration is that learning assessments will not provide merely a score, a label, a grade level, or a percentile, but also *instructional scoring* that makes apparent to the student and to the teacher the requirements for increasing competence.

ACKNOWLEDGMENT: This chapter is a version of a talk that appears in *The Redesign of Testing for the 21st Century*, Proceedings of the 1985 ETS Invitational Conference. Research support was provided by the Center for the Study of Learning of the Learning Research and Development Center with funds from the Office of Educational Research and Improvement, United States Department of Education; and by the Office of Naval Research, Personnel and Training Research Programs, Psychological Sciences Division.

REFERENCES

Ashcraft, M. H. (1982). The development of mental arithmetic: A chronometric approach. *Developmental Review, 2*, 213–236.

Brown, A. L., & Campione, J. C. (1984). Three faces of transfer: Implications for early competence, individual differences, and instruction. In M. Lamb, A. Brown, & B. Rogoff (Eds.), *Advances in developmental psychology*, (Vol. 3, pp. 143–192). Hillsdale, NJ: Erlbaum.

Brown, A. L., & Campione, J. C. (1986). Psychological theory and the study of learning disabilities. *American Psychologist, 41* (10), 1059–1068.

Brown, J. S., & Burton, R. R. (1978). Diagnostic models for procedural bugs in basic mathematics. *Cognitive Science, 2*, 155–192.

Brown, J. S., & VanLehn, K. (1980). Repair theory: A generative theory of bugs in procedural skills. *Cognitive Science, 4*, 379–426.

Chase, W. G., & Chi, M. T. H. (1981). Cognitive skill: Implications for spatial skill in largescale environments. In J. Harvey (Ed.), *Cognition, social behavior, and the environment*. Hillsdale, NJ: Erlbaum.

Chase, W. G., & Simon, H. A. (1973). Perception in chess. *Cognitive Psychology, 1*, 55–81.

Chi, M. T. H., Feltovich, P. J., & Glaser, R. (1981). Categorization and representation of physics problems by experts and novices. *Cognitive Science, 5*, 121–152.

Chi, M. T. H., Glaser, R., & Rees, E. (1982). Expertise in problem solving. In R. Sternberg (Ed.), *Advances in the psychology of human intelligence*. Hillsdale, NJ: Erlbaum.

Cronbach, L. J. (1970). [Review of *On the theory of achievement test items*]. *Psychometrika, 35*, 509–511.

de Groot, A. (1965). *Thought and choice in chess*. The Hague: Mouton.

de Groot, A. (1966). Perception and memory versus thought: Some old ideas and recent findings. In B. Kleinmuntz (Ed.), *Problem solving*. New York: Wiley.

Gelman, R., & Gallistel, C. R. (1978). *The child's understanding of number*. Cambridge: Harvard University Press.

Glaser, R., Lesgold, A. M., & Lajoie, S. (in press). Toward a cognitive theory for the measurement of achievement. In R. R. Ronning, J. Glover, J. C. Conoley, & J. C. Witt (Eds.), *The influence of cognitive psychology on testing and measurement*. Hillsdale, NJ: Erlbaum.

Greeno, J. G., Riley, M. S., & Gelman, R. (1984). Conceptual competence and children's counting. *Cognitive Psychology, 16*, 94–143.

Hinsley, D. A., Hayes, J. R., & Simon, H. A. (1978). From words to equations: Meaning and representation in algebra word problems. In P. A. Carpenter & M. A. Just (Eds.), *Cognitive processes in comprehension*. Hillsdale, NJ: Erlbaum.

Hull, G. (in press). Research on error and correction. In B. W. McClelland & T. R. Donovan (Eds.), *Perspectives on research and scholarship in composition*. New York: Modern Language Association.

Kintsch, W., & Greeno, J. G. (1985). Understanding and solving word arithmetic problems. *Psychological Review, 92*, 109–129.

Larkin, J., McDermott, J., Simon, D. P., & Simon, H. A. (1980). Expert and novice performance in solving physics problems. *Science, 208*, 1335–1342.

Linn, R. L. (1983). Testing and instruction: Links and distinctions. *Journal of Educational Measurement 20* (2), 179–189.

McCloskey, M., Caramazza, A., & Green, B. (1980). Curvilinear motion in the absence of external forces: Naive beliefs about the motion of objects. *Science, 210,* 1139–1141.

Messick, S. (1984). The psychology of educational measurement. *Journal of Educational Measurement, 21* (3), 215–237.

Perfetti, C. A., & Lesgold, A. M. (1979). Coding and comprehension in skilled reading. In L. B. Resnick & P. Weaver (Eds.), *Theory and practice of early reading.* Hillsdale, NJ: Erlbaum.

Resnick, L. B. (1982). Syntax and semantics in learning to subtract. In T. Carpenter, J. Moser, & T. Romberg (Eds.), *Addition and subtraction: A cognitive perspective* (pp. 136–155). Hillsdale, NJ: Erlbaum.

Resnick, L. B. (1984). Beyond error analysis: The role of understanding in elementary school arithmetic. In H. Cheek (Ed.), *Diagnostic and prescriptive mathematics: Issues, ideas, and insight* (pp. 181–205). Kent, OH: Research Council for Diagnostic and Prescriptive Mathematics.

Riley, M. S., Greeno, J. G., & Heller, J. I. (1983). Development of children's problem-solving abilities in arithmetic. In H. P. Ginsburg (Ed.), *The development of mathematical thinking* (pp. 153–196). New York: Academic.

Shaughnessy, M. (1977a). *Errors and expectations.* New York: Oxford University Press.

Shaughnessy, M. (1977b). Some needed research on writing. *College Composition and Communication, 28,* 317–321.

Siegler, R. S., & Shrager, J. (1984). Strategy choices in addition and subtraction: How do children know what to do? In C. Sophian (Ed.), *Origins of cognitive skills.* Hillsdale, NJ: Erlbaum.

Simon, D. P., & Simon, H. A. (1978). Individual differences in solving physics problems. In R. Siegler (Ed.), *Children's thinking: What develops?* Hillsdale, NJ: Erlbaum.

Simon, H. A., & Chase, W. G. (1973). Skill in chess. *American Scientist, 61,* 394–403.

Tatsuoka, K. K. (1981, January). *Diagnosing cognitive errors: Statistical pattern classification and recognition approach* (Research Report 85–1-ONR). Urbana-Champaign: University of Illinois at Urbana-Champaign.

CHAPTER 14

CHRISTOPHER M. CLARK
ROBERT J. YINGER

TEACHER PLANNING

Teacher planning is one of the central topics of research on teacher thinking. This is so, in part, because teacher planning plays an apparently pivotal role in linking curriculum to instruction and, in part, because teacher planning is a relatively accessible aspect of the mental lives of teachers. The studies summarized in this chapter provide interesting details about how experienced teachers plan and what relation their plans have to their classroom behavior. The research literature on teacher planning is not sufficiently mature to provide a solid empirical basis for deciding what the best ways to plan may be. But, even in its early descriptive stage, this research offers concepts and insights that can help us see and appreciate the complexities of the teacher's role in new ways. In particular, these descriptions of teacher planning support the image of the teacher as a reflective professional engaged in a complex and fluid design process. Seen in this way, research on teacher planning can be helpful in demonstrating ways in which teaching is similar to other design professions.

RESEARCH ON TEACHER THINKING

The thinking, planning, and decision making of teachers constitute a large part of the psychological context within which curriculum is interpreted and acted on and within which teachers teach and students learn. Teacher behavior is substantially influenced and even determined by teachers' thought processes. These are the fundamental assumptions behind the literature that has come to be called research on teacher thinking. Researchers on teacher thinking seek first to describe the mental lives of teachers fully. They also hope to understand and explain how and why the observable behaviors of teachers take on the forms and functions that they do. They ask when and why teaching is difficult and how human beings manage the complexity of classroom teaching. The ultimate goal of research on teachers' thought processes is to construct a portrait of the cognitive psychology of teaching for use by educational theorists, researchers, policy makers, curriculum designers, teacher educators, school administrators, and teachers themselves.

Jackson's (1968) book *Life in Classrooms* reports one of the earliest empirical attempts to describe and understand the mental constructs and processes that underlie teacher behavior. His descriptive study departed strikingly from contemporary research on teaching and from the then-dominant teacher-effectiveness research paradigm. In 1968, it was difficult to see how describing life in a few classrooms could contribute much to the quest for teaching effectiveness. Jackson's contribution to research on teaching, however, was conceptual. He portrayed the full complexity of the teacher's task, made conceptual distinctions (such as that between the preactive and interactive phases of teaching) that fit the teacher's frame of reference, and called educators' attention to the importance of describing the thinking and planning of teachers to achieving a fuller understanding of classroom processes.

In Sweden, Dahllof and Lundgren (1970) conducted a series of studies of the structure of the teaching process as an expression of organizational constraints. While this work was primarily concerned with the effects of contextual factors on teaching, it revealed some of the mental categories that teachers use to organize and make sense of their professional experiences. Dahllof and Lundgren's contribution, like Jackson's, was primarily conceptual.

Of particular significance in Dahllof and Lundgren's research was the phenomenon of the "steering group," a small subset of a class (ranging in achievement level from the tenth to the twenty-fifth percentile) that teachers used as an informal reference group for decisions about pacing a lesson or unit. During whole-class instruction, when the students in the steering group seemed to understand what was being presented, the teachers would move the class on to a new topic. But when the teachers believed that the steering group was not understanding or performing up to standard, the teachers slowed the pace of instruction for all. The steering group is important as a concept both because it is empirically verifiable and because it shows clearly how teachers' mental categories can have significant pedagogical consequences.

In June 1974, the National Institute of Education convened a week-long National Conference on Studies in Teaching to create an agenda for future research on teaching. The participants in this planning conference were organized into ten panels, and each panel produced a plan for research in its area of expertise. The deliberations of Panel 6, Teaching as Clinical Information Processing, were of particular importance to the development of research on teacher thinking. Lee S. Shulman, as chair of Panel 6, assembled a diverse group of experts on the psychology of human information processing, the anthropology of education, classroom interaction research, and the practical realities of teaching. Panel 6's report (National Institute of Education, 1975) provided a rationale for and defined the assumptions and the domain of a proposed program of research on teachers' thought processes. The panelists argued that research on teacher thinking is necessary if educators are to understand what is uniquely human in the process of teaching:

> It is obvious that what teachers do is directed in no small measure by what they think. Moreover, it will be necessary for any innovations in the context, practices, and technology of teaching to be mediated through the minds and motives of teachers. To the extent that observed or intended teacher behavior is "thoughtless," it makes no use of the human teacher's most unique attributes. In so doing, it becomes mechanical and might well be done by a machine. If, however, teaching is done and, in all likelihood, will continue to be done by human teachers, the question of the relationships between thought and action becomes crucial. (p. 1)

Beyond this logical argument for attending to teacher thinking, Panel 6's report went on to cite research on human information processing, which indicates that a person, when faced with a complex situation, creates a simplified model of that situation and then behaves rationally in relation to that simplified model. The resulting behavior, as indicated by Simon (1957):

> is not even approximately optimal with respect to the real world. To predict . . . behavior we must understand the way in which this simplified model is constructed, and its construction will certainly be related to [one's] psychological properties as a perceiving, thinking, and learning animal. (cited in National Institute of Education, 1975, p. 2)

To understand, predict, and influence what teachers do, the panelists argued, researchers must study the psychological processes by which teachers perceive and define their professional responsibilities and situations.

Panel 6's report is explicit about the view of the teacher that guided the panelists in their deliberations and recommendations for research:

> The Panel was oriented toward the teacher as clinician, not only in the sense of someone diagnosing specific forms of learning dysfunction or pathology and prescribing particular remedies, but more broadly as an individual responsible for (a) aggregating and making sense out of an incredible diversity of information sources about individual students and the class collectively; (b) bringing to bear a growing body of empirical and theoretical work constituting the research literature of education; somehow (c) combining all that information with the teacher's own expectations, attitudes, beliefs, purposes . . . and (d) having to respond, make judgments, render

decisions, reflect, and regroup to begin again. (National Institute of Education, 1975, pp. 2–3)

In short, Panel 6's report presented an image of the teacher as a
professional who has more in common with physicians, lawyers, and
architects than with technicians who execute skilled performances according to prescriptions or algorithms that others define. This view of
the teacher as professional has had a profound effect on the questions
asked, methods of inquiry employed, and the form of the results reported
in research on teacher thinking. Moreover, Panel 6's report influenced
new initiatives in research on teaching in a more instrumental way:
in 1975, the National Institute of Education issued a request for propos-
als for an Institute for Research on Teaching that would focus on research
on teaching as clinical information processing. Such an institute was
established at Michigan State University in 1976, and this organization
initiated the first large body of research on the thought processes of
teachers. With this as background, let us now focus more closely on
one part of the research on teacher thinking: research on teacher planning.

PLANNING DEFINED

As a subject of research, planning has been defined in two ways. First,
planning is a basic psychological process in which a person visualizes
the future, lists means and ends, and constructs a framework to guide
his or her future action—what Robert Yinger calls "thinking in the
future tense." This definition leads to research on the process of planning
that draws heavily from the theories and methods of cognitive psychology.

At another level, planning can be defined (somewhat circularly) as
"the things that teachers do when they say that they are planning."
This definition suggests a phenomenological or ethnographic approach
to research on teacher planning, in which the teacher assumes an important role as informant or even as research collaborator.

Both definitions of teacher planning are represented in the research
literature either explicitly or implicitly. We believe that the differences
in thought about the definition of planning account for the variety of
methods of inquiry in use and for the challenge that reviewers of this
literature face in summarizing coherently what has been learned. Planning is challenging to study because it is both a psychological process
and a practical activity.

Through examining the results of selected studies of teacher planning, we hope to answer three major questions that researchers have
been pursuing: (1) what are the types and functions of teacher planning?
(2) what models have been used to describe the process of planning?

and (3) what is the relationship between teacher planning and subsequent behavior in the classroom?

TYPES AND FUNCTIONS OF TEACHER PLANNING

What are the different kinds of planning that teachers do, and what purposes do they serve? The answer to both of these questions seems to be "many." But several recent studies of teacher planning provide more specific answers.

Two of these studies were designed to (among other things) determine what kinds of planning experienced teachers engage in. Yinger (1977) studied the planning decisions of one teacher who taught first and second grade over a five-month period. Using interviews and extensive classroom observations, and by having the teacher think aloud, Yinger determined that this teacher engaged in five different kinds of planning: yearly, term, unit, weekly, and daily. The teaching "activity" was found to be the basic unit of daily and weekly planning. The teacher drew heavily on routines, established early in the school year, that incorporated learning outcomes for students. These routines were seen as functioning to reduce the complexity and increase the predictability of classroom activities.

In a second study, by Clark and Yinger (1979), 78 teachers wrote descriptions of general characteristics of their planning and also selected and described three examples that represented the three most important types of planning that they did during the year. The teachers reported that they engaged in the following eight different types of planning (in order of frequency of mention): weekly, daily, unit, long-range, lesson, short-range, yearly, and term planning. Unit planning was most often identified as the most important type, followed by weekly and daily planning. Only 7 percent of the teachers listed lesson planning among the types of planning most important to them.

The dynamic relationships among different types of planning have also been studied to a modest degree. Two studies by Greta Morine-Dershimer (Morine-Dershimer, 1979; Morine-Dershimer & Vallance, 1976) suggest that teachers' plans are seldom fully reflected in their written plans. Rather, the details recorded in a written plan are nested within more comprehensive planning structures, which Morine-Dershimer calls "lesson images." These lesson images, in turn, are nested within a still larger construct that Joyce (1978–1979) calls the "activity flow." For elementary-school teachers, the activity flow encompasses the year-long progress of a class through each particular subject and the way teaching activities are balanced across subjects in a school day or week.

Further support for the idea that teacher planning is a nested process comes from a study by Clark and Elmore (1979). They interviewed and observed five elementary-school teachers during the first five weeks of the school year and found that their planning was primarily concerned with setting up the physical environment of the classroom, assessing student abilities, and establishing the social system of the classroom. By the end of the fourth week, a system of schedules, routines, and groupings for instruction had been established. These structural and social features of the classroom then persisted throughout the school year and served as the framework within which particular activities and units were planned. Other studies of the first weeks of school also support the conclusion that, to a significant degree, the "problem space" (after Newell & Simon, 1972) within which teacher and students operate is defined early, changes little during the course of the school year, and exerts a powerful, if subtle, influence on thought and behavior (see, for example, Anderson & Evertson, 1978; Buckley & Cooper, 1978; Shultz & Florio, 1979; Tikunoff & Ward, 1978).

Functions of Planning

The research that speaks to the functions of teacher planning suggests that there are almost as many reasons to plan as there are types of planning. In the Clark and Yinger (1979) study mentioned earlier, the teachers' written responses to a question about why they plan fell into three clusters: (1) planning to meet immediate personal needs (for example, to reduce uncertainty and anxiety, to find a sense of direction, confidence, and security); (2) planning as a means to the end of instruction (to teach the material, to collect and organize materials, to organize time and activity flow); and (3) direct uses of plans during instruction (to organize students, to get an activity started, to aid memory, to provide a framework for instruction and evaluation).

An ethnographic study of the planning of 12 elementary-school teachers by McCutcheon (1980) also confirmed that some teachers plan because they are required to turn in plans to the principal on a regular basis. These teachers also indicated that substitute teachers have to use special plans if the regular teacher is absent. These plans were special both because they included a great deal of background information about how the system in a particular classroom and school operates and because the regular teachers tended to reserve the teaching of what they judged to be important material for themselves, planning filler or drill and practice activities for the substitute. (Incidentally, we have long believed that a great deal could be learned about teacher thinking and planning from the vantage point of a substitute teacher. We hope that someday someone will do such a study.)

Planning and the Content of Instruction

The most obvious function of teacher planning in American schools is to transform and modify curriculum to fit the unique circumstances of each teaching situation. In one of the only studies of yearly planning to date, Clark and Elmore (1981) asked a second-grade teacher to think aloud while doing her yearly planning for mathematics, science, and writing. The primary resources she used in yearly planning were curriculum materials (especially the teacher's guides that accompany most textbooks), her memory of classroom interaction during the previous year, and the calendar for the coming school year. The process of yearly planning, typically done during the summer months, consisted of the teacher's reviewing the curriculum materials that she would be using during the coming year, rearranging the sequence of topics within curricula, and adding and deleting content to be taught. A broad outline of the content to be taught emerged from a process of mental review of the events of the past year, combined with adjustment of the planned sequence and pace of teaching to accommodate new curriculum materials and new ideas consistent with the teacher's implicit theory of instruction.

Through her review of the past year, reflection on her satisfaction with how things went, and modifications of the content, sequence, and planned pace of instruction, the teacher's yearly planning process served to integrate her own experience with the published materials, establishing a sense of ownership and control of content to be taught (Ben-Peretz, 1975). Yearly planning sessions satisfied this teacher that she possessed the resources to provide conditions for learning at least equal to those she had provided during the previous year. Yearly planning decreased the unpredictability and uncertainty that attend every teaching situation.

The Clark and Elmore (1981) study of yearly planning supports the idea that published curriculum materials have a powerful influence on the content and process of teaching. In a series of studies of teacher planning for sixth-grade science instruction, Smith and Sendelbach (1979) pursued this idea at the level of unit planning. Working with the SCIS (Science Curriculum Improvement Study) curriculum, Smith and Sendelbach compared explicit directions for a unit of instruction provided in the teacher's manual with four teachers' transformations of those directions into plans, and with the actual classroom behavior of one of the four teachers while teaching the unit.

Observation of the four teachers during planning sessions combined with analysis of think-aloud and stimulated-recall interview data revealed that the principal product of a unit-planning session was a mental picture of the unit to be taught, the sequence of activities within it, and of the students' probable responses. These mental plans were supplemented and cued by sketchy notes and lists of important points that the teachers wanted to be sure to remember. Smith and Sendelbach characterized the process of activating a unit plan as one of reconstructing the plan from memory, rather than of carefully following the directions provided in the teacher's guide.

Smith and Sendelbach are critical of the loose coupling between curriculum and instruction because they see the potential for distortions or significant omissions in the content of instruction. From their classroom observations of one experienced teacher implementing her unit plan, they concluded that the quality of instruction was diminished somewhat by both planned and unintended deviations from the SCIS materials. Smith and Sendelbach attributed these deviations to the teacher's limited knowledge of the subject matter and difficulty in finding information in the teacher's guide, and to the presence of inherently complex and confusing concepts. The researchers suggest that heavy dependence on teacher's guides in unit planning provides an opportunity to improve the quality of instruction by revising these guides to be more clear, comprehensive, and prescriptive.

Few studies have attempted to describe teacher planning in all its variety; all but two or three studies of teacher planning focus on a single type of planning. Educators could benefit from more studies that describe the full range of the kinds of planning that teachers do during the school year and the interrelationships among these different types of planning.

In addition, the modest-to-insignificant role of lesson planning for experienced teachers is interesting. Lesson planning is the one type that all teacher-preparation programs address directly. Yet experienced teachers rarely claim it as an important part of their repertoire. This anomaly suggests that perhaps some of our teacher-preparation practices are based on the "rational" models of the university rather than on studies of professional practice (see Chapter 15 for a description of the same phenomenon in medicine).

Finally, the functions of teacher planning that are not directly and exclusively concerned with a particular instructional episode have been slighted. Researchers and teacher educators should think more broadly about what teachers are accomplishing in their planning time and should avoid narrow comparisons of what was planned with what was taught as the only criterion for evaluation.

WHAT MODELS DESCRIBE TEACHER PLANNING?

A logic similar to that of an industrial production system has given educators the most widely prescribed model for teacher planning (Tyler, 1950). This linear model consists of a sequence of four steps: (1) specify objectives; (2) select learning activities; (3) organize learning activities; and (4) specify evaluation procedures. This linear model has been recommended for use at all levels of educational planning, and hundreds of thousands of educators have been trained in its use. It was not until 1970 that researchers began to examine directly the planning processes that teachers use and to compare what was being practiced with what had been prescribed.

Taylor (1970) conducted a study of teacher planning in British secondary schools. The study was directed toward examining how teachers plan course syllabi. Using group discussions with teachers, analyses of course syllabi, and a questionnaire administered to 261 teachers of English, science, and geography, Taylor came to the following general conclusions: the most common theme found across all of the modes of data collection was the prominence of pupils—their needs, abilities, and interests. Following these, in order of importance, were the subject matter, goals, and teaching methods. In planning for courses of study, evaluation emerged as being of little importance, as did the relation between one's own courses and the curriculum as a whole. Taylor concluded that most course planning was unsystematic and general in nature and that most teachers appear to be far from certain about what the planning process requires.

Through teacher ratings of the importance of various issues in curriculum planning and a factor analysis of their responses, Taylor identified four primary factors of interest to his sample of teachers. In order of importance, these were: (1) factors associated with the teaching context (such as materials and resources); (2) pupil interests; (3) aims and purposes of teaching; and (4) evaluation considerations. Rather than beginning with purposes and objectives and moving to a description of learning experiences necessary to achieve the objectives, as the linear-planning theorists propose, Taylor found that these teachers began with the context of teaching, next considered learning situations likely to interest and involve their pupils, and only then considered the purposes that their teaching would serve. Another difference between Taylor's data and the Tyler model was that criteria and procedures for evaluating the effectiveness of their course of teaching were only a minor issue. These findings led Taylor to conclude that curriculum planning should begin with the content to be taught and with important contextual considerations (such as time, sequencing, resources). This should be followed by considerations of pupil interests and attitudes, aims and purposes of the course, learning situations to be created, the philosophy of the course, the criteria for judging the course, the degree of pupil interest fostered by the course, and, finally, evaluation of the course.

Zahorik (1975) continued this line of inquiry by examining the use of behavioral objectives and different kinds of planning models, such as Eisner's (1967). Zahorik asked 194 teachers to write down the decisions that they made prior to teaching and the order in which they made them. He classified these decisions into the following categories: objectives, content, activities, materials, diagnosis, evaluation, instruction, and organization. He found that the kind of decision made by the greatest number of teachers concerned pupil activities (81 percent). The decision most frequently made first was content (51 percent), followed by learning objectives (28 percent).

Zahorik concluded from this study that teacher planning decisions do not always follow linearly from a specification of objectives and that, in fact, objectives are not particularly important for planning in terms of quantity of use. He also argued that certain models of planning did not appear to be functioning in reality, since relatively few teachers reported beginning their planning in ways suggested by the models of planning.

More recently, researchers have turned their attention to describing teacher planning by observing and audiotaping teachers thinking aloud during planning sessions. Peterson, Marx, and Clark (1978) examined planning in a laboratory situation as 12 teachers prepared to teach a new instructional unit to groups of junior-high-school students with whom they had had no previous contact. These units were taught to three different groups of eight students on three different days. During their planning periods, teachers were instructed to think aloud, and their verbal statements were later coded into planning categories including objectives, materials, subject matter, and instructional process. The primary findings of this study were that (1) teachers spent the largest proportion of their planning time dealing with the content to be taught; (2) after subject matter, teachers concentrated their planning efforts on instructional processes (strategies and activities); and (3) the smallest proportion of their planning time was spent on objectives. All three of these findings were consistent with those by Zahorik (1975) and Goodlad and Klein (1970). The third finding was also similar to results reported by Joyce and Harootunian (1964) and by Popham and Baker (1970).

The task demands on the teachers should be taken into account in interpreting these results. The researchers provided the teachers with unfamiliar materials from which to teach, and they limited preparation time to 90 minutes immediately preceding teaching on each day of the study. Since the teachers did not know their students in advance, it follows that the emphasis in their planning would be on content and instructional processes. Finally, the researchers did provide the teachers with a list of six general teaching goals, expressed in terms of content coverage, process goals, and cognitive and attitudinal outcomes for students. Under these circumstances, it is not surprising that the teachers devoted little planning time to composing more specific objectives and spent the largest part of their planning time to studying the content and deciding how to teach it.

The findings of a study conducted in a classroom setting by Morine-Dershimer and Vallance (1976) were consistent with those of Peterson, Marx, and Clark (1978). Morine-Dershimer and Vallance collected written plans for 2 experimenter-prescribed lessons (in mathematics and in reading) that 20 second- and fifth-grade teachers taught in their own classrooms to a small group of their own students. Teacher plans were described by the researchers in terms of: (1) specificity of written plans; (2) general format of plans; (3) statement of goals; (4) source of goal statement; (5) attention to pupil background and preparation; (6)

identification of evaluation procedures; and (7) indication of possible alternative procedures. In this study, teachers tended to be fairly specific and used an outline form in their plans. Their written plans reflected little attention to behavioral goals, diagnosis of student needs, evaluation procedures, or alternative courses of action. However, the teachers reported that writing plans for researcher-prescribed lessons was not typical of their planning, and observations of their classroom teaching behavior revealed that much of what the teachers had planned was not reflected in their written outlines (Morine-Dershimer, 1979).

In his five-month field study of one teacher, Yinger (1977) drew on his observations, interview data, and think-aloud protocols to create a theoretical model of the process of teacher planning. The following is a brief description of the model (from Clark & Yinger, 1977):

> Three stages of planning were represented in the planning model. The first stage, problem finding, was portrayed as a discovery cycle where the teacher's goal conceptions, her knowledge and experience, her notion of the planning dilemma, and the materials available for planning interact to produce an initial problem conception worthy of further exploration. The second stage in the planning process was problem formulation and solution. The mechanism proposed for carrying out this process was the "design cycle." In this cycle, problem solving was characterized as a design process involving progressive elaboration of plans over time. Elaboration, investigation, and adaptation were proposed as phases through which plans were formulated. The third stage of the planning model involved implementation of the plan, its evaluation, and its eventual routinization. This stage emphasized the contribution of evaluation and routinization to the teacher's repertoire of knowledge and experience which in turn play a major role in future planning deliberations. (p. 285)

One of the most significant contributions of Yinger's conceptualization of the planning process is that his model is cyclical in two senses. Internally, the Yinger model postulates a design cycle similar to the processes hypothesized to go on in the work of architects, physicians, artists, designers, and other professionals. Externally, the Yinger model acknowledges that schooling is not a series of unrelated planning-teaching episodes, but that each planning event draws from prior planning and teaching experiences and that each teaching event feeds into future planning and teaching processes. The cycle is a continuous, year-long process, in which the boundaries between planning, teaching, and reflection are not sharp or distinct.

A later study by Clark and Yinger (1979) involved asking five teachers to plan a two-week unit on writing that they had never taught before. The teachers kept journals documenting their plans and their thinking about planning during a three-week period, and they were interviewed twice each week. The journal keeping and interviews continued and were supplemented by observations during the two-week period when the plans were being put into effect.

Analysis supported the idea that unit planning was not a linear process moving from objectives through design of activities to meet objectives. Rather, it was a cyclical process, typically beginning with a general idea and moving through phases of successive elaboration. Some teachers spent a great deal of time and energy at the problem-finding stage, generating topics or ideas for their unit. The search process typical of this stage was distinctly different from the elaboration and refinement of the idea that took place in the subsequent problem-formulation/solution stage. These data are consistent with the planning process model that Yinger (1977) developed earlier.

Individuals differed in their use of the model. Two of the teachers' unit plans consisted of a short problem-finding stage, brief unit planning, and considerable reliance on trying out activities in the classroom. This approach to planning was called "incremental planning." Teachers who planned incrementally used a series of short planning steps, relying heavily on day-to-day information from the classroom. The remaining three teachers' unit plans were characterized as products of "comprehensive planning," in which the teachers developed a thoroughly specified framework for future action. Comprehensive planning involved more attention to the unit as a whole, and more time and energy were invested in specifying plans as completely as possible before beginning to teach. Both approaches to unit planning seemed to work well for the teachers who used them. Incremental planning saved time and energy while staying in touch with changing student states. Comprehensive planning provided a complete and dependable guide for teacher-student interaction for the whole course of a unit, reducing uncertainty and increasing the probability of achieving prespecified objectives.

A final note on the models-of-planning issue comes from a University of Alberta doctoral dissertation by McLeod (1981), who approached the question of learning objectives in planning by asking not whether they are the starting point for planning but when teachers think about them. McLeod did a stimulated-recall interview with each of 17 kindergarten teachers, using a videotape of a 20- to 30-minute classroom activity taught earlier that same day. The purpose of her interviews was to determine when intended learning outcomes were formulated in terms of four stages:

1. Preactive 1: before planning activities or selecting materials.
2. Preactive 2: after planning but before teaching.
3. Interactive: during the act of teaching.
4. Postactive: during reflection after a teaching episode (after Pylypiw, 1974).

The interviews also revealed how different types of intended learning outcomes (cognitive, social, and psychomotor) were distributed.

Averaging the responses across the 17 teachers, McLeod found that the largest percentage of intended learning outcomes occurred during the interactive stage (45.8 percent). This was followed by the first preactive stage (26.5 percent), the second preactive stage (19.5 percent), and the postactive stage (8.2 percent). The data also indicated that 57.7 percent of the intended learning outcomes were categorized as cognitive, 35 percent were classified as social or affective, and 7.2 percent as psychomotor or perceptual. Interestingly, the intended social/affective learning outcomes were primarily identified during the interactive stage, while cognitive outcomes predominated in the preactive and postactive stages.

The McLeod study can be criticized on the grounds that too much weight may have been placed on the stimulated-recall interviews. These data could have been supplemented to good effect by observations and by having teachers think aloud during the preactive stages. Nevertheless, this research does much to broaden the concept of goals, objectives, or intended learning outcomes and their roles in planning and teaching. Earlier research tended to dismiss learning objectives as a rare, and therefore unimportant, element in teacher planning, even going so far as to characterize teachers as interested only in activities rather than in outcomes. McLeod's study, though, suggests that teachers can and do think about acting to support both specific and general learning outcomes for their students, and that it is hazardous to study the process of teacher planning apart from interactive teaching and postactive reflection.

Summary of Research on Models of Planning

In summary, the research on descriptive modeling of teacher planning shows us that planning is not a single, straightforward process moving from specification of goals or learning objectives, through means to those ends, to instruction and evaluation. Each of these concerns (and more) may be attended to, explicitly or implicitly, as a teacher prepares to teach. Familiarity with the particular content to be taught and personal knowledge of the students to be taught can have dramatic effects on the detail present in a teacher's plan and on the focus of the planning process. And, whatever model describes a teacher's planning, the plan is seldom used as a rigid script but rather as a flexible framework for getting off to a good start and staying generally on course. In other words, planning does not end when instruction begins, but continues in the form of interactive decision making and adjustment of the plan to fit the unpredictable circumstances of classroom interaction. The research to date does not tell us which model of planning is most effective, but it does provide a clearer sense of the variety of approaches that experienced teachers use to prepare themselves for lessons, units, and longer episodes of teaching.

TEACHER PLANNING AND CLASSROOM INTERACTION

The third and final question addressed in this review has to do with the link between teacher planning and classroom behavior. Studies mentioned earlier demonstrate that the content of instruction and the sequence of topics are influenced by teacher planning (for instance, Clark & Elmore, 1981; Smith & Sendelbach, 1979). Several other studies examine how teachers' plans influence what actually happens in the classroom.

Zahorik (1970) compared the effects of the presence and absence of structured planning on teachers' classroom behavior. He provided 6 of 12 teachers with a partial lesson plan containing behavioral objectives and a detailed outline of content to be covered two weeks later. He requested that the remaining 6 teachers reserve an hour of instructional time to carry out a task for the researchers, not telling them that they were going to be asked to teach a lesson on credit cards until just before the appointed time. Zahorik analyzed recorded protocols of the 12 lessons, focusing on "teacher behavior that is sensitive to students" (p. 144). He defined this behavior as "verbal acts of the teacher that permit, encourage, and develop pupils' ideas, thoughts, and actions" (p. 144). In comparing the protocols of the planners and nonplanners, Zahorik judged that teachers who had been given plans exhibited less honest or authentic use of the pupils' ideas during the lesson. He concluded that the typical planning model—goals, activities and their organization, and evaluation—resulted in insensitivity to pupils by the teacher.

Unfortunately, Zahorik did not determine the degree to which the teachers who received the lesson plans in advance actually planned or elaborated the lesson. A competing explanation for these findings is that the teachers who had no advance warning about what they were to teach were forced by the demands of the task to concentrate on their students' ideas and experiences, while those teachers who knew the expected topic of instruction two weeks in advance could focus on the content rather than on their students.

Peterson, Marx, and Clark (1978) conducted a laboratory study of teacher planning, teaching, and student achievement. Twelve experienced junior-high-school teachers were given social studies materials dealing with life in a small French community, along with a list of desired cognitive and affective student learning objectives. The teachers were given a 90-minute period in which to think aloud while they planned a 3-hour instructional unit. After planning, the teachers were videotaped while teaching groups of eight students. At the end of the teaching day, the teachers were interviewed using a stimulated-recall process in which they viewed videotaped segments of their own teaching and responded to a series of questions about their thought processes while teaching. The students completed achievement tests and an attitude inventory immediately after class. This process was repeated on three separate days with three different groups of students.

A number of positive relationships between the focus of the teachers' planning statements and their classroom behavior emerged. For all teachers, planning on the first day of teaching was heavily weighted toward the content to be covered. However, the focus of their planning shifted on the second and third days, with planning for instructional processes becoming more prominent. The proportion of planning statements dealing with the learner was positively related to teacher behaviors classified as "group-focused." The proportion of planning statements dealing with the content was positively and significantly correlated with teacher behavior coded as "subject-matter-focused." These findings suggest that teacher planning is most related to the general focus or tone of interactive teaching, rather than to the specific details of verbal behavior. They also suggest that the nature of the work done during the preactive planning period changes with situation-specific teaching experience. As the task demands on the teacher change, so does the nature of appropriate preparation.

Carnahan (1980) studied the planning and subsequent behavior of nine fifth-grade teachers who taught the same two-week mathematics unit. The quality of the teachers' written plans was determined by rating plans that focused on large groups as low in quality and plans that focused on individuals or small groups as high in quality. (This criterion was chosen because the curriculum materials that the teachers were using incorporated a similar bias.) Classroom observers rated instruction for teacher clarity, use of motivation strategies, and student engagement. Carnahan found that no statistically significant relationship existed between his ratings of plan quality and of teaching quality. However, he did find a significant positive correlation between the total percentage of written planning statements about small groups or individuals and the teachers' observed use of small groups in the classroom. This and other findings in Carnahan's report indicated that the main relationship between written plans and subsequent classroom interaction is in the domain of organization and structuring of teaching, rather than in the domain of specific verbal behavior. During interactive teaching, the responses of students are unpredictable, and therefore verbal dialogue is not a profitable focus for teacher planning.

The influence of teacher planning on classroom processes in preschool teaching seems to be somewhat different from that observed in higher grades. Hill, Yinger, and Robbins (1981) studied the planning of the six teachers in a university developmental preschool. During a 10-week period, the researchers observed the teachers in their Friday afternoon group planning sessions, staff meetings, conferences with student-teachers, materials selection from the storeroom, and arrangement of classroom environments. They also interviewed the teachers about their planning processes and copied planning documents and records.

Hill, Yinger, and Robbins found that much of the teachers' planning centered around selecting and arranging manipulatable materials. The school storeroom was an important source of ideas for learning activities, and once the appropriate materials were identified, the planning process focused on how these materials would be arranged in the classroom for use by the children and on how the transitions into and out of these activities would be managed. The teachers were observed to spend three or more hours per week arranging the physical environments of their classrooms. When an activity did not go well, the first improvement strategy used by these teachers was to rearrange the physical environment. Because teaching in this setting was so heavily dependent on the materials selected and arranged by the teachers, it is clear that the nature of the children's learning opportunities was heavily influenced by teacher planning. It is also clear that the nature of the planning process was influenced by the demands of teaching in this setting.

These studies, taken together, suggest that teacher planning does influence opportunity to learn, content coverage, grouping for instruction, and the general focus of classroom processes. They also highlight the fact that the finer details of classroom teaching (say, specific verbal behavior) are unpredictable and are therefore not planned. Planning shapes the broad outlines of what is possible or likely to occur while teaching and is used to manage transitions from one activity to another. But once interactive teaching begins, the teacher's plan moves to the background and interactive decision making becomes more important.

Summary and Future Directions

Research on planning has systematically described an invisible and taken-for-granted set of teachers' activities and responsibilities. Regardless of the level of teaching, from preschool to university, teachers must go beyond the information provided in curriculum guides and materials. Planning is the process of studying, reorganizing, learning, and adapting the "what" of curriculum to prepare for the "how" of instruction. Planning as a process is sensitive to the experience of the teacher, the predictability or uncertainty that characterizes a particular classroom, and the chosen or assumed short- and long-range hopes and fears of both teacher and students.

Our review of the empirical research on teacher planning does not lead us to recommend a particular way to plan for either novices or experienced teachers. But the research does highlight the apparent links among teachers' knowledge of subject matter, awareness of student characteristics and limitations, attention to the social and physical constraints of the school setting, and availability of routines for teacher action. In short, improvements in teaching effectiveness may come as much from improved coordination of what teachers already know (through teacher planning) as from changing teachers' knowledge of and precision in performing pedagogical skills.

One practical implication of this claim is that teachers' professional development programs should include more time for teachers to spend in local planning and in making local adaptations of innovations and teaching techniques that are the focus of the staff development efforts. Teachers should be given the time, opportunity, encouragement, and rewards necessary to foster planning. Investment in teacher planning time is likely to pay off in more organized, coordinated, and coherent teaching and learning and also to boost the probability of improved professional communication among teachers in a given school.

Future research efforts in this area should include attention to teacher planning across the full school year to replanning and revision of plans, in addition to studies of preparation for first-time lessons, units, and curricula. A longitudinal approach to the study of teacher planning and behavior may also reveal how novice teachers become expert. Such a research program could lead to changes in the organization of schooling and in the content and timing of professional development efforts to match better the ways in which teachers think and act in complex, unpredictable situations.

THINKING FROM THE RESEARCH

We strongly believe that research on teachers' thought processes has taught us as much about how to think about teaching as it has about teachers' thinking. As we reflect on the findings of research on teacher planning, we have been able to develop new conceptions of teaching, which in turn have led us into new areas of inquiry and theorizing. In this section, we explore some of these ideas to show how the research on teacher planning has become a bridge to more powerful and productive visions of teaching and teachers.

Images of Teaching

Throughout history, the act of teaching has been described and guided by various metaphors and images drawn chiefly from the arts, agriculture, and the social sciences. Most recently, educators have been influenced by two dominant images: the teacher as skilled manager and the teacher as decision maker.

The image of the teacher as skilled manager has its roots in the industrialization of Western society. It came to fruition in the early 1950s, with the emergence of an "educational technology" based largely on the promise of behavioral psychology as a means of controlling human behavior. These notions, when combined with theories from the emerging areas of organizational development, systems science, and administrative science, lead to the development of the image of the teacher as one who effectively manages the learning of his or her charges.

Like other professions, the skill of the teacher was thought to be rooted in the mastery of technique, which in turn is grounded in "basic sciences" (for education, these are the social sciences, primarily psychology). In teaching, as in most other professional fields, this image became solidified and institutionalized in the guise of a model of "technical rationality" (Schön, 1983). This model asserts that skilled professional practice is possible only when the practitioner uses technical or "engineering" skills based on systematic knowledge that is specialized, scientific, and standardized. The model of technical rationality was exemplified in teacher education by the rise of competency-based models of training and behavioral systems for evaluating teacher effectiveness.

In recent years, the image of the teacher as skilled manager or technician has been joined (though not replaced) by the image of the teacher as decision maker. The new prominence of cognitive psychology has refocused the emphasis on technique and skill from the behavioral to the cognitive domain. Skills such as diagnosis and prescription, problem solving, and decision making have been named as basic teaching skills. But, in many cases, decision making has just become another skill or technique to be mastered and applied within the framework of technical rationality.

The influence of cognitive psychology has been much more apparent in the thinking of researchers who have turned their interests to studying teacher cognition. Their research has uncovered an unacknowledged richness and complexity in the realm of teaching practice. At the same time, it has failed to link the model of technical rationality to the actual practice of teachers. In fact, drastically different norms of rationality seem to be present.

The norms of rationality that are documented in teaching are very similar to those being described in recent research in other professions. All professions must deal with five general features of practical situations: complexity, uncertainty, instability, uniqueness, and value conflict. Russell Ackoff, one of the founders of operations research, paints a vivid picture of the world of the professional:

> Managers are not confronted with problems that are independent of each other, but with dynamic situations that consist of complex systems of changing problems that interact with each other. I call such situations *messes*. Problems are abstracted from messes by analysis; they are to messes as atoms are to tables and charts. . . . Managers do not solve problems; they manage messes. (Ackoff, 1979, cited in Schön, 1983)

The skills called for by these situations do not involve the systematic application of predetermined models or standardized techniques. Rather, these situations require the artful use of skills such as problem discovery and formulation, design, invention, and flexible adaptation. The orderly prescriptions of technology and science do not seem to match what professionals actually do in practice.

The image we see emerging from research and theory is that of the teacher as professional. We use this term to refer to practitioners who specialize in designing practical courses of action to serve the needs of a particular client group, and whose success depends on their ability to manage complexity and solve practical problems. The skill required is that of intelligent and artful orchestration of knowledge and technique. This image also portrays the richness of practice by emphasizing the importance of goal-directed action and design. We assume, based on previous research on teaching practice, that the images that dominate education today are insufficient to describe the work of teachers fully. We see a need to break from the model of technical rationality, which seems mismatched with the world of teaching, and to explore patterns of practice and knowledge that may be used as a basis for rethinking and reasserting teaching as a profession. Our firm belief is that teaching is in great need of a new image to revive and empower it. We believe that teacher as professional may be that image.

This image gains further power when compared to descriptions of professional behavior in other fields. Research on the professions (for instance, Argyris and Schön, 1974; Schön, 1983) has recently begun to portray the divergent activities of such professionals as planners, architects, engineers, and psychiatrists as being based on common mental operations and processes. Simon (1981) has labeled this common activity as "design": action aimed at bringing about desired states of affairs in practical contexts. Schön (1983) has depicted the activities of the professional as a "reflective conversation" with the immediate problem situation and has suggested that, to understand the practice of professionals, we need to understand their reflection-in-action. Some propositions that we have derived from this research include:

1. Not only can we think about things we do, but we can think about doing something while doing it. This reflection-in-action is central to the art that practitioners use to cope with divergent situations.
2. Reflection-in-action draws on implicit and situation-grounded ("action-present") cognitions, instead of the more explicit and deliberative cognitions associated with reflection *on* action.
3. Professional problem solving draws on a repertoire of practical knowledge that generates examples and metaphors for understanding new phenomena.
4. Professional problem solving often proceeds by reframing the initial problem, inquiry within the imposed frame, and reflection on the "back-talk" produced by this inquiry.

Recently, there has been much discussion both within and outside the teaching community about teaching as a profession. Questions abound about what a professional is, whether teachers are true professionals, and what must be done to establish teaching as a profession. We would argue that professionals are defined by the essential nature of their action, rather than their educational experiences, certification or licensing procedures, or governance of standards of practice. Therefore, we see teachers as professionals already, designing practical courses of action in complex situations. What allows them to do this is a thoughtful and purposeful consideration of practice. What is needed in education is a more thorough understanding of these processes. One aspect of this conception that needs to be further developed and researched is that of the relationship between reflection and action.

A Call for Research on Reflection and Action

To say "thoughtless professional" is to pose a contradiction. The essence of professional life is thoughtful deliberation, problem solving, and design. To say that teaching is a profession is to attribute the same characteristics to teachers. (It is a revealing commentary on the current image of teaching that the term "thoughtless teacher" would not seem self-contradictory.)

We suggested previously that one way to depict the activities of a professional is as a reflective conversation with the immediate situation. This notion of tying reflection to immediate context is somewhat contradictory to the ways in which many writers have defined reflection.

John Dewey's writings are often the reference of first choice when discussing the nature of reflection. In his books *How We Think* (1933) and *Democracy and Education* (1966), Dewey uses the word "reflection" almost synonymously with the word "thinking." Reflection, for Dewey, involves active, persistent, and careful consideration of behavior or practice. He says reflection is the means for meeting and responding to problems ("reflection" is also used interchangeably with "problem solving").

One of the most useful distinctions Dewey draws is between reflection and impulse and routine. To Dewey, reflection "converts action that is merely appetitive, blind, and impulsive into intelligent action" (1933, p. 17). Not only is reflection intelligent action, it is responsible action.

> The opposites . . . to thoughtful action are routine and capricious behavior. The former accepts what has been customary as a full measure of possibility and omits to take into account the connections of the particular things done. The latter makes the momentary act a measure of value, and ignores the connections of our personal action with the energies of the environment. It says, virtually, "things are to be just as I happen to like them at this instant," as routine says in effect "let things continue just as I have found

them in the past." Both refuse to acknowledge responsibility for the future consequences which flow from present action. Reflection is the acceptance of such responsibility. (Dewey, 1933, p. 140)

Thus for Dewey and most writers who have built on his writings, reflection has become that component of thought that is most intelligent and responsible. It is often portrayed as a type of rational analysis and contrasted to intuitive thought. In effect, reflection is defined as something that one does deliberately and deliberatively. One is portrayed as reflecting *on* action; the reflective posture is one of standing apart from the chaos of action and bringing reason to bear on it.

In contrast to this view of reflection stands a body of theory on practical reasoning. Most of this writing has been done by moral philosophers. They portray the relationship between thought and action as more general and intertwined. Maxine Greene (1984), for instance, says that "thinking about our craft often brings conscience to bear on the actions we undertake in the course of our work" (pp. 55–56).

Donald Schön has described the intermingling of thought and action as thought-in-action.

When someone reflects-in-action, he becomes a researcher in the practice context. He is not dependent on the categories of established theory and technique, but constructs a new theory of the unique case. His inquiry is not limited to a deliberation about means which depends on a prior agreement about ends. He does not keep means and ends separate, but defines them interactively as he frames a problematic situation. He does not separate thinking from doing, ratiocinating his way to a decision which he must later convert to action. Because his experimenting is a kind of action, implementation is built into his inquiry. (Schön, 1983, p. 68)

In describing the nature of the deliberation that occurs in practical reasoning, Wiggins (1978) supports Schön's description. Wiggins describes practical deliberation as a process of searching for an "adequate specification" of the situation, a constant remaking and re-evaluation of concerns, an evolving conception of the point of acting, and a reciprocal relation between the agent and the world. One of the keys to practical deliberation, according to Wiggins, is "situational appreciation," what he says Aristotle called "perception" (*aisthesis*). "The man of highest practical wisdom," Wiggins writes, "is the man who brings to bear upon a situation the greatest number of genuinely pertinent concerns and genuinely relevant considerations commensurate with the importance of the deliberative context" (pp. 146–147). Both of these conceptions of reflection contain some useful notions. It is apparent that reflection can take place subsequent to action, as one's thoughts return to the situation. It seems also apparent that we somehow think about practice in the midst of it and that this is an important process. In reality, we know very little about how these processes take place. Reflection has long been an admirable goal of practitioners, but there have been few empirical studies of this kind of thought in action. What kinds of products can we expect to result from research in this area? Wiggins suggests that the best we can hope for is not explanation or prediction of practical reasoning but:

> a conceptual framework which we can apply to particular cases, which articulates the reciprocal relations of an agent's concerns and his perceptions of how things objectively are in the world; and a schema of description *which relates the complex ideal the agent tries in the process of living to make real in the form which the world impresses, both by way of opportunity and by way of limitation, upon that ideal."* (1978, pp. 149–150, emphasis in original)

We believe the goal of research on teaching is to develop an image of teaching that provides the kind of schema Wiggins refers to. The nature of practice is such that improvement can be fostered only by the professional's own understanding of self and of the nature of the practical. Reflection obviously plays a big role here. The results of these efforts may not meet everyone's desires for a theory of practice. But we side with Wiggins when he says:

> I entertain the unfriendly suspicion that those who feel they *must* seek more than all this provides want a scientific theory of rationality not so much from a passion for science, even where there can be no science, but because they hope and desire, by some conceptual alchemy, to turn such a theory into a regulative or normative discipline, or into a system of rules by which to spare themselves some of the agony of thinking and all the torment of feeling and understanding that is actually involved in reasoned deliberation. (1978, p. 150)

CONCLUSION

Ten years of research on teacher planning have given us two insights: (1) an appreciation of the complexity of the psychological and practical demands that teachers must deal with as they decide what and how to teach; and (2) a starting point for advocacy of new and more empowering images of teaching as a profession. This program of research is not directed at discovering which methods or models of planning are most effective in some sense, but rather at influencing the ways in which teacher educators, curriculum developers, school administrators, and teachers themselves think about teaching. We hope that future research on teaching will continue to provide each of these audiences with provocative food for thought about the important role of teacher planning.

REFERENCES

Ackoff, R. (1979). The future of operations research is past. *Journal of Operations Research Society, 30,* 93–104.

Anderson, L. M., & Evertson, C. M. (1978). *Classroom organization at the beginning of school: Two case studies.* Paper presented to the American Association of Colleges for Teacher Education, Chicago, IL.

Argyris, C., & Schon, D. (1974). *Theory in practice: Increasing professional effectiveness.* San Francisco, CA: Jossey-Bass.

Ben-Peretz, M. (1975). The concept of curriculum potential. *Curriculum Theory Network, 5* (2), 151–159.

Buckley, P. K., & Cooper, J. M. (1978, March). *An ethnographic study of an elementary school teacher's establishment and maintenance of group norms.* Paper presented to the American Education Research Association.

Carnahan, R. S. (1980). *The effects of teacher planning on classroom processes* (Technical Report No. 541). Madison, WI: Wisconsin Research and Development Center for Individualized Schooling.

Clark, C. M., & Elmore, J. L. (1979). *Teacher planning in the first weeks of school* (Research Series No. 56). East Lansing, MI: Institute for Research on Teaching, Michigan State University.

———. (1981). *Transforming curriculum in mathematics, science and writing: A case study of teacher yearly planning* (Research Series No. 99). East Lansing, MI: Institute for Research on Teaching, Michigan State University.

Clark, C. M., & Yinger, R. J. (1977). Research on teacher thinking. *Curriculum Inquiry, 7* (4), 279–394.

———. (1979). *Three studies of teacher planning* (Research Series No. 55). East Lansing, MI: Institute for Research on Teaching, Michigan State University.

Dahllof, U., & Lundgren, U. P. (1970). *Macro- and micro approaches combined for curriculum process analysis: A Swedish education field project.* Goteborg, Sweden: Reports from the Institute of Education, University of Goteborg, mimeo.

Dewey, J. (1933). *How we think.* New York: Heath.

———. (1966). *Democracy and education.* New York: Free Press.

Eisner, E. W. (1967). Educational objectives: Help or hindrance? *School Review, 75,* 250–260.

Goodlad, J. I., & Klein, M. F. (1970). *Behind the classroom door.* Worthington, OH: C. A. Jones.

Greene, M. (1984). How do we think about our craft? *Teachers College Record, 86,* 55–67.

Hill, J., Yinger, R. J., & Robbins, D. (1981). *Instructional planning in a developmental preschool.* Paper presented at the annual meeting of the American Educational Research Association, Los Angeles, CA.

Jackson, P. W. (1968). *Life in classrooms.* New York: Holt, Rinehart & Winston.

Joyce, B. (1978–1979). Toward a theory of information processing in teaching. *Educational Research Quarterly, 3* (4), 73–77.

Joyce, B. R., & Harootunian, B. (1964). Teaching as problem solving. *Journal of Teacher Education, 15,* 420–427.

Joyce, B. R., & Weil, M. (1972). *Models of teaching.* Englewood Cliffs, NJ: Prentice-Hall.

McCutcheon, G. (1980, September). How do elementary school teachers plan? The nature of planning and influences on it. *Elementary School Journal, 81*, 4–23.

McLeod, M. A. (1981). *The identification of intended learning outcomes by early childhood teachers: An exploratory study.* Doctoral dissertation, University of Alberta.

Morine-Dershimer, G. (1979). *Teacher plan and classroom reality: The South Bay study, part IV* (Research Series No. 60). East Lansing, MI: Institute for Research on Teaching, Michigan State University.

Morine-Dershimer, G., & Vallance, E. (1976). *Teacher planning.* Beginning Teacher Evaluation Study, Special Report C. San Francisco, CA: Far West Laboratory for Educational Research and Development.

National Institute of Education. (1975). *Teaching as clinical information processing* (Report of Panel 6, National Conference on Studies in Teaching). Washington, DC: National Institute of Education.

Newell, A., & Simon, H. A. (1972). *Human problem solving.* Englewood Cliffs, NJ: Prentice-Hall.

Peterson, P. L., Marx, R. W., & Clark, C. M. (1978). Teacher planning, teacher behavior and student achievement. *American Educational Research Journal, 15* (3), 417–432.

Popham, J. W., & Baker, E. L. (1970). *Systematic instruction.* Englewood Cliffs, NJ: Prentice-Hall.

Pylypiw, J. (1974). *A description of classroom curriculum development.* Doctoral dissertation, University of Alberta, 1974.

Schon, D. (1983). *The reflective practitioner: How professionals think in action.* New York: Basic Books.

Shultz, J., & Florio, S. (1979). Stop and freeze: The negotiation of social and physical space in a kindergarten/first-grade classroom. *Anthropology and Education Quarterly, 10*, 166–181.

Simon, H. A. (1957). *Models of man.* New York: Wiley.

———. (1981). *The sciences of the artificial,* 2nd ed. Cambridge, MA: MIT Press.

Smith, E. L., & Sendelbach, N. B. (1979). *Teacher intentions for science instruction and their antecedents in program materials.* Paper presented to the American Education Research Association, San Francisco, CA.

Taylor, P. H. (1970). *How teachers plan their courses.* Slough, England: National Foundation for Education Research.

Tikunoff, W. J., & Ward, B. A. (1978). *A naturalistic study of the initiation of students into three classroom social systems* (Report A-78–11). San Francisco, CA: Far West Laboratory for Educational Research and Development.

Tyler, R. W. (1950). *Basic principles of curriculum and instruction.* Chicago, IL: University of Chicago Press.

Wiggins, D. (1978). Deliberation and practical reason. In J. Raz (Ed.), *Practical Reasoning.* New York: Oxford University Press.

Yinger, R. J. (1977). *A study of teacher planning: Description and theory development using ethnographic and information processing methods.* Doctoral dissertation, Michigan State University.

Zahorik, J. A. (1970). The effect of planning on teaching. *Elementary School Journal, 71*, 143–151.

———. (1975). Teachers' planning models. *Educational Leadership, 33*, 134–139.

PART VI

CONCLUSION

CHAPTER 15

LEE S. SHULMAN

THE WISDOM OF PRACTICE
Managing Complexity in Medicine and Teaching

Art is the solving of problems that cannot be expressed until they are solved.
PIET HEIN

The story is told of a young man who approached his rabbi for advice on the building of a *sukkah*, the ritual hut that is erected by religious Jews in celebration of the Feast of Tabernacles, Sukkot, the autumn festival that follows less than a week after Yom Kippur. Rather than simply telling his congregant how to build the sukkah, the rabbi urged that he read the appropriate sections of the Talmud, which includes an entire tractate dedicated to the laws pertaining to this holiday. The young man agreed and proceeded to spend several months in careful study of the designated volume.

When autumn arrived and Yom Kippur had passed, the small shelter was built precisely as the Talmudic text advised. Several days later, the visibly upset young man appeared once again at the rabbi's door. A moderate rainstorm had occurred the evening before and much to his dismay the sukkah had been blown flat. "How is it possible," implored the youthful builder, "that I could follow the instructions of the Talmud so religiously and yet have the structure blow over so easily?" The rabbi gazed at his visitor as he silently stroked his long beard. He sighed. "You know, many of the commentaries ask exactly the same question!"

The movement from theory to practice is frequently accompanied by embarrassments. The sukkah falls, the economy totters, a bridge collapses, crops wither, patients falter, pupils flounder. All too frequently we who conduct and interpret educational research are asked similar questions by the teachers whose work our scholarship is intended to inform. How can our theories, so carefully crafted and empirically grounded, frequently fail to hold up against even the most gentle winds

369

of practical exigency? What is the contribution of scholarly theory to the enhancement of practice?

A traditional stance for psychologists who wished to influence practice was to conduct research in their laboratories, to formulate theories or principles based upon the findings of their well-controlled studies, and then to prescribe those principles as the proper bases for grounded practice. An alternative research strategy is to study accomplished practice as it actually occurs and to ask how it has been achieved.

This focus on expert practice is a major strategy of contemporary cognitive psychological research in the information-processing tradition. This stream of inquiry, especially as exemplified by the "expert-novice" research programs, begins with the recognition that, in principle, the human animal is a very limited information processor. That is, given the modest limits within which the human short-term memory operates (the magic number seven plus or minus two was George Miller's estimate, apparently an overly optimistic one by more recent accounts), it is quite amazing what feats of intelligence we *Homo sapiens* are capable of performing. From Godel's Proof to the Sistine Chapel ceiling, the accomplishments of the human mind are quite substantial.

Regarding these achievements, the information-processing psychologist asks, "How can the human mind, a mechanism with so many limitations, produce works of art, intellect, and practice that are so complex and subtle?" Thus, the psychologist asks how the "expert" human thinker and problem solver manages to simplify the complexities of the world around him so they can fit through the bottlenecks of human memory and information processing. Such psychologists are typically interested in developing a theory *of* practice, a theoretical formulation adequate to explain the miracle of cognition in the expert thinker.

Articulating the relationships of theory to practice, of science to art, has been the prevailing theme in N. L. Gage's distinguished career. It is a problem that besets both scholarly practitioners and practical theorists. It is a central theme of this chapter.

I have had the opportunity during the past 20 years to engage in research on the professional activities of members of two professions: medicine and teaching. I have been particularly interested in the question of what makes the intellectual work of each occupation difficult. That is, as both physicians and teachers think their ways through the complex and demanding tasks that their respective clients and professional obligations place upon them, how do they manage? More specifically, since the hallmark of a profession is the presence of enormously complex and indeterminate problem situations, and the exercise of professional judgment characterizes such practice, how is complexity managed in the doing of both medicine and teaching?[1]

[1] This emphasis is particularly appropriate for the present volume. Nate Gage has maintained a lifelong commitment to the improvement of teaching practice through the study of effective practitioners. Both through his correlational and his experimental work, he

STUDYING THE WISDOM OF PRACTICE IN MEDICINE

I shall begin with a description of a program of research on the ways in which experienced physicians go about their diagnostic work. This was research I conducted in collaboration with Arthur Elstein and Sarah Sprafka during an eight-year period in the late 1960s and the 1970s (Shulman & Elstein, 1976; Elstein, Shulman, & Sprafka, 1978).[2]

We wished to understand how expert diagnosticians solved the complex clinical cases they encountered. We recognized that diagnosis represented only a limited portion of the physician's work. It left out the processes of medical management and follow-up as well as the all-important affective and interpersonal aspects of the doctor-patient relationship. Nevertheless, the intellectual processes of diagnosis were of great interest psychologically and were quite central to the education of physicians. Moreover, there could be connections between diagnosis in medicine and the kinds of strategies employed by teachers in the diagnosis of educational difficulties.

We had clear expectations regarding the strategies that expert physicians would use. First, through reading the standard medical textbooks and consulting with medical educators we found a clear consensus regarding how physicians ought to proceed in their diagnostic workups. Harrison's (1973) textbook of medicine, the most widely used among medical students, asserted "the clinical method is an orderly intellectual activity which proceeds from symptom to sign to syndrome to disease." We thus expected to observe a highly inductive process in which the physicians would first collect a large body of data, following the injunction to "keep an open mind," and only after gathering a rich data base would then begin to organize the data into larger units and move toward a diagnosis.

This expectation was also consistent with the then-current psychological understandings regarding the management of cognitive strain during information processing. Bruner, Goodnow, and Austin (1956), in their classic *A Study of Thinking*, had investigated the strategies employed by individuals attempting to learn a new concept from examination of positive and negative examples of that concept. For example,

---

has contended that research on teaching is generalizable to practice precisely because it comprises the study of practice. One need not speculate whether a real teacher is capable of engaging in the kinds of practice described in process-product research. The very fact that the behavior described is captured in the research program is evidence that real teachers engage in it. While I have quibbled with Gage regarding how closely his *composite* characterizations of effective teachers necessarily correspond to what any particular teacher might have done, I consider his work well within the traditions of wisdom-of-practice research programs. With Gage, it represents the twin efforts of the applied behavioral scientist and educator—whose goal is to better understand the processes of skilled professionals in order to educate those professionals more responsibly in the future.

[2] These studies of medical problem solving were conducted under grant support from the U.S. Public Health Service to the Office of Medical Education Research and Development (OMERAD) at Michigan State University.

they could provide participants in their studies with examples of dogs (collie, scottie, doberman, spaniel) and examples of non-dogs (cat, parakeet, mule, college professor) with the task of finding the general category or rule that could organize all the positive examples and exclude the negative ones. However, rather than use commonplace categories like dogs, tools, or "countries with seaports on the Indian Ocean with populations of less than 10,000,000" (the concepts can get very complicated), they used geometrical figures or similarly unfamiliar stimulus objects. What resulted was a Twenty-Questions-like game.

They concluded from their studies that the most frequently employed strategy in such instances was "conservative focusing," an inductive, step-by-step process in which the problem solver systematically reduced the field by ruling out alternatives. The alternative strategy, guessing particular hypotheses and testing them directly, was untenable. It simply placed too much strain on the fragile vessel of human memory. As soon as one tried to keep the results for more than one or two hypotheses in mind simultaneously, errors of memory increased rapidly. Thus, the findings of psychology and the principles of traditional medical lore concurred. We should expect to observe physicians employing a conservative, inductive strategy in diagnosis.

Through a survey of practicing internists in three geographical areas, we identified a small number of internists who were viewed by their peers as particularly gifted diagnosticians, physicians to whom you would turn for help with a particularly difficult case. For comparison purposes we also identified a group of similarly experienced and certified specialists who, while apparently competent, had not been so nominated by their colleagues. We expected to find that there would be differences in problem-solving strategies or abilities that distinguished the consistently more effective diagnosticians from their less wily colleagues.

Each physician came to our laboratory, which housed a simulated examination room with remote-controlled television cameras for taping the encounters between physician and patient. The patients were carefully trained actors and actresses who had been prepared to provide the medical histories that corresponded to the actual clinical cases we had selected for our simulations. For two of the cases—a hematology problem and a gastrointestinal disorder—the actors provided the history, a "resident" who had ostensibly conducted a comprehensive physical examination provided all requested physical information, and all possible laboratory tests could be ordered as they would normally. Unlike the real world, however, the results of lab tests were made available almost immediately.

For the third case, the actor was encountered in an "emergency room" setting, lying on an examining table complaining of inability to move or feel anything in her legs. The participating actors had been trained to simulate the sensory and motor losses associated with a neurological disorder—in this case the acute onset of multiple sclerosis—and a full physical examination could be conducted by the physician since all nonneurological symptoms were expected to be normal in any event.

I remember well the first pilot study we conducted using these procedures. The distinguished chief of medicine of a regional diagnostic and treatment center had agreed to come to our laboratory for two days and work on all three of the simulated cases. He sat in the simulated examination room/office, interviewing the "patient" as our television cameras silently tilted and panned, sending their signals to the videotape recorders. He alternated between asking sequences of questions and ruminating out loud about what he was thinking and what alternatives he was considering. An advantage to using the actors and refraining from any deception was that the physicians could think aloud without fear of traumatizing the patients. To our amazement, within 30 seconds of the patient's first descriptions of her ailment ("college student in a dorm . . . headache . . . fatigue . . . bad sore throat . . . some fever . . ."), he had already generated his first diagnostic hypothesis (infectious mononucleosis) to be followed less than a minute later by two others (infectious hepatitis; some kind of flu). And so did he proceed, working directly with specific diagnostic alternatives, at times three or four at a time, and organizing much of his questioning using the working hypotheses as a framework. He was apparently violating all the rules, whether they were those of medicine or cognitive psychology.

He continued to operate in that manner during his full two days in our lab, with all the cases we presented to him. When we did stimulated recall showing him his own videotapes for review, he confirmed his use of the strategy we had identified. We assumed he was an anomaly until, as the pilot studies continued and we proceeded into the full investigation, we came to realize that every physician we studied performed in the same manner. Inductive processing where early judgments were withheld, where one first gathered all the information one would need and only then began to diagnose, was by and large a myth. The wisdom of practice proceeded otherwise.

Moreover, the physicians characteristically generated *multiple competing hypotheses*, that is, pairs or triplets of diagnostic alternatives arrayed such that evidence that was positive for one was likely to be negative for the others. This in turn was related to another feature of their diagnostic work. Although constantly talking of the strategy of "rule-outs" in their approach, they in fact favored modes of inference in which they gathered evidence to confirm a particular hypothesis rather than to disconfirm it. Finally, we failed to find evidence of the general competence in medical diagnosis whose existence was an underlying assumption of our work. (Why else ask medical peers to nominate experts in diagnosis in general?) Indeed, as far as we could tell, medical diagnostic expertise was case- or domain-specific. Knowing that a physician was excellent in diagnosing diseases of the gastrointestinal tract was no help in predicting his or her competence with hematological or neurological complaints. Basic problem-solving strategies and proce-dures were remarkably similar across all physicians (a finding strikingly parallel to that of de Groot (1965) regarding different levels of chess expertise). The appropriate question was not "Who is a good physician?" but "When is a physician good?"

What, then, did we conclude from our studies of the wisdom of practice in medicine? Both traditional medical belief and the ostensible lessons of psychological research were misleading. In general, the clinician's competence in problem formulation and hypothesis generation was the key to diagnostic success. Both of these processes are closely related to the physician's substantive knowledge base and specific experiences in a particular domain. Strategies are employed to reduce the complex-ity of the problem-solving process and to reduce cognitive strain, just as Bruner and his colleagues asserted. However, unlike their laboratory studies with tasks for which the research participants had no relevant prior knowledge or experience, inductive processing is not most adaptive in situations where substantial prior knowledge, much of it well orga-nized, already exists. Diagnostic hypotheses form the schema, the intel-lectual scaffolding, on which the rest of the medical inquiry is suspended.

By respecting the wisdom of practice we had discovered the rules that governed medical diagnostic work. What's more, the rules were a real surprise to us because they appeared to break the rules, to violate the commonly held assumptions about the proper ways to do medical diagnostic problem solving. An important reason for understanding this was the likelihood that medical educators were teaching students a set of strategies that were in fact maladaptive in practice. The beliefs regarding how diagnosis ought to be conducted were the most significant determiners of how diagnosis was taught to medical students. Better empirical data on how expert physicians perform served to guide medi-cal teaching in important new ways.[3] The key to understanding why

[3] Several additional comments are in order. Professor Roy Maffly of Stanford University School of Medicine was sufficiently convinced of the validity of our findings to base a new instructional system upon them. He received a grant from the National Fund for Medical Education to support development of a computer-based learning system to help medical students learn to generate early diagnostic hypotheses most effectively and how to evaluate them critically.

Interesting things occurred when Elstein and I began to report these findings to members of the medical community. We anticipated strong resistance to the claim that medical work was being pursued in one way while being taught and written about in an utterly different manner. Instead, we were pleased to hear that our account of medical problem solving squared quite well with how individual practitioners intuitively recog-nized they were working. Somehow, each seemed to believe that he or she was alone in practicing in such an illegitimate manner. In general, physicians were quick to agree that what we described was precisely how they performed.

A final note. One physician who heard our report acknowledged that we had accurately described how he practiced but voiced disappointment that he did not proceed inductively because he had always wanted to feel that doing medicine was like doing science. We then informed him that most recent work in the philosophy of science (e.g., Peter Medawar) had argued that the typical working strategy of science was in fact hypothetico-deductive, not inductive in a Baconian manner. So our physician friend was thinking like a scientist after all.

physicians thought through medical problems as they did lay in the complexity they had to manage and the most powerful strategies available for controlling the intricacies of medical work.

WISDOM OF THE PRACTITIONER

In 1966 I coedited a book called *Learning by Discovery* in which David Hawkins, eminent mathematics and science educator and distinguished philosopher, wrote:

> Our efforts are being made, I believe, in an historical situation where the best practice excels the best theory in quite essential ways; this fact defines a strategy we ought to follow.

> There have often been times in the history of science when the personal knowledge of practitioners was significantly deeper than anything embedded in the beliefs and writings of the academically learned. Indeed, science has never started in a social vacuum, but has grown typically out of the interplay of Theorizein and those practically achieved mappings of nature embodied in the working arts. (Hawkins, 1966, p. 3)

Hawkins' observations were the first to alert me to the importance of the wisdom of practice as a source for understanding the complexities of skilled performance. The challenge is to get inside the heads of practitioners, to see the world as they see it, then to understand the manner in which experts construct their problem spaces, their definitions of the situation, thus permitting them to act as they do.

This notion of getting inside the head of the practitioner whose skills you wish to understand is reflected in a very different context in the writings of Thomas Kuhn. Kuhn has long been interested in how a historian of science can make sense of the writings of scientists who lived centuries or even millennia before. He especially reports his frustrations in attempting to understand the concept of mechanics found in Aristotle's *Physics*.

He was especially troubled by all the serious inaccuracies in the philosopher's reported observations of natural phenomena. He concluded that the only way to understand Aristotle was to avoid reading him within the framework of contemporary physics. When he came to understand Aristotle's physics in the light of the more general Greek worldview, the incongruities in the work of that ancient philosopher dissolved.

> Trying to transmit such lessons to students, I offer them a maxim: When reading the works of an important thinker, look first for the apparent absurdities in the text and ask yourself how a sensible person could have written them. When you find an answer, I continue, when those passages make sense, then you may find the more central passages, ones you previously thought you understood, have changed their meaning. (Kuhn, 1977, p. xii)

We thus treat the actions of the practitioner as, in principle, adaptive. That is, when practitioners are observed to behave in a manner that appears irrational, silly, maladaptive, or just plain foolish, we ask what would make their choice of behavior sensible.

Now, it may be that the observed behavior is just plain silly and we would be unwise to accept any observed performance of a veteran practitioner (or the rules we infer from detecting regularities in some particular individual's thoughts and actions) as adequate reason to stipulate that such rules ought to serve as grounds for the actions of others. Other decision rules are needed.[4] Strategies for avoiding this version of the naturalistic fallacy will be discussed at the conclusion of this chapter.

WISDOM OF PRACTICE IN TEACHING

The practice of teaching involves a far more complex task environment than does that of medicine. The teacher is confronted, not with a single patient, but with a classroom filled with 25 to 35 youngsters. The teacher's goals are multiple; the school's obligations far from unitary. Even in the ubiquitous primary reading group, the teacher must simultaneously be concerned with the learning of decoding skills as well as comprehension, with motivation and love of reading as well as word-attack, and must both monitor the performances of the six or eight students in front of her while not losing touch with the other two dozen in the room. Moreover, individual differences among pupils are a fact of life, exacerbated even further by the worthwhile policies of mainstreaming and school integration. The only time a physician could possibly encounter a situation of comparable complexity would be in the emergency room of a hospital during or after a natural disaster. Thus the question How do teachers manage the complexity of classroom life? is not only as legitimate to raise regarding teachers as it is for physicians, it is far more germane.

I shall illustrate this way of looking at the management of complexity in classrooms by focusing on a set of studies that are linked together by a common interest in the way teachers use *time*. As Gage (1978) has pointed out in a critique of the work of Berliner and his colleagues, time is an empty vessel, and simply looking at the amount of time

---

[4] The process-product researcher has fairly clear-cut decision rules for determining whether an observed behavior is worth emulating. The behavior should correlate significantly with a desired outcome in students. Preferably, it should be demonstrated that experimental manipulation of the behavior yields the desired outcome under controlled experimental conditions. Fenstermacher (1978), among others, has raised questions regarding the adequacy of these conditions for justifying the stipulation of the behaviors as desirable. Nevertheless, some decision rules are needed and process-product researchers are prepared to state them.

used by either teachers or students is in itself not particularly illuminating. But for Berliner, time is a proxy, a variable of interest because of what it hides, because of what it represents in the minds and motives of those whose lives center on classrooms. What fills the empty vessel of time are inferences about what teachers and students who use more or less time, or use the time in particular ways, are thinking, feeling, attending to, or withdrawing from as they confront the tasks of schoolrooms.

From a teacher's perspective, time is a precious resource, a commodity to be invested in both children and activities, a valuable resource that must be used carefully because it is available in such limited amounts.[5] One of the reasons classroom teaching is so complex is that a limited amount of time and energy must somehow be allocated among individuals and groups while promoting equity and achieving excellence. When a teacher provides time—in the form of a question addressed to a pupil, a chance to ask a question, to present an idea, to do a problem at the board with the teacher's assistance—the teacher is providing an opportunity to learn, an occasion for the student to respond, construct, and test a thought. Trade-offs are always necessary; some children inevitably remain untaught while others are receiving special attention. Cooperative learning and peer tutoring can help, but in the final analysis teachers must teach.

I shall give a couple of brief examples of how teachers manage the complexities of allocating opportunities to learn, the triage of turn taking. Time does not float though classrooms unpackaged. Indeed, most of classroom time, especially during recitations, discussions, and the monitoring of seatwork, is incorporated within that ubiquitous vessel of social interaction, the *turn*. One of the most important accomplishments of any child's development is learning how to take turns, whether waiting to bat in a softball game or waiting to buy a ticket in a movie line. Much of the commerce of classroom life is the management of a turn-taking economy.[6] Let's talk first about some studies of how teachers allocate turns and then move on to an examination of the internal anatomy of a turn, what a turn is made of.

[5] I was first led to think about time in this manner by two economist colleagues at the Institute for Research on Teaching, Byron Brown and the late Dan Saks. Their suggestion that microeconomic metaphors be applied to classrooms, seeing them as firms, as oil refineries, as automobile job shops, each of which suggested a different principle for organizing work and allocating resources, had great heuristic value for their colleagues— both teachers and researchers—as they studied classrooms. They subsequently conducted reanalyses of the Beginning Teacher Evaluation Study data employing some of these ideas.

[6] I first learned of the importance of turn taking and its rules while working as a preadolescent in my parents' Chicago delicatessen. My late mother, an immigrant from Lithuania, disliked the formalities of queuing systems where customers were told to take a number at the door. She preferred an honor system in which turns were allocated by responses to her repeated question, "Whose *next* is it?" A "next" was a turn in the Logan Delicatessen, and a precious one at that. By transforming an adjective of subsequence into a noun of consequence, Sonia Shulman made her own contributions to the wisdom of practice.

Anderson, Evertson, and Brophy (1979), in a study I am quite fond of citing, examined the behaviors of first-grade reading teachers that correlated significantly with pupil end-of-year achievement gains. Among the many questions they asked was one that relates directly to this question of turn allocation. How should turns be allocated within a primary-grade reading group? Every teacher who deals with groups of any size readily understands the dilemma of turn allocation. Basically three strategies are available: ordered turns, random turns, and volunteered turns. In an ordered strategy, youngsters are called upon in a predetermined order, usually the order in which they are seated. In a random approach, the teacher employs the weapon of surprise, calling on students guerrilla-style to maintain attention and an optimal level of adaptive anxiety. When the teacher permits volunteering, the children themselves take the initiative by either raising their hands or calling out.

Which of these strategies will, in general, yield the largest achievement gains over a year of work in first-grade reading groups? When this question is posed before experienced teachers in talks like this one, the general consensus is clear. Teachers assert that random turns will be best. Student attention has a tendency to wander; fear of a sneak attack will keep students on their toes. At times, Kounin's (1970) management principle of "group alerting" is also cited in support of the virtues of random turns.

Most often educational research is said to confirm the intuitively obvious, though Gage (1986) has argued persuasively that the "obvious" is not always readily apparent. In fact, it can be demonstrated that the same individuals will claim that both a particular assertion *and its opposite* are both true and obviously so! Nevertheless, what is particularly attractive about the Anderson, Evertson, and Brophy findings regarding turn taking is that the findings are counterintuitive. Contrary to expectations, those children who had the highest achievement gains in reading were members of reading groups whose teachers used *ordered turns*.

What would account for those surprising findings? First, keep in mind that the preferred alternative—random turns—probably does not exist. That is, most studies of classroom interaction reveal that it is nearly impossible for any teacher, however well motivated, to assign turns in a truly random (and, over the long haul, thus equitable) manner. Indeed, a relatively small group of students inevitably garners the bulk of opportunities to respond when a nonstructured turn-taking protocol is employed. This should not surprise us. Those who know the right answers will be more likely to volunteer and will also be called on more frequently by the teacher. Let's face it. Teachers need reinforcement too. After teaching your heart out all morning, you will tend to call on someone whose response will suggest that your teaching produced some learning. As Bruno Bettelheim once observed, teachers need to replenish their own narcissistic reserves too, and student performance is our major source of pride.

Thus, since random turns rarely occur, the *un*ordered turn strategy will usually yield patterns of participation in which many children do not have a chance to perform, to demonstrate their understanding and receive praise or to demonstrate their misconceptions and receive remediation—both necessary features of effective teaching. When a large portion of a classroom's participants is not called upon, it should not surprise that achievement is lower.

But is it not certainly the case that students pay more attention when they do not know who will be called on next? Here we must ask where attention is directed rather than merely whether students are attending. Interviews with students suggest that much of the time during classroom discussions is spent with students thinking about who the teacher is going to call on, more precisely, whether and when the teacher will call on them. Thus, while there may be an increase in attention associated with unordered turns, that attentional increment may not be devoted to the texts, ideas, or materials of instruction, but to the subtle cues from teachers regarding their next pedagogical moves. Instead of focusing on the texts, the students may be working at "psyching out" the teacher. Such patterns of attention are unlikely to lead to increased student achievement. The reasons for the apparent superiority of ordered turns, therefore, may be that the ordering strategy disciplines the teacher's allocation patterns thereby assuring a more equitable distribution of learning opportunities, as well as removing a source of ambiguity for the students, hence permitting them to dedicate more of their energy to concentrating on the academic tasks rather than the teacher's management strategy.[7]

I have discussed this particular study of turn allocation in great detail because it so beautifully exhibits how much can be learned about classroom teaching from careful examination of the character of turns. Some practitioners had already understood intuitively that ordered turns work best and were using them. But the bulk of teachers continue to believe that unstructured turns are best. At times the wisdom of practice is neither obvious nor universal.

---

[7] Of course, the results of this particular study do not dictate that ordered turns be employed by all teachers under all conditions. Indeed, the reasons behind these findings ought to be analyzed and used as principles to guide practice rather than the specific behaviors themselves. Teaching in ways that distribute opportunities to learn and to perform more equitably and in ways that produce student cognitions that focus on task-relevant characteristics of the teaching rather than on task-irrelevant, these are the proper principles to be learned from this research. Process-product research, like all research on teaching, is valuable for the principles it teaches us to employ as we think about our teaching, not because of the specific behavior that it prescribes for teachers to employ. The failure to understand this important precept regarding the proper relationship between research and practice, a relationship that Gage emphasized repeatedly in his discussions of art and science, has led to the misuse of the results of research in some policy settings (see Chapter 1 as well).

Now I would like to discuss a series of studies that explore turns in a very different way. What is the anatomy of a turn? If you dissect a turn, take it apart to examine its constituent parts and their interrelationships, what do you find?

A turn can be defined as a teacher's question, a pupil's response, and a subsequent teacher response. This is one particular kind of turn, a recitation turn; but since recitation remains the most frequently identified mode of group instruction, it is fairly typical of classroom life. Occupying the interstices that separate these three anatomical pieces of a turn is *time*. The teacher asks a question after which we find some time. A student responds and again we find some length of time. The teacher responds to the student and again we observe a passage of time. The pace of classrooms is largely determined by the amount of time that occupies those interstices. In rapidly paced classrooms question, answer and response follow on one another's heels with the speed of a machine gun. In more slowly paced arenas, the time dividing these acts is longer, the general pace of recitation is slower, less hectic. What is the significance of this temporal aspect of the anatomy of a turn?

Mary Budd Rowe (1974a; 1974b), a distinguished science educator, became interested in an aspect of the anatomy of a turn she called "wait-time." She designated as wait-times the amount of time between teacher's question and student response (or a teacher repeating, restating, or redirecting the question) and the subsequent amount of time between a student response and a teacher's reaction. She proceeded to ask how the length of wait-times, which appears to be very much under the control of the teacher, relates to student performance and achievement.[8]

The findings of her research, carried out over a decade ago, are by now well known in the educational community. Overall, longer wait-times were associated with higher-order responses on the parts of students. That is, the longer teachers waited after asking questions or following student answers, the more complex, analytic, or creative were the statements made by their students.[9] The importance of wait-time has by now made its way into many staff development programs for teachers.

When staff development programs are designed for the purpose of teaching teachers to increase their wait-times, the results are provocative. During the course of the workshops, teachers seem perfectly capable

[8] Rowe's interest in wait-time goes well beyond concern for the proper pacing of classroom questions. She is particularly interested in the attitudes that develop among students as a consequence of the ways in which classrooms are run. She has termed one of the those attitudes "fate control."

[9] Naturally, the teachers' questions needed to be appropriately higher order to elicit such responses. Asking in what year Columbus discovered America is not going to elicit higher-order thinking even if wait-time approaches eternity. Increased wait-time only yields higher-order responses when the questions permit (or encourage) such thinking.

of increasing their wait-times from the general average (about one second) to a veritable pedagogical eternity (about four seconds). Yet when they are observed upon returning to their own classrooms, the wait-times rapidly return to their earlier values. What accounts for this backsliding? Are teachers simply lazy and shiftless? Or are there good reasons why longer wait-times may look more attractive to researchers than to wise practitioners?

To understand the probable price teachers pay when extending their wait-times, think for a moment about where wait-times occur: in the interstices of turns. As we noted earlier, longer wait-times necessarily entail the slowing of a classroom's instructional pace and the punctuation of its flow with eddies of silence. Periods of reflection (for that is in fact what those wait-times represent) provide opportunities for analysis and deliberation, for cognition and metacognition, but are also likely to present, in their very emptiness, occasions for disruption and misbehavior. Students, like nature, abhor a vacuum. The slowed pace of classroom interaction is likely to exact a toll from the teacher in the form of more frequent classroom disruptions and interruptions. One reason why the wise practitioner may find wait-times unattractive is that they bring with them an increase in the problems of classroom management.

Let us imagine for a moment, however, that the jointly produced drama of the classroom can survive the slower pace through a well-designed classroom rule system, a well-wrought social contract among teacher and students, and the adoption of a more deliberate learning style in the group. What unintended consequences of increased wait-times might motivate teachers to consider reducing them once more? Consider the possibility that the improvements in learning produced through the longer wait-times might themselves be two-edged swords, blessings dipped in acid for teachers. Yet what could possibly be problematic about higher-level and more creative student responses?

I find it easier to think about that question in relation to another study, a dissertation conducted several years ago by Janet Shroyer (1981) at Michigan State University. She asked, "What makes mathematics teaching difficult?" What are those kinds of classroom interaction that place particular stress on the teacher—from a substantive point of view rather than from a management perspective? Shroyer concentrated on a category of event we called a critical moment.[10] The critical

---

[10] The idea of a critical moment emerged from a set of seminars that Professor Joseph Schwab was then conducting with the research staff of the Institute for Research on Teaching. Schwab suggested that teaching could be characterized as proceeding in a flow of interactions periodically punctuated by interruptions. We could call these "occurrences" or "occasions." Each word means an interruption (an *occlusion*) in the flow (*current*) of any set of events. An occasion such as a holiday, a wedding, a special visit acts as an occlusion in the flow or current of everyday life. That special category of classroom occurrences with which we were interested were dubbed *critical moments*.

moments all involved the consequences of questions asked by teachers and were therefore structurally related to the same kinds of events in which we spoke of wait-times.

We will consider three categories of critical moment. The first occurs when a teacher asks the class a question he or she knows everyone can answer—and no one can! The second occurs when the teacher asks the class a question he or she is confident no one can answer—and many do! In each case, the planned lesson or lesson segment has been disrupted because the expected understanding (or ignorance) has not been demonstrated.

The third kind of critical moment is the most discomfiting of all. Here the teacher asks a question with a range of expectable answers, or at least a sense of the "ball park" within which the possible responses will fall. Instead, someone produces a response that falls beyond the pale, an idea or invention that simply does not fit with the teacher's expectations and is not immediately discernable as right or wrong. This kind of unpredictability produced some of the most painful critical moments of all. It placed the greatest strain on the subject-matter competence of the teacher, who now had to delve into his or her understanding of mathematics to think of a way of coping with this strange, or at least unexpected, response.

I hope it is now clear why I am reminded of Shroyer's study of critical moments in thinking about why prolonged wait-times are not always seen as producing positive outcomes by teachers. Classroom life is characterized by unpredictability. The uncertainties inherent in any simple act of tutoring are multiplied enormously as one attempts to teach a room filled with 30 mindful bodies. A teacher must attempt to keep this unpredictability within an acceptable range at all times. The cognitive strains of teaching become intolerable when the uncertainty of classroom life exceeds a certain threshold, which certainly must vary from teacher to teacher. If the great virtue of wait-time is that it yields more inventive or creative responses from students, then its great liability is that by the same token it necessarily increases the unpredictability of classroom discourse. Most likely, increases in wait-time are accompanied by increases in the frequency and intensity of critical moments. Wait-times may not only make teaching better; they may make teaching more difficult and strainful.

This is not to say that just because increased wait-times may make teaching difficult they ought to be avoided. Indeed, the solution to the problem is not likely to be forgoing both the goals of higher-order thinking and the wait-times needed to foster it. Teachers and students can probably learn to engage in more complex forms of discourse involving longer wait-times and more complex and unpredictable student responses. But more careful preparation of teachers and of their classes may be needed to support such an effort. For one, a teacher may well have to develop deeper content knowledge and pedagogical content knowledge to respond adequately to higher frequencies of less predictable student contributions.

I have invoked these examples to emphasize that the wisdom of practice must be considered even when we are confronted with what appear to be examples of teachers' resistance to change and misunderstandings of the usefulness of new ideas. In the spirit of Kuhn's interpretations of Aristotle, we must always treat teachers and their activities with respect. We must try to understand teachers' actions and reactions from *their* perspective in the classroom, because what may look like foolishness to an observer in the back of the room may look like the only route to survival from behind the teacher's desk.

EMBARRASSMENTS OF PRACTICE

A cautionary tale. Practitioners are not always wise. Not only theory can err. There will be times when despite efforts to find a rationale that supports or explains practitioners' work, they will turn out to be dead wrong. I have two examples, one from medicine, the other from education. Beginning some 30 years ago, a series of studies was conducted to investigate how experienced radiologists interpreted chest x-rays (Garland, 1959; Yerushalmy, 1969). To the dismay of the researchers, they discovered that when the same films were placed in a pile of x-rays to check for reliability of judgment, the experienced radiologists were found to be unacceptably unreliable. They would provide quite different interpretations for the same chest x-ray when looking at it a second time.

More recently, a group of investigators at the Institute for Research on Teaching (Weinshank, 1982; Vinsonhaler, Weinshank, Wagner, & Polin, 1983) conducted a comparable series of studies with reading diagnosticians who were presented with alternate versions of the same case, with a few surface changes to make detection more difficult, within a couple of weeks of one another. The reliability of their diagnoses of the same cases hovered around zero. Could practice be considered wise when it changed radically over a short time? I doubt it. The lesson is thus to treat the wisdom of practice with respect, with deference, albeit with careful skepticism.

In our research, moreover, we do not fall into the trap of simply treating anything practitioners are observed to do as worthy of emulation. Treating what *is* as grounds for what ought to be has long been designated as the "naturalistic fallacy" in philosophy, and its dangers extend with equal validity to the world of practice. There are several ways in which we manage to avoid the excesses of overly celebrating the status quo. First, we do not find, in studying the wisdom of practice, that some uniform, monolithic image of "good practice" or "current practice" emerges. Indeed, we are particularly interested in detecting and documenting the variations among individual examples of practice. Wise practitioners vary. Those variations are responses to the diversity of youngsters whom they teach, the range of subject matters they instruct, the variety of grounded philosophies of education they espouse, or the styles of teaching they adopt. It would be foolish to seek to calculate some grand mean of wise practice, somehow aggregating across these variations to estimate one "best" system of teaching. Instead, we choose to examine those variations carefully and to attempt to understand the grounds on which they rest.[11]

Observed variations are then related to contextual or environmental constraints and opportunities (class size, availability of materials, pupil and community characteristics, prescribed curriculum, and so on), teachers' goals, plans, and strategies, and other conditions—both internal and external—that would help us understand why the actions taken were selected. Such research can only be undertaken through a combination of observation and interview, monitoring both performance and cognition. The behavior of teachers remains inscrutable unless it is understood as a function of the minds and motives of those who behave.[12]

My studies of practice in medicine and teaching have led inevitably to questions of comparison. How are teaching and medicine alike? How are they different? Which places the greater cognitive strain on the problem solver? In which case—teaching or medicine—is the management of complexity a greater challenge?

I have already suggested my response earlier in this chapter. There is little doubt that, from the perspective of complexity management, teaching is a far more demanding occupation than is medicine. Naturally there are many variations in the practice of each. But overall, the diagnosis and treatment of a single patient under circumstances that the physician controls are far easier than the management and teaching of 30 students under constraints of time, materials, and multiple sources of unpredictability. If there is any kind of medicine that resembles teaching, it may be emergency medicine on the battlefield. For an analogy to teaching in medicine, therefore, look to MASH rather than to St. Elsewhere.

---

[11] This strategy characterizes research my colleagues and I are currently conducting to develop better means for assessing teaching competence in a National Board for Teaching Standards. We have dubbed these "wisdom of practice" studies.

[12] In a lovely critique of my work on teacher decision making, Gage argued correctly that I had placed such great emphasis on teacher decision making and cognition that I had ignored the importance of teacher behavior entirely. He was reminded of a similar disagreement between two learning theorists, Guthrie (the behaviorist) and Tolman (the cognitivist), both of whom studied learning in rats. Guthrie had said of Tolman, "He leaves his rats lost in thought." Similarly, Gage admonished, "Shulman leaves teachers lost in thought." I finally have an opportunity to reply. "Professor Gage, I would rather leave teachers lost in thought than missing in action!"

STREAMS OF INQUIRY

Two streams of research flow in education, two strategies of inquiry to inform practice and policy. In one stream we strive to develop better theory through carefully conducted investigations and controlled conditions. In the second stream we study the variations of practice to discern the underlying causes and reasons for action. These studies of practice in turn enrich our theories and models. A dialectic must ensue between these two streams of inquiry—the theory driven and the practice driven—because through this alternation we begin to grasp both the potential for positive educational change as well as the limits of reform.

At this time the study of teaching and of schools is a rich research site in which the efforts of many disciplines—social sciences, natural sciences, humanities—can be and are fruitfully employed. Our call for continued inquiry may disappoint those who wish simple answers to the pressing problems of education, but one of our responsibilities is to inhibit glib prescriptions of simple solutions to complex dilemmas. One way to ensure that caution is through continued studies of the worlds of professional practice. Thus may the wisdom of practice enrich and inform us all.

ACKNOWLEDGMENT: Preparation of this chapter was made possible, in part, by support from the Spencer Foundation and the Carnegie Corporation of New York. The views expressed are the author's and not necessarily those of Stanford University or the funding agencies.

REFERENCES

Anderson, L., Evertson, C., & Brophy, J. (1979). An experimental study of effective teaching in first-grade reading groups. *Elementary School Journal, 79* (4), 193–223.

Berliner, D. C. (1979). Tempus educare. In P. L. Peterson & H. L. Walberg (Eds.), *Research on teaching.* Berkeley, CA: McCutchan.

Bruner, J. S., Goodnow, J. J., & Austin, G. A. (1956). *A study of thinking.* New York: Wiley.

de Groot, A. D. (1965). *Thought and choice in chess.* The Hague: Mouton.

Elstein, A. S., Shulman, L. S., & Sprafka, S. A. (1978). *Medical problem solving: An analysis of clinical reasoning.* Chicago: University of Chicago Press.

Fenstermacher, G. D. (1978). A philosophical consideration of recent research on teacher effectiveness. In L. S. Shulman (Ed.), *Review of research in education.* Itasca, IL: Peacock.

Gage, N. L. (1978). *The scientific basis of the art of teaching.* New York: Teachers College Press.

———. (1986). Hard gains in the soft sciences: The case of pedagogy. *Phi Delta Kappa Monographs.*

Garland, L. H. (1959). Studies on the accuracy of diagnostic procedures. *American Journal of Roentgenology, 82,* 25–38.

Harrison, T. R. (1973). *Harrison's principles of internal medicine,* 7th ed. New York: McGraw-Hill.

Hawkins, D. (1966). Learning the unteachable. In L. S. Shulman & E. R. Keislar (Eds.), *Learning by discovery: A critical appraisal.* Chicago: Rand McNally.

Kounin, J. (1970). *Discipline and group management in classrooms.* New York: Holt, Rinehart & Winston.

Kuhn, T. S. (1977). *The essential tension.* Chicago: University of Chicago Press.

Rowe, M. B. (1974a). Wait-time and rewards as instructional variables, their influence on language, logic, and fate control: Part I—Wait-time. *Journal of Research in Science Teaching, 11* (1), 81–94.

———. (1974b). Relation of wait-time and rewards to the development of language, logic, and fate control: Part II—Rewards. *Journal of Research in Science Teaching, 11* (4), 291–308.

Shroyer, J. (1981). *Critical moments in the teaching of mathematics: What makes teaching difficult?* Doctoral dissertation, Michigan State University, East Lansing, MI.

Shulman, L. S., & Elstein, A. S. (1976). Studies of problem solving, judgment, and decision making: Implications for educational research. In F. N. Kerlinger (Ed.), *Review of research in education* (Vol. 3). Itasca, IL: Peacock.

Vinsonhaler, J. S., Weinshank, A. B., Wagner, C. C., & Polin, R. M. (1983). Diagnosing children with educational problems: Characteristics of reading and learning disabilities specialists and classroom teachers. *Reading Research Quarterly, 18* (2), 134–164.

Weinshank, A. B. (1982). The reliability of diagnostic and remedial decisions of reading specialists. *Journal of Reading Behavior, 14* (1), 33–50.

Yerushalmy, J. (1969). The statistical assessment of the variability in observer perception and description of roentgenographic pulmonary shadows. *Radiologic Clinics of North America. 7,* 381–391.

ABOUT N. L. GAGE

Nathaniel Lees Gage, 1986

Margaret Jacks Professor of Education and, by courtesy, Professor of Psychology, Stanford University

CURRICULUM VITAE

BORN   Union City, N.J., August 1, 1917
MARRIED   To Margaret Elizabeth Burrows, 1942
CHILDREN Elizabeth, 1947   Thomas Burrows, 1950
          Sarah,   1955   Anne,   1958

EDUCATION

Public schools of west New York, N.J.
University of Minnesota, A.B., magna cum laude, with major in Psychology, 1938
Purdue University, Ph.D., Psychology, 1947
          Litt.D. (Honorary), 1978

ACADEMIC POSITIONS

Purdue University   **1947–1948**
University of Illinois **1948–1962**
Stanford University   **1962–**

387

HONORS (a selection)

Member, Research Team, National Training Laboratory for Group Development, Bethel, Maine   **1950**

Member, Summer Seminar on Person Perception, Social Science Research Council, Harvard University   **1955**

Fellow, Center for Advanced Study in the Behavioral Sciences   **1965–1966**

Special Fellow, U.S. Public Health Service   **1965–1966**

Diamond Jubilee Lecturer, School of Education, New York University   **1966**

Distinguished Alumni Lecturer in Psychology, Purdue University   **1968**

Fellow, John Simon Guggenheim Memorial Foundation   **1976–1977**

Julius and Rosa Sachs Visiting Professor of Psychology and Education, and Sachs Memorial Lecturer, Teachers College, Columbia University   **1977**

U.S. Information Service Lecturer, University of Hamburg and University of Heidelberg   **1978**

Recipient, Creative Leadership Award, School of Education, New York University   **1980**

Recipient, Phi Delta Kappa Biennial Award for Meritorious Contributions to Education through Evaluation, Development, or Research   **1981**

Visiting Fellow, Brasenose College, University of Oxford   **1983**

Distinguished Fulbright Lecturer, University of the Rio Grande of the South, Porto Alegre, Brazil   **1985**

Recipient, Thorndike Award, Division of Educational Psychology, American Psychological Association   **1985**

Recipient, Outstanding Writer Award, American Association of Colleges for Teacher Education (for Item 139 in List of Publications)   **1986**

MEMBERSHIPS

Phi Beta Kappa   **1938–**

Sigma Xi   **1940–**

American Psychological Association   **1942–**

    Fellow, Divisions of Educational Psychology   **1954–**
                                Personality and Social Psychology   **1954–**
                                Measurement and Evaluation   **1954–**

    Fellow of the Society for the Psychological Study of Social Issues   **1954–1975**

American Educational Research Association   **1946–**

Phi Delta Kappa   **1947–**

American Association for the Advancement of Science   **1948–1984**

National Society for the Study of Education   **1968–**

National Academy of Education   **1979–**

EDITORIAL POSITIONS

Consulting Editor, *Journal of Abnormal and Social Psychology*   **1956–1964**

Consulting Editor, *Sociometry*   **1956–1958**

Associate Editor, *Sociometry*   **1958–1960**

Editor, *Handbook of Research on Teaching* (a project of the American Educational Research Association)   **1957–1962**

Coeditor, *Readings in the Social Psychology of Education* (a project of the Society for the Psychological Study of Social Issues)   **1959–1962**

Consulting Editor, *American Educational Research Journal*   **1964–1970**

Consultant, *American Heritage Dictionary of the English Language*   **1965–1969**

Member, Board of Editors, *Encyclopedia of Educational Research*, Fourth Edition   **1965–1969**   Fifth Edition   **1979–1983**

Consulting Editor, *Journal of Educational Psychology*   **1963–1975**

Consulting Editor, *Contemporary Psychology*   **1967–1973**

Referee, *Journal for Research in Mathematics Education* (a publication of the National Council of Teachers of Mathematics)   **1969–1971**

Member, Editorial Advisory Board, *Current Contents: Social and Behavioral Sciences*   **1969–1983**

Consulting Editor, *Educational Studies: A Journal of Book Reviews in the Foundations of Education*   **1970–1975**

Advisory Editor, *Instructional Science*   **1971–1981**

Editor, *Psychology of Teaching Methods: The 75th Yearbook of the National Society for the Study of Education, Part I*   **1972–1976**

Consulting Editor, *Educational Research Quarterly*   **1976–**

Member, Editorial Advisory Board, *Texas Tech Journal of Education*   **1976–1982**

Member, Honorary Advisory Editorial Board, *International Encyclopedia of Education: Research and Studies*   **1980–1984**

Editor, *Teaching and Teacher Education: An International Journal of Research and Studies*   **1983–1986**

POSITIONS IN PROFESSIONAL ORGANIZATIONS (a selection)

President, Division of Educational Psychology, American Psychological Association   **1961–1962**

President, American Educational Research Association   **1963–1964**

Chairman, Committee on Relations Between Psychology and Education, American Psychological Association   **1960–1962**

Member, Advisory Committee, Curriculum Research Branch, U.S. Office of Education   **1964–1965**

Member, Committee of Consultants, National Program of Educational Laboratories, U.S. Office of Education   **1965–1966**

Member, National Advisory Committee on Educational Laboratories, U.S. Office of Education   **1966–1969**

Member, Research Advisory Committee, American Council on Education   **1966–1973**   Chairman   **1972–1973**

Consultant, International Association for the Evaluation of Educational Achievement   **1966–1972**

Member, Board of Directors, National Society for the Study of Education   **1969–1972**   **1976–1979**

Chairman, Board of Directors, National Society for the Study of Education **1971–1972** **1978–1979**

Member, Executive Committee, Council for Educational Development and Research **1970–1971**

Visiting Fellow, National Institute of Education (NIE) **1974**

Chairman, NIE Conference on Studies in Teaching **1974**

Consultant, International Institute for Educational Planning (Paris) **1973–1974**

Member, Research and Development Committee, National Teacher Examination Policy Council, Educational Testing Service **1979–1984**

Chairman, International Project Council, IEA Classroom Environment Study: Teaching for Learning, International Association for the Evaluation of Educational Achievement **1979–1981**

Member, Task Force on Impact, Ontario Institute for Studies in Education **1979–1980**

Consultant, Teaching Styles Project, National Foundation for Educational Research in England and Wales **1979–1984**

Visitor, USSR Academy of Pedagogical Sciences, Moscow, Leningrad **1985**

PUBLICATIONS

1. (With H. H. Remmers & Ruth Karslake) Reliability of multiple-choice measuring instruments as a function of the Spearman-Brown prophecy formula, I. *Journal of Educational Psychology* 31 (1940): 583–590.

2. (Coeditor with H. H. Remmers) *Two thousand test items in American history.* Lafayette, Ind.: Purdue University, State High School Testing Service for Indiana, 1941, p. 110.

3. (With H. H. Remmers) The scope and purposes of the State High School Testing Service. *The Indiana Teacher* (January 1943): 130, 142.

4. (With H. H. Remmers) The family, education, and child adjustment. *Review of Educational Research*, 13 (1943): 21–28.

5. (With H. H. Remmers) *Educational measurement and evaluation.* New York: Harper & Brothers, 1943, p. 580.

6. Some guidance implications of the Purdue Opinion Poll for Young People. Lafayette, Ind. Division of Educational Reference, Proceedings of the 12th Annual Guidance Conference, November 8 and 9, 1946, *Studies in Higher Education* 58: 45–50.

7. (With H. H. Remmers) Northern youth and an American dilemma. *The Purdue Opinion Poll for Young People, No. 13* (December 12, 1946): 19.

8. (With H. H. Remmers) *Student exercises in measurement and evaluation for education and guidance.* New York: Harper & Brothers, 1947, p. 101.

9. (With H. H. Remmers) Patterns of attitudes towards minorities among high school youth in the United States middle west. *International Journal of Opinion and Attitude Research* 1 (1947): 106–109.

10. (With H. H. Remmers) Does youth believe in the Bill of Rights? *The Purdue Opinion Poll for Young People, No. 14* (March 15, 1947): 19.

11. (With H. H. Remmers) Achievement and predictive testing in the Pharmaceutical Survey. *American Journal of Pharmaceutical Education* 11 (1947): 43–53.

12. (With H. H. Remmers) The predictive testing program of the Pharmaceutical Survey. *American Journal of Pharmaceutical Education* 11 (1947): 54–62.

13. Scaling and factorial design in opinion poll analysis. Further Studies in Attitudes, Series 10, Lafayette, Ind.: Purdue University, The Division of Educational Reference, *Studies in Higher Education* 61 (1947): 84.

14. Review of Leo J. Margolin, Paper Bullets: A brief story of psychological warfare in World War II. *Public Opinion Quarterly* 11 (1947): 462–463.
15. (With H. H. Remmers, R. L. Hobson, & B. Shimberg) Youth looks at war and peace. *The Purdue Opinion Poll for Young People, No. 16* 7 (November 1947).
16. (With H. H. Remmers) The abilities and interests of pharmacy freshmen. *American Journal of Pharmaceutical Education* 12 (1948): 1–65.
17. (With H. H. Remmers) Opinion polling with mark-sensed punch cards. *Journal of Applied Psychology* 32 (1948): 88–91.
18. (With H. H. Remmers & B. Shimberg) Youth ponders national headaches. *The Purdue Opinion Poll for Young People, No. 17* (March 1948).
19. (With H. H. Remmers & B. Shimberg) Youth looks at school and jobs. *The Purdue Opinion Poll for Young People, No. 18* (March 1948).
20. (With H. H. Remmers) *Student personnel studies in the Pharmaceutical Survey.* Washington, D.C.: American Council on Education, The Pharmaceutical Survey. Monograph No. 3, April 1949. 126 pp.
21. (With B. Shimberg) Measuring senatorial "progressivism." *Journal of Abnormal and Social Psychology* 44 (1949): 80–87. Also in G. F. Summers (Ed.), *Attitude Measurement*, Chicago: Rand McNally, 1970, pp. 451–457.
21a. (With H. H. Remmers & D. N. Elliott) Curricular differences in predicting scholastic achievement: Applications to counseling. *Journal of Educational Psychology* 40 (1949): 385–394.
22. (With H. H. Remmers) Reshaping educational policy. *Review of Educational Research* 19 (1949): 77–89.
23. Report of the Committee on the Evaluation of College Teaching. Urbana, Ill.: Office of the Dean, College of Education, University of Illinois, 1949. Mimeographed.
24. Review of P. F. Lazarsfeld & F. Stanton (Eds.), Communications research: 1948–49. *Journal of Educational Psychology* 41 (1950): 251–253.
25. (With Dora E. Damrin) Reliability, homogeneity, and number of choices. *Journal of Educational Psychology* 41 (1950): 385–404.
26. (With George J. Suci) Social perception and teacher-pupil relationships. *Journal of Educational Psychology* 42 (1951): 144–152. Also in J. Raths et al. (Eds.), *Studying teaching*. Englewood Cliffs, N.J.: Prentice-Hall, 1967, pp. 383–388. Also in J. Raths et al. (Eds.), *Studying teaching* (2nd ed.). Englewood Cliffs, N.J.: Prentice-Hall, 1971, pp. 373–379.
27. Review of D. Fryer & E. Henry (Eds.), Handbook of Applied Psychology. *Journal of Educational Psychology* 42 (1951): 372–381.
28. Judging interests from expressive behavior. *Psychological Monographs* 66 (1952) (Whole No. 350).
29. (As a member of the committee) Committee on Criteria of Teacher Effectiveness, American Educational Research Association, "Report of the Committee," *Review of Educational Research* 22 (1952): 238–263.
30. (With Jacob S. Orleans) Guiding principles in the study of teacher effectiveness. *Journal of Teacher Education* 3 (1952): 294–298.
31. (Chairman of the issue) Social framework of education. *Review of Educational Research* 22 (1952).
32. Review of Paul J. Brouwer & the Staff of the Cooperative Study in General Education, Inventory of Personal-Social Relationships: General Education Series. In O. K. Buros (Ed.), *Fourth Mental Measurements Yearbook*. New Brunswick, N.J.: Gryphon Press, 1953, p. 109–110.
33. (With Ralph V. Exline) Social perception and effectiveness in discussion groups. *Human Relations* 6 (1953): 381–396
34. (As a member of the committee) Committee on Criteria of Teacher Effectiveness, American Educational Research Association, Second Report of the Committee, *Journal of Educational Research* 46 (1953): 641–658
35. Explorations in the understanding of others. *Educational and Psychological Measurement* 13 (1953): 14–26.

36. Accuracy of social perception and effectiveness in interpersonal relationships. *Journal of Personality* 22 (1953): 128–141.

37. Review of Eli Ginzberg & Douglas Bray, The Uneducated. *Journal of Higher Education* 25 (1954): 167–168.

38. (With Gabriel M. Della Piana) Pupils' values and the validity of the Minnesota Teacher Attitude Inventory. *Journal of Educational Psychology* 46 (1955): 167–178. Also in B. N. Phillips et al. (Eds.), *Psychology at work in the elementary school classroom.* New York: Harper, 1960, pp. 92–106.

39. (With Lee J. Cronbach) Conceptual and methodological problems in interpersonal perception. *Psychological Review* 62 (1955): 411–422.

39a. (With H. H. Remmers) *Educational measurement and evaluation* (rev. ed.). New York: Harper, 1955, p. 650.

40. (With George S. Leavitt & George C. Stone) Teachers' understanding of their pupils and pupils' ratings of their teachers. *Psychological Monographs* 69 (1955, Whole No. 406).

41. (With George S. Leavitt & George C. Stone) The intermediary key in the analysis of interpersonal perception. *Psychological Bulletin* 53 (1956): 258–266.

42. Understanding your group. *Adult Leadership* 5 (1956): 57–59.

43. (With George C. Stone & George S. Leavitt) Two kinds of accuracy in predicting another's responses. *Journal of Social Psychology* 45 (1957): 245–254.

44. Logical vs. empirical scoring keys: The case of the MTAI. *Journal of Educational Psychology* 48 (1957): 213–216.

45. (With George S. Leavitt & George C. Stone) The psychological meaning of acquiescence set for authoritarianism. *Journal of Abnormal and Social Psychology* 55 (1957): 98–103.

46. Explorations in teachers' perceptions of pupils. *Journal of Teacher Education* 9 (1958): 97–101. Also in H. Toch & H. C. Smith (Eds.), *Social perception: The development of interpersonal impressions—An enduring problem in psychology.* Princeton, N.J.: Van Nostrand, 1968, pp. 219–226.

47. Toward a framework for research on teaching. In L. E. Metcalf & L. Wagner (Eds.), *Proceedings of the Conference on Economic Education, 1959.* Evanston, Ill.: Northwestern University, 1960.

48. Review of O. K. Buros (Ed.), Stanford Achievement Test. *The Fifth Mental Measurements Yearbook.* New Brunswick, N.J.: Gryphon Press, 1959, p. 75–80.

49. Review of G. W. Allport, P. E. Vernon, & G. Lindzey, A Study of Values. In O. K. Buros (Ed.), *The Fifth Mental Measurements Yearbook,* New Brunswick, N.J.: Gryphon Press, 1959, pp. 99–102.

50. An educational psychologist looks at teaching in pharmacognosy. *Proceedings, Teachers' Seminar on Pharmacognosy, 1959.* Chicago: American Association of Colleges of Pharmacy, 1959, pp. 170–184.

51. Ends and means in appraising college teaching. In W. J. McKeachie (Ed.), *The appraisal of teaching in large universities.* Ann Arbor: University of Michigan, 1959, pp. 58–64. Also as: The appraisal of college teaching: An analysis of ends and means, *Journal of Higher Education* 32 (1961): 17–22.

52. Perception. In C. W. Harris (Ed.), *Encyclopedia of educational research* (3rd ed.). New York: Macmillan, 1960, pp. 941–945.

53. (With B. B. Chatterjee) The psychological meaning of acquiescence set: Further evidence. *Journal of Abnormal and Social Psychology* 60 (1960): 280–283.

54. (With H. H. Remmers & J. F. Rummel) *A practical introduction to measurement and evaluation.* New York: Harper, 1960, p. 400.

55. (With C. Hagan, N. Garvey, & R. Payette) *Principles of democracy: A test of knowledge and understanding.* Chicago: Science Research Associates, 1960.

56. Review of G. G. Thompson, E. Gardner, & F. DiVesta, Educational psychology. *Contemporary Psychology* 5 (1960): 185–186.

57. (With P. J. Runkel & B. B. Chatterjee) *Equilibrium theory and behavior change: An experiment in feedback from pupils to teachers.* Urbana, Ill.: Bureau of Educational

Research, University of Illinois, 1960. Report No. 6, Studies in the behavioral corre-lates of social perception. Mimeographed.

58. Metatechnique in educational research. In *Proceedings, 12th Annual State Conference on Educational Research, San Mateo, November 1960.* Burlingame, Calif.: California Teachers Association and California Advisory Council on Educational Research, 1961, No. 16, pp. 1–12.

59. Plan of the *Handbook of research on teaching. Journal of Teacher Education* 13 (1962): 89–99.

60a. New directions in educational research. In *New directions in educational research.* Proceedings of the New York State Convocation on Educational Research. Albany, N.Y.: State Education Department, 1963, pp. 38–51.

60. Research design with special reference to the teaching of English. *Proceedings of the Allerton Park Conference on Research in the Teaching of English.* Urbana, Ill.: Dept. of English, University of Illinois, 1962, pp. 77–87.

61. (Editor) *Handbook of research on teaching.* Chicago: Rand McNally, 1963, pp. xiv + 1218. Also in German, edited by Karlheinz Ingenkamp in collaboration with Evelore Parey, as *Handbuch der Unterrichtsforschung: Teil I. Theoretische und Metho-dologische Grundlegung; Teil II.* Berlin: Verlag Julius Beltz, 1970.

62. Paradigms for research on teaching. In N. L. Gage (Ed.), *Handbook of research on teaching.* Chicago: Rand McNally, 1963, pp. 94–141. Also in German as "Paradigmen für die Erfonschung des Lehrens." In Franz Weinert (Ed.), *Pädagogische Psychologie.* Koln, Berlin: Kiepenheuer & Witsch, 1967, pp. 70–101. Also, translated into German by Hubert Feger (Uberzetzung) and Edmund von Trotsenburg (Bearbeitung), as Paradigmen für die Unterrichtsforschung. In Karlheinz Ingenkamp & Evelore Parey (Eds.), Handbuch der Unterrichtsforschung: Teil I. Theoretische und Methodolo-gische Grundlegung. Berlin: Verlag Julius Beltz, 1970, pp. 272–366.

63. (Coeditor with W. W. Charters, Jr.) *Readings in the social psychology of education.* Boston: Allyn & Bacon, 1963, pp. xxiv & 350.

64. (With P. J. Runkel & B. B. Chatterjee) Changing teacher behavior through feedback from pupils: An application of equilibrium theory. In W. W. Charters, Jr., & N. L. Gage (Eds.), *Readings in the social psychology of education.* Boston: Allyn & Bacon, 1963, pp. 173–181. Also in M. Argyle, (Ed.), *Social encounters: Readings in social interaction.* Chicago: Aldine, 1973, pp. 371–382.

65. A method for "improving" teacher behavior. *Journal of Teacher Education* 14 (1963): 261–266.

66. Psychological research on teacher education for the great cities. In B. J. Chandler et al. (Eds.), *Research seminar on teacher education* (Cooperative Research Project No. G-011). Washington, D.C.: Cooperative Research Program, U.S. Office of Educa-tion, 1963, pp. 43–74. Also in *Urban Education* 1 (1965): 175–196.

66a. This side of paradigms: The state of research on teaching English. In *Research design and the teaching of English: Proceedings of the San Francisco Conference, 1963.* Champaign, Ill.: National Council of Teachers of English, 1964, pp. 22–31.

67. Theories of teaching. In E. R. Hilgard (Ed.), *Theories of learning and instruction,* Yearbook, National Society for the Study of Education 63 (1964): Part I, 268–285. Also in R. D. Strom, *Teachers and the learning process.* Englewood Cliffs, N.J.: Pren-tice-Hall, 1971, pp. 258–272. Also in K. Yamamoto (Ed.), *Teaching: Essays and read-ings.* Boston: Houghton Mifflin, 1969, pp. 337–353. Also translated into Hebrew and published in Zvi Lamm (Ed.), *The concept of teaching.* Jerusalem: School of Education, Hebrew University, 1969.

68. Toward a cognitive theory of teaching. *Teachers College Record* 64 (1964): 408–412. Also in *Problems and issues in contemporary education: An anthology from the Harvard Educational Review and the Teachers College Record.* New York: Scott, Foresman, 1968, pp. 112–116. Also in R. F. Kuhlen (Ed.), *Studies in educational psychology.* Waltham, Mass.: Blaisdell, 1968, pp. 160–166. Also in C. G. Hass (Ed.), *Readings in secondary teaching.* Boston: Allyn & Bacon, 1972. Also in M. D. Glock (Ed.), *Guiding learning: Readings in educational psychology.* New York: Wiley, 1971, pp. 27–33. Also in M. C. Wittrock (Ed.), *Learning and instruction.* Berkeley, Calif.: McCutchan, 1977, pp. 603–609.

69. The evaluation of teaching. *Journal of the Student Personnel Association for Teacher Education* 3 (1964): 33–41.

70. Psychological theory and empirical research for teacher education. In *Freedom with responsibility in teacher education*, Proceedings, Annual Meeting of the American Association of Colleges for Teacher Education 17 (1964): 94–105.

71. Desirable behaviors of teachers, *Urban education* 1 (1965): 85–95. Also in M. Usdan & F. Bertolaet (Eds.), *Teachers for the disadvantaged.* Chicago: Follett, 1966, pp. 4–12. Also in J. Raths et al. (Eds.), *Studying teaching* (2nd ed.). Englewood Cliffs, N.J.: Prentice-Hall, 1971, pp. 10–17.

72. Education of teachers: Psychology of education. In R. H. Beck (Ed.), *Society and the schools: Communication challenge to education and social work*, Proceedings, Conference on Interprofessional Communication, Chicago, April 1964. New York: National Association of Social Workers, 1965, pp. 86–103. Also in M. D. Glock (Ed.), *Guiding learning: Readings in educational psychology.* New York: Wiley, 1971, pp. 741–744.

73. (With H. H. Remmers & J. Francis Rummel) *A practical introduction to measurement and evaluation* (2nd ed.). New York: Harper & Row, 1965, pp. xvii + 309.

74. A Step-Child? Review of P. F. Lazersfeld & S. D. Sieber, Organizing educational research: An exploration. *Contemporary Psychology* 10 (1965): 90–91.

75. Research on cognitive aspects of teaching. In *The way teaching is: A report of the Seminar on Teaching.* Washington, D.C.: Association for Supervision and Curriculum Development and the National Education Association, 1966, pp. 29–44.

76. (With Jimmie C. Fortune & Robert E. Shutes) Generality of ability to explain. Paper presented at the meetings of the American Educational Research Association, Chicago, Ill., February 19, 1966.

77. (With Robert W. Daw) Effect of feedback from teachers to principals. *Journal of Educational Psychology* 58 (1967): 181–188.

78. Psychological conceptions of teaching. *Educational Sciences: An International Journal* 1 (1967): 151–161.

79. Three pressing concerns of educational research. Burlingame, Calif.: California Advisory Council on Educational Research, *Research Résumé*, No. 33 (1967): 15.

80. The need for process-oriented research. In Calvin B. T. Lee (Ed.), *Improving college teaching.* Washington, D.C.: American Council on Education, 1967, pp. 244–248.

81. An analytic approach to research on instructional methods. In H. J. Klausmeier & G. T. O'Hearn (Eds.), *Research and development toward the improvement of education.* Madison, Wisc.: Dembar Educational Research Services, 1968, pp. 119–125. Also in *Phi Delta Kappan* 49 (1968): 601–606. Also in H. F. Clarizio, R. C. Craig, & W. A. Mehrens (Eds.), *Contemporary issues in educational psychology.* Boston: Allyn & Bacon, 1970, pp. 67–81. Also in A. Morrison & D. McIntyre (Eds.), *The social psychology of teaching: Selected readings.* Baltimore: Penguin Books, 1972, pp. 44–59. Also in H. D. Thornburg (Ed.), *School learning and instruction: Readings.* Monterey, Calif.: Books/Cole, 1973, pp. 107–120.

82. (With A. H. Yee) Determining causal relationships in socio-psychological inquiries: Four techniques. Research Memorandum No. 9. Stanford, Calif.: Stanford Center for Research and Development in Teaching, 1967, p. 39. Also as: Techniques for estimating the source and direction of causal influence in panel data. *Psychological Bulletin* 70 (1968): 115–126. Also in M. C. Wittrock & Wiley (Eds.), *The evaluation of instruction.* New York: Holt, Rinehart & Winston, 1970, pp. 462–483.

83. (With W. R. Unruh) Theoretical formulations for research on teaching. *Review of Educational Research* 37 (1967): 358–370. Also in R. C. Anderson et al. (Eds.), *Current research on instruction.* Englewood Cliffs, N.J.: Prentice-Hall, 1969, pp. 3–14. Also in H. D. Thornburg (Ed.), *School learning and instruction: Readings.* Monterey, Calif.: Brooks/Cole, 1973, pp. 42–53.

84. "I think you think I think. . . ." Review of *Interpersonal perception: A theory and a method of research* by R. D. Laing, H. Phillipson, & A. R. Lee. New York: Springer, 1966, pp. x + 179. Also in *Contemporary Psychology* 13 (1968): 78–80.

85. Research on the new roles of teachers required by educational innovations. Paper

prepared for the International Conference on the Changing Roles of Teachers Required by Educational Innovations, Berlin, October 16–19, 1967.

86. (With Maria Podlogar & Barak Rosenshine) The teacher's effectiveness in explaining: Evidence on its generality and correlation with students' ratings. Research Memorandum No. 10. Stanford, Calif.: Stanford Center for Research and Development in Teaching, 1967, p. 22.

87. See 21a

88. See 66a

89. Can science contribute to the art of teaching? *Phi Delta Kappan* 49 (1968): 399–403. Also in R. D. Armstrong & P. A. Lane (Eds.), *The education of elementary school teachers: Proceedings of the Second Invitational Conference on elementary education, Banff, Alberta, October 25–28, 1967.* Edmonton, Alberta: University of Alberta, 1967, pp. 7–17. Also in H. F. Clarizio, R. C. Craig, & W. A. Mehrens (Eds.), *Contemporary issues in educational psychology.* Boston: Allyn & Bacon, 1970, pp. 27–40. Also in Marguerite Pohek (compiler), *Teaching and learning in social work education.* New York: Council on Social Work Education, 1970, pp. 1–12. Also in *Selected readings in educational administration* (1971 ed.) Dept. of Educational Administration, Univ. of Alberta, Edmonton, Canada, p. 36–40. (Duplicated). Also in M. D. Glock (Ed.), *Guiding learning: Readings in educational psychology.* New York: Wiley, 1971, pp. 115–127. Also in Madan Mohan & Ronald E. Hall (Eds.), *Teaching effectiveness: Its meaning, assessment, and improvement.* Englewood Cliffs, N.J.: Educational Technology Publications, 1975, pp. 27–42.

90. The program of the Stanford Center for Research and Development in Teaching. Paper prepared for the Symposium on "Current Research on Teaching" at the Eleventh InterAmerican Congress of Psychology, Mexico City, December 19, 1967.

91. Conceptual integration in research and development centers. Remarks at the meeting of directors of research and development centers supported by the U.S. Office of Education, Madison, Wisc., June 15, 1967.

92. See 60a

93. Teaching methods. In R. L. Ebel (Ed.), *Encyclopedia of educational research* (4th ed.). New York: Macmillan, 1969, pp. 1446–1458.

94. (With Robert N. Bush) The Stanford Center for Research and Development in Teaching. *Journal of Research and Development in Education* 1 (1968): 86–105.

95. (With Maria Belgard, Daryl Dell, Jack Hiller, Barak Rosenshine, & W. R. Unruh) Explorations of the teacher's effectiveness in explaining. Technical Report No. 4. Stanford, Calif.: Stanford Center for Research and Development in Teaching, 1968, p. 57. Also in I. Westbury & A. A. Bellack (Eds.), *Research into classroom processes.* New York: Teachers College Press, Columbia University, 1971, pp. 175–217.

96. Contemporary formulations of the learning-teaching process. In R. Saxe (Ed.), *Educational comment, 1969: Contexts for teacher education.* Toledo, Ohio: College of Education, University of Toledo, 1969, pp. 87–93.

97. *Teacher effectiveness and teacher education: The search for a scientific basis.* Palo Alto, Calif.: Pacific Books, 1972.

98. What sort of teachers are needed [for moral education]?—2. *Moral Education* 1 (1969): 33–36.

99. Comments on Professor Lortie's paper, "The cracked cake of educational custom and emerging issues in evaluation." In M. C. Wittrock & D. Wiley (Eds.), *The evaluation of instruction.* New York: Holt, Rinehart & Winston, 1970, p. 167–172.

100. A tool-development strategy for research on teaching. In *How teachers make a difference.* Washington, D.C.: Bureau of Educational Personnel Development, U.S. Office of Education, 1971 [OE-58044], pp. 32–50.

101. Foreword. In J. Elashoff & R. E. Snow, *Pygmalion reconsidered.* Worthington, Ohio: Charles A. Jones, 1971, pp. iv–v.

102. IQ heritability, race differences, and educational research. *Phi Delta Kappan* 53 (1972): 308–312.

103. Replies to Shockley, Page, & Jensen: The causes of race differences in I.Q. *Phi Delta Kappan* 53 (1972): 422–427.

104. (With Zwirner, W. W., Cronbach, L. J., & Beck, W. R.) Pupil perceptions of teachers: A factor analysis of "About My Teacher." *Western Psychologist* 3 (1972): 78–98.

105. (Editor) *Mandated evaluation of educators: A conference on California's Stull Act.* Washington, D.C.: Capitol Publications, 1973, pp. x + 347.

106. Obeying and improving the mandate to evaluate educators: Some lessons from the conference on the Stull Act. In N. L. Gage (Ed.), *Mandated evaluation of educators: A conference on California's Stull Act.* Washington, D.C.: Capitol Publications, 1973, pp. 333–347.

107. Student ratings of college teaching: Their justification and proper use. In Naftaly S. Glasman & Berthold R. Killait (Eds.), *Second UCSB Conference on Effective Teaching.* Santa Barbara, Calif.: Graduate School of Education and Office of Instructional Development, University of California, Santa Barbara, Calif., 1974, pp. 72–86. Also in Dwight W. Allen, Michael A. Melnik, & Carolyn C. Peele (Eds.), *Improving university teaching: Reform, renewal, reward (based on the Proceedings of the International Conference on Improving University Teaching, October 4–8, 1974).* Amherst, Mass: Clinic to Improve University Teaching, University of Massachusetts, 1975, pp. 121–135.

108. Evaluating ways to help teachers behave desirably. In *Competency assessment, research and evaluation: A report of a national conference, University of Houston, March 12–15, 1974.* Washington, D.C.: American Association of Colleges for Teacher Education, pp. 173–185.

109. (With Philip H. Winne) Performance-based teacher education. In Kevin Ryan (Ed.), *Teacher education: The 74th Yearbook of the National Society for the Study of education,* Part II. Chicago: University of Chicago Press, 1975, pp. 146–172.

110. (With David C. Berliner) *Educational psychology.* Chicago: Rand McNally, 1975, pp. x + 869. Also translated into Germany by Gerhard Bach, as *Pädagogische Psychologie: Lehrerhandbuch. Erziehungswissenschaftliche Grundlagen für die Unterrichtspraxis.* Munich: Urban & Schwarzenberg, 1977.

111. Models for research on teaching. Stanford, Calif.: Stanford Center for Research and Development in Teaching, Stanford University, Occasional Paper No. 9, 1976. Also in *Toward continuous professional development: Designs and directions.* College Park: College of Education, University of Maryland, 1976, pp. 1–21.

112. (Editor) *The psychology of teaching methods: The 75th yearbook of the National Society for the Study of education.* Chicago: University of Chicago: University of Chicago Press, 1976.

113. (With David C. Berliner) The psychology of teaching methods. In N. L. Gage (Ed.), *The psychology of teaching methods: The 75th yearbook of the National Society for the Study of Education.* Chicago: University of Chicago Press, 1976, pp. 1–20.

114. A factorially designed experiment on teacher structuring, soliciting, and reacting. *Journal of Teacher Education* 27 (1976): 35–38.

115. Is it ready? Review of *Learning from teaching: A developmental perspective* by J. E. Brophy & C. M. Evertson. *Contemporary Psychology* 10 (1977): 108–109.

116. (With C. M. Clark, R. M. Marx, P. L. Peterson, N. Stayrook, & P. H. Winne) A factorially designed experiment on teacher structuring, soliciting, and reacting. Stanford, Calif.: Stanford Center for Research and Development in Teaching. R & D Memorandum, November 1976, 507 pp. A shortened version appeared as C. M. Clark, N. L. Gage, R. M. Marx, P. L. Peterson, N. Stayrook, & P. H. Winne, *Journal of Educational Psychology* 71 (1979): 534–552.

117. (With John Crawford) Developing a research-based teacher education program. *California Journal of Teacher Education* 4 (1977): 105–123.

118. *The scientific basis of the art of teaching.* New York: Teachers College Press, 1978, p. 122. Also an excerpt (pp. 24–41) reprinted as: The yield of research on teaching. *Phi Delta Kappan* 60 (1978): 229–235. Also in German, translated by Karl Heinz Siber, with a foreword by Franz E. Weinert, as *Unterrichten—Kunst oder Wissenschaft?.* Munich: Urban & Schwarzenberg, 1979. Also in Korean, translated by Yongnam Lee, as 敎授의 藝術性과 科學 , 1981.

119. Comments on Vernon H. Smith's "Learning vs. Teaching" (A review of N. L. Gage, *The scientific basis of the art of teaching* [see publication 118]). *Review of Education* 5 (1979): 163–165.

120. Should research on teaching be generic or specific? Stanford, Calif.: Program on Teaching Effectiveness, CERAS. September 1977, 32 pp. Also, in revised form, as: The generality of dimensions of teaching. In Penelope L. Peterson & Herbert J. Walberg (Eds.), *Research on teaching*, Berkeley, Calif.: McCutchan, 1979, pp. 264–288. Also, in German, translated by W. Söntgen, *Unterrichtswissenschaft:* Zeitschrift für Lernforschung in Schule und Weiterbildung, 9, Jahrgang, Heft 1, Marz 1981, pp. 82–102.

121. A reexamination of paradigms for research on Teaching. Stanford, Calif.: Program on teaching Effectiveness, CERAS, September 1977, 134 pp.

122. (With Alexis L. Mitman & Dale H. Schunk) Paradigms: An annotated bibliography with special reference to research on teaching. Stanford, Calif.: Program on Teaching Effectiveness, CERAS, September 1977, 43 pp.

123. (With Richard E. Snow, Lyn Corno, Robert N. Bush, & Christopher M. Clark) A systematic teacher training model: Part 1. Theory and research in teacher education. Stanford, Calif.: Program on Teaching Effectiveness, CERAS, September 1977, 109 pp.

124. (With Dale H. Schunk & Alexis L. Mitman) A systematic teacher training model: Part 2. The practice component of teacher education. Stanford, Calif.: Program on Teaching Effectiveness, CERAS, September 1977, 95 pp.

125. (With David C. Berliner) *Educational psychology* (2nd ed.). Chicago: Rand McNally, 1979, Pp. xiv + 800.

126. Doing right by a big course: A review of Donald J. Treffinger, J. Kent Davis, & Richard E. Ripple (Eds.), *Handbook of teaching educational psychology* (New York: Academic Press, 1977, pp. xv + 352). In *Contemporary Psychology* 24 (1979): 200–201.

127. (With Theodore Coladarci) *Replication of an experiment with a research-based inservice teacher education program.* Final report to the National Institute of Education on Grant No. NIE–G–79–0014. Stanford, Calif.: Program on Teaching Effectiveness, CERAS, 1980. Available as ERIC Document No. ED 18023.

128. New Prospects for educational research. *Australian Educational Researcher* 7 (1980): 7–75.

129. (With Torsten Husén & James W. Singleton) *Report of the Task Force on the Impact of the Research, Development and Field Activities of the Ontario Institute for Studies in Education.* Toronto: Ontario Institute for Studies in Education, 1981, pp. xvi + 198 + Annex and Appendixes.

130. (With Rose Giaconia) Teaching practices and student achievement: Causal connections. *New York University Education Quarterly* 12 (1981): 2–9.

131. (With Theodore Coladarci) Effects of a minimal intervention on teacher behavior and student achievement. *American Educational Research Journal* 21 (1984): 539–555.

132. When does research on teaching yield implications for practice? *Elementary School Journal* 83 (1983): 492–496.

133. What superintendents can give principals to help teachers. *The School Administrator* 40 (1983): 23–26.

134. The future of educational research. In F. H. Farley (Ed.), The future of educational research. *Educational Researcher* 11 (1982): 11–12.

135. A glance at research on students' ratings and collegial evaluation of teaching in higher education. *Campus Report*, Stanford University, May 11, 1983, pp. 22–23.

136. Contemporary approaches to research on teaching, teacher education and staff development. In Z. Lamm (Ed.), *New trends in education.* Tel Aviv: Yachdav United Publishers, 1983 (translated into Hebrew by Dov Porat), pp. 101–118.

137. (With David C. Berliner) *Educational Psychology* (3rd ed.). Boston, Mass.: Houghton Mifflin, 1984.

138. What do we know about teaching effectiveness? *Phi Delta Kappan* 66 (1984): 87–93.

139. *Hard gains in the soft sciences: The case of pedagogy.* Bloomington, Ind.: Phi Delta Kappa, 1985.

140. (With G. Mohlman & T. Coladarci) Comprehension and attitude as predictors of implementation of teacher training. *Journal of Teacher Education* 33 (1982): 31–36.

141. Editorial: The scope and purpose of Teaching and Teacher Education. *Teaching and Teacher Education: An International Journal of Research and Studies* 1 (1985): 1–3.

ABOUT THE CONTRIBUTORS

David C. Berliner is professor of educational psychology at the University of Arizona. He is coauthor with N. L. Gage of the text *Educational Psychology*, third edition. Thousands of hours and hundreds of days spent together in a tiny room writing have forged bonds of enduring respect and friendship between Berliner and Gage. "Never," Berliner has noted, "have two people come up with so many creative and self-delusional excuses to put off writing." Nevertheless, Berliner has written dozens of articles and book chapters about teaching and teacher education. He studies, among other things, uses of instructional time and teacher expertise. He has won two awards for distinguished writing from the American Association for Colleges of Teacher Education (AACTE). He is past president of the American Educational Research Association (AERA) and a fellow of the Center for Advanced Study in the Behavioral Sciences.

Jere Brophy is codirector of the Institute for Research on Teaching at Michigan State University and professor in the Department of Teacher Education and the Department of Counseling, Educational Psychology, and Special Education. His research interests include teacher expectations, teacher effects, classroom management, student motivation, and the dynamics of teacher-student interaction. He was the recipient of AERA's Palmer O. Johnson Award in 1983 for his article entitled "Teacher Praise: A Functional Analysis." He is author or coauthor of 9 books and over 100 other publications, including *Teacher-Student Relationships: Causes and Consequences*, *Looking in Classrooms*, *Educational Psychology: A Realistic Approach* (all with Thomas L. Good), *Learning from Teaching: A Developmental Perspective*, and *Student Characteristics and Teaching* (both with Carolyn M. Evertson).

Christopher M. Clark is professor of Educational Psychology at Michigan State University and senior researcher at the MSU Institute for Research on Teaching. He is a former Spencer Fellow of the National Academy of Education and recipient of the 1980 Palmer O. Johnson Award of the American Educational Research Association. He has served as associate editor of the American Educational Research Journal, chair of the AERA Special Interest Group on Teacher and Student Cognitions, and chair of the North American Steering Committee of the International Study Association on Teacher Thinking. His published works include journal articles, book chapters, and reviews of research on teacher thinking ("Teachers' Thought Processes," "Teachers' Reports of their Cognitive Processes During Teaching"), the teaching of writing ("Understanding Writing in School"), and the relationship between research and practice ("Research in the Service of Teaching").

Lyn Corno is associate professor of education at Columbia University's Teachers College in New York City. She completed graduate work at Stanford University, where she received a Ph.D. in educational psychology in 1978. From 1977 until 1982 Professor Corno was a member of the faculty at Stanford University, serving as assistant professor of education. Her primary research interest is the study of student learning and motivation in classrooms and how teaching can foster both. She is an advisory editor of the *Journal of Educational Psychology* and has published articles in journals such as *American Educational Research Journal, Journal of Educational Psychology, Educational Psychologist, Journal of Educational Measurement*, and *Curriculum Inquiry*. She has also contributed chapters to several specialized scholarly books.

Carolyn M. Evertson is professor of education in the Department of Teaching and Learning at Peabody College, Vanderbilt University. She teaches both graduate and undergraduate courses for preservice teachers. Professor Evertson received her doctorate in Educational Psychology from the University of Texas, Austin, and is a fellow of the American Psychological Association. Her research interests include issues in effective instructional practices, classroom management, teacher education, and observational methods. She has written widely on these topics and has coauthored four books on effective instruction and classroom management: *Learning from Teaching, Student Characteristics and Teaching* (both with Jere Brophy), *Classroom Management for Elementary Teachers*, and *Classroom Management for Secondary Teachers* (with Edmund Emmer and others).

Elizabeth Fennema is professor of Curriculum and Instruction (mathematics education) at the University of Wisconsin at Madison. Her research specialty is gender-related differences in mathematics. Besides publishing much original research, she has written many interpretive articles for both preservice and in-service teachers.

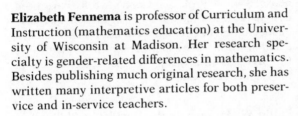

Robert Glaser is director of the Learning Research and Development Center and University Professor of Psychology and Education at the University of Pittsburgh. His current research focuses on the acquisition of knowledge and thinking skills, the development of expertise in scientific and technical fields, and computer laboratories for science instruction. He is a past president of AERA, of the National Academy of Education, and of the APA's Divisions of Educational Psychology and Evaluation and Measurement. He serves on committees and national commissions on research and its applications, most recently on Project 2061 of the AAAS, and on the Mathematical Sciences Education Board and the Committee on Research in Mathematics, Science, and Technology Education of the NRC. He is editor of the series *Advances in Instructional Psychology* and has recently edited a

special issue of the *American Psychologist* entitled "Psychological Science and Education." Glaser's continuing concern has been the development of scientific bases for instruction.

Thomas L. Good is a professor of Curriculum and Instruction in the College of Education and a research associate at the Center for Research in Social Behavior in the graduate school at the University of Missouri, Columbia. Professor Good's teaching and writing interests lie in the area of the analysis of instructional behavior, including the study of teacher expectation, teacher management, and teacher instructional issues. He is the editor of the *Elementary School Journal* and an advisory editor for the *Journal of Educational Psychology*. He is an active researcher and has published over 75 articles and book chapters and more than 15 books. Two of Professor Good's works have been designated Citation Classics because of their frequent citation by peers: a textbook, *Teacher-Student Relationships: Causes and Consequences* (with Jere Brophy) and an article, "Teacher Effectiveness in the Elementary School."

Philip W. Jackson is the David Lee Shillinglaw Distinguished Service Professor in the Departments of Education and Behavioral Sciences, and the College, at the University of Chicago. He is currently the director of the Benton Center for Curriculum and Instruction in the Education Department. His most recent book is *The Practice of Teaching*.

Ronald W. Marx is professor and director of graduate programs in the Faculty of Education at Simon Fraser University. Dr. Marx also coordinates international programs and studies in Asia-Pacific education at Simon Fraser University and is currently vice-president of the Canadian Educational Researchers' Association. Recent honors include a Social Sciences and Humanities Research Council of Canada leave fellowship and an award from the Canadian Guidance and Counseling Association for the research article entitled "Rational Emotive Counselling and Self-instruction Training for Test

Anxious High School Students." His research interests are in the areas of students' perceptions of teaching and cognitive approaches to the study of instructional effects. Recent publications are "Classroom Organization and Perceptions of Student Academic and Social Status," "Studying Student Cognition During Classroom Learning," and "Student Perception in Classrooms."

Greta Morine-Dershimer is a professor and coordinator of the doctoral program in Teaching and Curriculum in the Division for the Study of Teaching, School of Education, at Syracuse University. She is an experienced elementary teacher (10 years), teacher educator (15 years), and researcher (10 years). Her research focuses on teacher and pupil thinking about classroom instruction. Her most recent book is *Talking, Listening, and Learning in Elementary Classrooms*. Her articles have appeared in *Teachers College Record, Journal of Teacher Education, Elementary School Journal, American Educational Research Journal, Educational Theory*, and *Theory Into Practice*.

Margaret Needels is assistant professor at California State University, Hayward, where she is coordinator of the Secondary School Teacher Preparation Program. She studied under Professor N. L. Gage at Stanford and worked with him on the IEA Classroom Environment Study. Dr. Needels is author of two research reports of the study of classroom teaching and is coauthor of several other reports. Currently, she is conducting research on the teaching of writing at the secondary school level.

Penelope L. Peterson is Sears Roebuck Foundation–Bascom Professor of Educational Psychology at the University of Wisconsin at Madison. She received her M.A. and Ph.D. degrees from Stanford University where she worked for five years with N. L. Gage studying effective teaching. Since 1977 she has been principal investigator and program-area coordinator in the Wisconsin Center for Education Research. Peterson has also directed several other major research projects concerned with classroom mathematics instruction funded by the National Science Foundation. She has published numerous articles and book chapters on classroom teaching and learning, and she has edited books on teaching and grouping in schools. In 1980 she received the AERA's Palmer O. Johnson award for her research article on teacher decision making during interactive classroom teaching. In 1986 she received the AERA's Raymond B. Cattell Early Career Award. She is currently editor of the *Review of Educational Research*. She was a member of the consulting and writing team for the Holmes Group—a consortium of the School of Education deans of the major research universities who are engaged in a reform of teacher education.

Barak V. Rosenshine was a student of N. L. Gage when the Stanford Center for Research and Development in Teaching began in 1965. His dissertation, "A Study of the Ability to Explain," was part of a project headed and developed by N. L. Gage and was one of the first studies done at the Stanford Center. Rosenshine first taught at Temple University. Since 1973 he has been a professor of Educational Psychology at the University of Illinois at Urbana-Champaign. He is best known for his review articles on the study of teaching and has published chapters in both the second and third editions of the *Handbook of Research on Teaching*.

Lee S. Shulman is professor of Education and affiliated professor of Psychology at Stanford University. He did undergraduate and graduate work at the University of Chicago, where he received a Ph.D. in educational psychology. From 1963 to 1982 he was a member of the faculty at Michigan State University, serving as professor of Educational Psychology and Medical Education and as founding codirector of the Institute for Research on Teaching. He is a member of the National Academy of Education and past president of the American Educational Research Association. His research interests include the study of teaching and teacher education, comparative cross-professional studies, and the development of new approaches to the assessment of teachers. His publications include *Medical Problem Solving* (with Elstein and Sprafka) and the *Handbook of Teaching and Policy* (edited with Sykes).

Georgea Mohlman Sparks is currently assistant professor in the Department of Teacher Education at Eastern Michigan University and a researcher and writer who has consulted with teachers and administrators across the United States. Her graduate work in teacher effectiveness was completed at Stanford University in Palo Alto, California. Georgea Sparks is particularly interested in designing preservice and in-service programs that enable teachers to use the recent research on effective teaching and learning in their classrooms. She has collaborated with Madeline Hunter on a study of the impact of Dr. Hunter's model on students' academic learning time and student achievement. Dr. Sparks has made numerous presentations at national educational conferences and has published her work in such journals as *Educational Leadership, American Educational Research Journal, Journal of Staff Development,* and *Journal of Teacher Education.* She is also the coauthor of the ASCD videotapes *Effective Teaching for Higher Achievement* and *School Improvement through Staff Development.* She has taught at the secondary and university levels and has visited countless classrooms throughout the country in her supportive efforts to help teachers grow.

Jane Stallings was a classroom teacher for ten years prior to earning her Ph.D. from Stanford in 1970. Her classroom experience served her well in the evaluations she conducted of Head Start, Follow Through, National Day Care Centers, and secondary reading classes while she worked at the Stanford Research Institute. Her studies have focused on how teachers teach and how students learn. Her specialty has been developing, using, and training others to use teacher-focused and child-focused observation systems. She has worked on a number of projects with N. L. Gage. To carry out staff development using findings from research on teaching and schooling, Dr. Stallings founded the Stallings Teaching and Learning Institute. In 1983 she became director of the Peabody College of Effective Teaching at Vanderbilt University. Dr. Stallings currently is department chair of Curriculum Instruction at the University of Houston.

Philip H. Winne is professor in the Faculty of Education and director of the Instructional Psychology Research Group at Simon Fraser University. His contribution to this volume was written while he was Simon Fraser University research professor and a distinguished visiting professor at the Max Planck Institute for Psychological Research in Munich, West Germany. He is past-president of the Canadian Educational Researchers' Association and a fellow of the American Psychological Association's Division of Educational Psychology. His research focuses on cognitive models that describe how students learn from teaching and on teaching effectiveness. Currently, he is working to develop artificially intelligent computer software to assist teachers in planning for teaching. Two of his recent publications are "Cognitive Processing in the Classroom" and "Steps Toward Promoting Cognitive Achievements."

Robert J. Yinger is an associate professor of Education at the University of Cincinnati. He received his Ph.D. from Michigan State University where he was an intern and postdoctoral research associate at the Institute for Research on Teaching. His research interests are in the areas of teacher planning, teachers' interactive thinking, and instructional theory and design.

INDEX